Basics of the Theoretical System of Socialism with Chinese Characteristics

edited by Xu Hongzhi & Qin Xuan

translated by Yang Xu

CANUT INTERNATIONAL PUBLISHERS

Istanbul - Berlin - London - Santiago

Basics of the Theoretical System of
Socialism with Chinese Characteristics

Edited by Xu Hongzhi & Qin Xuan

Translated by Yang Xu

The English version is published in cooperation with China Renmin
University Press

Chinese Title: 中国特色社会主义理论体系概论, ISBN: 9787300148939

Copyright © CRUP China, 2011

Canut International Publishers

Canut Intl. Turkey, Teraziler Cad. No.29. Sancaktepe, Istanbul, Turkey

Canut Intl. Germany, Heerstr. 266, D-47053, Duisburg, Germany

Canut Intl. United Kingdom, 12a Guernsay Road, London E11 4BJ, England

Copyright © Canut International Publishers, 2017

ISBN: 978-605-9914-56-7

Printed in UK

Lightning Source Ltd. UK

Chapterhouse, Pitfield Kiln Farm

MK11 3LW

United Kingdom

www.canutbooks.com

About the Editors

Xu Hongzhi, Professor and PhD. tutor in Marxism School of Renmin University of China, has wrote many academic works, such as the History of Marxism, The History of Mao Zedong Thought , the concise history of Marxism, The Comprehensive Power of Deng Xiaoping Theory and co-edited the book titled An Outline of Deng Xiaoping Theory.

Qin Xuan, born in December 1963 in Jingmen, Hubei Province, doctor of law, he is PhD. tutor in Marxism School of Renmin University of China, chief editor of Journal of Teaching and Research published by China Renmin University and former dean of School of Marxism. He also served as Chief Expert of the "Introduction to Mao Zedong Thought and Theoretical System of Socialism with Chinese Characteristics", and Vice President of the Chinese Scientific Socialism Society, Vice President of the Beijing Institute of Scientific Socialism, and Marxism School of China Renmin University.

Acknowledgements

The book we present is written by the most prominent researchers of Marxism in China, and reviewed by Qin Xuan and Xu Zhihong the two senior scholars of Renmin University. In 14 chapters they have demonstrated the most important component parts of the CPC's socialism building concept in the Chinese particlarity, which is a meta-system theory, with interrelated sub-theories. At the time when Deng Xiaoping proposed this new concept which emphasized Chinese particularity, he has added new meanings to it, when compared with Mao Zedong's understanding of applying Marxism to Chinese conditions: he strived to thoroughly revise the prevalent concepts of socialism building and open a new chapter in the history of socialist movement in regards, how to define and build socialism in China. It was a tremendously hard task, when the trials in the eastern European countries were still in development and exploration, especially when the Soviet model of socialism building established by Stalin was deemed as the only universally applicable one, except the Yugoslavian model. The CPC when choosing this term has given a clear signal that each socialist or communist party should better determine its own path in building socialism, and external interference wouldn't be favorable.

The meta-theory of socialism with Chinese characteristics has been gradually improved with the development of social practice and times, and is still in development, but its essence and ultimate goal remain the same. It has made great breakthroughs in the cognition of socialism and socialism building and in the aspect of how socialism relates with capitalism and how it step by step dialectically sublates it.

This academically processed but easily readable book will give the reader a comprehensive understanding of this theory and enable them to compare the previous cognition of socialism and socialism building with the current one.

Daivya Jindal
December, 2017
London, UK

Editor's Note

In 2007, the 17th National Congress of the Communist Party of China has made clear that our party will persist in following the important strategic thought of Deng Xiaoping Theory, the important thought of the 'Three Represents' and the Scientific Concept of Development which was formed by theoretical and practical innovation, generally referred to as the "Theoretical System of Chinese Socialism" and stressed: the report stated: "In contemporary China, to stay true to Marxism means to adhere to the system of theories of socialism with Chinese characteristics." Since the 17th National Congress of the Communist Party of China (CPC), the CPC Central Committee has done a scientific deployment of how to cultivate the builders and successors who will hold high the cause of socialism with Chinese characteristics and on how to use theoretical system of socialism with Chinese characteristics, to educate the leaders of the youth across the country. The high-level Office for The Marxist Theory Research and Construction Project pays meticulous and consistent efforts to prepare all kinds of cognitive learning materials, which will reflect and expound on the brand new academic achievements attained in the study of Chinese Marxism. Among them, the textbook "Mao Zedong Thought and The Theoretical System of Socialism with Chinese Characteristics," has been a unique work which has been highly praised by readers from all walks of people, promising young people including college students. By courtesy of the ministry of education, colleges and universities across the country have made great contributions and achievements in transforming the rich contents of the theoretical system of socialism with Chinese characteristics into teaching materials, a part of which can be utilized in schools. This book—*The Basics of the Theoretical System of Socialism with Chinese Characteristics*—we present to readers was prepared by the most prominent scholars of the subject from the Marxism School of the Renmin University of China especially designed for college students. Throughout the writing and editing of this book, we have both enjoyed the advantage of certain comprehension basis, and a certain degree of difficulty, certain comprehension basis as an advantage, firstly because we had already edited the "Introduction to Deng Xiaoping Theory", "Introduction to the Important Thought of Three Represents", since their publication in 2003, the titles were re-published for dozens of times, and the aggregate print of them has nearly reached 3 million, most of which have reached the readers. Secondly, the writers of this textbook are all in the front line of teaching and research, they have a certain degree of research accretion on the theoretical system of socialism with Chinese characteristics and have abundant teaching experience on the subject. Thirdly, the academic community has made abundant research on "Deng Xiaoping Theory", and on the "Important Thought of Three Represents" and also on "The Scientific Concept of Development" and other major strategic thoughts, which are component parts of the theoretical system of socialism with Chinese characteristics, and have produced numerous precious research results. These above favorable conditions have laid a virtuous foundation in the writing and editing of this book.

We have faced a certain degree of difficulty, firstly because the theoretical system of socialism with Chinese characteristics still encounters enrichment and perfection. The academic circles have different understandings of its theme, its historical starting point, main content and the logical structure of this theoretical system. There still exist differences in the understanding and interpretation of many major issues regarding it. Secondly, we have encountered a considerable difficulties, as in the following, how to break through the previous framework of Deng Xiaoping Theory and unify the three strategic thoughts of—Deng Xiaoping Theory, Important Thought of Three Represents, and The Scientific Concept of Development—and integrate them into one and same book, because all the three not only represent major theoretical achievements having their own unique characteristics, but also have succession and development relations among them, besides they follow the same strain and have included successive times characteristics. Thirdly, since the 17th National Congress of the CPC, our party's understanding on the theoretical system of socialism with Chinese characteristics was further deepened, and many new propositions have been put forward. As Comrade Hu Jintao in his speech at the commemoration of the 90th anniversary of the founding of the Communist Party of China, has put forward and summarized a new conception of "the socialist system with Chinese characteristics", also the 6th Plenary Session of the 17th Central Committee of the CPC put forward the proposition of "the path of socialist cultural development with Chinese characteristics." Regarding these new propositions, the academic community also lacks in-depth research, our understanding is not accurate, yet, which is also a major problem encountered in the preparation of teaching materials. The textbook is the crystallization of collective wisdom, including the designing of its outline, the final draft to be published has been the result of collective deliberation.Scholars from the School of Marxism attached to Renmin University of China who have contributed to this book include Prof. Xu Zhihong (edited Chapter II and V), Prof. Qin Xuan (Chapter I and VII), Prof. Yang Fengcheng (Chapter XI and XIV), Prof. Huang Jifeng (Chapter III and IX), Prof. Wang Xiangming (Chapter VIII and X), Prof. Qi Pengfei (Chapter XII and XIII), Prof. Zhang Xin (Chapter IV, and VI).

The book was finally reviewed by Professor Xu Zhihong and Professor Qin Xuan. We are grateful to Prof. He Yaomin, the President of the Renmin University Press, and Prof. Zhou Weihua, the editor-in-chief of the Renmin University Press, who have paid great attention to the to the compilation and publication, and to Guo Xiaoming, the head of the public administration department, who has paid a lot of hard work for this book. Our starting point and innermost desire has been preparing a comprehensive and accurate book that will comprehensively and accurately reflect the theoretical system of socialism with Chinese characteristics. Objectively speaking, such a complex work can never be perfect, cannot avoid certain shortcomings and deficiencies. We sincerely welcome criticism, from all quarters, including all aspects, so that we can make it more perfect in future editions.

Qin Xuan
October, 2012
Beijing

Contents

CHAPTER ONE

Formation and Development of the Theoretical System of Socialism with Chinese Characteristics

Section I

Social and historical conditions behind the formation of the theoretical system of socialism with Chinese characteristics

First, the historical basis: evaluating the positive and negative aspects of socialist construction experiences

The theoretical system of socialism with Chinese characteristics is formed and developed on the basis of the Party's summarizing and absorbing the historical experience of our socialist development and drawing lessons from other socialist countries. Since the beginning of the new period, our Party has attached great importance to the summary of historical experience. In the 3rd Plenary Session of the 11th CPC Central Committee, the Party seriously summed up the positive and negative experiences, drew lessons from the "Cultural Revolution", restored the ideological line of Marxism, and resolutely made the major historical choice of transferring the work center of the Party and the state to the economic construction and carrying out the reform and opening up. The 6th Plenary Session of the 11th CPC Central Committee adopted The Resolution on Some Historical Issues of the Party Since the Founding of the PRC through which the Party conscientiously cleared up major historical rights and wrongs and adhered to and inherited all the positive achievements made by our Party in the practice of the long-term socialist construction, marking the completion of the Party's bringing order out of chaos in the ideological line, political line and organizational line. In the process of reform and opening up and modernization construction, our Party earnestly draws lessons from other countries, especially the Soviet union, eastern Europe and other socialist countries, which provides an important reference for the better development of the socialism with Chinese characteristics. As Deng Xiaoping said: if there was no profound summarization of historical experience and lessons, "It would be impossible to formulate the ideological line, the basic line, politics, organizational lines and a series of policies we have established since the 3rd Plenary Session of the 11th CPC Central Committee."[1] It can be said that the development and expansion of the socialist path with Chinese characteristics and the formation and development of the theoretical system of socialism with Chinese characteristics are inseparable from our Party's adeptness and efforts in summing up and absorbing the positive and negative experiences.

Second, the basis of establishment: Basic national conditions of China in the primary stage of socialism

Accurately grasping the basic national conditions of the primary stage of socialism in China is the fundamental starting point for our Party to promote the theoretical innovation and formulate the correct line, guideline and policy. In the 13th CPC National Congress, the Party expounded the issue of the primary stage of socialism in a systematic way and emphasized the need to fully understand the long-term, arduous and complex nature of the socialist construction and to constantly enhance the consciousness of starting from the reality that China is in the primary stage of socialism. This issue was reiterated in the 14th, 15th and 16th CPC National Congress which stressed that we should not proceed from the subjective wishes, from the various foreign modes, but from the biggest reality that China is in the primary stage of socialism in doing things, making decisions and thinking about issues.

It was further emphasized in the 17th CPC National Congress that the basic national conditions of our country that it is still in the primary stage of socialism and the principal contradiction between the increasing material and cultural needs of the people and the backward social production remain unchanged. We shall recognize this basic national condition, grasp the phase characteristics of the century and new phase, and take it as the fundamental basis of advancing the reform and planning the development. It can be said that during the reform and opening up for more than 30 years, our Party's theory, line, guideline and policy are correct and play a huge role in promoting the social development and progress in practice because they are based on the realities of the primary stage of socialism and on the sober understanding and accurate grasp of the basic national conditions and stage characteristics of this primary stage.

1   Selected Works of Deng Xiaoping, 1st Edition, Vol.3, p.272, Beijing, People's Publishing House, 1993.

Third, the realistic basis: the party leadership sets things right and starts the vivid practice of opening-up and modernization

Reform and opening up is the main theme of contemporary China, the only way to develop socialism with Chinese characteristics, and also the important foundation for the development of the theoretical system of socialism with Chinese characteristics. Since the reform and opening up for more than 30 years, the theoretical system of socialism with Chinese characteristics has deepened and enriched with the deepening practice. From the rural reform to urban reform, from the economic system reform to various system reforms, from the establishment of the special economic zone and the opening of the coastal cities to the opening of the inland border cities, the cities along the river and the provincial capitals, from the proposal of the planned commodity economy to the establishment of the socialist market economy, from grasping the two links of material civilization and spiritual civilization to comprehensively promoting the modernization construction in accordance with the "Four-in-one" overall layout, and from strengthening and improving the Party's leadership to comprehensively promoting the new great project of the Party's construction, our Party has continuously studied and resolved the new contradictions and problems in advancement and vested the new connotations of the age and practical requirements in the theoretical system of socialism with Chinese characteristics. It can be said that whenever the reform and opening up advances by one step, our Party's understanding of socialism with Chinese characteristics can be deepened and the enrichment and development of this theoretical system can be promoted. The theoretical system of socialism with Chinese characteristics is vigorous because it is the scientific theory rooted in the great practice of the reform and opening up.

Fourth, the source of power was the rich and creative experience of the people

Insisting on summarizing experience and absorbing wisdom from the vivid practice of the people is an important way to develop the theoretical system of socialism with Chinese characteristics. Deng Xiaoping said that many things in the reform and opening up were put forward by the masses in practice and embodied the wisdom of the masses. Jiang Zemin said that a good solution does not fall from heaven nor is it inherent in our minds, in the final analysis correct theories come from the people's practice of creating history. Hu Jintao pointed out: "Respecting the people's practice and drawing ideological nutrition from the people's great creation and elevating it to a theoretical form are the inexhaustible sources of our party's theoretical innovation."[2]

---

2   CPCCC Party Literature Research Office: "Selection of Important Literature since the 16th National Congress" (Vol.2), p.595, Beijing, Central Literature Publishing House, 2008.

Much of the experience in reform and innovation during the past more than 30 years of reform and opening up has come from the grassroots level and the masses of people. Our Party has always been adhering to the Marxist ideological line "from the masses, to the masses", enthusiastically supporting, encouraging, protecting and guiding the great creation of the people, and profoundly summing up the practical experience of the people, from which the laws of the socialist modernization construction can be mastered and the Marxist theoretical innovation can be constantly promoted. It can be said that the theoretical system of socialism with Chinese characteristics is formed and developed due to our party's effort to closely rely on the people, widely mobilize the people's enthusiasm, initiative and creativity and gather strength and wisdom from the people.

Fifth, the background: the profound changes in the international situation and the new trends in world development

Since the 1970s, great changes have taken place in the whole world, and the intensity and profundity of these changes is far beyond the expectation. The most significant change is that peace and development have become the theme of the times, the trend of world multi-polarization and economic globalization has developed in an accelerating way, and the competition in the comprehensive national strength is becoming increasingly fierce. In particular, the new science and technology revolution and the following wide applications of the great science and technology discoveries and inventions have promoted the unprecedented profound changes in production mode, way of life and economic society all over the world and also unprecedented major changes in the global economic pattern, interest pattern and security pattern. In the face of such profound and major changes, our Party should constantly emancipate the mind and vigorously promote theoretical innovation and then the new development of the cause so as to better solve the new issues and meet the new challenges raised by the times and usher in new situations for the development of the party and the people. It can be said that the theoretical system of socialism with Chinese characteristics, including Deng Xiaoping Theory, the important thought of "Three Represents", the scientific outlook on development and other major strategic thoughts, is formed and developed on the basis of our Party's effort to follow the world development trend, draw on the experience and lessons from the ups and downs of other countries and critically absorb all the civilization achievements created by human society.

Section II

Stages in the development of the theoretical system of socialism with Chinese characteristics

First, the preliminary exploration of the path of socialism with Chinese characteristics by the CPC

It is pointed out in the 17th CPC National Congress that the theoretical system of socialism with Chinese characteristics is the scientific theoretical system that includes Deng Xiaoping Theory, the important thought of "Three Represents", the scientific outlook on development and other major strategic thoughts.

China has experienced a long process of exploration, choice and struggle before embarking on the socialist path. Since modern times, the Chinese nation has faced two historical tasks: one is to seek the national independence and people's liberation; the other is to realize the national prosperity and mighty and people's affluence. After the opium war, China was reduced to a semi-colonial and semi-feudal country. In order to save the nation from peril, the Chinese people made a long-term exploration and strenuous struggle, including the Westernization Movement, the Hundred Days' Reform, Taiping Rebellion led by Hong Xiuquan, the Boxer Rebellion and the Revolution of 1911 led by Sun Yat-sen, which all ended in failure. And the social nature of China as a semi-colonial and semi-feudal society and the people's miserable fate remain unchanged, for which a fundamental reason is that no scientific theoretical guidance is provided. The advanced Chinese have tried various ideological weapons in order to seek the way of saving the country and their people. After making the fierce struggle and difficult choices, Marxism gradually took rooted in Chinese society because of its popularity among the progressive youth and even the Chinese people. It is the history that has chosen Marxism and it is Marxism that has profoundly changed the fate of China. Mao Zedong points out that the Chinese people have turned from the passive status into the active status and created a new outlook of Chinese revolution since the introduction of Marxism-Leninism. Thanks to the guidance of Marxism, the repeated comparison and profound thinking, and especially the influence of the Russian "October Revolution", the advanced Chinese have made a clear choice of the scientific socialist path. The founding of the Communist Party of China in 1921 ushered in a new era of the Chinese revolution. At the beginning of the founding, our Party made it clear that the ultimate direction of the democratic revolution led by it is socialism. Under the leadership of the Party and Mao Zedong, our Party founded Mao Zedong Thought and opened up a revolution path that was in line with the realities in China by combining the Marxism-Leninism and China's realities and overcoming the erroneous tendency to dogmatize Marxism and sanctify the resolutions of the Communist International and the experience of the Communist Party of the Soviet Union that enjoyed great popularity at one time. After 28 years of arduous struggle, the Communist Party of China overthrew the three big mountains (imperialism, feudalism and bureaucrat-capitalism), won the New Democratic Revolution, and founded the New China, which indicated the realization of the national independence and people's liberation that several generations of Chinese dreamed about since the modern times and the completion of the first historical task of the great rejuvenation of the Chinese nation.

During the 28 years between the founding of the New China and the end of the "Cultural Revolution", the Party's first collective leadership, with Mao Zedong as the core, led the whole party and people of all ethnic groups throughout the country to rapidly heal the trauma of the war and restore the national economy, and then to propose the general line in the transition period, carry out the socialist transformation, and establish the basic system of socialism without losing any time, resulting in the realization of the most profound and greatest social transformation in China. However, how to build socialism is a brand new exploration for our Party. Mao Zedong said at that time that we should realize "the second combination" of the basic principle of Marxism-Leninism and the concrete realities of China, and find out the correct way of socialist construction in China. Some important ideas on the socialist construction in China, concerning the economy, politics, culture, national defense, diplomacy and other aspects, were put forward in Mao Zedong's *Ten Major Relationships, Issues on Correctly Handling the Contradictions among the People* and other works, and the documents of the 8th CPC National Congress, which marked the beginning of our Party to independently explore the socialist construction path suitable for our country's national conditions. Under the leadership of the Party and Mao Zedong, China has gradually established an independent, relatively complete industrial system and national economic system, and accumulated important experience in socialist construction. As a new subject in the Marxism and socialism development history, the socialist construction in such a backward eastern country in China was doomed to experience errors and setbacks, given the lack of regular understanding on how to combine the socialist path with the national conditions and the influence of the complex international environment at that time. These errors and setback have left deep historical experience and lessons and China paid a huge price for them.

Our Party's victory in the revolution and exploration of the socialist construction path in China under Mao Zedong's leadership provided the fundamental political premise and institutional foundation for all the development and progress in contemporary China, and exerted a profound influence on the opening up and emergence of the socialist path with Chinese characteristics. As indicated in the 17th CPC National Congress, we must always bear in mind that the great cause of reform and opening up is based on the valuable experience of the Party's first collective leadership with Mao Zedong as the core in leading the whole Party and people of all ethnic groups throughout the country to build the New China, make the great achievements in the socialist revolution and construction and explore the laws of socialist construction.

Second, The initial formation of the theoretical system of socialism with Chinese characteristics

When the "Cultural Revolution" came to an end in 1976, what stood in front of our Party was the China with many things waiting to be done and an urgent problem about whether China continued adhering to the wrong line in the "Cultural Revolution" period or opened up a new path reflecting the trend of the times and the China's conditions by getting rid of the "leftist" ideological shackles. The 3rd Plenary Session of the 11th CPC Central Committee held at the end of 1978 re-established the Party's ideological line, political line and organization line, which brought order out of chaos in the guiding ideology and initiated a new exploration of socialist construction. It is in this session when the Party's second central collective leadership with Deng Xiaoping as the core was formed, which marked the entry of our country into the new period of socialist modernization construction. In the new historical period, Deng Xiaoping was keenly aware that the Marxism we adhere to is the science and truth and that the socialist system established in our country is a good system, but the question is: what is Marxism, how can we uphold Marxism what is socialism and how can we build socialism, of which our understanding was not completely clear enough in the past. Our experience is rich enough, but what matters most is to clarify this question. Hence, at the beginning of the new period, our party insisted on combining Marxism with China's realities, and carried out the in-depth theoretical exploration on how to build socialism in economically and culturally backward countries like China, marking the initiation of the new course of localized Marxism in China. In September 1982, Deng Xiaoping made it clear in the opening speech of the 12th CPC National Congress that "we should take our own path and build socialism with Chinese characteristics". The proposition of this important conclusion points out the direction of our Party's theoretical and practical exploration in the new period.

From 1978 to 1992, our Party, under Deng Xiaoping's leadership, combined the basic principles of Marxism with the specific realities of China and the features of the times, put forward a series of creative ideas, and initially formed the theoretical system of socialism with Chinese characteristics. Deng Xiaoping, based on the new changes of the world situation, clearly argued that "peace and development are two major problems of the contemporary world", and that it was one of the three tasks in the new period to oppose hegemonism and safeguard world peace; he also emphasized that we must insist on the basic line that takes the economic construction as the center and upholds the Four Cardinal Principles and reform and opening up, and establish the modernized socialist country of prosperity, democracy and civilization by "three steps", given China's national condition that China is and will be in the primary stage of socialism in the long run when the essential task is to develop the productivity; he also underscored that science and technology are the primary productive force and their modernization is the key to realizing the modernization of China, considering their new development situation in the world; that we should develop the socialist democracy and construct the socialist legal system because there would be no socialism nor the socialist modernization if no democracy exists, and that we should grasp both the material and spiritual civilization with equal importance attached to each because the good development of the two is

the real socialism with Chinese characteristics, since the socialism is the requirement of the society with an all-around development; that the socialism can also adopt the market economy since both the plan and the market are the means rather than the essential difference between socialism and capitalism, according to the development law of the world economy and China's realities; that we should construct a modern, strong and regularized revolutionary army and unswervingly take the path of fewer but better troops with Chinese characteristics, given the new requirements of the world military reform; that we should combine the Marxist theory of the state with the concrete realities of China, and propose solving the problems of Hong Kong, Macao and Taiwan in accordance with the concept of "One Country, Two Systems"; that the key to China's problems is the Party and we should thus concentrate on Party's construction and make our Party a Marxist one with fighting capacity and a strong core that leads the whole nation in constructing the socialist modernization, according to the change of the Party's historical orientation.

In the 13th CPC National Congress held in 1987, the theory of the primary stage of socialism was expounded in a systematic way, the Party's basic line in this stage was proposed, the modernization goal of "being prosperous, democratic and civilized" was established, and the development strategy of realizing the modernization by three steps until the middle of the 21st century was formulated. It was clearly indicated in this congress that the combination of Marxism with China's practice experienced two great leaps. The first one occurred in the period of the new democratic revolution when the Chinese communists finally found the revolutionary path with Chinese characteristics and led the revolution to victory due to the repeatedly exploration and the summary of experience in the successes and failures. The second one occurred when the Chinese communists began to find a way to build socialism with Chinese characteristics after the 3rd Plenary Session of the 11th CPC Central Committee by summing up the positive and negative experience during the past more than 30 years since the founding of China and studying the international experience and world situation, which opened up a new stage of socialist construction. In the report of the 13th CPC National Congress, the new theoretical ideas proposed by our Party in the process of paving the socialist path with Chinese characteristics are reduced into 12 articles which constitute the outline and mark the initial formation of the theoretical system of socialism with Chinese characteristics.

Deng Xiaoping made a southern speech in 1992 in which he summed up a series of major issues concerning the development of socialism with Chinese characteristics, and proposed that the basic line should be kept for a hundred years, the criteria for judging all aspects of work should be "Three Favorables", and that the essence of socialism is to liberate and develop the productive forces, eliminate exploitation and polarization between the rich and poor, and finally achieve the common prosperity. This speech boosted the ideological emancipation of the whole Party and Chinese people and advanced the cause of reform and opening up. In 1992, the 14th CPC National Congress made a summary of the new idea of the theoretical innovations of our Party during the period when Deng Xiaoping reigned, which was called "Deng Xiaoping's theory of building socialism with Chinese characteristics". In 1997, the 15th CPC National Congress made a further summary and discussion on it and named it "Deng Xiaoping Theory", which was included into the Party Constitution as the guiding ideology.

Third, the further development of the theoretical system of socialism with Chinese characteristics

Socialism encountered unprecedented sharp challenges in the world after the 13th CPC National Congress: the drastic changes in Eastern Europe in the late 1980s and the disintegration of the Soviet Union in the early 1990s. These events that shocked the world are the most serious and profound crises when socialism turned from the theory into practice. The same situation happened domestically in the course of reform and development: political turmoil occurred; the economy was overheated and had to be improved and rectified; in terms of the system reform, no significant breakthrough was made in state-owned enterprises, and a dual system existed for a long time with serious contradictions and loopholes due to the lagging reform in the state tax system, financial system and price system. The whole situation was rather grim. In June 1989, the 4th Plenary Session of the 13th CPC Central Committee elected Jiang Zemin as the General Secretary of the Central Committee, and formed the third CPC collective leadership with Jiang Zemin as the core. However, it became quite urgent for this new leadership to figure out how to continue promoting the socialist cause with Chinese characteristics according to the new changes of the world, China and the Communist Party.

After the 4th Plenary Session of the 13th CPC Central Committee, the Communist Party of China with Jiang Zemin as the main representative continued promoting the great cause of socialism with Chinese characteristics by putting forward a series of new ideas and new statements, and enriched and developed the theoretical system of socialism with Chinese characteristics. Confronted with the austere political situation at home and abroad and the arduous task of the reform and development in the late 1980s and early 1990s, this new leadership stressed clearly that the lines and basic policies formulated since the 3rd Plenary Session of the 11th CPC Central Committee should be maintained steadfastly and implemented comprehensively. Jiang Zemin pointed out that building socialism with Chinese characteristics was "a major project", of which the basic ideas and principles have been established by Deng Xiaoping, and our task was to continue implementing this project in a good way. In this process, Jiang Zemin also proposed a series of innovative ideas, which are mainly manifested in the following 7 aspects. Firstly, he argued that the goal of economic system reform was to establish the socialist market economy system and that the combination of socialism with market economy was a great innovation, according to Deng Xiaoping's important view that "socialism can also adopt the market economy". Secondly, the basic economic system that public ownership plays the leading role and diverse forms of ownership develop side by side, the distribution system with distribution according to work being the main form and the multiple ways of distribution co-existing, and the basic political system should be adhered to and improved, according to the basic principles of Marxism and the national conditions of China in the primary stage of socialism. Thirdly, he, combining the issue of development with the nature and power-exercising philosophy of our Party, made it clear that development was the first task of our Party in governing and rejuvenating the country, and that the advanced nature of our Party and the superiority of the socialist system should be put into practice to develop advanced productive forces, advanced culture, to realize the fundamental interests of the majority of the people, and to promote the all-round social progress and human development. Fourthly, the strategy of rejuvenating the country through science and education, the strategy of sustainable development, and the opening-up strategy that combines "bringing in" with "going out" should be vigorously implemented, the new path of industrialization should be taken, and the rational layout and coordinated development of regional economy should be promoted. Fifthly, he stressed that according to the development and changes of the situation at home and abroad at the turn of the century, our Party should strengthen its construction under the new historical conditions, insist on examining itself according to the requirement of the times, improve itself at the spirit of reform, earnestly work out the two major historical problems of how to improve the Party's leadership and governance capability and its ability to resist corruption and risk, comprehensively promote the Party construction——a new great project—so as to make it the Marxist political party that is utterly consolidated ideologically, politically, and organizationally, always ahead of the times, and can withstand all kinds of risks and lead the whole nation in building socialism with Chinese characteristics. Sixthly, the national defense and army construction should be strengthened and the military reform with Chinese characteristics should be advanced in addition to the main tasks of developing the market economy and keeping the Party's advanced nature, according to the new situation of the army and national defense construction in the new period. At last, the world multi-polarization and democratization of international relations should be boosted according to the new world situation after the cold war.

This new collective leadership with Jiang Zemin as the core adhered to the reform and opening up, kept pace with the times, led the whole Party and the people of all ethnic groups in the whole country through the political storm, economic risks and other ordeals at home and abroad, and founded the important thought of "Three Represents" on the basis of a profound and accurate understanding of the situation changes of the world, China, and the Party. This important thought is a significant part of the theoretical system of socialism with Chinese characteristics. In the 16th CPC National Congress in 2002, the Party summed up the basic experience of our Party in leading people to build socialism with Chinese characteristics since reform and opening up, especially the 4th Plenary Session of the 13th Central Committee, expounded the fundamental requirements of the important thought of "Three Represents", explicitly proposed the Party's goal and guidelines and policies in various aspects in the first 20 years of the new century, and made a comprehensive deployment of the socialist economy, politics, culture, and Party building with Chinese characteristics, and other work. It is in this congress when the important thought of "Three Represents" was established along with Marxism-Leninism, Mao Zedong Thought and Deng Xiaoping Theory as the guiding ideology that our Party must adhere to for a long time, another time when our Party's guiding ideology advanced with the times.

Fourth, opening of the new realm in the development of the theoretical system of socialism with Chinese characteristics

Since the 16th CPC National Congress, the CPC Central Committee with Hu Jintao as its General Secretary, guided by Deng Xiaoping Theory and the important thought of "Three Represents", followed the development and changes of the situation at home and abroad, carried forward the spirit of seeking truth and forging ahead, continued promoting the theoretical and practical innovation, and proposed a series of important theoretical ideas, strategic thoughts and work arrangement and formed the newest achievements of the socialist theoretical system with Chinese characteristics in the course of developing socialism with Chinese characteristics.

In the new stage of the new century, our Party, starting from the history and the times, the basic national conditions of China at the primary stage, the stage characteristics and practice of China's development, the world development trend, the development experience of foreign countries, and the new development requirements, puts forward a series of ideas, such as being people-oriented, realizing the comprehensive, coordinated and sustainable development, building the harmonious socialist society, the new socialist countryside, the innovation-driven country, the socialist core values system, and the socialist concept of honor and disgrace, and boosting the construction of a harmonious world, which together answered such basic questions as what socialism is and how to build it. Facing the opportunities and challenges in the 21st century, our Party has made it clear that the construction of its advanced nature is the essence of the Marxist party to survive, develop and expand. As a result, the Party's governing capacity and advanced nature construction should be taken as the main line of the Party's construction, the great new project that should be comprehensively promoted at the spirit of the reform and innovation, so as to make the Party always the arduous, honest, clean, energetic, united and harmonious ruling party of Marxism built for the public and exercising state power for the people, and seeking truth and being pragmatic. Centering on this goal, the CPC Central Committee has put forward a series of important new ideas on strengthening and improving the Party's construction in the new stage of the new century. Centering on the central issue of development, our Party has made a creative exploration of what development is, why and how to develop, for whom the development is, on whom the development depends, who is to share the development achievements and other major issues, and emphasized the correct understanding and proper treatment of the major relations related to the cause of socialism with Chinese characteristics, so as to strive for scientific, harmonious and peaceful development. In the

17th CPC National Congress, the historical status and background, scientific connotation, spiritual essence and fundamental requirements of the scientific outlook on development were profoundly elaborated and taken as an important guideline for China's economic and social development and a major strategic thought that has to be adhered to and carried out for the development of socialism with Chinese characteristics.

Since the founding of the New China, especially the reform and opening up, our Party's theories and practices have been centering on the theme of socialism with Chinese characteristics. It is during the process of the reform and opening up when the theoretical system of socialism with Chinese characteristics was formed and developed. Deng Xiaoping Theory, "Three Represents" and the scientific outlook on development, formed in different periods, focused on exploring and answering the new contradictions and new problems encountered at different periods and different stages, and made their unique contributions to both theoretical innovation and theoretical development. They are interconnected and progressive layer by layer, reflecting the inherent consistency of the scientific system, stage achievements and developmental requirements of our Party's theoretical innovation achievements since the new period. They were summarized as "the theoretical system of socialism with Chinese characteristics" in the 17th CPC National Congress, which marks the further maturity of the theory and practice of socialism with Chinese characteristics.

In 2011, when commemorating the 90th anniversary of the founding of the Chinese Communist Party, Hu Jintao further pointed out: "We have embarked on the path of socialism with Chinese characteristics, formed a system of theories of socialism with Chinese characteristics and established a socialist system with Chinese characteristics. These achievements made over 90 years of endeavors, innovation, and enrichment, should be valued, upheld on a long-term basis and continuously built upon by our Party and people." In this speech Comrade Hu Jintao, for the first time used the term of theoretical socialist system with Chinese characteristics" into the overall framework of socialism with Chinese characteristics, which has further deepened our Party 's understanding of Socialism with Chinese Characteristics.[3]

In 1990, when commemorating the 90th anniversary of the founding of the Communist Party of China, Hu Jintao further pointed out: "We have embarked on the path of socialism with Chinese characteristics, formed a system of theories of socialism with Chinese characteristics and established a socialist system with Chinese characteristics. These achievements made over 90 years of endeavors, innovation, and enrichment, should be

3   See Hu Jintao, "Speech at the 90th Anniversary of the Founding of the Chinese Communist Party", Beijing, People's Publishing House, 2011.

valued, upheld on a long-term basis and continuously built upon by our Party and people." In this speech Comrade Hu Jintao, for the first time used the term of "theoretical socialist system with Chinese characteristics" into the overall framework of socialism with Chinese characteristics, which has further deepened our Party 's understanding of Socialism with Chinese Characteristics.

Section III

Theoretical system of socialism with Chinese characteristics and its main contents

First, The theoretical system of socialism with Chinese characteristics: a scientific theoretical system with a rich compound

It was clearly stated in the report of the 17th CPC National Congress that "the theoretical system of socialism with Chinese characteristics mainly includes Deng Xiaoping Theory, "Three represent", and the scientific outlook on development", which is a brand new generalization of this theoretical system. Looking back to the development process of the socialist theory with Chinese characteristics, we can see clearly that our Party's generalization of this theoretical system is deepening in a gradual way.

In the 13th CPC National Congress in 1987, the new ideas formed in our Party's theoretical exploration on socialism with Chinese characteristics were divided into 12 aspects which have constituted the outline of the socialist theory with Chinese characteristics, preliminarily answered the basic questions of China's socialist construction, such as the stages, task, motivation, conditions, layout and international environment, and planned the scientific track of our way forward.

In 1992, the Party's 14th National Congress summarized the theory of socialism with Chinese characteristics from 9 aspects. The 14th National Congress of the Communist Party of China made it clear that the theory of building socialism with Chinese characteristics is the product of the integration of the fundamental tenets of Marxism-Leninism with the reality of present-day China and the special features of our times, a continuation and development of Mao Zedong Thought, a crystallization of the collective wisdom of the entire Party membership and the whole Chinese people, and an intellectual treasure belonging to them all.[4]

---

4 CPCCC Party Literature Research Office: "Selection of Important Literature since the 14th National Congress" (Vol. I), p. 13, Beijing, Central Literature Publishing House, 1996.

In 1997, when explaining the historical status and guiding significance of Deng Xiaoping Theory, the 15th National Congress of the Communist Party of China explicitly pointed out for the first time: "Deng Xiaoping Theory constitutes a new, scientific system of the theory of building socialism with Chinese characteristics. It has been gradually formed and developed under the historical conditions in which peace and development have become the main themes of the times, in the practice of China's reform, opening up and modernization drive, and on the basis of reviewing the historical experience of successes and setbacks of socialism in China and learning from the historical experience of the rise and fall of other socialist countries. For the first time it has given preliminary but systematic answers to a series of basic questions concerning the path to socialism in China, the stages of development, the fundamental tasks, the motive force, the external conditions, the political guarantee, the strategic steps, Party leadership, the forces to be relied on, and the reunification of the motherland. It has guided our Party in formulating the basic line for the primary stage of socialism. It is a fairly complete scientific system which embraces philosophy, political economy and scientific socialism and covers, among other things, the economy, politics, science and technology, education, culture, ethnic, military and foreign affairs, the united front and Party building. It is also a scientific system which needs to be further enriched and developed in all aspects.

In July 2003, after the formation of the important thought of the "Three Represents", at the theoretical seminar on the important thought of the "Three Represents", Comrade Hu Jintao made commented: The important Thought of the Three Represents, has solved the major issues concerning the ideological line, the path of development, development stages, development ways, the fundamental tasks, the motive forces of development, the comprehensive national power, the international strategy, the leading forces, and the fundamental goals of socialism with Chinese characteristics. The Thought of Three Represents fulfills the common wishes of the Chinese people and forms the foundation of nation building in the new century. This thought enriches and develops the basic tenets of Marxism with a series of new ideas, views and theses and profoundly embodies the integration of history with reality in the development of the theory of Marxism, it has answered a series of questions on what socialism is, and how to build it, which are closely linked and integrated. The important thought of Three Represents creatively takes the theory of building the party in office as its main subject and answers what kind of party we should build, and how to build it.[5]

5   CPCCC Party Literature Research Office: "Selection of Important Literature since the 16th National Congress" (Vol. I), p.361, Beijing, Central Literature Publishing House, 2005.

Since the 16th CPC National Congress, the CPC Central Committee taking Hu Jintao as the General Secretary, starting from the overall situation of the Party and the country in the stage of the new century, has profoundly summarized the lessons and experience in the foreign and domestic economic and social development, constantly advanced the theoretical innovations, and explicitly proposed a series of major strategic thoughts, such as the scientific outlook on development, the construction of the harmonious socialist society, the innovation-driven country and the new socialist countryside, the strengthening of the construction of the Party's governance capacity and advanced nature, the building of the socialist concept of honor and disgrace, and the path of peaceful development. These important strategic thoughts are elaborated around the socialist theory with Chinese characteristics.

The theoretical system of socialism with Chinese characteristics is always elucidated around the four closely related basic questions: what is Marxism and how to deal with it, what is socialism and how to build it, what kind of party is to be built and how to build it, and what kind of development is to be achieved and how to achieve it, with a rich compound. In terms of the first question, the system stresses that Marxism keeps pace with the times and its essence is to seek truth from facts, which provides a creative answer to how to adhere to and develop Marxism under the new historical conditions, enriches and develops Marxism with a series of new thoughts and ideas, and opens up a new realm for Marxism in China. In terms of the second question, the system creatively answers how to build, consolidate and develop socialism in a country with backward economic and cultural background after the establishment of the socialist system, and provides a series of new thoughts and ideas on how to develop socialism by not only upholding the basic principles of scientific socialism but also considering the conditions of the times and people's desire, which has raised our Party's understanding of socialism to a new level. As for the third question, the system answers in a creative way how to adhere to the Party's foundation, consolidate the ruling foundation and strengthen the power source when the Party's historical orientation experiences profound changes, and puts forward a series of new ideas that the nature of the Marxist ruling party should be adhered to, the Party's governance capacity be improved, and the Party's advanced nature be maintained and developed, which have enriched and developed the Marxist theory of Party construction. In terms of the fourth question, the system gives a creative answer to what development is, why it is necessary to develop, how to develop, for whom the development is, on whom the development depends, who is to share the development achievements, and proposes a series of new thoughts and ideas on development connotation, concepts, thoughts and problems, and on how to achieve scientific development, which elevates our Party's understanding of development issues to an unprecedentedly high level.

The theoretical system of socialism with Chinese characteristics is scientific in that it is in line with Marxism-Leninism, the essential guiding ideology for our Party and country to be well-established and the action guide and powerful ideological weapon for us to learn about and transform the world, and advances with the times. It is the outcome of the combination of the basic principles of Marxism with China's concrete realities and the characteristics of the times. It adheres to the Marxist world outlook and methodology of dialectical materialism and historical materialism, to the highest ideal and value pursuit of communism, to the leading core—the proletariat—and the power source of the history—the broad masses of the people, to the fundamental task—emancipating and developing productive forces, to the essential characteristics of socialist democratic politics—people are the masters of the country, to the guiding position of Marxism in the field of Marxist ideology, and to the fundamental driving force of the socialist development—reform and innovation. By adhering to and applying the basic principles of Marxism on scientific socialism, this system analyzes the realities of the world and contemporary China, and thus makes a series of theoretical innovations and embodies the spirit of keeping pace with the times. It is a model of upholding and developing Marxism as well as a scientific theory consistent with Marxism-Leninism.

The theoretical system of socialism with Chinese characteristics is a theoretical system which is in line with Mao Zedong Thought and keeps pace with the times. The theoretical system of socialism with Chinese characteristics has its profound theoretical roots in Mao Zedong Thought and it is a continuation and development of Mao Zedong's arduous exploration and achievements regarding laws of building socialism. As Deng Xiaoping pointed out: "we have been restoring the correct things advocated by Comrade Mao Zedong, The basic points of Mao Zedong Thought are still those we have enumerated. In many respects, we are doing things Comrade Mao suggested but failed to do himself, setting right his erroneous opposition to certain things and accomplishing some things that he did not. All this we shall continue to do for a fairly long time. Of course, we have developed Mao Zedong Thought and will go on developing it."[6]

Both Mao Zedong Thought and the theoretical system of socialism with Chinese characteristics insist on emancipating the mind, seeking truth from facts, keeping pace with the times, adopting the Party's mass line and walking on its own way independently. This is their common ground on the basic aspects, such as the positions, views, methods, etc.. Today, these two should be still upheld and developed.

6   Selected Works of Deng Xiaoping, 2nd Edition, Volume 2, p. 300, Beijing, People's Publishing House, 1994.

The theoretical system of socialism with Chinese characteristics is a constantly developing and open theoretical system. It is also true for Marxism. It is clearly stated in the report of the 17th CPC National Congress: The theoretical system of socialism with Chinese characteristics is an open system that keeps developing. Keeping pace with the times is the theoretical quality of Marxism and theoretical innovation is an essential feature of Marxism and an inexhaustible source of its vitality forever. Practices since the publication of the "Communist Manifesto" nearly 160 years ago have proved that only when Marxism is integrated with the conditions of a specific country, advances in step with the times and is tied to the destiny of the people can it demonstrate its strong vitality, creativity and its appeal. The theoretical system of socialism with Chinese characteristics, as the latest theoretical achievement in adapting Marxism to Chinese conditions, the Party's invaluable political and intellectual asset, is also an open theoretical system itself and also a scientific system that requires constant enrichment and development. As a new great revolution, reform and opening up cannot win an easy victory and cannot be accomplished in one go.

Over the past 30 years of reform and opening up, the socialism with Chinese characteristics has made remarkable achievements. China has scored achievements in development that have captured world attention. However, the basic reality that China is still in the primary stage of socialism and will remain so for a long time to come has not changed, nor has Chinese society's principal contradiction–the one between the ever-growing material and cultural needs of the people and the low level of social production. Our country is the largest developing country in the world. Its international status has not changed."[7]

Meanwhile, quite a lot of difficulties and problems still exist in the course of continuing to promote the socialist cause with Chinese characteristics. All the achievements and progress made over the past 30 years of development can be essentially owed to the fact that our Party has paved the path of socialism with Chinese characteristics and formed the theoretical system of socialism with Chinese characteristics. Looking into the future and in order to solve the complex problems in the development of the socialist cause with Chinese characteristics and seize the new victory of building a well-off society in a comprehensive way, our Party is required to hold high the great banner of socialism with Chinese characteristics, unswervingly follow the socialist path with Chinese characteristics, and continue to deepen the study of the socialist theory with Chinese characteristics; to insist on the scientific Marxist principle and spirit, be good at grasping the objective changes and summarizing the fresh experience created by the people in practice, enrich

---

7   Hu Jintao: Speech at the Meeting Celebrating the 90th Anniversary of the Founding of the CPC, p. 20.

and develop the theoretical system of socialism with Chinese characteristics, continuously endow the contemporary Chinese Marxism with distinctive features in terms of the practice, nation and times, constantly open up new horizons for the Marxist theoretical development, and strive to a wider socialist path with Chinese characteristics.

Second, the main contents of the theoretical system of socialism with Chinese characteristics

The theoretical system of socialism with Chinese characteristics runs through the important strategic thoughts: Deng Xiaoping Theory, "Three Represents" and the scientific outlook on development. It is unified and scientific in that it has formed a series of interconnected basic views on such major issues as the socialist development path, development stage, fundamental task, development motivation, external conditions, political guarantee, strategic steps, leadership and supporting group, and reunification of the motherland. It includes the following 14 aspects:

——The ideological line. It is the essence of the theoretical system of socialism with Chinese characteristics as well as the soul of Deng Xiaoping Theory, "Three Represents", and the scientific outlook on development. It stresses emancipating the mind, seeking truth from facts, keeping pace with the times, starting from the reality, examining and developing the truth in practice, vigorously carrying forward the spirit of seeking truth and being pragmatic, vigorously promoting the theoretical and practical innovation, and making efforts to realize the ideological liberation, theoretical development and practical creations.

——The fundamental task. It is the central issue of the theoretical system of socialism with Chinese characteristics. It stresses that development is the key to solving all problems in China. In essence, socialism is to liberate and develop the productive forces, eliminate exploitation and polarization, and finally achieve common prosperity. We should adhere to the unity of the center—economic construction—and the two basic points—the four basic principles and the reform and opening up, and to the principle of focusing on construction and development, grasp the development laws, innovate the development concept, transform the development mode, solve the development problems, improve the development quality and efficiency, and strive to achieve the scientific, harmonious and peaceful development.

——The development stage and development strategies. It is the strategic goal and grand blueprint proposed by our Party according to the basic national conditions of contemporary China. It is emphasized that we should be soberly aware that China is and will be for a long time in the primary stage of socialism and that the main contradiction of the society is the conflict between the growing material and cultural needs of the masses and the backward social production. We should accurately grasp the stage characteristics of China's development, make full use of the important strategic period, better implement the strategy of rejuvenating the country through science and education, the strategy of strengthening China through talents, and the strategy of sustainable development, adhere to the basic requirements of comprehensive, coordinated and sustainable development and the basic methods of making overall plans and taking all factors into consideration, comprehensively promote the economic, political, cultural, social and ecological construction according to the four-to-one overall layout, and realize enough food and clothing, the well-off society and modernization through three steps, and build a strong, prosperous, democratic and civilized modern socialist country.

——The development motivation. It stems from the profound understanding of the contradiction movement between the socialist productive forces and productive relations, and the economic base and the superstructure, and reveals the vitality source of the development and progress of our Party and country. It emphasizes that the reform and opening up, a new great revolution, is the path to the powerful nation. We should always adhere to the correct direction of reform and opening up, carry out the spirit of reform and innovation to all aspects of country governance, promote the reform of all areas, and advance the self-improvement and development of our socialist system. In addition, we should improve the scientific nature of the reform decision-making and the coordination of concrete measures, and correctly understand and properly handle the relationship among the reform, development and stability. At last, we should adhere to the basic national policy of opening up to the outside world, make it happen in all aspects, a higher level and wider areas, better combine the "bringing in" and "going out", and form the new advantage of participating in international economic cooperation and competition at the background of the economic globalization.

——The fundamental purpose. It reflects the starting point and foothold of developing socialism with Chinese characteristics and our Party's fundamental purpose——serving the people wholeheartedly. It is emphasized that the Party should always be built for the public and exercise power for people, adhere to the principle of being people-oriented, uphold the people's principal role in the cause of socialism with Chinese characteristics, carry forward the people's initiative spirit, realize, maintain and develop the fundamental interests of the majority of the people, safeguard people's various rights and interests, promote people's all-round development, so as to realize the development for the people, development relying on the people, and development achievements shared by the people.

——The economic construction. It stresses that we should establish and improve the socialist market economy system, adhere to and improve the basic economic system that public ownership plays the leading role and diverse forms of ownership develop side by side, accelerate the transformation of the economic development mode, and vigorously promote the strategic adjustment of the economic structure. By adhering to the status of science and technology as the first productive force, we should improve the independent innovation capability, promote the coordinated development between urban and rural areas, improve the macro-control system and the level of open economy, and promote the sound and fast development of the national economy. The civilized development path that we develop through production, enjoy in affluence, live in ecologically good environment.

——The political construction. It emphasizes that people's democracy is the life of socialism and thus we must adhere to the political development path of socialism with Chinese characteristics, the organic unity of CPC's leadership, people's status as the masters of the country and ruling by law, adhere to and improve the people's congress system, the CPC-led multi-party cooperation and political consultation system, the system of national regional autonomy and the grass-roots democratic system, and constantly promote the self-improvement and development of the political socialist system. We should adhere to the correct political direction, deepen the political system reform, ensure the people's status as the masters of the country, set the goal of enhancing the vitality of the Party and the country and mobilizing people's enthusiasm, expand socialist democracy, build a socialist country ruled by law and develop the political socialist civilization.

——The cultural construction. It stresses that we need to adhere to the direction of advanced culture, vigorously develop the national, scientific and popular socialist culture that is oriented to modernization, the world, and the future, promote the socialist cultural development and prosperity, and give rise to a new upsurge of the socialist cultural construction. By adhering to the guiding position of Marxism in the field of ideology, equipping people with the scientific theory, guiding people with the right public opinion, shaping people with the lofty spirit, inspiring people with excellent works, and approaching the reality, the life, and the masses, we should focus on constructing the socialist core values system, consolidating and expanding the mainstream ideological public opinion, promoting cultural innovation, deepening cultural system reform, developing cultural undertakings and industries, and improving the soft power of the national culture, so as to make the people's basic cultural rights and interests better guaranteed, the social and cultural life more colorful and people more high-spirited.

——The social (society) construction. It stresses that social harmony is the essential attribute of socialism with Chinese characteristics. As a result, to guarantee and improve people's livelihood must be carried out as a major task that concerns the overall situation, so as to promote social fairness and justice and enable all people to live a decent and dignified life in which they can be taught when they want to learn, get paid when they work, get treated when they are ill, be looked after properly when they turn old, and have a place for them to live in. We should also adhere to and improve the distribution system with distribution according to work being the main form and multiple ways of distribution co-existing, and promote the participation of such productive forces as the labor, capital, technology and management into the distribution. Special efforts shall be made to solve the most direct and realistic issue of interests that concern people the most, to correctly handle the contradictions among the people, to maximize the social vitality for creations and the harmonious factors, and to minimize the factors of disharmony.

——The national defense and army building. It stresses that we should, standing at the height of the national security and development strategy, integrate the economic construction with national defense construction, adhere to the Party's absolute leadership in the army and to the fundamental purpose of the people's army, implement the strategic military guideline in the new period, accelerate the military reform with Chinese characteristics, comprehensively strengthen and coordinate the advancement of the revolutionary construction, modernization and normalization of the army, and resolutely safeguard the integrity of the state sovereignty, security and territory, so as to make the prosperous country powerful in its army as well.

——Basic forces it depends on. It stresses that the working class including intellectuals, and the broad masses of farmers are the fundamental strength that promotes the development of advanced productive forces and the all-round social progress in our country; and the social classes newly emerging in the social transformation are constructors of the socialist cause with Chinese characteristics. We should fully implement the guideline of respecting the labor, the knowledge, the talent, and the creation, mobilize all positive factors in the broadest and fullest way, develop and expand the patriotic united front, unite all forces that can be united, and promote the harmony of party relations, ethnic relations, religious relations, relations among social strata, and relations among foreign and domestic compatriots at home and abroad.

——Promoting the great cause of the national reunification. We must unswervingly implement the highly autonomous principle of "One Country, Two Systems", "Hong Kong self-rule", and "Macao self-rule" and act strictly by the basic laws of the special administrative region, so as to maintain the long-term prosperity and stability of Hong Kong and Macao; adhere to the principle of "peaceful reunification, and One Country, Two Systems", the 8 proposals for developing the cross-straits relations and promoting the peaceful reunification process of the country, and the four points of view on the development of the cross-strait relations under the new situation, so as to initiate a new situation of the cross-strait relations and achieve the complete reunification of the country.

——The foreign diplomacy and international strategy. It stresses that we should hold high the banner of peace, development and cooperation, unswervingly follow the path of peaceful development, the independent foreign policy of peace, and the opening-up strategy of mutual benefit and win-win result, and develop itself through the maintenance of world peace and maintain world peace through its own development. Besides, we should develop the friendly cooperation with all countries on the basis of the five principles of peaceful coexistence and promote the construction of a harmonious world characteristic with lasting peace and common prosperity; the national sovereignty, security and development interests shall be safeguarded.

——The leadership core. It makes clear the leadership and fundamental guarantee of socialism with Chinese characteristics. It is emphasized that the key to China's problems lies in the Party and thus the Party construction, a new great project, should be connected with the great cause of socialism with Chinese characteristics, and be strengthened at the spirit of reform and innovation. It thus follows that we shall adhere to the principal line of the Party's governing capacity and advanced nature construction, persist in policing itself and imposing strict discipline on its members, strengthen the Party's ideological, organizational, work-style, institutional, and anti-corruption construction, so that the Party will always be the strong leadership core of the socialist cause with Chinese characteristics.

Generally speaking, the theoretical system of socialism with Chinese characteristics is not only a scientific, integrated and logically rigorous system in that it involves various aspects such as reform, development and stability, the domestic and foreign affairs and the national defense, and the administration of the Party, country and army, and covers the construction in such various areas as the economy, politics, culture, society, Party, national defense and army modernization, but also an open one that is constantly developing and will continue to enrich and develop with the development of the socialist practice with Chinese characteristics.

Section IV

Historical status, role and guiding significance of the theoretical system of socialism with Chinese characteristics

First, The correct theory guiding the Chinese people to victories in reform and opening and in promoting socialist modernization

The 17th National Congress of the Communist Party of China has written the theoretical system of socialism with Chinese characteristics into the party constitution and clearly pointed out that the theoretical system of socialism with Chinese characteristics ""upholds, develops and represents the Party's adherence to and development of Marxism-Leninism and Mao Zedong Thought and embodies the wisdom and hard work of several generations of Chinese Communists leading the people in carrying out tireless explorations and practices. It is the latest achievement in adapting Marxism to Chinese conditions, the Party's invaluable political and intellectual asset, and the common ideological foundation for the concerted endeavor of the people of all ethnic groups."[8]

This is our party's high evaluation of the historical status and guiding significance of the theoretical system of socialism with Chinese characteristics and reflects the common aspirations of the people of all ethnic groups throughout the country.

In the final analysis, the historical position of a scientific theory is determined by practice and determined by its historical pros and cons. Since the reform and opening-up for the past 30 plus years and more, under the guidance of the theoretical system of socialism with Chinese characteristics, we have achieved rapid and steady long-term development that was unprecedented in modern times and has won great successes that have attracted worldwide attention. From 1978 to 2007, China's GDP has increased from 364.5 billion yuan to 24.95 trillion yuan, with an average annual growth rate of 9.8%. This is more than three times the growth rate (annual) of the world economy. China's total economic aggregate has risen to fourth rank in the world fourth. We rely on our own strength in solving the food problem of our 1.3 billion people. China's total import-export volume has increased from 20.6 billion US dollars to 2.1737 trillion US dollars, ranking third in the world. Its foreign exchange reserves rank the first in the world, consequently China's foreign investments has increased substantially. And actually utilized foreign capital investments in China has reached nearly

---

8 CPCCC Party Literature Research Office: "Selection of Important Literature since the 17th National Congress" (Vol.I), p.9, Beijing, Central Literature Publishing House, 2009.

100 billion US dollars. The per capita disposable income of urban residents in China increased from 343 yuan to 13,786 yuan, an increase of 6.5 times in real terms. The per capita net income of farmers has increased from 134 yuan to 4,140 yuan, an increase of 6.3 times in real terms. The number of poor people in rural areas has dropped from 250 million to about 14 million. Urban per capita housing construction area and rural per capita housing area has doubled. We can see that people's household property, food, drinking and living standards have seen significant improvement.

The constant enhancement of the economic strength and comprehensive national strength, the remarkable achievements in political, cultural and social construction and the well-off status of people's living standards on the whole, and the historic changes of the Chinese people, the socialist China and the Communist Party of China, prove that the theoretical system of socialism with Chinese characteristics is the correct theory that has guided the Chinese people in successfully promoting the socialist modernization in the reform and opening up. In contemporary China, none but this theoretical system can instruct us to achieve the state prosperity and people's affluence and complete the historical task of the great rejuvenation of the Chinese nation.

Second, the basic goal of building a moderately well-off society

Since the reform and opening up, especially after entering the new stage of the new century, we have made steady steps towards the goal of building a well-off society in an all-round way which is supposed to be reached by 2020. In the course towards this goal, we face not only important development opportunities but also many contradictions and problems which are manifested in the following 8 aspects. First of all, the structural contradiction and extensive economic development mode formed in a long time remain without fundamental changes, with the relatively low-level productive forces and the less strong capability of independent innovation. Secondly, the institutional and mechanism obstacles in the development and the deep-level contradictions and problems in the further reform in difficult areas still exist. Thirdly, the trend of the widening income distribution gap has not been fundamentally reversed with the number of urban and rural poverty-stricken people and low-income people still considerable and the overall consideration of interests in all areas more difficult. Fourthly, the task of narrowing the gap between urban and rural areas and different regions and promoting the socially and economically coordinated development remains arduous considering the unchanged weak agricultural foundation and lagging rural development. Fifthly, the political system reform needs deepening since the construction of democracy and legal system is not fully adapted to the requirements of expanding people's democracy and economic and social development. Sixthly, people have increasing spiritual and cultural needs and their thoughts and activities are increasingly independent, variable, and diverse with more choices, which poses higher requirements for the development of advanced socialist culture. Seventhly, the social structure, social organizational form and social interests pattern have undergone profound changes, and the social construction and management are facing many new problems. Eighthly, the increasingly intense international competition, the advantages of the developed countries in the economy and science and technology over developing countries, and the increasing predictable and unpredictable risks, form a higher requirement for making overall plans of the domestic development and opening up to the outside world. In the face of such complex contradictions and problems and difficulties and challenges ahead, and in order to continue to promote reform and opening up and modernization, we have to adopt the scientific theory as the guidance. Only by adhering to the theoretical system of socialism with Chinese characteristics can we have a clearer understanding of the basic national conditions, the stage characteristics of development, and the objective laws of the socialist construction in our country, put forward the correct solutions to these contradictions and problems, and smoothly advance the great cause of building a well-off society in an all-round way and developing socialism with Chinese characteristics.

Third, common ideological basis for the struggles of the whole party and people from all nationalities

Common ideological foundation is the fundamental premise so that a party, a country and a nation can depend on and can maintain its existence and development. Without a common ideological foundation, the party will collapse and the country will be dissolved and its people will be divided. Mao Zedong emphasized: it is of great importance in achieving a common language in the Party, and that socialist countries should have "the will of unity". Deng Xiaoping emphasized: "in order to advance our cause "the most important thing is the unity of people. To achieve unity, people must have common ideals and firm convictions." Jiang Zemin pointed out: "If a country does not have its own spiritual supporting pillar, it means that it has no soul, and will lose its national cohesion and vitality."[9]

Hu Jintao pointed out: "lofty ideals and firm convictions are the great banners that unite people and inspire them to make new progress. They are the source of strength to overcome difficulties and win new victories."[10]

---

9   Selected Works of Jiang Zemin, Vol.2, pp.230-231, Beijing, People's Publishing House, 2006.
10   CPCCC Party Literature Research Office: "Selection of Important Literature since the 16th National Congress" (Vol. II) p.729, Beijing, Central Literature Publishing House, 2008.

As a new social system, socialism is not only a social movement, but also a pursuit of the ideal and value, which definitely requires us to unify people's thoughts with the common thought and will. The Soviet Union gave us a lesson on what kind of theory can be used to unify the Party's and people's thoughts. In the Soviet Union, the Party's theory was rather unattractive to the Party members and the masses considering the long-standing ideological rigidity and prevalence of dogmatism within the Party. After coming into power, Gorbachev put forward "the humane and democratic socialism", "new thinking", "openness", "democratization", "pluralistic guiding ideology", "political pluralism", and "multi-party system", which confused the thoughts of party members and the masses. Some western scholars explained that the reason for the collapse of the Communist Party of the Soviet Union was "the disintegration of the Marxist theory", which deprived the socialist system of its legitimacy. It shows that we should not only adhere to Marxism but also develop Marxism and unify people's thoughts and guide the practice with the developing Marxism. The ruling party with more than 80 million party members, confronted with a population of more than 1.3 billion in China, profound changes in the international and domestic environment, and people's diverse, variable, and pluralistic views and ideas, must adhere to the education of the Party and people with the developing Marxism and the theoretical system of socialism with Chinese characteristics. This theoretical system, integrating the socialist development with the historical task of national rejuvenation, the realization of socialist modernization with the common prosperity of the people, and the national security, danger, honor and disgrace with people's happiness, is the strong spiritual force leading and inspiring the people of all ethnic groups in the country and the backbone conquering all risks and challenges. Only by unifying the thoughts of the whole party and the people with this system can the people of different social classes and different interest groups be able to get united to the largest extent and work together for the common goal.

Fourth, a new breakthrough in the development of Marxist theory

Marx and Engels discussed the possibility of constructing socialism and how to build it in countries with backward economy and culture but failed to put it into practice for the absence of conditions. Lenin made some explorations according to Russia's realities, turned socialism from theory to reality, and achieved valuable results. Based on the experience of the Soviet Union and China's realities, Mao Zedong made deep reflections and practical explorations, which resulted in many creative ideas. However, Marxist classical writers cannot provide ready-made answers for how to build, consolidate and develop socialism in China today. Deng Xiaoping said: We cannot expect Marx to provide ready answers to questions that arise a hundred or several hundred years after his death, nor can we ask Lenin to give answers to questions that arise fifty or a hundred years after his death. A true Marxist-Leninist must understand, carry on and develop Marxism-Leninism in light of the current situation.[11]

After the 3rd Plenary Session of the 11th CPC Central Committee, our Party has been soberly aware that building socialism cannot proceed from the books nor from the inherent mode but from the concrete realities of China. It is stressed that we should not only adhere to the basic principles of Marxism and carry forward the revolutionary tradition but also compose a new epic of Marxism, create new experience, and guide the new practice of building socialism with Chinese characteristics with the developing Marxism. Our party has combined the basic principles of Marxism with the concrete practical realities of contemporary China, paved the socialist path with Chinese characteristics, formed the theoretical system of socialism with Chinese characteristics, systematically answered the major theoretical and practical problems of how to build, consolidate and develop socialism in China, added new content and made historic contributions to the Marxist theory.

---

11   Selected Works of Deng Xiaoping, 1st edition, Vol.3, p.291.

CHAPTER TWO

Ideological Line of Socialism with Chinese Characteristics

Section I

The enrichment and development of the party's ideological line

First, the re-establishment (correction) of the party's ideological line

"Ideological line", philosophically called cognitive line, refers to the world outlook and methodology hold by people in the activities of understanding and reforming the world. The fundamental question that it wants to answer and solve is the relationship between the subjective and objective and that between theory and practice. This question is in fact the concrete embodiment in actual work of the basic philosophical question, namely, the relationship between matter and consciousness and that between being and thinking. Dialectical materialism and historical materialism are scientific world outlook and methodology; the fundamental cognitive line of dialectical materialism and historical materialism and the ideological line of the proletariat and its political party is to proceed from reality in all work, achieve correspondence between subjectivity and objectivity, and integrate theory with practice.

The ideological line of the CPC is to proceed from reality in all work, integrate theory with practice, seek truth from facts and verify and develop the truth through practice. An important content and a scientific summary of this ideological line is to emancipate the mind, seek truth from facts, and advance with the times. However, seen from the historical development, emancipating the mind, seeking truth from facts, and advancing with the times, were not proposed at the same time but experienced a process of continuous enrichment and development. It can be said that Mao Zedong created this ideological line during the New Democratic Revolution, and summarized it as "seeking truth from facts". Deng Xiaoping re-established and developed it in the new period of socialist construction and summarized it as "emancipating the mind and seeking truth from facts". Jiang Zemin further developed it in the new century and summarized it as "emancipating the mind, seeking truth from facts, and advancing with the times".

During the period from the 1920s to 1930s, the "left-dogmatism" and the right-dogmatism in the CPC, especially the "left-dogmatism" represented by Wang Ming, carried out the cognitive line of proceeding from books only. Divorced from the actual situation of the Chinese society and the Chinese revolution, they blindly copied the experience of the October Revolution (Union of Soviet Socialist Republics) and the resolutions of the Communist International. They depended on rote memorization of the books of Marxism-Leninism to solve the extremely complex problem in China, namely how should China carry out revolution in a semi-colonial and semi-feudal society, which almost drove the Chinese revolution to the last ditch. The CPC, represented by Mao Zedong, followed the cognitive line of proceeding from reality in all work and combined the basic principles of Marxism-Leninism with the concrete reality of the Chinese revolution. Their shifts depending on time, place and conditions had repeatedly saved Chinese revolution. In the actual activities of leading the Chinese revolution, Mao Zedong deeply realized the harm of dogmatism and bookishness inconsistent with the reality of China to the CPC. In order to overcome various wrong ideas widely found in the Party and ensure the smooth development of the Chinese revolution, Mao Zedong summed up the basic cognitive line of dialectical materialism and historical materialism—proceeding from the realities—with four characters "seeking truth from facts" in the 1940s, and established it as the ideological line of the Chinese communists. Under the guidance of this ideological line, the Chinese communists overcame the obstacles on the way forward, found China's own revolutionary path, won the new-democratic revolution and established the People's Republic of China. After the founding of the new China, under the guidance of this ideological line, the Chinese communists quickly restored the national economy, successfully realized the socialist transformation of agriculture, handicrafts and capitalist industry, established a socialist system and developed the socialist economy, politics and culture.

In the 1980s, during the struggle against the wrong thinking of "Two Whatevers", Deng Xiaoping mentioned "emancipating the mind" and "seeking truth from facts" together, proposed a new summary of the fundamental cognitive line of dialectical materialism and historical materialism according with the needs of the development of times, re-established the ideological line of seeking truth from facts, and added "emancipating the mind" to this ideological line, so as to break the long-standing social situation characteristic with the ideological rigidity, ideological conservatism and ideological confinement, eliminate the ideological restraints of personal superstition and personal worship on the whole Party and all the people, get rid of the harmful effects of the "Cultural Revolution" and create a new historical development period. Guided by the ideological line of emancipating the mind and seeking truth from facts, the whole Party and all the people started from the reality of the primary stage of socialism, made trials and errors, and have created a socialist path with Chinese characteristics and made great groundbreaking achievements on this path.

Second, the enrichment and development of the ideological line

Just after entering the 21th century, in the report of the 16th National Congress of the Chinese Communist Party, Jiang Zemin pointed out: "Persisting in the party's ideological line, emancipating the mind, seeking truth from facts, and advancing with the times are the decisive elements for our party to adhere and maintain to its advanced nature and enhance its creativity."[1]

This new argument is the new summary of the fundamental cognitive line of dialectical materialism and historical materialism made by the Chinese communists in the new stage of the new century, according to the new situation, new tasks and new requirements. This new summary is consistent with the development needs of the times. It not only adheres to the ideological line of emancipating the mind and seeking truth from facts, but also adds the new content of "advancing with the times" to this ideological line.

In January 2004, at the 3rd Plenary Meeting of the Discipline Inspection Committee of CPC Central Committee, General Secretary Hu Jintao put forward the new requirements of "being realistic and pragmatic" to the whole Party. The essence of being realistic and pragmatic is to ask the whole Party to continuously seek for the truth of the basic national conditions in the primary stage of socialism in China and adhere to long-term and arduous struggle; seek the law of socialist construction and human social development, and do a good job at development which is the first priority of the Party in governing and rejuvenating the country; seek the historical status and function of the masses, and develop the fundamental interests of the overwhelming majority of the people; seek the law of the governance by the communist party and strengthen and improve the Party construction. To adhere to being realistic and pragmatic, we should strive to: effectively strengthen ideological education, constantly improve the consciousness of the party members and cadres of being realistic and pragmatic; insist

1   CPCCC Party Literature Research Office: "Selection of Important Literature since the 16th National Congress" (Vol.I) p.9, Beijing, Central Literature Publishing House, 2008.

on serving the people wholeheartedly, and straighten out the relationship with the masses; correctly understand the national conditions, formulate the guidelines and policies and carry out the work according to the national conditions; understand, grasp, follow and apply the laws. In short, being realistic and pragmatic is to closely focus on the implementation of the work of the Party and the country, put theory into practice, translate idea into action and achieve results.

From "seeking truth from facts" established by Mao Zedong to Deng Xiaoping's "emancipating the mind and seeking truth from facts", to Jiang Zemin's "emancipating the mind, seeking truth from facts and advancing with the times", and to the new demand of "being realistic and pragmatic" put forward by the former General Secretary Hu Jintao, we can clearly see the continuous enrichment and development of the ideological line of the CPC in revolution, construction and reform practice. With such a continuous enrichment and development, the various undertakings of the Party and China have been given a strong spiritual driving force, and the Party's theoretical innovation given a fountain head.

Section II

Theoretical qualities and essence of Marxism

First, theoretical qualities and essence of Marxism-Leninism

Marxism is a scientific theory that has evolved with the development of social practice. Emancipating the mind, seeking truth from facts, advancing with the times are the theoretical qualities and essence of Marxism. Marxism was born in the 1840s.

Before the creation of Marxism, capitalist society was shrouded in a kind of innocent "myth". When the bourgeoisie created a productivity that was larger in amount and greater than all productivities created before during its rule which only lasted less than one hundred years and when the capitalist system showed progress and superiority over the feudal system in all aspects of social life, the bourgeois thinkers, theorists and politicians were so absorbed in such a victory, believing that the capitalist society was the best and most desirable society in the mankind history and that the capitalist system would be sacred and unshakeable.

Although some economists, philosophers and historians had found that capitalism was not perfect with many defects and full of many evils through studies and observations in various fields, they still strove to speak for the capitalism and demonstrate the sanctity of the capitalist system. In the 1940s, Marx and Engels, starting from the actual conditions of the age when they lived and critically inheriting all outstanding ideological achievements created before and at that time, carried out an in-depth study on the operation characteristics, basic contradiction and development trend of capitalist economy, politics, culture and social life, and finally reached a scientific conclusion that capitalism was bound to death and socialism was bound to success. They founded Marxism, declared the failure of the myth that capitalism was sacred and unshakeable with the power of truth, and created a new realm of understanding the law and direction of human society development, thus establishing a scientific ideological system for the liberation movement of the proletariat and all mankind.

Although Marxism, with its critical and scientific spirit, has been warmly welcomed by the proletariat and the masses in the world and has so many strong believers and followers, thus it has become the guiding ideology and theoretical weapon of the proletarian political party, Marx and Engels have never regarded their theories as absolute truths, nor have they treated the specific conclusions that they have arrived under particular historical conditions as definite and rigid formulas, besides they have also opposed others who treated their theories as such.

They always emphasized repeatedly: "Our theory is a theory of evolution, not of dogma to be learned by heart and to be repeated mechanically."[2]

For example, *The Communist Manifesto*, which is the creation as well as the first programmatic document of Marxism, played a great guiding role in the vigorous development of the workers movement. But the practice in 1872 developed on the basis of the practice at the time when *The Communist Manifesto* was issued, and as a result, Marx and Engels pointed out clearly in the preface to the second edition of *The Communist Manifesto*: "However much that state of things may have altered during the last twenty-five years, the general principles laid down in the Manifesto are, on the whole, as correct today as ever. Here and there, some detail might be improved. The practical application of the principles will depend, as the Manifesto itself states, everywhere and at all times, on the historical conditions for the time being existing...., no special stress is laid on the revolutionary measures proposed at the end of Section II. That passage would, in many respects, be very differently worded today.... "But since then, the Manifesto has become a historical document which we have no longer any right to alter."[3]

2　Selected Works of Marx and Engels, 2nd edition, Vol.4, p.681, Beijing, People's Publishing House, 1995.
3　Selected Works of Marx and Engels, 2nd Edition, Vol.1, pp.248-249, Beijing, People's Publishing House, 1995.

Nowhere did Marx indicate this more clearly as when he wrote in his 1877 letter to the Editor of the Petersburg literary-political journal Otechstvennye Zapiski, which printed an article by Nicolai K. Mikhailovski, who treated the analysis found in his book *Capital* as iron-clad historical laws in non-European settings: He must by all means transform my historical sketch of the development of capitalism in Western Europe into a historical philo-sophical theory of universal development predetermined by fate for all na-tions, whatever their historic circumstances in which they find themselves may be,.... But I beg his pardon. (That mistaken understanding, does me at the same time too much honor and too much insult)."[4]

For example, when Engels wrote about how to treat materialism, he pointed to the powerful and ever more rapidly onrushing progress of natu-ral science, technology and industry, which have profoundly changed the connotation and denotation of social practice, and he explicitly stressed: "with each epoch-making discovery even in the sphere of natural science it has to change its form."[5]

The adherence to obtaining theory from practice, putting theory into practice for the test of practice and developing theory together with practice run through the life of Marx and Engels.

Born in the turn of the 19th century and the 20th century, Leninism is the Marxism appearing when capitalism developed into imperialism. In the late 1800s and early 1900s, the capitalism entering the imperialist stage underwent quite a lot of changes and found many new characteristics in economy, politics, culture, society and other aspects, comparing to that in the era of free competition. Then, how to rediscover the conditions, paths, methods, means and strategies of proletarian revolution according to the changing situation and practice and turn scientific socialism from theo-ry into practice became a major subject that need be taken seriously and solved by Marxists. However, some people did not proceed from reality but from the books. They rigidified and dogmatized the concrete conclusions of Marx and Engels made in specific historical period and under specific his-torical conditions. They insisted that the socialist revolution could only be successful through simultaneously breaking out in the developed European and American capitalist countries. They argued that the revolution could never break out in the economically and culturally backward countries, let alone achieving the success of socialist revolution. However Lenin insisted that: Marxism is not a dogma but a guide to action.

---

4   Selected Works of Marx and Engels, 2nd Edition, Vol.3, p.342, Beijing, People's Publishing House, 1995; Marx's 1877 Letter to the Editor of the Petersburg Literary-political journal Otechstvennye Zapiski.
5   https://www.marxists.org/archive/marx/works/1886/ludwig-feuerbach/ch02.htm.

For the present, it is essential to grasp the incontestable truth that a Marxist must take cognizance of real life, of the true facts of *reality*, and not cling to a theory of yesterday, which, like all theories, at best only outlines the main and the general, only *comes near* to embracing life in all its complexity. "Theory, my friend, is grey, but green is the eternal tree of life."[6]

Starting from this, Lenin combined the basic principles of Marxism with the characteristics of the times and the specific realities of the Russian revolution. Based on the new historical conditions and social practice and through in-depth study of the basic contradictions and development trend of the political and economic relations within and between the imperialist countries, he discovered the imbalance between the economic development and political development of capitalism, and further concluded that: under the new development conditions, the socialist revolution could succeed first in one or several countries in the weak link of the imperialist domination.

"On the Slogan for a United States of Europe" in August 1915, Lenin wrote: Uneven economic and political development is an absolute law of capitalism. Hence, the victory of socialism is possible first in several or even in one capitalist country alone."[7] In 1917, in his "The Military Programme of the Proletarian Revolution" he wrote: The development of capitalism proceeds extremely unevenly in different countries. It cannot be otherwise under commodity production. From this it follows irrefutably that socialism cannot achieve victory simultaneously *in all* countries. It will achieve victory first in one or several countries, while the others will for some time remain bourgeois or pre-bourgeois."[8]

The victory of the Russian October Revolution and the victory of the socialist revolution of the countries with relatively backward economy and culture in the later period proved that Marx and Engels' thought that the success of socialist revolution could only be achieved simultaneously in several developed capitalist countries did not conform to the new historical conditions and Lenin's revision of Marx and Engels' conclusions based on the new practice was completely correct. His revision is a significant theoretical innovation to Marxism, creating a new realm of understanding the socialist revolution.

Lenin pushed Marxism into a new stage, namely the stage of Leninism, and turned scientific socialism from theory into practice. However, Lenin did not become complacent because of his great theoretical contribution to the development of Marxism, nor did he absolutize the Russian path because of obtaining the first success of socialist revolution. On the issue of

6 https://www.marxists.org/archive/lenin/works/1917/apr/x01.htm.

7 https://www.marxists.org/archive/lenin/works/1915/aug/23.htm.

8 https://www.marxists.org/archive/lenin/works/1916/miliprog/i.htm.

theoretical development and revolutionary path, he, like Marx and Engels, respected practice, insisted on correctness and corrected mistakes. For example, with regard to the socialist path, Lenin pointed out that all nations would eventually go to socialism, which was the universal law of the history of the world. However, socialism cannot be achieved simultaneously in various countries in accordance with the same pattern. Because of the different conditions in the construction of socialism in various countries, such as nationality differences, national differences, local differences, the characteristics of economic structure, lifestyle and other aspects, there are various forms for the countries to move to socialism. And the richer the diversity is, the more reliable and the faster the process moving towards socialism is.

Lenin pointed out, in his attitude towards Marxism: We do not regard Marx's theory as something completed and inviolable; on the contrary, we are convinced that it has only laid the foundation stone of the science which socialists must develop in all directions if they wish to keep pace with life. We think that an independent elaboration of Marx's theory is especially essential for Russian socialists; for this theory provides only general guiding principles, which, in particular, are applied in England differently than in France, in France differently than in Germany, and in Germany differently than in Russia.[9]

Moreover, after the proletariat gained power, how to transit to socialism and carry out socialist construction is a new and unprecedented undertaking. In order to seek the path for an economically backward country to transit to socialism, Lenin tried "wartime communist policy", and envisioned a direct transition to communism spanning market and merchandise money relations, namely the transition to the unified production and distribution organized by the country. However, it was found that the approach had many problems and was not applicable. Lenin stopped it decisively, and admitted the failure bluntly.

Lenin decisively stopped this policy and frankly admitted that he "made a lot of mistakes in this regard." He also emphasized in particular: "The responsibility of the Communists is not to conceal the weaknesses of their own movement, but to openly criticize the weaknesses so that they can be overcome quickly and thoroughly."

"The attitude of a political party toward its own mistakes is critical in respect whether this party is solemn and whether it truly fulfills one of the most important and credible missions it has assumed for the class and the working masses."[10]

---

9   http://www.marx2mao.com/Lenin/ARG99.html.

10   Ibid., p.167.

Second, the theoretical qualities and the essence of Mao Zedong Thought

Born in the 1940s, Mao Zedong Thought is the first theoretical achievement of Marxism in China. From 1840 to 1920, the Chinese progressive people and political forces had explored for 80 years in order to revitalize the Chinese nation. However, they still failed to truly rescue China from sufferings. The October Revolution sent Marxism-Leninism to China, "Follow the path of the Russians—that was the conclusion". In 1921, the CPC, which was armed with Marxism-Leninism, was founded. And since then, the Chinese revolution has taken on a new look. However, the development of the Chinese revolution was not plain sailing, and the final victory of the revolution was not won easily.

In the history of our party, in a period of time, some so-called real Marxists in the CPC could not correctly understand the true meaning of "taking the path of Russia." Instead of proceeding from the actual situation in China they have proceeded from Marxist books on the series of questions regarding the nature, path, motive forces, strategy and tactics of the Chinese revolution. Instead of exploring the various questions encountered by the Chinese revolution independently, they have absolutized the experiences of the Soviet revolution and sanctified the resolutions of the Comintern, which, has for several times caused the thriving revolutionary movement into frustration. Comrade Mao Zedong resolutely opposed this subjectivism and dogmatism in the Party that did not conform with realities, and who blindly copied others' experiences. He insisted that "the victory of the China's revolutionary struggle will depend relies on the Chinese comrades" understanding of Chinese conditions".

He emphasized: It is up to the Chinese comrades to create a new situation in the revolutionary struggle, it is necessary to learn to apply the basic theory of Marxism-Leninism to the specific environment of China and integrate it with the actual situation in China. He said: to use a common expression, it is by "shooting the arrow at the target". As the arrow is to the target, so is Marxism-Leninism to the Chinese revolution.

With that in mind, Mao Zedong combined the basic principles of Marxism with the actual situation of Chinese revolution and followed the standpoint, viewpoint and method of dialectical materialism and historical materialism. Based on the changes of historical conditions and practice, the in-depth study of Chinese social class, social bracket and Chinese economic, political and cultural structure, and the summary of the experience and lessons of success and failure, he correctly answered Chinese social nature, revolutionary nature, revolutionary path, revolutionary stage, leading class, supporting power and other major problems, founded Mao Zedong

Thought, and realized the first historical leap of combining Marxism with practice in China.

For example, on the nature of the Chinese revolution, Mao Zedong gave a thorough analysis of the colonial, semi-colonial and semi-feudal nature of Chinese society: Since Chinese society is colonial, semi-colonial and semi-feudal, since the principal enemies of the Chinese revolution are imperialism and feudalism, since the tasks of the revolution are to overthrow these two enemies by means of a national and democratic revolution in which the bourgeoisie sometimes takes part, and since the edge of the revolution is directed against imperialism and feudalism and not against capitalism and capitalist private property in general even if the big bourgeoisie betrays the revolution and becomes its enemy—since all this is true, the character of the Chinese revolution at the present stage is not proletarian-socialist but bourgeois-democratic."[11]

However, in present-day China the bourgeois-democratic revolution is no longer of the old general type, which is now obsolete, but one of a new special type. We call this type the new-democratic revolution and it is developing in all other colonial and semi-colonial countries as well as in China. The new-democratic revolution is part of the world proletarian-socialist revolution."[12]

With regard to the stage of the Chinese revolution, Mao Zedong pointed out that: since the Chinese society is colonial, semi-colonial and semi-feudal, the Chinese revolution should be divided into two steps. The first step is the new democratic revolution, and the second is the socialist revolution. The two revolutionary steps are like the first part and the second part of one article. The New-Democratic Revolution is the first part, and the Socialist Revolution is the second part. Only after completing the first part can the second part be started. The first part is the necessary preparation, and the second part is the inevitable outcome of the first part. And no dictatorship of bourgeoisie appearing between the two parts should be allowed. We may turn to the path of the Chinese revolution. What kind of path should Chinese revolution take? Mao Zedong did not proceed from books, but from the specific realities of China. He pointed out that: in China, due to the weak force of proletariat, the large cities in China were completely in the hands of the reactionary ruling class. Therefore, the European revolution path of creating revolutionary surge through revolts in central cities did was not applicable at all. On the contrary, China had vast rural area where there was relatively weak domination of the reactionary forces. The rural area could provide a wide margin for revolutionary forces, and there were the most reliable allies of the proletariat, namely the peasants. Only by relying

11 http://radicaljournal.com/essays/the_chinese_revolution_party.html.
12 Ibid.

on the rural areas, arming the workers and peasants, creating the red regime, and encircling the city from the rural areas can the proletariat finally win the success. Therefore, the path of the Chinese revolution is different from the Russian path. It can only be the path of encircling the cities from rural areas and seizing power by armed people. Moreover, in terms of the transition to socialism, Mao Zedong proceeded from the reality of China. After winning the victory of the new democratic revolution, there was a period of new democratic society. Then, there was socialist transformation of agriculture, handicrafts and capitalist industry and commerce from new democracy. In this way, the transition to socialism was achieved in a peaceful way. All these are pioneering work, adding new and valuable content to the development of Marxism-Leninism.

Although Mao Zedong made serious mistakes in his later years and once deviated from the ideological line of seeking truth from facts established by him, he was still a great Marxist seen from his whole life. Without his creation of the special path of the Chinese revolution, successful exploration of the transition of the backward countries to socialist and pioneering work in other aspects, it would be impossible to have the victory of the Chinese revolution and the establishment of the socialist system of China. Even the mistakes made by Mao Zedong in his later years also provided a useful lesson for Deng Xiaoping to explore the construction of socialism with Chinese characteristics seen from the dialectical point of view. Deng Xiaoping's theory exactly generated, formed and developed on the basis of inheriting forefathers, pioneering and innovating, and insisting on correctness and correcting mistakes.

Third, the theoretical qualities and the essence of Deng Xiaoping Theory

Formed in the 1980s, Deng Xiaoping Theory is an important theoretical achievement of Marxism in China as well as an important part of the theoretical system of socialism with Chinese characteristics. In the late 1970s, China's society was at a critical juncture in its development. The whole Party and the national people had three paths to choose. One was the old path. The second was the crooked path and the third was a new path. The old path was to continue to follow the "Cultural Revolution", namely the path of "Two Whatevers". The crooked path was to deny the socialist path on the excuse of denying the "Great Cultural Revolution" and any mistakes made before, namely the capitalist path. The new path was not only different from the old path, but also different from the crooked path. It was a path leading to the bright. Which way would China go? The answer was related to the future of socialism and the future of the Party and the country. With extraordinary courage, Deng Xiaoping led the whole Party to break through the constraint of "Two Whatevers"a new way by rejecting the old path.

Then, he definitely criticized the ideological trend of denying socialism, refusing the crooked path. He insisted on combining the basic principles of Marxism with the contemporary Chinese practice and the characteristics of the times, and insisted on taking practice as the only standard to test the truth. He constantly summed up experiences, affirmed achievements, corrected mistakes, and led the whole Party and the national people to make bold breakthrough and trial. Finally, he carved out a new path, namely the socialist path with Chinese characteristics.

In the process of paving this new path, Deng Xiaoping's greatest characteristic is that he was not dogmatic but insisted on emancipating the mind, even in questions such as what is Marxism and what is socialism.

Deng Xiaoping said: For many years there has been a question of how to understand Marxism and socialism…. Nobody was clear about exactly what changes had taken place over the century since Marx's death or about how to understand and develop Marxism in light of those changes. We cannot expect Marx to provide ready answers to questions that arise a hundred or several hundred years after his death, nor can we ask Lenin to give answers to questions that arise fifty or a hundred years after his death. A true Marxist-Leninist must understand, carry on and develop Marxism-Leninism in light of the current situation."[13]

Lenin was a true and great Marxist because it was not books that enabled him to find the revolutionary path and to accomplish the October socialist revolution in backward Russia but realities, logic, philosophical thinking and communist ideals. It was not by reading the works of Marx and Lenin that the great Marxist-Leninist Mao Zedong learned how to accomplish the new-democratic revolution in backward China. Could Marx predict that the October Revolution would take place in backward Russia? Could Lenin foresee that the Chinese revolutionaries would win by encircling the cities from the countryside?"[14]

The reason why Lenin is a true and great Marxist is that he found the revolutionary path from reality, logic, philosophy and communism ideal instead of books, and obtained the success of October Socialist Revolution in a backward country. Mao Zedong, the great Marxist-Leninist of China, did not seek the way to win the victory of the New-Democratic Revolution in the backward China from the books of Marx and Lenin. Could Marx expect the success of the October Revolution in a backward Russia? Could Lenin predict that China will win victory by encircling the cities from the rural areas?" The same is true when the question is how to build up a country. After winning the revolution, the countries should build socialism on their

13   https://archive.org/stream/SelectedWorksOfDengXiaopingVol.3/Deng03_djvu.txt.
14   Ibid.

own terms. There is and will be no fixed pattern. It is precisely this spirit that makes Deng Xiaoping become the founder of Deng Xiaoping Theory.

From Marx to Deng Xiaoping, from the scientific socialist theory to practice, from one nation's practice to multiple nations' practice, from the Soviet model socialism to the socialism with Chinese characteristics, the development history of Marxism fully proves that the history of Marxism is the history of emancipating the mind, seeking truth from facts and advancing with the times since its birth. The reason why Marxism is the truth is that it insists on emancipating the mind, seeking truth from facts, advancing with the times, and developing with the development of the times; Marxism is a theoretical weapon because it emancipates the mind, seeks truth from facts, keeps pace with the times and is able to solve the major practical problems. The classical Marxist writers never regard their own theories as a dogma, but as a guide to action and a scientific method of understanding and solving problems; they never regard their theories as changeless thing and irrevocable ultimate truth. On the contrary, they always enrich and develop their own theories with the development of practice and according to new practical experience, so as to make their theories accept the test of the society. And they will correct incorrect understanding and judgment according to the test of the society. Emancipating the mind, seeking truth from facts and advancing with the times profoundly reveals the practicality, scientificity and expansibility of Marxism, and provides a scientific perspective for us to understand the development law and vitality of Marxism.

41

Section III

Advancing with the times

First, the ideological connotations and the relationship between emancipating the mind, seeking truth from facts and advancing with the times

Emancipating the mind, seeking truth from facts, advancing with the times, the 3 principles contain rich ideological contents. The so-called emancipation of the mind is to bravely break the shackles of backward traditional concepts and be good at starting from reality and strive to forge ahead"[15]

It is manifested in three aspects. First of all, the premise of emancipating the mind shall be the guidance of Marxism. Mind emancipation will be impossible if non-Marxism or even anti-Marxism rather than Marxism is taken as the guidance. Secondly, mind emancipation shall aim at break

15 CPCCC Party Literature Research Office: "Selection of Important Literature since the 13th National Congress" (Vol.II) p.2081, Beijing, People's Publishing House, 1993.

the habitual force and subjective prejudice. If it does not aim to break the habitual force and subjective prejudice, but the correct ideas and practices meeting the needs of social development, it shall not be regarded as mind emancipation. Thirdly, the purpose of emancipating the mind shall be studying the new situation, solving new problems and forging ahead. If mind emancipation only remains in the empty slogan and the "revolution" in the mind instead of solving practical problems and forging ahead, it shall not be regarded as mind emancipation. The true mind emancipation shall be the integration of all these three aspects.

According to Mao Zedong's argument seeking truth from facts, includes the following of cessation: "Facts" are all the things that exist objectively, "truth" means their internal relations, that is, the laws governing them, and "to seek," means to study. We should proceed from the actual conditions inside and outside the country, the province, county or district, and derive from them, as our guide to action, laws that are inherent in them and not imaginary, that is, we should find the internal relations of the events occurring around us. And in order to do that we must rely not on subjective imagination, not on momentary enthusiasm, not on lifeless books, but on facts that exist objectively; we must appropriate the study material in detail and, guided by the general principles of Marxism-Leninism, draw correct conclusions from it.[16]

To be simple, seeking truth from facts is to require people to adhere to proceeding from reality, understanding things according to their original appearance, seeing through the appearance to perceive the essence, striving to grasp the internal relations and development of things, guiding actions with the understanding of the development law of things, and consciously realizing the historical unity of subjective and objective, theory and practice in the activities of understanding and reforming the world.

"Keeping pace with the times means that all the theory and work of the Party must conform to the times, follow the law of development and display great creativity."…"Its content includes the organic combination of these three aspects: the characteristics of times, regularity and creativity."[17]

Emancipating the mind, seeking truth from facts, advancing with the times is an organic whole. The three aspects are interrelated, mutually promoted and indivisible. Emancipating the mind is the premise and condition of seeking truth from facts. Seeking truth from facts is the essence and foundation of emancipating the mind. The two are unified in the social practice. In the final analysis, they are unified in the process of advancing with the times. The key of adhering to the Party's ideological line, emancipating the

16 https://www.marxists.org/reference/archive/mao/works/red-book/ch23.htm.
17 http://www.fmprc.gov.cn/mfa_eng/topics_665678/3698_665962/t18872.shtml; Selected Works of Jiang Zemin, Volume 3, p. 537, Beijing, People's Publishing House, 2006.

mind, seeking truth from facts and advancing with the times is to carry on truth-seeking and pragmatic spirit and adhere to advancing with the times. Whether this can be achieved consistently determines the future of the Party and the country.

Second, keeping up with the times as the key link

Why is "keeping up with the times" the key link?

To correctly understand and grasp this problem, we must first correctly understand and grasp the concept of "times". The so-called "times" is an important philosophical category.

Philosophically, its biggest characteristic is that it is one-dimensional, just like time. In other words, it moves in one direction, which is irreversible. Time is continuous, but it is manifested through different stages of development. The larger time span can be called the era, and the smaller time span can be called the development stage or historical period. Whether it is the era, the stage of development or the historical period, the question of the times discussed now is to emphasize that the present is not the past. It is necessary to recognize the difference between the present and the past, the changes since the publication of *The Communist Manifesto*, and the new situation and new features presented at current development stage compared with the previous development stages. It is because of the characteristics of the times that Jiang Zemin had repeatedly stressed that adhering to advancing with the times is to recognize the major changes in politics, economy, culture, technology and other aspects over the past more than 160 years since the publication of *The Communist Manifesto*, the major changes in the socialist construction of China, and the major changes in the work, living conditions and social environment of the vast party members and cadres and the masses. It is also necessary to take full account of the serious challenges and new subjects put forward by these changes to the Party, correctly understand the historical process of socialist development, and have a correct understanding of the historical process of the socialist development and capitalist development, the influence of the practice of Chinese socialist reform on the thoughts of people, and the influence of current international environment and international political struggle. Great changes have taken place in the times, and the history has entered a new stage of development. The situation has changed, and the problems are different. In this way, the theory, ideas, methods and measures to solve the problem cannot remain unchanged. If we indiscriminately copy the old theory, ideas, methods and measures to face the new situation, solve the new problems, and create new things, we will inevitably get into trouble on all sides and encounter failure. This is why the adherence to advancing with the times should firstly ensure that "all theories and the work of the Party accord with the times".

Secondly, to correctly understand and grasp that the key is to advance with times, we should also correctly understand and grasp the relationship between the times and regularity and the significance of regularity. Whether in philosophy or science, "time" is not an empty frame existing independently. It is always closely related to things, and is the form of existence and development of things. When "time" changes, things will change too. And the internal relationship among things and the development rule and development trend formed by such relationship will also change inevitably. Based on this, we have every reason to say that situation changes when time changes. The past has its own situation, so does the present. Only by grasping the present can we grasp the current situation, go with the flow, and ride on the momentum. If we stand still, we will go against the flow and will inevitably encounter failure. Throughout the development history of human society, the current age is different from the age more than 160 years ago, and the current situation is different from that more than 160 years ago. The times have changed, and the situation is different. As a result, the development law and development trend of social politics, economy, culture and other aspects of social life will also change inevitably.

To advance with times, we must study new situation and new problems, grasp the new laws and new trends of the development of things, and guide our actions with the understanding and grasp of new laws. Otherwise, nothing will be done. Why the formal Chairman Jiang Zemin repeatedly stressed that all party members should focus on the practical problems of China's reform and opening up and modernization construction, things we are doing, the application of Marxist theory, the theoretical thinking on practical problems, new practices and new developments? That is the reason; and that is also the reason why the adherence to advancing with the times is to "make all theories and work of the Party... should accord with the laws of development".

Finally, to understand and grasp that the key is to advance with times, the most important is to correctly understand and grasp the "advancing". The achievement of advancing with the times, after all, should be reflected in the ability to "keep pace". "Advancing" is to move forward. However, moving forward cannot be realized passively. It should be a kind of conscious behavior. This requires forging ahead and bold innovation. We need to open a path in the thorns, and even a path in the place where there is no path. If there is no forging ahead, there will be no new path. Without innovation, there will be no new ideological realm. The discovery of the special path of the New Democratic Revolution in China and the opening of the path of socialist construction with Chinese characteristics has proved the importance of innovation. In the 1960s, Mao Zedong once pointed out that human beings have to constantly sum up, discover, invent, create, and move forward. Attitudes of cessation, pessimism, inaction and complacency are all wrong.

He added: Ideas of stagnation, pessimism, inertia and complacency are all wrong. They are wrong because they agree neither with the historical facts of social development over the past million years, nor with the historical facts of nature so far known to us (i.e., nature as revealed in the history of celestial bodies, the earth, life, and other natural phenomena)."[18]

By entering into the 21st century, Jiang Zemin explicitly pointed out: "Innovation is the soul driving a nation's progress and an inexhaustible source of a country's prosperity and development, also the source of the eternal vitality of a political party."[19]

In the report of the 16th CPC National Congress, he highlighted the importance of innovation again through summarizing the development history of human society, the social development history of Chinese society, especially that since the modern times, and the struggling course of the CPC since its establishment.

Innovation is manifested in the theory, institution, science and technology, culture and other aspects of the society. In these innovations, theoretical innovation is the premise and key to the development of the Party and the country. System innovation is the guarantee of the development of the Party and the national cause. Scientific and technological innovation and cultural innovation are the driving force and intellectual support for the development of the Party and the country.

The classical Marxist writers once made clear that the theory is the forerunner of action and there will be no real revolutionary movement without the correct revolutionary theory; once the correct theory is mastered by the masses, it will be transformed into a great material force to transform the world. Therefore, to obtain the continuous development of the cause of the Party and the country, it is necessary to continuously develop theory at first. The theoretical innovation should be carried out, otherwise all new developments will indulge in empty talk.

However, theoretical innovation does not drop from the skies, nor generate by itself. It is driven by social practice and its needs. Marx made it clear that the degree of implementing a theory in one country depends on the degree to which the theory meets the needs of the country. The content of theoretical innovation comes from the scientific induction, summary and sublimation of new practical experience; theoretical innovation depends on absorbing all the outstanding ideological achievements made

18   https://www.marxists.org/reference/archive/mao/works/red-book/ch22.htm.
19   Selected Works of Jiang Zemin, Vol.3, p.64.

by predecessors and contemporaries; whether the theoretical innovation is true or false should be tested and judged by practice; the innovative theory can be the guide of new practice. Practice, need, inheritance and new practice guidance are indispensable elements and functions of theoretical innovation.

The vitality of Marxism lies in constant theoretical innovation; the vitality and vigor of the CPC also lies in constant theoretical innovation.

In his article "Insist on the Scientific Method in the Study of Marxism and Start from Practical Problems", Jiang Zemin pointed out: "Attaching importance to theoretical construction and theoretical guidance is one of the fundamental characteristics of our party. And emphasizing the building of the party ideologically is an important political experience of our party. At every moment of the development of our enterprise, our party has paid due attention to the supreme priority of theoretical construction. Our 80-year historical experience shows that paying attention to theoretical innovation is an important guarantee for the advancement of the party's cause. As long as we closely the principle linking theory with practice and continuously push forward the theoretical innovation, the cause of the Party is full of vigor and vitality, and when the development of theory lags behind the practice, the cause of the party will be harmed and even setbacks will occur."[20]

In his speech at the meeting celebrating the 80th anniversary of the founding of the Chinese Communist Party, Jiang Zemin further pointed out: "Many changes have taken place in the present world and the time we are in, as compared with the past. We face many problems both at the international level and domestic level, therefore new problems and new situations must be answered and resolved theoretically and practically or we will not be able to move forward smoothly. We must keep pace with the times and continue to enrich and develop Marxism. If we allow the trend of old age and stagnation, we will be out of date, and our party will face with the risk of losing its advanced nature and leadership qualifications."[21]

When celebrating the 90th anniversary of the founding of the Chinese Communist Party, Hu Jintao pointed out: "For Marxism, practice is the source of its theory, the basis for its development, and the criterion for testing its truth. Any actions that stick to dogma, ignore practice, or overstep or lag behind real life will not succeed."[22]

Based on China's national conditions, we find that the world is changing when we open our eyes to the whole world and look forward to the future. China's reform and opening up and modernization is moving forward, and

20　Jiang Zemin: "On Party Building", p.536, Beijing, Central Literature Publishing House, 2001.
21　http://www.china.org.cn/e-speech/a.htm.
22　http://en.people.cn/90001/90776/90785/7426643.html.

the great practice of the masses are developing. All these urge the Party to take the theoretical courage of Marxism to summarize the new experience of practice, draw lessons from the beneficial results of contemporary human civilization, expand new horizons in theory and make new summaries. Only in this way can the Party's ideological theory guide and inspire the whole Party and the people to continuously push forward with the cause of socialism with Chinese characteristics.

Section IV

Treating Marxism with a scientific attitude

First, adherence to Marxism

The premise for carrying on theoretical innovation is that we must adhere to the basic position, basic ideas and basic methods of Marxism, and adhere to the basic principles of Marxism. Why should we insist on this premise? It is because the truth of Marxism is irrefutable and is the guiding ideology and theoretical weapon of the Party. Deng Xiaoping had repeatedly stressed that we are engaged in reform and opening up and socialist modernization without forgetting our ancestor; we should not forget our ancestor. If we lose our ancestor, we lose our root.

In the spring of 1992, Deng Xiaoping also confidently pointed out in a conversation in the South Speeches: I am convinced that more and more people will come to believe in Marxism, because it is a science. Using historical materialism, it has uncovered the laws governing the development of human society. Feudal society replaced slave society, capitalism supplanted feudalism, and, after a long time, socialism will necessarily supersede capitalism. This is an irreversible general trend of historical development, but the path has many twists and turns."[23]

In July 2001, Jiang Zemin pointed out in his speech to the 80th Anniversary of the Founding of the CPC that: "Marxism is the fundamental guiding ideology of the Party and the country and a common theoretical basis for the unity of the people of all ethnic groups. The basic principles of Marxism should be adhered to at any time, otherwise we will wander from the course and even lose our cause due to the loss of right theoretical foundation and ideological soul. "This is why we must always uphold the basic tenets of Marxism."[24]

---

23   Selected Works of Deng Xiaoping, 1st edition, Vol.3, pp.382-383 and https://archive. org/stream/SelectedWorksOfDengXiaopingVol.3/Deng03_djvu.txt.
24   Selected Works of Jiang Zemin, Vol.3, p.282.

Second, the development and enrichment of Marxism

To carry out theoretical innovation, we must constantly enrich and develop Marxism on the basis of new practice. Why should we do that? It is because although the theory is gray, the tree of life is evergreen. Practice is always moving forward without limit. Thus, theory should also develop together with practice. And the innovation also has no limits. Jiang Zemin pointed out that Marxism is the science of development. It believes that the nature, society and people's thinking is always in constant movement, change and development. It does not recognize any ultimate condition and ultimate truth in the world. This requires that we should combine the basic principles of Marxism with the reality of socialist modernization and the reform and opening up as well as the new developments and changes of the times and world situation, and enrich and develop Marxism in the practice of Marxism. If we ignore the historical conditions and the changes of reality and adhere to certain individual conclusions and concrete action programs made by classical Marxist writers under specific historical conditions and specific situations, we will be unable to go forward smoothly and even make mistakes due to divorcing from the actual situation. This is why we should always oppose the dogmatic approach to Marxism.

In the report to the 16th National Congress of the CPC, Jiang Zemin further pointed out: "We will surpass our predecessors, and future generations will certainly surpass us. This is an inexorable law governing social advancement. We must adapt ourselves to the progress of practice and test all things in practice. We must conscientiously free our minds from the shackles of the outdated notions, practices and systems, from the erroneous and dogmatic interpretations of Marxism and from the fetters of subjectivism and subdued and subversive metaphysics."[25]

On this point, we must be firm and never allow vagueness.

The historical process of China's reform and opening up is a process of always adhering to the basic tenets of Marxism and constantly emancipating the mind, seeking truth from facts, advancing with the times, make innovations in a pioneering spirit and being pragmatic.[26]

Therefore, in the report to the 16th National Congress of the CPC, Jiang Zemin solemnly demanded from the entire party: "While upholding the basic tenets of Marxism, we must add new chapters of theory to it. While carrying forward the revolutionary tradition, we must acquire new experience. We should be good at seeking unity in thinking through the emancipation of our minds and guiding our new practice with the developing Marxism."[27]

---

25   Ibid., p.538.
26   Ibid., p. 536.
27   Selected Works of Jiang Zemin, Volume 3, p. 538.

Guiding the new practice with the developing Marxism faced with the new century, new stage and new situation, requires us to guide our new practice with the scientific outlook on development. The scientific outlook on development is consistent with the Marxism-Leninism, Mao Zedong Thought, Deng Xiaoping Theory and the important thought of "Three Represents". It reflects the new requirements of the developments and changes of contemporary world and contemporary China for the work of the Party and the country. It is a powerful theoretical weapon to promote comprehensive and coordinated sustainable development of Chinese economy and society, strengthen and improve the Party construction. It is the crystallization of the collective wisdom of the whole Party and the people. It is a major strategic thought that should be adhered to for a long time in the socialist construction with Chinese characteristics.

CHAPTER THREE

Development Stages of Socialism and the Strategies to Develop Socialism in the Theory of Socialism with Chinese Characteristics

Section I

The theory of the primary stage of socialism

First, the formation and development of the theory of the primary stage of socialism

Regardless of both the revolution and socialist construction, we must proceed from the basic national conditions of our country. As early as during the democratic revolution, Mao Zedong pointed out: "Understanding China's national conditions is the fundamental basis for grasping all the questions of Chinese revolution."[1]

The basic national conditions not only refer to the general national conditions of China, such as our country having a long history, a vast territory and a huge population. More importantly, it refers to the real nature of the Chinese society and the stage of historical development in which it is developing. In his speech at the meeting celebrating the 70th anniversary of the founding of the Chinese Communist Party, Jiang Zemin pointed out: "when recognizing China's national conditions, the most important thing is to recognize all the favorable and unfavorable realistic factors that have a significant impact on the Chinese revolution and construction, especially the nature of Chinese society and the stage of development it is in, understand their major social contradictions, their development and changes."[2]

---

1 Selected Works of Mao Zedong, 2nd edition, vol.2, p.633.
2 CPCCC Party Literature Research Office: "Selection of Important Literature since the 17th National Congress", p.1634.

In designing the path of Chinese revolution, why did the Communist Party of China aim to launch a new-democratic revolution and not directly engage in the socialist revolution? This was determined by the nature the country, i.e. its semi-colonial and semi-feudal old society.

The New Democratic Revolution led by the Communist Party of China was able gain victory, because the first generation of the central collective leadership with Mao Zedong as the core accurately grasped that our country was still a semi-colonial and semi-feudal society, correctly analyzed the basic national conditions, so as to correctly solve the basic issues of new Democratic revolution, i.e. its goal, nature, motive forces and its future prospects and so on. In the current stage when we are building socialism in China, there is also the question of how to understand the basic national conditions of the country. China is in and will be in the early stage of socialism, for a long time in the future which is the scientific judgment of the Communist Party of China and Deng Xiaoping, which was evaluated on the basic national conditions of contemporary China.

This judgment provides a scientific theoretical basis for the Chinese Communist Party to put forward the correct basic line and basic program of the CPC for this stage. The theory of the primary stage of socialism has gone through a long process of practice and cognition.

The founders of Marxism have put forward the basic ideas regarding the future development stages of human society. In the *Critique of the Gotha Program*, Marx divided the future communism into the first stage and the higher stages of communism according its degree of maturity. Lenin referred to these two stages as socialism and communism. Lenin further elaborated on the development stages of socialism.

After the victory of the October Revolution, Lenin pointed out that in economically backward Russia, only "primary form of socialism" could be built, and cannot immediately build the "advanced socialism." This contains the concept that a socialist society should from a low level to higher one and from incomplete to a more complete development stage. The implementation of the "New Economic Policy" was based on this concept. But Lenin has mainly answered the question of how Russia would transit to socialism, and was not yet able to elucidate on the future development stages of the socialist system. After the death of Lenin, when Stalin led the Soviet people in the process of socialist construction, his evaluations and practice on the development stages of socialism, has gone beyond the reality. Shortly after the establishment of the socialist system in 1936, Stalin proposed that the Soviet Union had already entered the stage of completing socialist construction and gradually transiting to communism.

After the end of the World War II, after a period of economic reconstruction, in 1952 he had announced that the Party's main task was to transit from socialism to communism. Stalin's successors also overestimated the development stages of socialism in the Soviet Union. Eastern European socialist countries and the Soviet Union have shared similar views, basically that they had entered the stage of "developed socialist society."

China's cognition regarding the development stages of socialism has also experienced a tortuous development process. After the socialist transformation was basically completed in 1956, Mao Zedong believed that China's socialist system had just been established and had not yet been fully completed and needed a process of further consolidation. Due to the hasty and early entry into socialism, we didn't accumulate enough experience to enable us to have a very clear understanding on the issues of social development. Throughout the "Great Leap Forward" and the People's Commune Movement in 1958, there had occurred a blind optimism of targeting "the realization of communism in our country, which is no longer a distant future", and thus made a serious and erroneous estimation on the development stages of socialism.

Although later Mao Zedong and others, when trying to correct the mistakes of the "Great Leap Forward", held good discussions on the stage of the development of socialism in China, and pointed to the confusion regarding the difference between socialism and communism, criticized the viewpoints of denying the law of value and equivalent Exchange in the economic life, but in general, the prevalent "left" tendency could not be corrected.

As Deng Xiaoping pointed out: As early as the second half of 1957 we began to make "Left" mistakes. To put it briefly, we pursued a closed-door policy in foreign affairs and took class struggle as the central task at home. No attempt was made to expand the productive forces, and the policies we formulated were too ambitious for the primary stage of socialism."[3]

After the 3rd Plenary Session of the Party, after the comparison of our both positive and negative experiences, the Chinese Communist Party has gradually made a scientific conclusion that China is in and will be in the primary stage of socialism.

The resolution "On The Historical Issues of The Party since the founding of the People's Republic of China adopted by the 6th Plenary Session of the 11th CPC Central Committee in 1981, pointed out that "of course, our (socialist) system will have to undergo a long process of development before it can be perfected," and made another clear statement as "our socialist

3   Selected Works of Deng Xiaoping, 1st Edition, Vol. 3, p.269 and https://archive.org/stream/SelectedWorksOfDengXiaopingVol.3/Deng03_djvu.txt.

system is still in its early phase of development" our socialist system is still in its early phase of development".

The CC report to 12th CPC National Congress in 1982 once again pointed out: "China's socialist society is still at an early stage of development." And on the eve of the thirteenth Chinese Communist Party Congress in 1987, Deng Xiaoping emphasized: "The 13th National Party Congress will explain what stage China is in: the primary stage of socialism. Socialism itself is the first stage of communism, and here in China we are still in the primary stage of socialism–that is, the underdeveloped stage. In everything we do we must proceed from this reality, and all planning must be consistent with it."[4]

The 13th National Congress of the CPC systematically expounded the theory of the primary stage of socialism, clearly defined the meanings of the primary stage of socialism, clarified the main contradictions in the primary stage and the way to solve it, and put forward the mode of party work in the primary stage of socialism, elucidation of this basic line in this Congress marks the formation of the theory of the primary stage of socialism.

The 15th Party Congress once again expounded on the issues of primary stage of socialism, Party Congress further systematically summed up the 9 characteristics of the primary stage of socialism, and for the first time elaborated the basic sub-stages of the primary stage of socialism, thus our cognition on the issue has reached a new height.

When the 16th National Congress of the Communist Party of China in 2002, put forward the goal of building a well-off society in an all-round way, it has emphasizes that: "We must be aware that China is in the primary stage of socialism and will remain so for a long time to come. The well-off life we are leading is still at a low level; it is not all-inclusive and is very uneven", and added that "we need to work hard over a long period of time to consolidate and uplift our current well-off standard of living."

The 17th National Congress of the Communist Party of China in 2007 has analyzed a series of new characteristics of the development of our country since entering the new century. It has pointed out that this is the concrete manifestation of the basic national conditions in the new stage of the new century.

The Congress emphasized the unremitting efforts of Chinese people since the founding of new China, especially since the reform and opening up, and added: China has scored achievements in development that have captured world attention, and experienced far-reaching changes in the

4   Selected Works of Deng Xiaoping, 1st Edition, Vol. 3, p.352 and https://archive.org/stream/SelectedWorksOfDengXiaopingVol.3/Deng03_djvu.txt.

productive forces and the relations of production, as well as in the economic base and the superstructure. However, the basic reality that China is still in the primary stage of socialism and will remain so for a long time to come has not changed, nor has Chinese society's principal contradiction–the one between the ever-growing material and cultural needs of the people and the low level of social production. The current features of development in China are a concrete manifestation of that basic reality at this new stage in the new century. Stressing recognition of the basic reality is not meant to belittle ourselves, wallow in backwardness, or encourage unrealistic pursuit of quick results. Rather, such recognition will serve as the basis of our endeavor to advance reform and plan for development. We must always remain sober-minded, base our efforts on the most significant reality that China is in the primary stage of socialism, scientifically analyze the new opportunities and challenges arising from China's full involvement in economic globalization, fully understand the new situation and tasks in China's advance toward an industrialized, information-based, urbanized, market-oriented and internationalized country, have a good grasp of the new issues and problems we face in development, follow more conscientiously the path of scientific development, and strive to open up a broader vista for developing socialism with Chinese characteristics."

It is just due to the basic understanding of the basic conditions of socialism and the correct grasp of the basic conditions of socialism, we have succeeded in blazing a new trial of building socialism with Chinese characteristics, and have made remarkable achievements.

Second, the scientific connotations and the main features of primary stage of socialism

The theory of primary stage of socialism includes two meanings: firstly, China is already a socialist society, must adhere to and stick to the path of socialism; secondly, China's socialist society is still in the primary stage, it has not fundamentally got rid of poverty and in an undeveloped state, we must proceed from the actual conditions of this primary stage, and not attempt to go beyond it. The meaning of the former layer refers to the social nature of the primary stage, and the latter meaning points to the degree of development of our socialist society.

When analyzing the basic national conditions of our country, we must first be certain that the basic elements of socialism have already been achieved: the basic dominant position of socialist public ownership and the basic system of socialism have been established. The people's democratic dictatorship as the state system has been established and the guiding position of Marxism in the superstructure of the society has been established.

It is due to these basic achievements that have made the Chinese people stand up, so that China could attain the status of a socialist country among the community of world nations and have established the prerequisites for completing realizing socialist modernization in the mid of this century.

At the same time, we must also see that the level of productive forces in our country still lags far behind the developed capitalist countries. Thus, building the material and technical base necessary for building the advanced socialism must go through a long historical period.

To fully and correctly understand the concept of the primary stage of socialism, we must first fully grasp the meaning of these above two aspects.

Only by correctly recognizing and grasping the 8 Chinese characters of "socialism" and "primary stage", we can unify and grasp the basic national conditions, which means unifying the nature of the socialist society in our country with its degree of development.

If we cannot grasp the current social nature of our country, it will be impossible to make a correct analysis of the basic characteristics, major contradictions, fundamental tasks and development orientation of society, and it will be impossible to formulate the correct path, basic line, basic program and policies. Failure to correctly understand the current stage of development of society, it may appear that we may take a working path which goes beyond the stage or may passively fall behind the situation, which will lead us wrong measures and decision. The basic characteristics of the primary stage of socialism, if summed up in a single sentence is "underdeveloped stage of socialism".

The 13th Party Congress in 1987 has summarized the basic characteristics of the primary stage of socialism in China from the aspects of population structure, industrial development level, regional development differences and level of scientific education and cultural development.

The 15th Congress of the CPC has further systematically summed up the 9 characteristics of the primary stage of socialism:

(1) This stage is to gradually transcend the underdeveloped state, and the historical stage within which the basic realization of socialist modernization will be achieved, which is its general overall characteristics.

(2) This historical stage is in which a significant proportion of population involves in agricultural production, mainly relying on manual labor, and which will gradually be transformed into non-agricultural population and urban population becomes the majority, a stage which will lead us to a modern agriculture and service industry, an industrialized country.

(3) This is a historical stage, wherein the natural economy and semi-natural economy accounts for a large proportion, and will be gradually transformed into a highly developed market economy.

(4) This is a historical stage, wherein we have a large proportion of illiterate and semi-illiterate population, which lack education of science and culture is backward, which will be gradually transformed into a relatively advanced level of science and technology, education and culture.

(5) This is a historical stage, wherein the poor population accounted a high proportion and wherein people's living standards are relatively low, which will be gradually transformed into a state the whole people will achieve remarkable prosperity.

(6) This is a historical stage, wherein the regional economic and cultural development levels are quite uneven, wherein through the development achieved in the primary stage, the gaps will be gradually narrowed.

(7) This is a historical stage, wherein we will through reform practice and exploration, establish and improve a more mature and dynamic socialist market economic system, socialist democratic political system and other aspects of the socialist system.

(8) At this stage, the broad masses of people will be able to firmly establish the common ideals of building socialism with Chinese characteristics, strive for self-improvement, forge ahead, hard work, diligence and creativity, and strive to build spiritual civilization and achieve to realize coordinated development of the two civilizations, energetically promote spiritual civilization while advancing material civilization.

(9) This stage is a historical stage wherein we will gradually narrow the gap with the world's advanced level and achieve the great rejuvenation of the Chinese nation on the basis of socialism. These 9 aspects fully embody the procedural characteristics of the historical development of the primary stage of socialism.

In the process of the development of the primary stage of socialism, it is necessary to go through a number of specific sub-stages of development, which demonstrates distinct qualities.

The 17th National Congress of the Communist Party of China, in 2007 has carried a thorough analysis and made a new generalization which included 8 aspects of the sub-phasal status of the primary stage, when China entered into the new century.

(1) In the current situation, economic strength is significantly enhanced, while the overall level of productive forces is not high, independent innovation capability is not strong, the status of long-term structural contradictions

still exist and extensive economic growth mode has not fundamentally transcended.

(2) In the current situation, the initial establishment level of socialist market economic system is achieved, while institutional mechanisms that hinder the development still exist, the reform is faced with deep-seated contradictions and problems.

(3) In the current situation, in general people's living standards have achieved a well-off level, while the widening trend of gap regarding the income distribution gap widening trend has not fundamentally reversed, there is a considerable number of urban and rural poor and low-income population in China we need to undertake comprehensive efforts to regulate and optimize the interests of all quarters of the society.

(4) In the current situation, we have made significant achievements in coordinated development, while the agricultural base is still weak, the situation of rural development has not changed. We are faced with the arduous tasks of narrowing development gap between the city and rural areas, between regions and strike a coordinated economic and social development.

(5) In the current situation, the building of socialist democratic politics is developing continuously and our basic strategy of governing the country according to law is carried out. At the same time, the requirements of democracy and legal system construction and expansion of people's democracy and economic and social development are not fully met, the reform of political system needs to be deepened.

(6) In the current situation, the socialist culture has achieved more prosperous level, and the people's spiritual and cultural demands are becoming more and more vigorous. We see obvious enhancement of independence, selectivity, diversity and difference in people's ideological activities, which brings forward higher requirements for the development of advanced socialist culture by us.

(7) In the current situation, our society has become evidently more dynamic, but profound changes have taken place in the structure of society, in the way society is organized and in the pattern of social interests, and many new issues have emerged in social development and management.

(8) In the current situation, China is opening wider to the outside world, but international competition is becoming increasingly acute, pressure in the form of the economic and scientific dominance of developed countries will continue for a long time to come, both predictable and unpredictable risks are increasing, and the need to balance domestic development and opening to the outside world is greater than ever. .

At present, the phasal status characteristics of China's development given above are the concrete presentation of the basic national conditions of the primary stage of socialism in the sub-stage when China has entered into the new century.

Only by firmly grasping the great historical stage of the primary stage of socialism and seriously analyzing the specific characteristics of the sub-stages in different periods, can we accurately judge the mainstream and direction of our country's social development and formulate the correct development strategies and policies.

Third, the long-term nature of the primary stage of socialism

That, China is in the primary stage of socialism, is not conclusion based on general principles, but a scientific conclusion drawn from the concrete realities of China.

The 13th CPC National Congress pointed out: "the primary stage socialism" does not refer that generally to the initial stage that any country should pass through when proceeding towards socialism "but refers specifically to the backwardness of our country with relatively backward productive forces, and with an the underdeveloped commodity economy, it is certain stage of development that our socialism is bound to go through."[5]

China's socialism must go through a long-term primary stage.

Firstly, this truth is determined by the historical premises of our entry into socialism.

The main historical premise of China's entering socialism is the economic and cultural backwardness attached to the semi-colonial and semi-feudal society of China.

The concrete historical conditions of the modern world and China have determined that China's bourgeoisie would not lead the democratic revolution to victory, thus China would not be able to realize industrialization, economic modernization and marketization under capitalism. The only way out for China was to reject capitalist path and strive for the goal of socialism, through new democracy under the leadership of the Chinese Communist Party. These have historically imposed China to establish a socialist system whence the full development of capitalism was not there. However, this does not mean that China should pass through the stage of full development of capitalism, but at the same time this does not mean that we are allowed to by-pass beyond the stage wherein the great development of productive forces and full development of the commodity economy is

---

5 CPCCC Party Literature Research Office: "Selection of Important Literature since the 13th National Congress" (Vol. I), p.12, Beijing, People's Publishing House, 1991.

achieved. Socialism is based on the highly advanced productive forces, and industrialization based on high degree of socialization of production, which is accompanied by the full development of the commodity economy, in order to fully demonstrate its superiority over capitalism. When China has entered the socialism building, it was far behind the developed capitalist countries in terms of the level of development of productive forces, in terms of the socialization of production, marketization and economic modernization. All these determines that, our country must use a whole historical stage under socialism conditions to realize the socialization of production, marketization and modernization of the economy and industrialization—all of which were realized under capitalism conditions in many other countries—in order to establish and develop socialism it needs to develop the basis regarding the level of productive forces.

Secondly, when evaluating the realities of our national situation, China has not exceeded the primary stage of socialism.

Although after 50 plus years of socialist construction, especially with the rapid development we have achieved after the 3rd Plenary Session of the 11th Central Committee of the CPC, China has undergone profound changes, productivity has been a huge development, our cause has made great progress, comprehensive national strength of China is greatly enhanced and the people's living standards in general have reached a well-off level.

However, in general, the level of productive forces in China is not high yet, our socialist system is not perfect, the socialist economic system is not yet mature, the socialist democracy and the legal system is not sound enough, the backward situation of education regarding science and technology, and cultural level has not been fundamentally changed, the sphere of societal construction and social management are also faced with many new issues. The major social contradiction between people's ever growing material and cultural needs and the backward social production did not yet enter a new situation.

Thirdly, and finally, the characteristics of the times and the general international environment we are surrounded with determines that the socialist modernization drive of China have to go through a relatively long primary stage. Advance and mature socialism requires that we should continue to develop and improve our material and technical foundation, as well as scientific and technological progress.

In today's world, the productive forces of the developed countries is highly advanced, and looking at the world-wide environment we see that scientific and technological revolution has developed rapidly. Surrounded with this context, in the process of modernization, in addition to the conventional historical task of industrialization, China is also faced with the informationization to meet the challenges of the new scientific and technological revolution surrounding our country, which means that China's comparative comprehensive national strength is under a great pressure of foreign competition. All these determine that China must go through a long primary stage to develop into a more advanced and mature socialism. In short, our country is still in and will be in the early stages of socialism for a long time to come.

To achieve modernization, to build our country into a prosperous, democratic, civilized and harmonious socialist country, there is still a long way to go, till the middle of the 21st century in order to basically realize modernization, from 1956 into the socialist society. The primary stage of the work takes at least a hundred years. In 1992, Deng Xiaoping pointed out in his speech in the south tour: We have been building socialism for only a few decades and are still in the primary stage. It will take a very long historical period to consolidate and develop the socialist system, and it will require persistent struggle by many generations, a dozen or even several dozens. We can never rest on our oars."[6]

Capitalism has consummated centuries to modernize itself. Only by seizing the opportunities and utilizing them successfully so as to speed up the development, it is possible to achieve this magnificent vision of achieving socialist modernization in 2049.

Recognizing the long-term nature of the primary stage of socialism will help us to keep a clear mind and avoid us from making "left" or right mistakes, in our thinking and actions, and raise our consciousness of upholding the party's basic line and basic program, thus will promote the socialist modernization drive.

Section II

The basic line and basic program of the primary stage of socialism

First, the main social contradictions in the primary stage of socialism

One of the core issues of the theory of the primary stage of socialism is the correct judgment of the major social contradiction, which is the objective basis for formulating the basic line of the Party in the primary stage of socialism.

---

6   Selected Works of Deng Xiaoping, First edition, Vol.3, pp.379-380 and https://archive.org/stream/SelectedWorksOfDengXiaopingVol.3/Deng03_djvu.txt

After the socialist transformation in our country was basically completed in 1956, the 8th National Congress of the Party in 1956 pointed out: The contradiction between the proletariat and the bourgeoisie in our country has basically been resolved. The history of the class exploitation system which had lasted for thousands of years has basically ended. "The principal contradiction within the country is no longer the contradiction between the proletariat and the bourgeoisie but the one resulted from the need of the people for rapid economic and cultural development which fell short of their requirements. The chief task confronting the entire nation is to concentrate all efforts on developing the productive forces, change our country from an underdeveloped agricultural country to an advanced industrial country as soon as possible, and gradually meet the people's growing economic and cultural needs."[7]

The 8th Congress of our Party's judgment on the major social contradiction of China was basically correct, and in line with China's national conditions, but due to variety of subjective and objective reasons, we failed to stick to this correct understanding and judgment.

The failure of expansion of the "anti-rightist" struggle in 1957 was, theoretically speaking, a reflection of rejecting the correct analysis we have made regarding major social contradiction and meant that we regarded the contradiction between the proletariat and the bourgeoisie as the main social contradiction of our society, which led to the rise of the "left" thoughts.

In 1962, the class contradiction was further emphasized as the main contradiction and extended to be the main contradiction throughout the whole period socialism, and the line of "taking class struggle as the key link" was put forward, leading to the occurrence of the "Cultural Revolution" which caused serious setback in our socialist cause.

The 3rd Plenary Session of the 11th Central Committee of the CPC decisively corrected the erroneous judgments regarding the main contradiction and the erroneous line of "taking class struggle as the key link", and shifted the focus of the work of the party and the state to the socialist modernization drive.

In 1979, in his important speech "Adhere to the Four Cardinal Principles," Deng Xiaoping clearly answered the main contradictions at this stage: As for the question of what is the principal contradiction in the current period—what is the main issue or central task confronting the Party and the people in the current period—actually this question was answered by the decision of the 3rd Plenary Session of the 11th Central Committee to shift the

---

7   CPCCC Party Literature Research Office: "Selection of Important Literature since the Founding of PRC" (Vol. IX), pp.341-342, Beijing, Central Literature Publishing House, 1994.

focus of our work to socialist modernization. The level of our productive forces is very low and is far from meeting the needs of our people and country. This is the principal contradiction in the current period, and to resolve it is our central task."[8]

"The resolution on The Historical Issues of The Party since The Founding of The People's Republic of China, decided at the 6th Plenary Session of the 11th Central Committee CPC, in 1981 further pointed out that after the socialist transformation was basically completed, the main contradiction to be solved by our country was that "between the ever growing material and cultural needs of the people and the backward social production."

The 13th Party Congress in 1987 more comprehensively expounded and affirmed the theory of the primary stage of socialism and pointed out that the main contradiction throughout the primary stage of socialism in our country was that "between the ever growing material and cultural needs of the people and the backward social production."

But as a result of international and domestic factors, class contradictions and class struggle in China will continue to exist within a certain range, and may also intensify, under certain conditions. We must have a clear understanding of this issue, and take the correct attitude and methods to solve it. But the main contradiction of society is "between the ever growing material and cultural needs of the people and the backward social production." This main contradiction runs through the whole process of socialism in our country and demonstrates itself in the various aspects of social life, which determines that we must take economic construction as the center, all the work of the Party must obey and serve this central task.

Deng Xiaoping has always stressed the importance of this idea, by saying "even if there is a large-scale invasion by foreign enemies, we must not shake and change our judgment regarding the main contradictions and central task, nothing should interfere the determination of our party's concentration over the cause of socialist modernization, must not repeat the mistake we have made regarding the 8th Party Congress judgment, shake the central task work center and turn back to error of "taking class struggle as the key link".

The 16th National Congress of the Communist Party of China stressed that in the stage of building a well-off society in an all-round way, it is necessary to adhere to the economic development work as the central task and solve the problems regarding the development. It emphasized: we should promote social progress, and continuously improve people's living standards, and ensure that people share the fruits of development, by firmly

8   Selected Works of Deng Xiaoping, 2nd edition, Vol. 2, p.182 and https://archive.org/stream/SelectedWorksOfDengXiaopingVol.1/Deng02_djvu.txt.

focusing on the task of economic development. Only by firmly grasping the main contradictions and central task of the primary stage of socialism and concentrating on the development of productive forces can we fundamentally change the backwardness of our country and continuously meet the people's growing material and cultural needs.

Second, the formation and content of the basic line of the of the primary stage of socialism

The basic line, also known as the general line, is the description of the general goals and tasks of the CPC for a certain historical stage and the pathways and roads set to achieve this goal. The basic line of the primary stage of socialism was established on summing up the past experience and lessons, and was gradually formed in the course of reform and opening up and the practice of socialist modernization.

In the eve of the 3rd Plenary Session of the 11th CPC Central Committee in 1978, Deng Xiaoping pointed out that the realization of the four modernizations should be understood as a great revolution. We should carry out comprehensive and major reforms in the economic front and at the same time reform the relations of production and adjust the superstructures so that they can serve the base.

The 3rd Plenary Session of the 11th Central Committee decided to shift the focus of Party and state work to economic construction and made the great decisions of reform and opening up.

Evaluating the doubting thoughts in the society towards the viability of socialist system after certain failures, and in order to control the erroneous thought of negating the Mao Zedong Thought, Deng Xiaoping put forward the Four Cardinal Principles: adhere to the socialist path, adhere to the people's democratic dictatorship, adhere to the leadership of the Communist Party of China, adhere to our guiding ideology of Marxism-Leninism and Mao Zedong Thought. In 1980, Deng Xiaoping pointed out in his speech at the 5th Plenary Session of the 11th CPC Central Committee that the political line of our Party at this stage is to engage in four modernizations.

In 1981, in the 6th Plenary Session of the 11th Central Committee established the goal of building our country into a socialist country with modern agriculture, modern industry, modern defense and modern science and technology, with a high degree of democracy and a high degree of civilization.

By 1982 the 12th National Congress of the Party has proposed the Party task as "one center, two basic points" which was a further summarization of the above concept. At this Congress, Deng Xiaoping for the first time put forward "follow a path of our own, and build socialism with Chinese characteristics" as an important proposition. In 1986, as suggested by Deng

Xiaoping, the 6th Plenary Session of the 12th CPC Central Committee defined the overall comprehensive layout of China's socialist modernization task, that is, "take economic construction as the central task, unswervingly carry out economic reform, unswervingly carry out political reform, strengthen the construction of spiritual civilization."

On the eve of the 13th CPC National Congress held in 1987, Deng Xiaoping made it further clear:

"It is our basic line to carry out socialist modernization. If we are to do so and to make China a prosperous and developed country, we must, first, follow the policies of reform and opening up, and second, we must adhere to the Four Cardinal Principles."[9]

While systematically expounding the theory of the primary stage of socialism, the Party's 13th CPC National Congress formally formulated the party's basic line in the primary stage of socialism: "In the initial stage of socialism, our party's basic line of building socialism with Chinese characteristics is: "To lead and unite the people of all ethnic groups across the country, taking economic construction as the central task, uphold the Four Cardinal Principles, persist in reform and opening up, see that people of the whole country will rise to do hard pioneering work and bring about a great rejuvenation of the Chinese nation, thus we will strive to build our country into a prosperous, democratic and civilized modern socialist country."[10]

65

After the 4th Plenary Session of the 13th CPC Central Committee, the third generation of the central collective leadership, with Jiang Zemin as its core leader, has gradually put forward the major strategic task of building a socialist harmonious society.

The report of the 16th National Congress of the Communist Party of China combined the task of building a socialist harmonious society, with the important goal of building a well-off society in an all-round way.

After the 16th CPC National Congress in 2002, the Party Central Committee with Hu Jintao as General Secretary made further cognitive reforms. Consequently at the 6th Plenary Session of the 16th CPC Central Committee the goal of "harmonious society" and "prosperity and advanced democracy" was defined as the goal of socialist modernization. All these show that after years of practice and exploration, our party's cognition regarding the goal of the struggle has gradually deepened, it has attained a more comprehensive understanding on how to achieve the overall cause of socialism with Chinese characteristics and how to combine various related

9   Selected Works of Deng Xiaoping, 1st edition, Vol.3, p.248 and https://archive.org/stream/SelectedWorksOfDengXiaopingVol.3/Deng03_djvu.txt.
10   CPCCC Party Literature Research Office: "Selection of Important Literature since the 13th National Party Congress" (Vol. I), p.15.

tasks as organic unity to achieve our goals. The party's basic line, deeply summarizes the Party's goals, fundamental ways to follow and fundamental guarantees to achieve the goals, defines the leadership tasks and reliance on the fundamental principles of the socialist primary stage and the basic principle of achieving it.

Firstly, the phrase "to build China into a prosperous, democratic, civilized and harmonious socialist modern country", which is the party's goal in the primary stage of socialism, embodies the requirements of the comprehensively advanced socialist society.

Prosperity is the goal and requirement regarding the economic field; democracy is the goal and requirement of the political field; civilization is the goal and requirement in the field of ideology and culture; lastly "harmonious" refers to the goal and requirement of the societal sphere.

The goals of prosperous, democratic, civilized and harmonious are in fact linked with the acts of the of economic construction, political construction, cultural construction and construction of unity and cohesiveness in the society, i.e. social construction.

Secondly, "one center, two basic points", which is the party's basic line refers to the most important content we must bear in mind and practice, in order achieve the goal of socialist modernization goals.

Taking "economic construction as the focus" aims to answer the fundamental task of socialism, embodies the essential requirement: the development of productive forces.

"Adhere to the Four Cardinal Principles" is one of the two basic points, which is our political guarantee, when we are struggling for the liberation and the development of productive forces, it also embodies the requirements of the basic socialist system.

"Adhere to reform and opening up" is another basic point, aims to answer the question of how to deal with external conditions, when developing Chinese socialism, it also embodies the essential requirement of the liberation of productive forces. As explained above "one center" and "two basic points" concept is an indivisible whole.

China's economic construction is based on the Four Cardinal Principles as its political guarantee, reform and opening up as a powerful driving force; reform and opening up, to further the liberation and development of productive forces, the consolidation and development of the socialist system for the purpose of the Four Cardinal Principles, To ensure that reform and opening up and economic construction in the right direction, but also from the new practice continue to draw new experience to enrich and develop.

If we give up the economic construction as our central task, all the development and progress of socialist society will lose its material basis; and if we give up both adhering to Four Cardinal Principles and the reform and opening up principle, economic construction will lose both its key soul and its high vitality.

"One center, two basic points" embodies the strategic layout of China's construction of socialist modernization, and reveals the objective laws and development path of socialism with Chinese characteristics.

Thirdly, "leading and uniting the people of all nationalities" refers to the leadership of Party and also motive social force we rely in order to achieve the goal of socialist modernization.

The Communist Party of China is the core of leadership of the cause of socialism with Chinese characteristics. The people of all ethnic groups in the whole country are the forces we depend when fighting for the cause of socialism with Chinese characteristics.

Fourthly, "self-reliance and arduous pioneering" are the fine traditions of the Chinese Communist Party and the fundamental foothold and basic guideline for realizing our goals in the primary stage of socialism. As Deng Xiaoping had emphasized: "we must work hard and with a pioneering spirit. This spirit is essential if we are to achieve the four modernizations. The fact that China is poor, has weak economic foundations and is backward in education, science and culture means that we have to go through a hard struggle."[11]

The basic line of the party in the primary stage of socialism embodies the requirements of the nature of socialism, reflects the fundamental law of development of socialism in China, and determines the path of development of socialism with Chinese characteristics. Therefore, we must with no vacillation uphold the principles of the party's basic line. Deng Xiaoping emphasized: "We should adhere to the basic line for a hundred years, with no vacillation. That is the only way to win the trust and support of the people."[12]

Adhering to the party's basic line, the key is to adhere to taking the economic construction as the focus unwaveringly. Taking economic construction as the focus has summed our bitter lesson of the past, when we took "class struggle as the key link" which has caused major setbacks in the socialist construction task.

---

11 Selected Works of Deng Xiaoping, 2nd edition, Vol.2, p.257.
12 Selected Works of Deng Xiaoping, 1st edition, Vol.3, pp.370-371 and https://archive.org/stream/SelectedWorksOfDengXiaopingVol.3/Deng03_djvu.txt.

We can only consolidate and improve our socialist system and maintain social harmony; if we can be able to withstand the pressure of hegemonism and power politics, and safeguard China's sovereignty and independence against foreign pressures and if we can be able to maintain people's living standards and to strengthen the socialist system. Sovereignty and independence; in order to fundamentally get rid of the backward situation, among the world's modern forest.

In short, whether to adhere to the economic construction as the focus, decides the success or failure of China's socialist modernization, related to the future of socialism and the fate of our great cause.

Therefore, we must always take economic construction as the focus, all the other work spheres must obey and serve this central task, and all the other work spheres should not separate from this focus, and we should see that nothing should interfere and frustrate our central task.

Adhering to the party's basic line means we must unite the two: reform and opening up policy and adhering to the Four Cardinal Principles.

The Four Cardinal Principles reflect the ideals and the cause pursued by our country. It is the political foundation of our party and the political guarantee for China's survival and development. It also plays key role as the political guarantee of the reform and opening up policy and the modernization goal. Reform and opening up is the path we follow so as to inject energy and vitality into China's development and progress. Thus the Four Cardinal Principles and reform and opening up, the two are mutually linked and interdependent.

If we ignore the Four Cardinal Principles and talk about reform and opening up, the latter will inevitably lose its correct political orientation, it will never proceed smoothly. Reversely if we ignore the reform and opening up and talk about the Four Cardinal Principles, the latter will not be able to innovate and advance with the times, will become a rigid doctrine. Adhering to the two basic points, i.e. the Four Cardinal Principles, adhering to the reform and opening—must obey and serve the central task of economic construction. Unswervingly upholding the basic line of the party suited to the primary stage of socialism, i.e. the economic construction as the center and the Four Cardinal Principles, and reform and opening up as the two basic points is the great practice, regarding the construction of socialism with Chinese characteristics, which constitutes the most valuable experience of the CPC since 1978.

Third, the basic program of the primary stage of socialism

The basic program of the Chinese Communist Party throughout the primary stage of socialism is the concretization of the basic line of the Party. The corrective re-establishment of the party's ideological line in 1978 has provided the necessary ideological premise for the development of the path of socialism with Chinese characteristics. The establishment of the basic theory of the "primary stage of socialism", the formulation of the basic line of "one center and two basic points" has laid the theoretical basis for CPC's practice. The new basic line of the Party was also gradually developed.

In 1991, Jiang Zemin made a speech on the 70th anniversary of the founding of the Communist Party of China, which summed up the experience of reform and opening up practiced for more than 10 years, he defined the contemporary historical mission of the Chinese Communist Party and the basic economic, political views required in implementing the basic line, expounded on the basic content of culture to be constructed in the new era, and other basic policies that should be followed in the construction of socialism. In this speech, Jiang Zemin has made profound analysis and discussion, and laid the foundation of the basic program of the Party in the primary stage of socialism.

Deng Xiaoping's important speeches he made in an inspection tour to the South in 1992 and the report of the 14th Party Congress, have provided direct theoretical contributions for the formation of the Party's basic program.

Several Plenum meeting resolutions' explanations by the Central Committee of the 14th National Congress between 1992-97 and in particular, Jiang Zemin's contributions on the twelve major issues of China's socialist modernization construction goal have further clarified China's path of economic system reform, and the basic goals and basic policies of social development strategy, construction of spiritual civilization and the issue of party building in the era, all have laid the foundation for the further formation of the basic program.

On the basis of above achievements, the 15th Party Congress formulated the basic program of the Party in the primary stage of socialism, and thus defined the requirements of the basic line in the primary stage of socialism.

The 17th Party Congress has further enriched the content of the basic program: "the construction of a socialist economy with Chinese characteristics is to develop an advanced market economy under the conditions of socialism, to continuously liberate and develop productive forces, to achieve sound, sustainable and rapid economic development, and to ensure that people share the fruits of reform and development. That the political construction of socialism with Chinese characteristics is based on the 3 pillars: party leadership, people assuming as masters of their own destiny and the managing of state affairs, and the rule according to law of law, the development of socialist democratic politics, the realization of social stability, clean and efficient government clean and efficient, and creation of a fully enlivened political situation wherein the people of all ethnic groups enjoy harmony.

The construction of the culture of socialism with Chinese characteristics should be guided by Marxism, with the aim of cultivating citizens with ideals, good morals, and culturally advanced and having discipline consciousness. We should promote Chinese culture and build the common spiritual home for the Chinese nation, promote an advanced public socialist culture with the essentials of modern conduct, world-oriented, future-oriented. We should build a socialist core value system, and promote the great development and prosperity of the socialist culture.

Building a harmonious socialist society means to follow the principles of democracy and the rule of law, social fairness and justice, honesty and fraternity, vigor and vitality, stability and order. Building a harmonious socialist also means seeking for harmony between man and nature and following the policy of all the people building and sharing a harmonious socialist society, we will spare no effort to solve the most specific problems of the utmost and immediate concern to the people and strive to create a situation in which all people do their best, find their proper places in society and live together in harmony, so as to provide a favorable social environment for development.

To achieve the tasks of the basic stage of socialism, the basic program must correctly understand and deal with the dialectical relationship between the party's maximum and minimum programs.

The socialist construction that we carrying out today is, in the final analysis, in order to create conditions for the realization of communism, i.e. our maximum program, and the two are dialectically unified throughout the historical process of communist movement. The program of building socialism with Chinese characteristics is the minimum program of the Chinese Communist Party at this current stage. This minimum program and the maximum program of realizing communism form an organic unity and indivisible.

The maximum program sets the direction for the formulation of the minimum program, and the minimum program creates the conditions for the achievement of the maximum program.

The unity of the two, embodies the unity of ideals and reality, the unity of direction and the path, the unity of purpose and process, the unity of continuous development and development stage, also the unity of revolutionary spirit and scientific attitude.

This requires that we should not only talk about the party's minimum program, and forget the party's maximum program, and should not only talk about the party's maximum program, while ignoring the party's minimum program.

While firmly establishing the lofty ideal of communism, we should establish a firm conviction of building socialism with Chinese characteristics. In his speech at the meeting celebrating the 80th anniversary of the founding of the Chinese Communist Party, Jiang Zemin pointed out: "All comrades in the Party should set up a lofty communist ideal, fortify their conviction and spur themselves on by holding to high ideological and moral standards. More importantly, they should make unremitting efforts in a down-to-earth manner to realize the Party's basic program for the current stage and put their heart into each single piece of work now. To care about the immediate interests only while forgetting the lofty ideal will result in the loss of direction of progress. But to talk big about the lofty ideal without doing any practical work will get one divorced from reality."[13]

Throughout the primary stage of socialism, we must adhere to the unity of minimum program and maximum program, unswervingly implement the basic line and basic program of the party suited to the primary stage of socialism, and push forward the cause of socialism with Chinese characteristics.

Section III

Development strategies to deepen the primary stage of socialism

First, the "three-step" development strategy

The realization of socialist modernization is the long-cherished inspiration of the Chinese Communists and the Chinese people. Mao Zedong as the core figure of the first generation of the central collective leadership of the party has repeatedly put forward the grand idea of building our "four modernization tasks" till the end of the 20th century. However, due to the lack of consistent understanding of major issues such as the historical stage, major contradictions and fundamental tasks of our country's socialism and how to build it, China's socialist modernization has undergone through a tortuous process. With the ending of the "Cultural Revolution", Deng Xiaoping has seriously considered how to proceed from China's national conditions so as to achieve socialist modernization. In September 1978, when Deng Xiaoping met a group of guests from the Japanese press,

13   Selected Works of Jiang Zemin, Vol.3, p.293 and http://www.china-un.ch/eng/zgbd/smwx/t85789.htm.

he gave a new explanation of China's "four modernization" goals to be achieved by the end of the 20th century.

He said: "At the end of this century, even if we will achieve our goals of four modernizations, and build a well-off society, our level will not reach that of Japan". During this period Deng Xiaoping's visits to the United States, Japan and other countries, had also deepened his understanding of modernization.

In March 1979, Deng Xiaoping pointed out in his speech at the forum meeting regarding the theoretical work of the party: Now, in our national construction, we must likewise act in accordance with our own situation and find a Chinese path to modernization."[14]

In October the same year, Deng Xiaoping put forward a new point of view at the Political Bureau of the Central Committee. He said: By the political task, we are referring to the four modernizations. We used to have the ambitious goal of realizing the four modernizations by the end of the century. Later we changed the goal the 'Chinese-style" modernizations, intending to lower the standard a little."[15]

In January 1980, Deng Xiaoping divided the coming 20 years into the two decades, initially proposed two steps concept to achieve well-off society level.

The 12th Party Congress has formally proposed the two-step strategy concept based on his idea. The first step was to use the first 10 years to double the GNP (gross national product) by constant prices in order to solve the people's food and clothing problem. By the end of the twentieth century, the gross national product (GDP) would be quadrupled (with the constant prices of 1980) so that people's living standards will reach a well-off level.

By the end of the 20th century to achieve quadrupling the GNP, and then move forward the strategic goal that was defined as follows, by Deng Xiaoping: "As The first step Quadrupling the GNP will be a significant achievement… It will provide a new starting point from which, in another 30 to 50 years, we shall approach the level of the developed countries. I am talking about production and living standards."[16]

In April 1987, when he met with the Spanish guests, Deng Xiaoping for the first time, proposed a new development strategy which included three steps to achieve modernization.

---

14   Selected Works of Deng Xiaoping, 2nd edition, Vol.2, p.163, and https://archive.org/
stream/SelectedWorksOfDengXiaopingVol.1/Deng02_djvu.txt.

15   Ibid.

16   Selected Works of Deng Xiaoping, 1st edition, Vol.3, p.79 and https://archive.org/
stream/SelectedWorksOfDengXiaopingVol.3/Deng03_djvu.txt.

According to Deng Xiaoping's suggestions, in the same year in October, the Party's 13th Congress agreed on the "three-step" strategic conception.

The first step, from 1981 to 1990, will be the realization of doubling gross national product of the year 1980, so as to solve the people's food and clothing problems. The second step, from 1991 to the end of the 20th century, further doubling the gross national product so that people's living standards will reach a well-off level. The third step, in the 50 years to the middle of the 21st century, per capita GDP would reach the level of moderately developed countries, wherein people living standards will be more affluent, and the socialist modernization will be basically realized then, move forward on this basis.

According to Deng Xiaoping's three-step approach, targeting the basic realization of modernization in 2049, China through its effort according to three five-year plan periods, the 2000 goals were achieved in 1995, ahead of time.

In March 1996, in order to link the second-step and the third-step well, the State Council promulgated the "Ninth Five-Year Plan for National Economic and Social Development and Outline for Long-term Target for the Year 2010."

In 1997, the strategic goals for the third step, further defined third stage: in the first decade of the 21st century, we will realization the doubling of the gross national product of the 2000, and achieve a well-off life which is more affluent for people, and achieve the formation of a relatively complete socialist market economic system. After 10 years of efforts, between 2010-2021 till 100th anniversary of the founding of the CPC, we will a more developed national economy and more perfect socialist systems in all aspects. And in 29 years till the mid-21st century, by the 100th anniversary of anniversary of the founding of the PRC, modernization will be basically realized and we will "build a prosperous, strong, democratic, culturally advanced, civilized socialist country. This definition has made the "three-step" strategy and its steps more specific and clear.

The "three-step" strategy was put forward by the central leading collective of the Party on the basis of summing up the historical experiences of the development of modernization at home and abroad. And has been a profound embodiment of the characteristics of China's national conditions and characteristics of times and the correct reflection regarding the objective law of modernization.

The above development strategy which has started from the realities of the primary stage of socialism has reflected the unity of ideal and seeking truth from facts; considered the economic development and improving people's living standards as a unity, adhering to the economic development and the realization of the socialist character in gradual steps as another unity.

Building a prosperous, strong, democratic, culturally advanced, civilized socialist country, i.e. the goals of socialist modernization and adhering to comprehensive and coordinated development of economy and society, and guiding the whole party and the people in building of socialism with Chinese characteristics, has defined the program of action.

The 19th Party Congress in 2017 led by Xi Jinping further clarified the above strategy as follows:

The period between 2017 and 2020 will be decisive in finishing the building of a moderately prosperous society in all respects. We must follow the requirements on building this society set out at our 16th, 17th, and 18th National Congresses, act in response to the evolution of the principal contradiction in Chinese society, and promote coordinated economic, political, cultural, social, and ecological advancement. We must show firm resolve in implementing the strategy for invigorating China through science and education, the strategy on developing a quality workforce, the innovation-driven development strategy, the rural vitalization strategy, the coordinated regional development strategy, the sustainable development strategy, and the military-civilian integration strategy. We must focus on priorities, address inadequacies, and shore up points of weakness. In this regard, I want to stress that we must take tough steps to forestall and defuse major risks, carry out targeted poverty alleviation, and prevent and control pollution, so that the moderately prosperous society we build earns the people's approval and stands the test of time.

The period between the 19th and the 20th National Congress is the period in which the timeframes of the two centenary goals converge. In this period, not only must we finish building a moderately prosperous society in all respects and achieve the first centenary goal; we must also build on this achievement to embark on a new journey toward the second centenary goal of fully building a modern socialist country.

Based on a comprehensive analysis of the international and domestic environments and the conditions for China's development, we have drawn up a two-stage development plan for the period from 2020 to the middle of this century.

In the first stage from 2020 to 2035, we will build on the foundation created by the moderately prosperous society with a further 15 years of hard work to see that socialist modernization is basically realized. The vision is that by the end of this stage, the following goals will have been met:

* China's economic and technological strength has increased significantly. China has become a global leader in innovation.

* The rights of the people to participate and to develop as equals are adequately protected. The rule of law for the country, the government, and society is basically in place. Institutions in all fields are further improved; the modernization of China's system and capacity for governance is basically achieved.

* Social etiquette and civility are significantly enhanced. China's cultural soft power has grown much stronger; Chinese culture has greater appeal.

* People are leading more comfortable lives, and the size of the middle-income group has grown considerably. Disparities in urban-rural development, in development between regions, and in living standards are significantly reduced; equitable access to basic public services is basically ensured; and solid progress has been made toward prosperity for everyone.

* A modern social governance system has basically taken shape, and society is full of vitality, harmonious, and orderly.

* There is a fundamental improvement in the environment; the goal of building a Beautiful China is basically attained.

In the second stage from 2035 to the middle of the 21st century, we will, building on having basically achieved modernization, work hard for a further 15 years and develop China into a great modern socialist country that is prosperous, strong, democratic, culturally advanced, harmonious, and beautiful. By the end of this stage, the following goals will have been met:

* New heights are reached in every dimension of material, political, cultural and ethical, social, and ecological advancement.

* Modernization of China's system and capacity for governance is achieved.

* China has become a global leader in terms of composite national strength and international influence.

* Common prosperity for everyone is basically achieved.

* The Chinese people enjoy happier, safer, and healthier lives.

The Chinese nation will become a proud and active member of the community of nations.

Second, the goal of building a moderately prosperous society

Through the concerted efforts of the whole party and the people of all ethnic groups across the country, by the end of the 20th century, China has achieved the first two goals of the "three-step" strategy of modernization, and the people's living standard has reached a well-off level in general. This has marked a new milestone in the history of the Chinese nation.

After the people's living standards have reached the well-off level, the Fifth Plenary Session of the 15th CPC, Central Committee in 2000, has proposed that China will enter a new stage of building a well-off society in an all-round way and accelerate the socialist modernization.

The 16th National Congress of the Communist Party of China in 2002, put forward the goal of building a well–off society in an all-round (comprehensive) way in the first 20 years of the new century. The 17th National Congress of the Communist Party of China in 2007, put forward new and higher requirements on the basis of the goal of building a well-off society as compared to the 16th National Congress of the CPC.

How to understand the different terms in the Party documents, such as: low-level well-off, well-off society, and the term of the well-off society in an all-round way. Low-level well-off means that we have just entered the threshold of comprehensively well-off society, also means that we have solve the basic needs of survival, but we are also far away from comprehensively well-off (not comprehensive).

Still not comprehensive (all-round) well-off level mainly refers that the currently achieved well-off level includes a moderate level of material civilization, but it does not include comprehensive levels of spiritual civilization, political civilization, ecological environment, sustainable development due to lack of enough attention. The development being quite uneven, means we have just entered the threshold of comprehensively well-off society but the national income distribution among the population is unbalanced, which also means there is a huge gap between urban and rural areas, between the eastern and western regions, and means that there is a widening gap, between different income groups and widening gap of economic development of people as well as living standards of people.

The goal and requirements of building a well-off society in an all-round way are as the following:

- Enhancing the mode of coordinated development, and strive to achieve sound and rapid economic development.

Changing the mode of development, making significant progress in optimizing the economic structure, improve efficiency, reduce waste of human and natural sources, protect the environment on the basis of quadrupling the per capita GDP between 2000-2020. The socialist market economic system becomes more perfect. The ability of independent innovation improves significantly, and the contribution rate of scientific and technological progress to economic growth rises sharply and China enters among the ranks of innovative countries. Residents' consumption level encounters steady increase, the formation of coordinated growth pattern of three pillars: consumption, investment, export driven growth pattern. Coordinated and interactive development mechanism of urban and rural areas, among different regions. Significant progress will be made in the construction of new socialist countryside. The proportion of urban population will increase significantly[17].

- Expanding socialist democracy and better protect people's rights and interests and improve social equity.

Citizens' political participation will be enhanced in an orderly manner. The basic strategy of governing the country in accordance with the law will be deepened, the rights of the people to participate and to develop as equals will be adequately protected. The rule of law for the country, the government, and society is basically in place. Institutions in all fields are further improved; the modernization of China's system and capacity for governance is basically achieved. Grassroots democracy becomes more perfect. The ability of the government to provide basic public services will be significantly enhanced.

- Strengthening cultural construction, the civilization quality of the whole population will be improved significantly.

The socialist core value system will enjoy a strong popular support, and the good virtues of people and morality will ascend to a higher level.

A public cultural service system covering the whole society will be basically established, the establishment of cultural industry encounters a significantly increase in its proportion in comparison to total national economy. The international competitiveness regarding accessing to more rich cultural products will be significantly enhanced to meet the needs of the people.

- Accelerating the development of social undertakings, and comprehensively improve people's lives.

Modern national education system will be more perfect, lifelong education system will be basically formed, the education level of all people and innovative personnel training level will be improved significantly. Social employment pattern becomes more adequate. The social security system covering all the urban and rural residents will be basically established, where everyone enjoys basic living standards and social security.

Reasonable and equitable distribution of income will be basically formed, the size of the middle-income group has grown considerably and becomes the majority, the ultimate elimination of poverty is basically achieved. Everyone enjoys basic medical and health services. Social management system is more sound.

---

17   The above goals will be achieved by 2021.

- The concept of ecological civilization across the whole society will be firmly established, the construction of ecological civilization encounters remarkable progress. The basic form of energy conservation and protection of the ecological environment of the industrial structure, growth, consumption patterns will be formed. Circular economy ascends to a larger scale, the proportion of renewable energy increases significantly. The discharge of pollutants in the main will be effectively controlled, the quality of the ecological environment will be significantly improved. Sustainable development capacity is increasing.

By 2020, when we will achieved the goal of building a well-off society in an all-round way, our long history of civilization and the developing socialist country will encounter the following: industrialization will be basically realized, the comprehensive national strength is significantly enhanced, the overall size of the domestic market will rank in the forefront of the world, the whole people will achieve a higher degree of affluence, the quality of life has been improved and the ecological environment has been improved. Thus China will become a country with more full democratic rights and higher moral quality and spiritual pursuits. It has become a more perfect system and a more dynamic and stable society. China will become more open to the outside world, will have more affinity to other nations of the world, and China will make greater contributions to human civilization.

Building a well-off society in an all-round way is the necessary stage we must pass through realizing the strategic goal of socialist modernization in three-steps. It is an important strategy for the new stage of socialism with Chinese characteristics. The goal of this struggle is in line with China's basic national conditions and the law of modernization, in line with the aspirations of the broad masses of the people, leads us in our efforts to continue to move forward in the new century, points to our direction.

Section IV

Promoting a sound and rapid economic development

First, taking the path of new industrialization

Industrialization is the basis and premise of modernization, highly developed industrial society is the main symbol of modernization. What kind of path should be followed as the path to industrialization is a major issue facing our country.

The 16th National Congress of the Communist Party of China (CPC) in 2002, pointed out that it should adhere to industrialization combined by informatization, promote the informationization of industries, and blaze a new path of industrialization with high technological content, virtuous economic efficiency, low resource consumption, less environmental pollution and improvement of qualified human resource advantages. This are the major strategic decisions made by the Party Central Committee, to enable China achieve a well-off society in an all-round way and accelerate the advancement of socialist modernization in the new stage of development.

The concept of taking the new path to industrialization, is the right choice evaluating the realities of both China and the world's science and technological development.

Since the 1990s, the world economic and technological development has undergone tremendous advances: firstly, the new scientific and technological revolution has developed by leaps and bounds, high-tech, especially the extensive application of information technology, has become a strong driving force for economic and social development, and men's production activities and social has begun to enter the era of information and automation. Secondly, economic globalization has encountered in-depth development, the world's economic and trade development and capital movement and technology transfer movement has imposed to speed up the economies and markets to further open and interdependence among countries has increased remarkably.

On the other hand, in the above defined context of globalization, we cannot close our doors when engage in the industrialization efforts, and we cannot follow the traditional Western path of colonialist industrialization, also we need to strictly engage in informationization. In the above context, we cannot achieve the industrialization without blazing new path to industrialization.

After the founding of new China, especially since the reform and opening up, China's economy has made great achievements, China saw rapid progress of industrialization.

But in the past few decades, China's economic development has relied too much to expand the scale of investment and focused on increasing investments on material economy, this means an extensive economic growth, this mode of development has caused excessive waste of resources, environmental pollution, expansion of urban and rural gap, thus we have paid huge price for economic development. The contradictions regarding energy, resources, environment has become more and more acute and unsustainable.

This requires us to change the mode of economic growth, take the path of new industrialization, mainly by saving from the consumption of material resources and mainly rely on scientific and technological progress, improve the quality of workers, management innovation, shift from extensive development to intensive one, so as to achieve that we achieve sustainable and rapid development.

In order to take a new path of industrialization, we must firmly grasp the strategic adjustment task regarding the economic structure, as the main task, promote the optimization and upgrading of industrial structure.

The grand policy of adhering to develop an industrialized, information-based, urbanized, market-oriented and internationalized country, considers the formation of high-tech industries as the guiding sectors, the basic industries and manufacturing sectors as the supporting part, and includes the comprehensive development of the service industry.

High-tech industry is based on the IT-industry as the representative sector of the high-tech development in the emerging industries of the world, which is characterized by high level technological content, it is an important driving force for rapid development, regarding the national economy and social life and greatly contributes to economic growth. It is becoming the lifeline of both the whole industry of the national economy, it is also the basic material condition for the further development of modern social productive forces.

On the other side, the manufacturing industry is at the center of industrial structure, is the basis and prerequisite for accelerating the realization of national industrialization and modernization. Its development can promote and support the development of other industries of the national economy.

The prosperity and proportion of the service industry in the economic structure is the main feature of economic modernization. The proportion of service industry in the national economy is the main symbol to measure the degree of economic and social development and also the modernization level of a country.

To this end, the 17th National Congress of the Party, said: we will develop a modern industrial system, integrate IT application with industrialization, push our large industries to grow stronger, invigorate the equipment manufacturing industry, and eliminate outdated production capacities. We will upgrade new- and high-technology industries and develop information, biotechnology, new materials, aerospace, marine and other industries. We will develop the modern service industry and raise the level of the service sector and its share in the economy. We will step up efforts to improve basic industries and infrastructure and accelerate development of a modern energy industry and a comprehensive transport system. We will ensure the quality and safety of products. We will encourage formation of internationally competitive conglomerates.

Second, the construction of a new socialist countryside

The document titled as "The New Ideas in the Work of Agriculture, Countryside and Farmers" embodies the major strategic decision made by China's central leadership to meet the requirements of the new stage of economic and social development and realize the grand goal of building a well-off society in an all-round way which is the goal of full socialist modernization, in the new era of reform and opening up.

The problems of agriculture, rural areas and peasants, shortly "the three rural issues" has always been the fundamental problem of China during—revolution, construction and reform—the three periods.

The achievements of our party's leadership over revolution, construction and reform works are inseparable from its achievements in resolving the "three rural issues".

After the reform and opening up, especially since the 16th CPC National Congress in 2002, our Party has adopted a series of measures to solve the problem of "agriculture, rural areas and farmers", so that agriculture would be strengthened, rural areas to be developed, the benefits of farmers to be increased, and considered the three issues as the important premise of promoting economic and social development and maintain social stability.

However, it must be seen that the deep-seated contradictions that restricts the agriculture and rural development has not yet been eliminated, and the long-term mechanism for the sustainable and stable increase of farmers' incomes has not yet been formed. The lagging situation of rural economic and social development, in comparison to urban regions has not changed fundamentally.

Solving the problem of "three rural" is still a long-term task. The "three rural issues" a term in China to summarize rural issues is the key problem in the process of building a well-off society in an all-round way.

Building a moderately prosperous society is the most arduous task when applied to rural areas. If the peasants are not well-off of the peasants, the well-being of the people of the whole country will not be achieved. There will be no achievement of modernization of the whole China without the modernization of the countryside.

The virtuous development of the rural economy, building qualified and healthy farmer homes, so that farmers live a well-off life is a must to ensure that all people share the fruits of economic and social development and serves to the goal of continuously expanding domestic demand and thus promoting sustained, rapid and coordinated development of the national economy.

Since the 16th National Congress of the Communist Party of China (CPC) in 2002, our Party has stressed that it is necessary to solve the problem of "agriculture, rural areas and farmers" as the top priority of the work of the whole party and further stressed a coordinated urban and rural development.

At the 4th Plenary Session of the 16th CPC Central Committee, Hu Jintao put forward the important idea of "two trends", that is, in the initial stage of industrialization, agriculture supports industry and provides accumulation for industrialization being a general trend. But as the second trend, after a degree of industrialization (middle and late stage) is achieved, industry should nurture and support agriculture, urban regions should support rural areas, "we should achieve coordinated development of the industry and agriculture, urban and rural regions. At present, China has generally entered the development stage wherein we should promote agriculture, with the support of urban regions. The Fifth Plenary Session of the 16th CPC Central Committee further proposed that building "a new socialist countryside" is a major historical task in the process of modernization of our country.

In 2006, the CPC Central Committee and State Council co-issued the "Opinions on Promoting the Construction of New Socialist Countryside", and made a comprehensive plan for coordinating the economic and social development of urban and rural areas and promoting the construction of new socialist countryside.

The central government put forward the general requirements of constructing a new socialist countryside, as follows: development of agricultural productive forces, well-off life, rural civilization, clean and tidy villages, democratic village level management.

The comprehensive development of agricultural productive forces, is the central link in building a socialist new countryside… material basis and key link to achieve other objectives of the whole project. Making "increases in farmers' income" so that they lead a better life is the central task and the purpose of building a socialist new countryside but also the basic scale to measure the success of our work.

Township civilization, policy is the reflection of the quality of farmers, which reflects the requirements of spiritual civilization in rural regions. We should boost spiritual civilization and accelerating the development of education and culture in rural areas to cultivate "new-type" farmers.

Clean and tidy villages policy aims to achieve the harmonious development of man and the environment which will meet long-term requirements, but also a symbol of building a modern civil society in rural areas which means boosting harmony, caring for the lives of farmers, improving health and strengthening social administration in the countryside.

Improving grass-roots democracy is the political guarantee of building a socialist new countryside means showing respect for and maintenance of the peasant masses' political rights. We should boost grass-roots democracy in the countryside and improve transparency in village affairs. We should fully exert the leading core function of the grass-root party organization to provide solid political and organizational guarantee for the construction of a new socialist countryside.

The above policies form an organic whole, which summarizes the basic connotation and requirements of building a socialist new countryside, the policies have not only sketched out the prospects for the longed pleasant picture for a modern countryside, but also put forward the systematic ideas to solve the "three rural" problem.

Building a socialist new countryside, has been a systematic project, so as to actively promote the coordinated development of urban and rural areas to be carried out under the premise of orderly, planned and gradual methods.

In order to strengthen the basic status of agriculture, take the path of agricultural modernization with Chinese characteristics, the establishment of labor to promote agriculture, to urban long-term mechanism with the township, has the formed a new pattern of integration and coordination of urban and rural economic and social development.

We should adhere to promoting the development of modern agriculture, take the prosperity of the rural economy as a primary task, strengthen the construction rural infrastructures, improve rural markets and agricultural service system.

We should increase supports to agricultural development, enforce the protection of arable farming land plots strictly, increase agricultural investments, promote the progress of agricultural science and technology, comprehensively enhance the agricultural production capacity.

We should take increasing of farmers' income as the core task, promote the development of township enterprises in rural areas, strengthen the county level economies, explore and establish diverse channels for shifting the employment of farmers in non-farming occupations, which is one fundamental problem to solve for increasing farmers' incomes, employment. We should vigorously increase targeted efforts for poverty alleviation by agricultural development. We should deepen the comprehensive reform in rural areas and promote the reform and innovation of the rural financial system. We should adhere to the policy of improve the basic management system in rural areas, stabilize and improve the contract based land use relationship, in accordance with the principle of voluntary compensation in accordance with the law, improve the land transfer and management rights contract market. We should explore for more effective forms of collective economy, i.e. promote the development of professional and specialized farmers' co-operative associations and organizations in order to support the industrial-ization of agriculture and also promote the development of leading enter-prises. All of which can play an important role in helping farmers operate in modern value chains, by providing technical training and information.

We should also promote the development of leading enterprises in rural areas. Leading enterprises concept defines leading enterprises as important components of the industrial system of modern agriculture and key to in-dustrialized operations in agriculture.

We should cultivate culturally developed, science and technology friend-ly, new type of farmers, so that hundreds of millions of Chinese farmers can fully play their role in building a new socialist countryside.

Third, improve the ability of independent innovation, building an innovative nation

Innovation is the soul of a nation's progress, and an inexhaustible mo-tive force for the prosperity of a country. Hu Jintao as the general secretary of the Party Central Committee, has evaluated the development trend of the world and the historical stage of our country, made a far-sighted judgment to promote independent innovation, building China into an innovative country.

This has been a major strategic decision made by our Party to adopt the strategy of rejuvenating the country through science and education and the strategy of strengthening the country through talents. Building an in-novative country has become an objective requirement to improve Chinese international competitiveness. In today's world, human society is experi-encing an evolution from industrial society to knowledge economy soci-ety. Scientific and technological innovation has become the core driving force of national development, and will finally determine the international competitiveness of a country. In the new round of global science and tech-nological competition, developed countries are using their technological advantages to maximize their interests.

If developing countries can improve their abilities to innovate, they may have the opportunity and initiative to develop better. Otherwise, they will further widen the development gap with the developed countries.

If development is our highest priority, we should put science and tech-nology in a strategic position, accelerate the pace of independent innova-tion, build an innovative country, drive China's productive forces further forward to achieve a qualitative leap in order to grasp the opportunities in the fierce international competition and enhance our initiative to push the development.

Building an innovation-oriented country is a major step in implementing the scientific concept of development and building a well-off society in an all-round way. It is an urgent requirement to solve the outstanding contradictions and problems facing China's current development.

Only by vigorously promoting scientific and technological progress and innovation, only enhancing our ability of independent innovation, and promote China's economic growth mode from resource-dependent mode to innovation-driven mode, can we continue to maintain stable, rapid and sustainable economic growth.

The strategic decision to build an innovative country has not only been significant step forward but also a realistic step.

It is based on the scientific analysis of China's basic national conditions and comprehensive judgment on the strategic requirements of China, but also aims to launch the full potential of China's superiority as being a socialist country, superiority of socialism should be given full play. China which already has a good basis of economic and technological strength, should utilize this basis by independent innovation strategy.

Although there is still a big gap between China's current overall level of science and technology with the world's advanced level, although China's current overall level of science and technology, possess many holes or weak points which hinder its economic and social development, we cannot ignore the achievements made since the founding of new China, especially since the reform and opening up, with the establishment of a socialist market economic system, and after we have achieved sustained and rapid economic and social development: China's total number of scientific and technological human resources and the total number of R & D personnel in the forefront of the world, has significantly increased, we have formed a relatively complete research discipline system regarding natural sciences, therefore in some important areas of research and development capabilities China has entered among the ranks of world's advanced countries. All these have laid an important foundation and presents favorable conditions for building China as an innovative country.

Innovative country means we should focus to science and technological innovation as a basic strategy, try to achieve a substantial increase in scientific and technological innovation, strive to have an increasingly strong competitive advantage against our competitors.

At present, the world's leading innovative countries are the United States, Europe, Japan and so on. The common characteristics of these countries are: contribution of innovative industries, scientific and technological progress to their output is more than 70% of the total. And their R & D investment expenditures are generally more than 2% of their GDPs; their foreign dependency indicators regarding independent innovation capability, their dependency to external technology are usually less than 30%.

In building an innovative country, starting from the reality of our country, the core task is to enhance the ability of independent innovation as a strategic basis for the development of science and technology. We should follow a path of independent innovation with Chinese characteristics, in order to promote the development of science and technology by leaps and bounds.

In order to enhance China's ability of independent innovation as a national strategy, China aims to stimulate the whole nation's innovative spirit, cultivate high-level innovative talents, form an institutional mechanism conducive to independent innovation, vigorously promote theoretical innovation, system innovation, scientific and technological innovation, and constantly consolidate and promote the great cause of socialism with Chinese characteristics.

The 12th Five-Year Plan of China emphasized the following: "we should change the development mode and strive to create a scientific development pattern" "and as the focus of accelerating the transformation of the economic development pattern, the building of resource saving and environment-friendly society is a key factor. Obviously, the green economic growth is of extraordinary importance in forming a resource saving and environment-friendly society, and is an inevitable choice in coping with increasingly serious resource and environmental constraints. In pursuit of a green growth, endeavors on enhancing the sense of environmental crisis, accelerating energy saving and emission reduction, and constructing an energy-saving and environment-friendly production pattern are urgently needed."

The ability of independent innovation is the core of a nation's international competitiveness and the fundamental way to realize the goal of building an innovative country.

The practice of science and technology development in the world shows that, in order to enhance our initiative and grasp opportunities in the fierce international competition, the only way to success can be having a strong independent innovation capability.

Especially in the key areas of our national economic lifeline and in the key areas of our national economic security, and in core technology development areas, and in the areas of key technology we cannot buy from outside, therefore China must rely on independent innovation.

In all our works regarding science and technology, i.e. according to the guideline for scientific and technological work in order to improve our abilities of home-grown, independent innovation, firstly, we should focus to master a number of core technologies, targetly plan to produce a number of independent intellectual property rights which belong to us, create a number of internationally competitive enterprises, thus reach a substantial increase in national competitiveness.

In order to promote the path of independent innovation with Chinese characteristics, we must adhere to the above guideline (guideline for scientific and technological work) which focuses "home-grown innovation, leapfrog advancement in key areas, supportive development and leading for the future".

Independent home-grown innovation, means to enhance the national innovation capacity, means to strengthen the indigenous innovation capacity, integrated innovation and means in our technological innovation efforts we should adopt the policy of digestion and assimilation in technological innovation instead of copying and imitating.

Focusing on leapfrog advancement in key areas means we should insist on doing something wrong, choose such innovation areas where we have a certain degree of foundation and advantages, and strike a good balance when choosing key areas of innovation, i.e. strike a good balance between the needs of people's livelihood and key national security areas and link them appropriately. It means we should concentrate our efforts, to make breakthroughs in some major areas and achieve leapfrog development.

Focusing on supportive development means we should start from the realities of our urgent problems that needs to be solved in order to support the sustained and coordinated economic and social development. And in order to support the sustained and coordinated economic and social development, we should strive to make breakthroughs in the areas of key technologies and common technologies.

Leading the future, means to look forward with long term vision, strive to advance deployment of cutting-edge technologies and promote basic scientific and technological research, create new market demand, foster the development of the new industries, so as to lead the future economic and social development.

This guideline of focusing on "home-grown innovation, leapfrog advancement in key areas, supportive development and leading for the future" is a summarization of the practical experiences of developing of science and technology in China for more than half a century. It is an important choice for the future of our country and related to our cause of great rejuvenation of the Chinese nation. We must stick to this guideline through the whole process of the development of science and technology in China.

At the beginning of 2006, the State Council formulated "the Outline of the National Medium- and Long-term Science and Technology Development Plan", and put forward the major strategic task of bringing China into the ranks of innovative countries of the world within 15 years.

The overall goal of building an innovation-oriented country includes the following goals:

By 2020, our capability of independent and indigenous innovation will be significantly enhanced, the ability of our science and technological basis to promote economic and social development and to safeguard national security will be significantly enhanced, it will be able to provide a strong support for building an overall well-to-do society. By 2020, the comprehensive strength of basic science and cutting-edge technology research will be significantly enhanced, and a batch of scientific and technological achievements that will have a significant impact in the world arena will be achieved, thus we will enter among the ranks of innovative countries, and all these will lay the foundation for becoming a world scientific and technological power by the middle of the 21st century.

Accelerating the construction of national innovation system is an important task for building an innovative country. The national innovation system in China an institutional system led by the government which gives full play to the market's role in the allocation of scientific and technological resources, this institutional system includes various innovation entities which are closely linked and effectively interact with each other. To further deepen the reform of science and technology system, we should give full play to the role of enterprises in technological innovation, give full play to the backbone of national scientific research institutions and give full play to leading the role of these scientific research institutions, give full play to the role of universities and fully use their research basis.

To this end, we must strive to build a technology innovation system with enterprises as the main pillar of the system, build a market orientated system , we should combine production, teaching and research, scientific research and research by higher education institutions. We should also combine military and civilian research for innovation. Achieving the establishment of a comprehensive system of scientific and technological innovation, will provide a major guarantee in building China as an innovative country.

Creating a contingent of innovative S & T talents is the key in building an innovative country.

We must adhere to the strategic thinking that human resources are the primary forces and regard training innovative talents as an important strategic measure in building an innovative nation. We must strive to create world-class scientists and leading scientists in the sphere of science and technology, we should focus on cultivating front-line creative talents, so that innovative spirit and wisdom of the whole society will blossom vigorously, thus China will have numerous innovative talents, who are capable in all aspects.

Fourth, co-ordinated and balanced regional development

China covers a vast geographical land wherein its regions are faced with unbalanced development. Since the reform and opening up, the eastern, central and western regions have made great progress. However, due to the gaps regarding, the level of economic development in the eastern, central and western regions has been widening due to the differences in their respective foundations, i.e. their historical basis of social and economic development, natural geographical environment, their histories and cultures, and the speed of economic development levels are quite different. These gaps demonstrate a widening trend. On China to co-ordinate regional development, and narrowing the development gap between regions has become a critical problem that cannot be ignored. It is not only related to the overall situation of our modernization task, but also the stability of society and the long-term stability of the country. Our party has always attached importance to regional coordinated development. Mao Zedong in the famous "On the Ten Major Relations," urged to care for the development gap between Eastern and Western regions among major issues.

During the reform and opening up era, in 1980s Deng Xiaoping put forward the idea of "two-step sequential strategy to achieve an overall balanced development" : the first step would be to let the eastern coastal areas, develop first and help in speeding up the opening up, in the next step after eastern regions becomes rich, they will vigorously support the development of the western regions.

The third generation of the central collective leadership, with Jiang Zemin as its core, at the turn of the century (2000), put forward the strategy of implementing the western development as a priority, following Deng Xiaoping's concept of "two-step sequential strategy to achieve an overall balanced development", he declared: At the current stage, we should study and formulate overall plan for west development. We should have long term strategic thinking for west development. Through hard work of several generations, until mid of 21st century when China basically realize modernization, a new West will be built. This new West is of economic prosperity, progressed society, national unity, beautiful mountains and rivers, and happy lives.

In the new century, evaluating the current situation of China's regional development and with the vision of comprehensively promoting the requirements of modernization, Hu Jintao as the general secretary of the Central Committee of the CPC, put forward the coordinated regional development strategy as follows: We should give high priority to large-scale development of the western regions, fully revitalize old industrial bases in northeast China, work vigorously to promote the rise of the central regions, and support the eastern region in taking the lead in development. Encourage reasonable division of labor, we should promote distinctive, complementary advantages of regional industrial structure, and promote common development of all regions.

The 17th Party Congress in 2007 further discussed the idea and advocated the coordinated regional development: We should promote balanced development among regions and improve the pattern of land development. To narrow the gap in development among regions, we must work to ensure their equal access to basic public services and guide a rational flow of factors of production between regions. Following the general strategy for regional development, we will continue to carry out large-scale development of the western region, rejuvenate northeast China and other old industrial bases in an all-round way, boost the development of the central region and support the eastern region in taking the lead in development. We will strengthen land planning, improve policies for regional development and adjust the geographical distribution of economic operations in accordance with the requirement to form development priority zones. In compliance with the laws governing the market economy, we will work beyond administrative divisions to form a number of close-knit economic rims and belts that will provide a strong impetus to the development of other areas. In locating major projects, we must give full consideration to supporting development of the central and western regions and encourage the eastern region to help them develop. We will give more support to the development of old revolutionary base areas, ethnic autonomous areas, border areas and poverty-stricken areas. We will help transform the economies of areas where natural resources are exhausted. We will have the special economic zones, the Pudong New Area in Shanghai and the Binhai New Area in Tianjin play a major role in reform, opening up and independent innovation. Taking a path of urbanization with Chinese characteristics, we will promote balanced development of large, medium-sized and small cities and towns on the principle of balancing urban and rural development, ensuring rational distribution, saving land, providing a full range of functions and getting larger cities to help smaller ones. Focusing on increasing the overall carrying capacity of cities, we will form city clusters with mega cities as the core so that they can boost development in other areas and become new poles of economic growth.

Fifth, building a resource-saving and environment-friendly society

The Fifth Plenary Session of the 16th CPC Central Committee, in 2005, put forward the goal of building a resource-saving and environment-friendly society relying on the scientific development concept and relying on the concept of building a socialist harmonious society. The concept of building a socialist harmonious society, has been a new leap in our party's understanding of the law of socialist modernization. It is a major measure to coordinate the harmonious development of man and nature and promote the realization of sustainable development.

Resource-saving society, refers to the efficient use of energy resources in production process, to save the way to consumption as the fundamental characteristics of the community.

Resource-saving society does not only reflect the transformation of economic growth mode, but also a new model of social development, it requires that, in all spheres of production, circulation, consumption and in all aspects of economic and social development, we should save energy resources and improve the efficient use of energy resources as the core, with energy saving, water saving, materials saving, land, and suggests comprehensive utilization of resources as the focus, with the smallest possible consumption of resources, access to the greatest possible economic and social benefits, so as to promote the sustainable development of socio-economic structure.

Environment-friendly society, advocates the harmonious development of man and nature, through the harmonious development of man and nature. Specifically, it is a kind of harmony between man and nature as the goal, makes an evaluation of carrying capacity of ecological environment, on the basis of respecting the laws of nature as the core, it takes supporting green technology as the driving force, and takes protection of environment as priority. Environment-friendly society concept.

For an environment-friendly society we should develop an orderly and rational division of functional areas, promote an environment-friendly culture and ecological civilization understanding , we should promote the coordinated development of economy, society, and the environment.

Building a resource-saving and environment-friendly society is one major requirement of realizing our goal of building a well-off society in an all-round way.

Building a well-off society in an all-round way not only includes the tasks of economic construction, political construction, cultural construction, social construction, but also the construction of ecological civilization, so that the whole society will embark on the path of civilized development which includes development of production development, affluence life of people and a virtuous ecology.

We must see that it is remarkably difficult to meet the requirements of the resource-saving and environment-friendly society which will be the mark of the well-off society in an all-round way.

In the future, as the total economy continues to expand and the population continues to increase, the demand for energy resources will grow greatly, the amount of pollutants will continue to increase, pressures on ecological environment will further increase, environmental problems will become prominent. People's demands for environmental quality is constantly increasing, with the continuous improvement of material quality of their life.

In the process of building a well-off society in an all-round way, we must pay more attention to the conservation of resources and effectively protect the environment. At the same time, we should take effective measures to achieve the effective control of the main pollutant discharge and improve the quality of the ecological environment while we try achieving economic targets such as gross domestic product. We should build a new concept of GDP which includes, ecological standards.

Building a resource-saving and environment-friendly society is one major requirement of implementing the strategy of sustainable development. China is a country with a large population and which faces shortage of natural resources. Since the reform and opening up, China's economic and social development has made remarkable achievements.

However, since our economic growth was mainly based on high consumption, high pollution, i.e, the traditional development model, which had caused relatively high environmental pollution and ecological damage, the contradiction between the environment and development has become increasingly prominent. The relative shortage of resources, fragile ecological environment, limitedness in the carrying capacity of environment, all these 3 have gradually become a major issue negatively affecting the development. At present, China is in a stage wherein industrialization and urbanization has accelerated thus faces a lot of resources and environmental pressures. It is impossible to have a sustainable economic growth by utilizing excess resources and sacrificing the environment.

The history of human development has shown that the development and survival of human civilization is closely related to the resources and environment.

Resource conditions, especially the deterioration of the ecological environment will not only undermine people's living conditions, but may even lead to the demise of human civilization. If we do not attach importance to saving resources and protecting the environment, we may make mistakes that will be difficult to correct in the future.

We should adhere to the government policy of energy and resource conservation and ecological environmental protection which relates to the vital interests of the people and the survival and development of the Chinese nation.

The 17ᵗʰ Party Congress further emphasized the need to build a resource-saving and environment-friendly society put these tasks to a prominent position in our industrialization and modernization strategy, and include every unit and every family in the implementation of these tasks.

The report said: we must adopt an enlightened approach to development that results in expanded production, a better life and sound ecological and environmental conditions, and build a resource-conserving and environment-friendly society that coordinates growth rate with the economic structure, quality and efficiency, and harmonizes economic growth with the population, resources and the environment, so that our people will live and work under sound ecological and environmental conditions and our economy and society will develop in a sustainable way.

We should improve the laws and policies that are conducive to save energy resources and protect the ecological environment, and speed up the formation of a mechanism for sustainable development. Implementation of energy-saving emission reduction responsibility system.

We should develop and promote advanced technologies for conservation, substitution, recycling and pollution control, develop clean and renewable energy utilization, promote the protection of land and water resources, build a scientific and rational energy resources utilization system and improve energy efficiency.

We should develop an environment protection industry, increase investments for energy conservation and environmental protection, focusing on strengthening water, air, soil pollution prevention and control, thus improve urban and rural living environment.

We should strengthen water conservancy, forestry, grassland protection, strengthen desertification control, promote ecological restoration.

We should strengthen capacity building to fight against climate change, and make active contribution to the protection of global climate.

In short, we must profoundly understand the importance of strengthening energy conservation and ecological and environmental protection, with a spirit of being responsible to the state, to the nation and to the next generations, and earnestly put the building of a resource-saving and environment-friendly society in a prominent position in the strategy of industrialization and modernization so that we can better promote all-round, coordinated, sustainable economic and social development.

CHAPTER FOUR

Fundamental Task of Socialism with Chinese characteristics

Section I

The fundamental task of socialism is to liberate and develop productive forces

First, the conception of the fundamental task of socialism and its basis

1. The fundamental task of socialism

Marxist classic writers have always attached great importance to the role of productive forces in social development. They have held that productive forces are the decisive force for the development of human society and held that the superiority of a social system depends on whether productive forces meet the requirements of the continuous development of productive forces, which one key measure to recognize the superiority of a social system. In *The Communist Manifesto*, Marx and Engels made it clear that once the proletariat seizes power, all measures should be taken to "increase the total of productive forces as rapidly as possible."[1]

This scientific prediction of future socialism includes the idea that the fundamental task of socialism is to develop the productive forces. After the victory of Russia's October Revolution, Lenin repeatedly stressed that to create an economic system superior to capitalism and to enhancing the labor productivity is the "fundamental task" of the Soviet Union. The Soviet regime "either ends up in peril or surpasses the economies of the advanced nations."[2]

---

1 Selected Works of Marx and Engels, 2nd edition, vol. 1, p.293.
2 Selected Works of Lenin, Vol. 23, p. 271.

Obviously, an initial understanding that the fundamental task of socialism is to develop the productive forces is already included but implicitly into the thoughts of Marxist classical writers.

Since the founding of the New China, Mao Zedong underscored several times that the fundamental task of the socialist society was to develop the productive forces and the economy. He stated that the large-scale and storming class struggle of the masses had gone away with the establishment of the socialist system and our task was to launch the cultural revolution and technology revolution and fight against the nature. In particular, it was in the 8th CPC National Congress when the main contradiction of the socialist society was analyzed and it was pointed out that the main task of all the people was to bring together all the strength to develop the social productive forces, realize the national industrialization and gradually meet people's growing material and cultural needs. This fundamental task of developing the productive forces, however, was replaced by the "class struggle as a guiding principle", due to the exacerbation of the left-deviation errors in the Party's guiding ideology, which devastated the socialist construction.

Since the reform and opening up, Deng Xiaoping, on the basis of China's practical experience and the Marxist thoughts, further developed the Marxist thoughts on productivity development and clearly proposed that the current China was still in the primary stage of socialism and that the "primary task", "first task" and "fundamental task" was to liberate and develop the productive forces. He emphasized that the most fundamental task of the socialist stage was to develop the productive forces, for the greatest importance was attached to the development of productive forces, according to Marxism. We say that socialism is the primary stage of communism. According to Marxism, communist society is based on material abundance. Only when there is material abundance can the principle of a communist society—that is, from each according to his ability, to each according to his needs"—be applied. Socialism is the first stage of communism. This requires that social productive forces develop at a high level and that the material wealth of society be greatly enriched. Therefore, the most fundamental task in the socialist stage is to develop the productive forces."[3]

Therefore, it is the fundamental idea of Marxism that the fundamental task of socialism is to liberate and develop the productive forces. It is on this occasion when Deng Xiaoping explicitly proposed this fundamental task of socialism for the first time in the socialist development history.

---

3   Selected Works of Deng Xiaoping, 1st edition, Volume 3, p. 63.

2. Why is it established as the fundamental task of socialism to liberate and develop the productive forces?

The reasons can be summarized as follows.

First of all, this fundamental task is the fundamental manifestation of the superiority of socialism. The largest and most fundamental superiority of socialism is that socialism can better liberate and develop the productive forces than capitalism. In the capitalist society, the contradiction between the private ownership of means of production and the socialized production makes the capitalism the fetter of the productivity development; while in the socialist society, the private ownership of means of production is eliminated, which can provide a better and more favorable environment for the productivity liberation and development. As Deng Xiaoping pointed out, "The superiority of the socialist system is demonstrated, in the final analysis, by faster and greater development of those forces than under the capitalist system. As they develop, the people's material and cultural life will constantly improve."[4]

Since our socialist system is built on the basis of the backward economy and culture in the semi-colonial and semi-feudal society, it is a long historical development process to improve the relatively more backward productive forces, economic and cultural development and people's material and cultural standards compared with the developed capitalist countries. The establishment of the socialist system in our country provides the possibility to greatly shorten this process which still needs the efforts of several generations of our people. Only by vigorously developing the social productive forces can the "potential" superiority of the socialist system become an actual one and the solid material foundation for the victory over the capitalist system be created.

Secondly, it is determined by the historical mission of socialism, that is, to create the material basis for communism. Communism is the inevitable trend of the socialist development as well as the advanced stage of socialism. The transition from the socialist society to the communist society requires a variety of conditions which can generally be summed up in the two aspects: material and humans. The material condition refers to the highly developed social productive forces, the abundant social material wealth, and on this basis the gradual elimination of various social differences and the work according to ability and distribution according to demand; the human condition refers to human's own free and comprehensive development with the labor not only a means of livelihood but also the first need of life. Among these conditions, the highly developed productive forces is the most basic one and is thus the material basis for the realization of

97

---

4 Ibid.

other conditions. Without the highly developed productive forces nor the abundant material wealth, the realization of the communist ideal will be an empty talk. Therefore, in order to realize the transition to communism, we need to create a series of necessary material and spiritual conditions, and the most fundamental is to create the highly developed social productive forces.

Deng Xiaoping pointed out: "A Communist society is one in which there is no exploitation of man by man, there is great material abundance and the principle of from each according to his ability, to each according to his needs is applied. It is impossible to apply that principle without overwhelming material wealth. In order to realize communism, we have to accomplish the tasks set in the socialist stage. They are legion, but the fundamental one is to develop the productive forces so as to demonstrate the superiority of socialism over capitalism and provide the material basis for communism."[5]

Thirdly, it is the essential condition for the socialist consolidation and development. Human history has proved that a new social system is superior to the old one, because, in the final analysis, the former can create a higher labor productivity than the latter; the former can overcome the latter and be well-established, because, in the final analysis, the former is more conducive to the productivity development and can better meet the material and cultural needs of the masses of people.

It should be noticed as well that there still exists a considerable gap between the socialist country and capitalist country in the productivity development, since the socialist system is established in countries with relatively backward economy and culture. This situation not only makes the socialist countries in a disadvantageous position in the competition with the capitalist countries, but also provides the excuse and material conditions for the capitalist to attempt to subvert and destroy the socialist system. The evolution of the socialist countries in eastern Europe and the disintegration of the first socialist state of the Soviet Union demonstrate that socialist countries will find it impossible to realize the consolidation, development and final victory if they fail to develop their productive forces or catch up with and surpass capitalism in terms of the economy, technology and labor productivity. In this regard, Deng Xiaoping made it clear that "the socialist political system and economic system cannot be fully consolidated, nor the national security guaranteed under the dictatorship of the proletariat when the modernization is not launched, the science and technology and social productive forces remain backward, and the national strength and the people's material and cultural life remain at a low level. To build China into a modern socialist power we should more effectively consolidate our

98

---

5   Selected Works of Deng Xiaoping, 1st Edition, Vol.3, p.137.

socialist system and cope with the aggression and subversion of foreign powers and ensure that we are gradually creating the material conditions and advance toward the great ideal of communism."[6]

"If China wants to withstand the pressure of hegemonism and power politics and to uphold the socialist system, it is crucial for us to achieve rapid economic growth and to carry out our development."[7]

In today's world where socialism and capitalism coexist and compete fiercely, the development of productive forces in socialist countries determines the fate of socialism and the future of mankind.

Second, the liberation and development of productive forces is the inherent requirement of the essence of socialism

1. The scientific connotation and characteristics of the essence of socialism

After the 3rd Plenary Session of the 11th CPC Central Committee, Deng Xiaoping summed up the historical lessons that we had been talking about socialism in an abstract way disregarding the productive forces over many years and treating something uncharacteristic of the socialist nature and fettering the development of the productive forces as "socialist principles" and defending it tenaciously but something conducive to the development of productive forces under the socialist conditions as "something capitalist" and opposing it. After the in-depth thinking, he provided a new generalization of the socialist nature, which deepened the understanding of socialism. He made a new scientific judgment about the essence of socialism: "The essence of socialism is liberation and development of the productive forces, elimination of exploitation and polarization, and the ultimate achievement of prosperity for all."[8]

Deng Xiaoping's new theoretical generalization of the socialist nature enables us, starting from the fundamental question of "what socialism is and how to build it", to deeply understand the fundamental task of socialism, that is, liberating and developing the productive forces, and to realize that it is the intrinsic demand of the socialist nature.

In the early 1980s, Deng Xiaoping first proposed the concept of the essence of socialism when he expounded on the issue how to demonstrate the superiority of the socialist system. He pointed out: ""Socialism" is a good term, but if we fail to have a correct understanding of it and adopt correct policies for establishing it, we will not be able to demonstrate its essence."9

6   Selected Works of Deng Xiaoping, 2nd edition, Vol.2, p.86.
7   Selected Works of Deng Xiaoping, 1st edition, Vol.3, p.356.
8   Selected Works of Deng Xiaoping, 1st edition, Vol.3, p.373.
9   Selected Works of Deng Xiaoping, 2nd edition, Vol.2, p.313.

According to him, the development of productive forces comes first for socialism, because only in this way can the superiority of socialism become prominent. The key to judge whether the socialist economic policy is right lies in whether the productivity is developed and people's income increases. He described the production development and income increase as the overriding criterion, which was in fact the core content of the socialist nature. He also made a profound analysis of the thought that is incompatible with the socialist nature, such as the poverty, slow development, egalitarianism, polarization, and lack of democracy, which are not characteristics of socialism.

To develop productivity and increasing people's livelihood and ultimately achieving common prosperity of all. This is the fundamental requirement of socialism. In September 1986, when he replied to a US reporter's report on the relationship between the China's slogan of "To get rich is glorious" and socialism or communism, Deng Xiaoping commented: "Wealth in a socialist society belongs to the people. To get rich in a socialist society means prosperity for the entire people. The principles of socialism are: first, development of production and second is common prosperity."[10]

This passage can be seen the prototype of Deng Xiaoping's ideas on the essence of socialism. In December 1990, Deng Xiaoping once again commented on the issue of common prosperity and pointed out: "Since the very beginning of the reform we have been emphasizing the need for seeking common prosperity; that will surely be the central issue some day. Socialism does not mean allowing a few people to grow rich while the overwhelming majority live in poverty. No, that's not socialism. The greatest superiority of socialism is that it enables all the people to prosper, and common prosperity is the essence of socialism."[11]

On the basis of a comprehensive summary of the historical experience in socialist practice and the fresh experience in reform and opening up, Deng Xiaoping clearly put forward the famous statement on the socialist nature in the speech made in his 1992 visit to the South.

Deng Xiaoping's new generalization regarding the essence of socialism nature is rich in its connotations.

First of all, it profoundly reveals that the socialist nature is the unity of liberating productive forces and developing productive forces, which is why the socialism exists and develops and superior over the capitalism. Deng Xiaoping stressed the liberation and development of productive forces as a

---

10   Selected Works of Deng Xiaoping, 1st edition, Vol.3, p.172 and https://archive.org/stream/SelectedWorksOfDengXiaopingVol.3/Deng03_djvu.txt.

11   Selected Works of Deng Xiaoping, 1st edition, Vol.3, p.364 and https://archive.org/stream/SelectedWorksOfDengXiaopingVol.3/Deng03_djvu.txt.

key part of the socialist nature, which happened in the history of scientific socialism for the first time and was a major development of Marxism. It is well-known that Marxist classical writers have always stressed the decisive role of productivity in social development, and treated social production as the basis for the existence and development of human society and the fundamental force promoting social development, and the adaptation to the productivity development as an essential measure of the advanced social system. Based on this essential standard, Marxist classical writers made a scientific analysis of the capitalist system and pointed out that the capitalist system in essence has become a hinder to the development of productive forces, and therefore is doomed to be replaced by the socialist system. The root cause for this replacement is that the socialist system can adapt to and promote the development of productive forces. Deng Xiaoping, based on the basic views of Marxism and the profound summary of the historical experience of socialist construction, clearly put forward -the scientific concept of the socialist nature for the first time, and treated the liberation and development of productive forces as the essential prescription of socialism, which is undoubtedly a significant development of scientific socialism.

Treating the liberation and development of the productive forces as the essential prescription of socialism fully affirms the great role of socialist system in promoting the productivity development, on the one hand; on the other hand, it shows that socialism can liberate and develop the productive forces only when it makes constant reforms. According to the historical experience in China's socialist construction, Deng Xiaoping pointed out that the establishment of socialist system could not guarantee the natural promotion and development of productive forces, since facts show that it takes time to perfect the socialist system and to give a full play to its superiority. In particular, when the socialist system was established in our country, it was greatly influenced by the Soviet Union, which made it defective and disadvantageous. As a result, the development of productive forces in our country was seriously fettered and the superiority of socialism was damped. To change this situation, we must deepen the political and economic system reform. Deng Xiaoping pointed out: "Revolution means the emancipation of the productive forces, and so does reform. The overthrow of the reactionary rule of imperialism, feudalism and bureaucrat-capitalism helped release the productive forces of the Chinese people. This was revolution, so revolution means the emancipation of the productive forces. After the basic socialist system has been established, it is necessary to fundamentally change the economic structure that has hampered the development of the productive forces and to establish a vigorous socialist economic structure that will promote their development. This is reform, so reform also means the emancipation of the productive forces. In the past, we only stressed expansion of the productive forces under socialism, without mentioning the need to liberate them through reform. That conception was incomplete. Both the liberation and the expansion of the productive forces are essential."[12] According to him, the reform must be based on the condition of productive forces, which requires us to establish the political system and economic system that can fully liberate and develop productive forces under the premise of adhering to the socialist basic system so as to fully reflect the essential requirements of socialism.

Secondly, the fundamental goal of eliminating exploitation and polarization and achieving the common prosperity was revealed on the basis of liberating and developing the productive forces. While exploring what socialism is, Deng Xiaoping repeatedly stressed that the greatest advantage of socialism was the common prosperity, something that embodies the socialist nature. In this new generalization about the socialist nature, Deng Xiaoping includes the elimination of exploitation and polarization and the realization of common prosperity as the fundamental goal of the socialist nature, which links it with the liberation and development of productive forces and thus further reveals the socialist nature in the light of the unity of productive forces and relations of production. If the liberation and development of productive forces reflect the nature and superiority of socialism in promoting the development of productive forces, then the elimination of exploitation and polarization and the achievement of common prosperity reflect the essential requirements of socialism in relations of production, because eliminating exploitation and polarization, and finally achieving common prosperity exists only in the socialist relations of production. At the same time, this also reflects the socialist nature in both the social development goal and the value goal and also shows the essential difference between the socialist society and the society ruled by the exploiting class, in regard to the goal of developing productive forces.

Deng Xiaoping's generalization of the essence of socialism has very distinct characteristics.

First of all, Deng Xiaoping's new generalization of the socialist nature reveals the inherent consistency and dialectical relationship among the essential requirements, the fundamental task and the social development goals of socialism. To eliminate exploitation and polarization, and eventually achieve common prosperity is the fundamental goal of the socialist development, while the liberation and development of productive forces is the premise and foundation of this goal. Without the development of productive forces, the fundamental goal cannot be achieved; the process of achieving this fundamental goal is in fact the process of liberating and developing

---

12   Selected Works of Deng Xiaoping, 1st edition, Vol.3, p.370.

the productive forces. The liberation and development of the productive forces must be based on the premise and condition that we should adhere to the socialist path for common prosperity, so that we can truly liberate and develop the productive forces.

Deng Xiaoping emphasized: "Economic development must lead to the path of common prosperity and always see that polarization is avoided."[13]

Departing from the fundamental goal, productive forces can neither be truly liberated nor be rapidly developed; our ideal for being a great power will vanish into naught and modernization will fail.

Secondly, this new generalization has corrected the erroneous tendency in the past that the nature and superiority of socialism is only embodied in the relation of production with the development of productive forces neglected. Deng Xiaoping profoundly revealed that the essential requirement, fundamental task and historical mission of socialism were to liberate and develop the productive forces, which was more important especially in the primary stage of socialism. He also pointed out that after the establishment of the socialist basic system, the productive forces should be further liberated through reforms, in order to give full play to the superiority of socialism and promote the rapid development of productive forces. It also emphasizes that the liberation and development of productive forces must adhere to the fundamental goal of which the realization can only be based on the former. Considering the low-level productive forces and the primary stage of socialism in China, we have to be soberly aware that we have to go through a long period of constantly liberating and developing the productive forces before achieving the socialist social development goal. It is thus repeated by Deng Xiaoping that we must insist on the economic construction as the center and whether it is conducive to the development of productive forces, to the enhancement of the comprehensive national strength of the socialist country, and to the improvement of the people's living standard as the standard for the correctness of the work or policy. From this, we can clearly see that Deng Xiaoping stressed the liberation and development of the productive forces because it can help achieve the fundamental goal of eliminating exploitation and polarization and finally achieving common prosperity, create the material basis for communism, and realize the full and free development of humans, which is the fundamental value goal he and the Chinese communists have always insisted on.

103

13   Selected Works of Deng Xiaoping, 1st edition, Vol.3, p.149 and https://archive.org/stream/SelectedWorksOfDengXiaopingVol.3/Deng03_djvu.txt.

2. Liberating and developing productive forces is the fundamental task of socialism with Chinese characteristics

First of all, the historical premise of socialism in China and the characteristics of the times determine that we must vigorously liberate and develop the productive forces, and realize the socialist modernization as soon as possible. The socialism was established in China under the historical premise that the old China was a semi-colonial and semi-feudal country with very backward economy and culture and had not experienced the stage of full development of capitalist economy. It thus followed that the socialist countries like China would inevitably fall behind the developed capitalist countries in productive forces and science and technology for a long historical period. Besides, in the process of building socialism, China also faces the challenges of the times which include, on the one hand, those from the traditional industrial revolution which had been completed in developed capitalist countries from the middle 1700s to the middle 1900s, and on the other hand, the others from the new scientific and technological revolution. This requires us to vigorously develop and improve the science and technology and focus on developing productive forces and carrying out modernization in double efforts, so as to narrow the gap with the developed capitalist countries and enhance our comprehensive national strength as soon as possible. Only in this way can we fully demonstrate the superiority of our socialist system and improve our position in the world.

Secondly, the resolution of various social contradictions and problems in the primary stage of socialism depends on the continuous development and liberation of productive forces. In addition to the main contradiction—the conflict between the growing material and cultural needs of the people and the backward social production, quite a number of other social contradictions and problems also exist in the primary stage of socialism in our country, including such contradictions as that among the state, the collective and the individual workers, between the central and local, different local places, and various departments, and between workers and peasants, urban and rural, and mental labor and manual labor; and such problems as the huge and unequal difference in people's possession of means of production and their income, and in particular the uneven regional economic development, since there is still a considerable number of poverty-stricken areas and population. These contradictions and problems can be essentially attributed to the low-level productive forces in China and thus be solved only through the continuous development and liberation of productive forces.

Thirdly, the construction of a high degree of the socialist democratic politics and spiritual civilization, the fundamental requirement for the realization of socialist modernization, also depends on the development and liberation of productive forces. However, it is in need of a solid material base and certain economic conditions. At present, the democratic politics and spiritual civilization in our country have not reached the height required by socialism, with some imperfect or weak points, which can be fundamentally attributed to the low-level productive forces and backward economy and culture in this stage in China. It can thus be said that the construction of democratic politics and spiritual civilization in our country still has a long way to go, and in order to create conditions for it, we should definitely take developing productive forces as the most fundamental task.

Finally, the international and domestic situation China faces also requires us to vigorously develop and liberate the productive forces. Judging from the international situation, the opposition against hegemonism for world peace is inseparable from the development of productive forces. International competition in any era is based on strength. Whoever falls behind is to be beaten. Whether China can withstand the pressure of power politics, adhere to the socialist system, and play a greater role in international affairs, mainly depends on whether China can achieve the best development, realize our development strategy and strengthen our material base. Judging from the domestic situation, the adherence to the "One Country, Two Systems" and the peaceful reunification of China are inseparable from the development and liberation of productive forces. Deng Xiaoping once said that Taiwan's return to the motherland and the reunification of the motherland, require us, in the final analysis, to do our own things well. We should be superior to Taiwan not only in the political and economic system but also in the economic development, since only when the economy is developed can we make difference in the realization of the national reunification.

Section II

Science and technology are the primary productive forces in promoting and advancing the development of productive forces

First, science and technology are primary productive forces

1. The scientific proposition of "science and technology is the primary productive force"

In today's world, science and technology play a decisive role in the development of productive forces, so in order to liberate and develop productive forces in China, we must gain a profound understanding of Deng Xiaoping's thought that "science and technology is the primary productive forces", and vigorously promote the development of science and technology in China.

By examining the development history of human society, especially the great role of modern science and technology in the transformation from the handicraft industry to the modern industry and in the development of capitalism, Marx made an analysis of the science and technology as a whole. He argued that science and technology is part of the productive forces and that it is a powerful force in the productivity and social development. The Communist Party of China has always attached importance to the position and role of science and technology in the national economic and social development, and enriched and developed the theory that science and technology is the productive forces in the relevant practice. In 1953 when the New China began its first five-year plan, Mao Zedong proposed that we should learn advanced science and technology and then apply it to the construction of our country. In 1956, Zhou Enlai, on behalf of the CPC Central Committee, put forward the slogan of "marching to science".

In early 1958, Mao Zedong proposed the technological revolution, and required that the Party's work should focus on the technological revolution which was suspended later due to the development of "leftist" thought. After the 3rd Plenary Session of the 11th CPC Central Committee, Deng Xiaoping explicitly proposed that "science and technology is the primary productive forces", considering the huge driving effect of the rapid development of world science and technology on the productive forces. This statement was later revised by Jiang Zemin to "science and technology is the primary productive forces and the centralized embodiment and main symbol of the advanced productive forces", and then complemented by Hu Jintao's important statement that science and technology "is the revolutionary force promoting the progress of human civilization", which has become an important part of the socialist theory with Chinese characteristics.

Deng Xiaoping attached great importance to the status and role of developing science and technology in socialist construction. He pointed out that modern science and technology was undergoing a great revolution, which was manifested not only in individual scientific theory, production technology, and the progress and reform in the general sense, but also in almost every field of science and technology, the emergence of new leaps and a series of emerging science and technology that had and would be coming up.

Evaluating the new trend of scientific and technological revolution and the rapid development of productive forces across the world, Deng Xiaoping further pointed out in September 1988: "Marx said that science and technology are part of the productive forces. Facts show that he was right. In my opinion, science and technology are a primary productive force."[14]

14 Selected Works of Deng Xiaoping, 1st edition, Vol.3, p.274 and https://archive.org/stream/SelectedWorksOfDengXiaopingVol.3/Deng03_djvu.txt.

Later, he stressed that the economy with a faster growth must rely on science and technology and education. We should promote science, since it brings us hope. This famous statement enriches and develops the theory of Marxism on science and technology and productive forces, reveals the primary role of science and technology in contemporary productivity development and social and economic development, and is of epoch-making theoretical and practical significance.

2. The connotations of "science and technology is the primary productive forces"

First of all, the role of science and technology in the national economic growth has been gradually lifted to the first place. In the early 1900s when the world just entered the modern science and technology development stage, the economic growth mainly depended on the input of manpower, material and capital, about 20% of which came from science and technology. After the WWII, the knowledge and information played an increasing role in economic development, while mineral resources and cheap labor force played a decreasing role in it. According to the world bank, scientific and technological progress contributed 49% on average to the national economic growth in developed countries between 1950 and 1970, and the proportion rose to 60-80% in 1980s, due to the thriving development of the emerging new technology industries. In other words, about 2/3 of the national economic growth in today's developed countries is achieved by science and technology.

Secondly, science and technology has been penetrated into various elements of modern productive forces system. In ancient times, the production development, the increase of labor productivity and the economic growth depended on the manual labor. In modern times, this situation underwent some changes. In modern productive forces system, the science is applied into the production or technological process, penetrated into other various elements of the productive forces, and can be transformed into the actual direct productive forces. Human beings have entered an era of relying more on knowledge, intelligence and science and technology, in which science and technology can greatly improve the knowledge content and added value of products. The workers' scientific and cultural quality today has become an important symbol of measuring the level of productivity development. According to statistics, in the primary stage of mechanization, the proportion of manual labor and intellectual labor consumption in production was about 9:1; in the medium stage of mechanization, the ratio changed to 3:2; in the highly automated and intelligent phase, the ratio reversed to 1:9. It can be seen how important science and technology is in productive forces development in today's society.

Thirdly, modern science and technology makes management work more modern and scientific. In the development of social productive forces, science and technology combines the elements of objects and humans, that is, management is the key to the transformation of the potential productive forces into the actual one. The extensive combination of science and technology with economy makes management an important category of productive forces. Production management is science, knowledge, and also technology. Science, technology, and management are called the three important factors of modern economic development.

Finally, the role of high-tech in knowledge economy is more prominent. Knowledge economy is based on knowledge and depends directly on the market, dissemination and use of knowledge and information. It takes intellectual resources and intangible assets as the first element, high-tech industry as the pillar, and high-tech products and new knowledge generated through information as the main consumed objects. Therefore, the development and industrialization of high-tech is the fundamental way to promoting the rapid development of productive forces.

3. The enrichment and development of the thought that "science and technology is the primary productive force" in the new period

Jiang Zemin and Hu Jintao inherited and developed Deng Xiaoping's thought that "science and technology is the primary productive forces". In the light of the science and technology progress and new situations of social development, they complemented that science and technology is not only the primary productive forces but also the centralized embodiment and main symbol of advanced productive forces, and that science and technology progress and innovation is the decisive factors for the development of productive forces. They emphasized that in response to the challenges from the rapid development of the world science and technology and the rapid emergence of knowledge economy, what mattered most was to adhere to innovation. Innovation, the nature of science, mainly relies on talents who can grow and develop mainly through education. The strength of science and technology and the level of national education are always the important symbol of the comprehensive national strength and the degree of social civilization, and two indispensable flywheels for each country to prosper. Therefore, the CPC Central Committee has successively put forward the strategy of rejuvenating the country through science and education and the strategy of reinvigorating the country through human resource management.

The basic meaning of the strategy of rejuvenating the country through science and education is to fully implement the idea that "science and technology is the primary productive forces", adhere to the basic role of education, put science and technology and education in an important place of economic and social development, strengthen the national scientific and technological strength and its capability of being transformed to the actual productive forces, improve the scientific and cultural quality of the whole nation, carry out the economic construction by relying on the scientific and technological progress and the improvement of workers' quality, and accelerate the realization of the national prosperity and strength. The basic meaning of the strategy of reinvigorating the country through human resource management is that: talents should be regarded as the key factor in promoting the great cause of building socialism with Chinese characteristics, and as a result, we are supposed to build a large-scale, reasonably-structured and high-quality team of talents that is made up of hundreds of millions of high-quality workers, tens of millions of special talents and a large number of top-notch creative talents, so as to create a new situation that great talents appear successively and everybody is let to display his talents fully and to transform our country from one with a great population into one with a large number of talents.

Second, the development of advanced productive forces is the fundamental mission and fundamental undertaking of our party as a ruling party

1. The development of human society is the historical process in which advanced productive forces continuously replace the backward productive forces

The development of human society is the historical process in which advanced productive forces continuously replace the backward productive forces. The struggle of the Communist Party of China is the historical process in which the advanced productive forces is continuously liberated and developed. Our Party has always followed the objective law of social and historical development and taken the liberation and development of China's advanced productive forces as its fundamental mission, making great contributions to the development of China's advanced productive forces. The Party's historical experience has repeatedly proved that our cause prospers when the development direction of advanced productive forces is represented, but it suffers from turns and twists when we go against it.

The history of human development is first of all the development process of productive forces. If the human society is to develop, we must constantly replace the backward productive forces with the advanced, which is the law of productive forces and of social development. Advanced productive forces reflects the achievement and height of the latest science and technology and plays a decisive role in promoting social development. Dating back to the history, we can find that the changes and reforms of social system stemmed from the emergence of advanced productive forces, that is, the old social system and social relations become the shackles of advanced productive forces, so a new relation of production is needed to correspond to the development requirements of advanced productive forces.

"In acquiring new productive forces men change their mode of production; and in changing their mode of production, in changing the way of earning their living, they change all their social relations."[15]

The "new productive forces" Marx mentioned hereby is precisely the advanced productive forces. The continuous acquisition and development of advanced productive forces, will lead to the change of the "mode of production". The change of "the way of earning their living" eventually leads to the change of "social relations" and the establishment of a new social system. "The hand-mill gives you society with the feudal lord; the steam-mill society with the industrial capitalist."[16]

Advanced social system and relation of production represent the onward direction and development level of advanced productive forces.

2. Always representing the development requirements of China's advanced productive forces

Always representing the development requirements of and vigorously promoting the development of China's advanced productive forces is the fundamental embodiment and requirements of the CPC's standing at the forefront of the times and keeping the advanced nature as well as the fundamental mission and responsibilities of the CPC as the ruling party.

The statement that always representing the development requirements of and promoting the development of China's advanced productive forces is the fundamental requirements and path of the CPC's keeping the advanced nature as the ruling party is decided by the law of the human society development, that of the socialist construction, and the ruling law of the communist party. The CPC's advanced nature is essentially reflected in its ability to represent the development requirements of China's advanced productive forces and promote its development.

Since its establishment, the CPC has been representing the development requirements of advanced productive forces in China. It is the vanguard of the Chinese working class who is the representative of modern advanced productive forces. Therefore, all policies and guidelines of the Party must be conducive to the continuous development of productive forces, especially the advanced productive forces, in order to truly reflect the nature of the vanguard of the working class and represent the fundamental interests of the working class and the Chinese people.

15　Complete Works of Marx and Engels, Chinese 1st edition, Vol.4, p.144, Beijing, People's Publishing House, 1958.
16　Ibid.

The new democratic revolution led by the CPC aimed to abolish the privilege of imperialism in China, eliminate the exploitation and oppression by the landlord class and the bureaucratic bourgeoisie, change the feudal comprador relations of production and the decadent superstructure rising over such an economic base, establish a new political system at the core of the people's democratic dictatorship, and fundamentally liberate the fettered productive forces. After the founding of the New China, the CPC, as the ruling party, need lead the masses of the people to seek the road and way of developing advanced productive forces. To this end, our Party carried out the socialist transformation on agriculture, handicrafts and capitalist industry and commerce, established the socialist relations of production, and further perfected the socialist superstructure on such economic base so as to continue to liberate and develop the advanced productive forces in China. After the 3rd Plenary Session of the 11th CPC Central Committee, China carried out reform and opening up to further liberate and develop advanced productive forces. In a word, the revolution, construction and reform led by the CPC all aim to promote the liberation and development of advanced productive forces in China.

3. Promoting the development of advanced productive forces in China

The development of advanced productive forces is closely related to the continuous improvement of the relations of production and the superstructure. To promote the development of advanced productive forces in China, we should make sure that its development requirements are reflected in all aspects of relations of production and the superstructure. Therefore, we must unswervingly adhere to the reform, improve the socialist relations of production and superstructure, and pave a broader way for the liberation and development of productive forces.

Man is the most active factor in productive forces. To develop advanced productive forces, we must give full play to the enthusiasm, initiative and creativity of all people, constantly improve the ideological and moral qualities and scientific and cultural qualities of workers, peasants, intellectuals, other laboring masses, and all other people, and constantly improve their labor skills and creativity. It reflects the efforts and fundamental shift of the ruling party in the development of advanced productive forces, different from the behaviors and practices of the exploiting class who contempt and fear the people. Besides, we should actively build a social environment that respects talents and encourages entrepreneurship, form a good mechanism for talents to stand out and display their talents fully, create a new situation in which talents come forth in large numbers and their enthusiasm and creativity can be given a full play, and provide a strong guarantee for the reform and opening up and modernization construction.

The development of advanced productive forces also requires us to vigorously promote the scientific and technological progress and innovation and strive to achieve the leapfrog development of productive forces. Advanced productive forces is something armed with advanced science and technology. The rapid development of science and technology in the world today has brought great impetus to the productive forces and the economic development of human society, and its importance for the economic and social development has never been so prominent. The future scientific and technological development will still give rise to new major leaps. The Party must grasp this objective trend sensitively, always pay attention to the combination of the superiority of our socialist system with the mastery, application and development of advanced science and technology, vigorously promote the scientific and technological progress and innovation, continuously transform and improve the national economy with advanced science and technology, in an effort to achieve the leapfrog development of China's productive forces. This is also the important responsibility that the Party, as the representative of the development requirements of China's advanced productive forces.

Section III

112 Development is the overriding issue in order to promote the comprehensive development of society

First, development is the overriding issue, and the first priority in governing and rejuvenating the country

Development is the overriding issue

With the human society undergoing profound changes and development the theme of the times, the global competition in the economic strength and comprehensive national strength is unprecedentedly intense. Neither country nor nation can stand aloof in front of this global competition. History has repeatedly shown that seizing the opportunity to accelerate development, the backward countries and nations may realize the new leap of development and walk in the forefront of the times; without seizing development opportunities, the originally strong countries and nations may become the laggards of the times. Whether we can seize new opportunities to solve new problems and achieve new development is a major test of our Party's governing capability as well as of our national cohesion and creativity. It is the root of China's invincible position and the CPC's historical responsibility for the country, the nation and the people to cling to the important strategic opportunity period and make an effective use of it, and to strive to take the initiative in this large-scare competition to develop and expand our country.

On the basis of profoundly summarizing historical experiences and lessons and accurately grasping the theme of the present era, Deng Xiaoping pointed out: "Development is the overriding issue, absolute principle"[17], "development is the key to solve all the problems of China"[18].

Development is the overriding issue. To take the development of productive forces as the fundamental task of socialism is the fundamental view of the scientific socialism and the inevitable requirement of consolidating and developing the socialist system. Whether socialism can consolidate and develop itself and reflect its superiority in the contest with capitalism fundamentally relies on whether its productive forces can develop in a faster and better way than that of capitalism does. Deng Xiaoping pointed out: "To give full play to the superiority of socialism means, in the final analysis, it is necessary to make arduous efforts to develop social productive forces and gradually improve and enhance people's material and spiritual life."[19]

Only when the productive forces are developed can people's living standards be improved and the social stability be achieved, which will create material conditions for the construction of the socialist democratic politics, spiritual civilization and harmonious society and fundamentally consolidate the socialist system. Only the socialist development can make those who do not believe in socialism gradually have faith in it and those who do so firmly believe it.

113

That development is the overriding issue is a profound summary of the historical experience and lessons of the socialist construction. In the 20 years before the reform and opening up, the socialist modernization did not go well, an important reason for which is that the development of productive forces was not realistically taken as the fundamental task of socialist construction in a long time. Deng Xiaoping pointed out that if shortcomings existed after the founding of the New China, then we might have neglected developing productive forces to some extent. According to him, neither the long-term economic stagnation nor the long-term low-level living standard of the people can not be called socialism. Socialism is not an empty talk and it cannot be built on the low-level productive forces and poverty for a long time. To develop the socialism, we must take economic construction as the center and vigorously develop the social productive forces. We have to rely on our own development in face of all problems, which is the most important conclusion after our Party's scientific analysis of the lessons learned from the socialist construction at home and abroad.

17　Selected Works of Deng Xiaoping, 1st edition, Volume 3, p.377 and https://archive.org/stream/SelectedWorksOfDengXiaopingVol.3/Deng03_djvu.txt.

18　Ibid., p.265.

19　Selected Works of Deng Xiaoping, 2nd edition, Vol.2, p. 251 and https://archive.org/stream/SelectedWorksOfDengXiaopingVol.1/Deng02_djvu.txt.

That development is the overriding issue is the reflection and require-ment of the theme of the times. Peace and development are the two main themes of the world today, and the global strategic issues. As a socialist country, China maintains peace and stability and is an important factor in developing the world peace forces. The more developed China is, the more secure the world peace is. China's development is beneficial to the peace and stability of the world and the Asia-Pacific region. By the time China is developed, the forces of peace that restrict the war will be greatly en-hanced. Besides the world peace, the resolution of the world development is in need of China's development. China is the largest developing country in the world with 1/5 of the world's population. Its development concerns not only China itself but also the world peace and development. The good development momentum of China's economy will not only benefit the Chinese people of 1.3 billion but also bring enormous opportunities to other countries. As the economic globalization deepens, China's development is becoming a new driving force of the world economic development. In this respect, China's development is of global strategic significance.

To better adhere to the strategic thought that development is the over-riding issue, we should establish and implement the people-oriented, com-prehensive, coordinated and sustainable scientific outlook on development, which is the generalization of the experience in the reform and opening up, the urgent requirement of advancing the comprehensive construction of a well-off society, and the requirement of advancing socialism with Chinese characteristics. In order to realize the grand blueprint of building a well-off society in an all-round way and promote the continuing development of socialism with Chinese characteristics, we must adhere to the concept of people-oriented development and promote the comprehensive, coordinated and sustainable social development.

2. Development is the first priority of the party in governing and rejuve-nating the country

In the process of leading the whole nation to build socialism with Chinese characteristics, the Party faces many problems and all kinds of important and urgent tasks, but the primary and most important task is to develop.

That development is the first priority of the party in governing and re-juvenating the country is determined by the Party's historical mission and responsibilities. After the Opium War, China was gradually reduced to a semi-colonial and semi-feudal society in which the society was war-torn, the government was overwhelmed with the enduring impoverishment and long-standing debility, and the people were plunged into an abyss of misery. Under the CPC's leadership and after the arduous and heroic struggle of the Chinese people, China finally realized the national liberation and embarked on the socialist path. However, due to the enduring impoverishment and long-standing debility, China began to build socialism on the basis of the backward economy and culture. Until now, the most prominent problem facing us today is still the backward economy and culture and the main contradiction of the Chinese society is and will be the conflict between the people's growing material and cultural needs and the backward social production for a long period to come. This decides that the CPC, as the ruling party and the vanguard of the Chinese working class, Chinese people and Chinese nation, must always take development as the first priority at any time in the great course of leading the people of all ethnic groups in China in developing socialism with Chinese characteristics and striving to achieve the national rejuvenation.

Whether the CPC can solve the problem of development in the process of leading people in modernizing China, a great developing country with backward economy and culture, directly decides whether the people are for or against and the cause rises or falls. The party, as the ruling party that represents the fundamental interests of the people of China, must always cling to this first priority in governing and rejuvenating the country—development, and adhere to its advanced nature and give a full play to the superiority of the socialist system by developing the advanced productive forces and advanced culture and realizing the fundamental interests of the overwhelming majority of the people, so as to promote the all-round social progress and development of human beings. Clinging to the first priority, we can thoroughly understand the aspirations and fundamental interests of the people, grasp the nature of the socialist modernization, so as to constantly consolidate the ruling status of the Party and constantly meet the requirements of enforcing the country and enriching the people.

Whether the CPC can solve the problem of development in such a great developing country like China is directly related to the rejuvenation of the Chinese nation and the future and fate of socialism. The CPC's ruling status was chosen by the people, fundamentally because it can lead China to the national prosperity and people's wealth and the rejuvenation of China. Only by grasping this first priority can the Party realize its historical mission in the new stage of the new century. Development plays an inevitable role both in achieving the grand goal of building a well-off society in a comprehensive way, further improving people's material and cultural life, enhancing China's comprehensive national strength and realizing the great rejuvenation of the Chinese nation, and in realizing the complete reunification of the motherland and promoting the lofty cause of world peace and development. Only by taking the development as the theme can we thoroughly understand the aspirations of the people, continuously consolidate and develop the mass base of the Party's ruling status, push forward the socialist cause with Chinese characteristics, and create more advanced productive forces than capitalism through the efforts of several, more than ten or even dozens of generations, so that the people can enjoy more practical benefits and socialism can better display its own superiority.

Second, taking development as the key in solving all kinds of problems

1. Taking development as the key in solving all kinds of problems is an important experience gained in the process of our socialist modernization practice

Development is the overriding issue and the key in solving all kinds of problems in China. To solve problems occurring in advancement with development methods is an important experience gained in the process of our socialist modernization practice.

Since the reform and opening up for more than 30 years, the Party's lines, guidelines and policies have gained the support of the masses of the people, we have gone through the international and domestic waves, and our international status and influence has been constantly improving, to which the key is that we firmly grasp the theme of development. Practice has proved that development plays an indispensible role in enhancing the comprehensive national strength, constantly improving people's living standards and achieving the "three-step" strategic goal of national development; in consolidating and improving the socialist system and strengthening the cohesion and vitality of socialism with Chinese characteristics; in maintaining social stability, promoting social harmony, and achieving the long-term peace and order of the state; in enhancing the international competitiveness to have the initiative in hands in the international contest; and in accomplishing the reunification of the motherland and the great cause of the rejuvenation of the Chinese nation. Only by focusing on the construction and development can we calmly deal with the difficulties and challenges and firmly have the initiative in hands. The prosperity of the country and the wealth of the people is in the final analysis the issue of economic strength, so is the international competition. Without a strong economy, how can we participate in the international competition; without the development of productive forces, how can socialism overcome capitalism. Only when the economy has greatly developed, the economic strength and comprehensive national strength have greatly increased, and the people's livelihood has gradually improved can the country gain the long-term peace and order, our back be straightened, our words in the international community carry weight, and socialism be better tomorrow. The continuous improvement of social productive forces is not only the base of the improving living standard of the people but also the material base of building a socialist harmonious society. Without development, the people's life will be difficult to be guaranteed and improved; there must be quite a number of unstable factors underlying in the society where the wealth is extremely deficient, let alone the real social harmony. The mansion of the socialist harmonious society is by no means built on poverty. At any time, we should insist on economic construction as the center in a steadfast way and concentrate on how to develop the economy.

To solve the problems in advancement with the methods of development is a profound summary of the experience in the socialist construction in our country. At the beginning of the New China, socialism was constructed at an economically poor and culturally blank background. For decades, the people's living standard has been marching towards a higher level of the well-off society, for which the continuous advancement of the socialist modernization can account. At present, with the continuous progress of the society, the people have put forward higher demands on the economic and social development, and a series of new challenges have appeared in the economic and social development process, which require us to take them seriously and make efforts to solve them. In a word, to solve these problems in advancement, in the final analysis, depends on the continuous development of the socialist society.

Solving the problems in advancement with the methods of development requires us to cling to the economic construction as the center, adhere to the guidance of Deng Xiaoping Theory and "Three Represents", and implement the scientific outlook on development. According to the scientific outlook on development, we should adhere to the development as the first priority, the people-oriented development as the core, the comprehensive, coordinated and sustainable development as the basic requirements, and making overall plans and taking all factors into consideration as the fundamental approach. In accordance with the requirements in making overall plans about the urban and rural development, the regional development, economic and social development, the harmonious development of man and nature, and domestic development and opening up to the outside world, we should make efforts to learn about the development laws, innovate the development concept, transform the development mode, solve development difficulties, and promote the cause of socialist modernization. In addition, we should better implement the strategy of revitalizing the country through science and education, the strategy of reinvigorating the country through human resource management, and the strategy of sustainable development, accelerate the strategic economic restructuring, build an innovation-driven country by speeding the improvement of the capability of independent innovation, accelerate the building of a resource-saving and environment-friendly society, continuously enhance the economic strength, scientific and technological strength, and comprehensive national strength, and enhance the international competitiveness and risk-resistance, so as to lay a solid foundation for the development of socialism with Chinese characteristics.

2. Concentrating on the construction and development

Concentrating on the construction and development is to be absorbed in the socialist modernization and the development of socialism with Chinese characteristics. In his speech at the 30th anniversary of the 3rd Plenary Session of the 11th CPC Central Committee, Hu Jintao pointed out that as long as we unswervingly promote reform and opening up and follow the socialist path with Chinese characteristics, we will absolutely be able to achieve the set magnificent blueprint and goals.

Since the reform and opening up for more than 30 years, China's economic and social development has displayed an unprecedentedly good situation. We not only withstood the test of the drastic changes of the Soviet Union and eastern Europe, successfully responded to a series of serious challenges from natural disasters, but also promoted the rapid development of the socialist cause in China, the enhancement of the comprehensive national strength, the constant improvement of people's material and cultural life, and the flourishing of the socialist cause with Chinese characteristics. All of these achievements can be mainly attributed to our adherence to the economic construction as the center of the work.

In the 21st century, peace and development are still the themes of the times, and seeking peace, development and cooperation has become an irresistible trend of the times. The world today is in the midst of great changes and adjustments, such as the irreversible world multi-polarization, the deepening development of the economic globalization, and the accelerating advancement of the science and technology revolution. However, it should be seen that the world is still very restless. Hegemonism and power politics still exist, local conflicts and hot issues arise, the global economic imbalance exacerbates, the gap between the north and the south is widening, traditional security threats and non-traditional security threats are intertwined, and world peace and development face many difficulties and challenges. Confronted with this situation, we must seize this strategic opportunity period at the beginning of the new century to accelerate our own development, solve China's problems in the economic and social development, continuously enhance the comprehensive national strength of the socialist China and improve people's material and cultural life, in an effort to achieve the "Three-step" development strategy in the middle 2000s. Whether we can seize this opportunity to accelerate development decides whether a country or a nation can win the initiative and advantage. To this end, we must unswervingly promote the reform and opening up, take the socialist path with Chinese characteristics, cling to the economic construction as the center, and continue to concentrate on the construction and development. Only in this way can we continuously strengthen the ability of the state to deal with various risks and realize the grand blueprint of building a well-off society in an all-round way; only in this way can the great rejuvenation of the Chinese nation be built on a solid foundation and the great cause of socialism with Chinese characteristics be increasingly prosperous.

Focusing on the construction and development requires us to deal with the relationship between the economic construction and the development of other areas in a good way in the process of developing socialism with Chinese characteristics. We should firmly grasp the fundamental task of socialism of liberating and developing the productive forces, since the development of other socialist undertakings must be based on the development of the socialist productive forces. Without the development of productive forces, the socialist cause will definitely fail. In any case, we must work on the central task of economic construction and promote the better and faster development of the social productive forces, in order to lay a solid foundation for the further development of socialism.

Third, to achieve scientific development, harmonious development, peaceful development, and promote the comprehensive development of society

1. To achieve scientific development, harmonious development and peaceful development

The report of the 17th CPC National Congress stresses that efforts should be made to achieve a people-oriented, comprehensive, coordinated, sustainable, and scientific development, to realize the organic unity of different undertakings and the harmonious development of all members of the society, and to bring about the peaceful development of the country through the maintenance of the world's peace and vice versa, and clearly points out that we must adhere to scientific development, harmonious development and peaceful development, which is the basic way to realize socialist modernization of our country.

Adhering to the scientific development requires the economic and social development to follow the objective laws of social and human development, and the coordinated development between man and nature, based on the actual conditions of our country, so that a people-oriented, all-round, coordinated and sustainable development can be achieved, which in essence can ensure the sound and rapid economic and social development. Insisting on the harmonious development means to uphold the concepts and requirements of fairness and justice, democracy and rule of law, honesty and fraternity, vitality, stability and order, harmony between man and nature, so that we can coordinate economic development with social development, promote social development while achieving economic development, make progress in an all-round way, realize the organic unity of all undertakings, unite all the members of the society, maintain social harmony and stability, and let all the people share the fruits of reform and development. Upholding peaceful development means that we must adhere to peace, development and cooperation, strive to the realize the development of our country through the maintenance of the world's peace and vice versa, and work with other nations together to promote the building of a harmonious world of lasting peace and common prosperity.

Scientific, harmonious and peaceful development embody the historical materialism's thinking on the dominant position of the masses of the people and reflect the fundamental interests and common wishes of the overwhelming majority of them. These development principles stem from the ideas of developing for the people, depending on the people, and the fruits of development shared by the people. Scientific development should be people-oriented and aim at achieving comprehensive, coordinated and sustainable development, which requires us to set the all-round development of the people as the fundamental goal and to continuously meet their growing material and cultural needs so that the fruits of development can be shared by all.

The goal of harmonious development is to achieve the organic unity of all undertakings, and the unity and harmony of all members of the community, which requires us to comprehensively promote the economic, political, cultural and social construction of socialism according to the overall layout of socialism with Chinese characteristics, and to solve the problems concerning the interests that are most practical and that people are most concerned about and most directly related to, so as to bring about the best of the people's ability, make each find the proper place and realize the harmonious coexistence of all. The essence of peaceful development, as part of China's national development strategy and the natural extension of it in foreign affairs, is to maintain world peace through self-development and vice versa. In the great practice of developing socialism with Chinese characteristics, the Chinese people have always cherished the value of peace highly. Therefore, while concentrating on building the country, they regard favorable surroundings and international environment as an important external condition for safeguarding the country's development.

Scientific, harmonious and peaceful development are strategies made based on our national conditions of being at the initial stage of socialism, so they are in line with the features of our current development stage, aiming at promoting the sound and rapid economic and social development. After the founding of New China, especially since the reform and opening up, we have made remarkable achievements that attract worldwide attention in economic and social development. However, the basic national condition that our country is still in the primary stage of socialism and will remain so for a long time to come has not changed, neither does the major social contradiction between people's ever-growing material and cultural needs and the backward social production. It is known that the initial stage of our socialism will last a long period of time and have different characteristics in different periods of development. The current characteristics show that China has entered a crucial period of development and reform, with prominent social contradictions. With profound changes in the economic system, social structure, pattern of interests, and ideology and concepts, it faces tremendous pressures on population, resources and environment on the one hand, and great potentials for development on the other hand. Therefore, in order to seize the unprecedented opportunities, cope with the hitherto unknown challenges, and solve the contradictions and problems that will emerge, we should stick to the path of scientific, harmonious and peaceful development.

Sticking to scientific, harmonious and peaceful development reflects the Party's profound insight and accurate understanding of the theme of the times and the development tendency of contemporary China and the world. It is a wise choice which complies with the trend of the times. After World War II, mankind has made unprecedented achievements in economic growth. However, due to the excessive emphasis on economic growth, various problems emerge in the world development. As a result, people have been constantly reflecting on and deepening their understanding of the development ideas. In the meantime, under the background of economic globalization, the interdependence of all countries has been deepened. Therefore, only by creating a peaceful environment can all the countries develop themselves, and only by strengthening exchanges and expanding cooperation can they achieve common development. After summing up experiences of the world's development, drawing lessons from the theoretical results of human development, and accurately grasping the trend of world development, the Party puts forward the scientific, harmonious and peaceful development, which conforms to the trend of the times, concurs with the theme of the times, and demonstrates the foresight and the great breadth of vision of the CPC.

Scientific development, harmonious development, and peaceful development are intrinsically unified: scientific development is the foundation, without which economic development cannot be realized, and harmonious and peaceful development will lose its backing; harmonious development is the goal. Scientific and peaceful development aim to create better conditions to improve the people's livelihood and promote social fairness and justice, so that all the people can share the fruits of reform and development.

Meanwhile, harmonious development also provides conditions for scientific and peaceful development; peaceful development is the guarantee. Without a peaceful international environment, mutual benefit and win-win result, scientific and harmonious development will also be affected. The "three developments", having different focuses but are closely linked with and beneficial to each other, form an organic whole in the great practice of comprehensively implementing the scientific outlook on development and building socialism with Chinese characteristics, and becomes the fundamental guarantee for realizing the grand goal of socialist modernization. Therefore, people of all ethnic groups across the country must closely rally around the CPC, accept the leadership of the Party, work together, and forge ahead in unity, in order to achieve scientific development, harmonious development and peaceful development.

2. To comprehensively promote economic, political, cultural, social and ecological civilization construction: Five constructions

The report of the 17th CPC National Congress, which systematically elaborates some important issues such as promoting economic, political, cultural, social and ecological civilization construction in an all-round way, is the political declaration and guideline for developing socialism with Chinese characteristics and building an overall well-to-do society in the new era. In the construction of the socialist modernization with Chinese characteristics, the coordinated promotion of economic, political, cultural, social and ecological civilization construction is the essential requirement of the development of socialist society and the main task of comprehensively promoting modernization.

First of all, adhering to the coordinated promotion of economic, political, cultural, social and ecological civilization construction is determined by the basic contradiction of socialism, i.e. the contradiction between the relations of production and the productive forces, or in other words, between the superstructure and the economic base, which is mainly manifested in the incompatibility of them. In particular, at a stage where economic development is backward, the rapid changes in productivity can easily lead to its incompatibility with the relations of production, which is mainly manifested in political, cultural, social and ecological civilization's lagging behind the economic construction. Actually, coordinating the relations among the above five constructions will open the way for the development of productive forces and create conditions for the all-round development of socialism in China.

Secondly, upholding the coordinated promotion of economic, political, cultural, social and ecological civilization construction is determined by the major contradiction our country is facing at the present stage. Major contradiction, as the concentrated expression of social development at a certain stage, plays a dominant and decisive role in the development of the society at that time. In the primary stage of socialism, the main contradiction of our country is that between people's ever-growing material and cultural needs and the backward social production. Whether this contradiction can be correctly understood and whether the focus of work and fundamental tasks are set accordingly determines the future and destiny of socialism. However, the material and cultural needs of the broad masses of the people are manifested in many aspects, including not only material but also spiritual and development needs. Therefore, to meet these needs, we must coordinate and promote the economic, political, cultural, social and ecological civilization construction.

Thirdly, adhering to the coordinated promotion of economic, political, cultural, social and ecological civilization construction is also a conclusion drawn from past experiences and lessons, which reflects the deepening of the Party's understanding of the laws of the construction of socialism with Chinese characteristics. In terms of the ways to achieve modernization, although we can learn a great deal from countries first embark on the path to modernization, China, as a populous nation that develops quite late, faces not only a special historical background but also enormous pressures on population, resources and environment. What's more, there are significant differences between China and other countries in the objectives, basic requirements and ways of development. As a result, if we simply copy other nation's experience, with the focus on economic development only, lacking guarantee and support from political, cultural and social development, we will not only pay a heavy price, but may also ruin the achievements already made.

In order to adhere to the coordinated development of economic, political, cultural, social and ecological civilization construction, we must be guided by the scientific outlook on development, which is the fundamental guiding ideology of and the essential way and method for building an overall well-to-do society. In fact, the basic requirement of the scientific outlook on development is to achieve comprehensive, coordinated and sustainable development, which is an important manifestation of realizing the cause of socialism with Chinese characteristics from an overall perspective, reflecting our Party's profound understanding of the laws of the socialist modernization, and revealing the ways to implement the scientific outlook on development in all aspects. By thoroughly implementing the outlook, we can coordinate all links in and all aspects of the construction of modernization and comprehensively promote socialist economic, political, cultural, social and ecological civilization construction.

Insisting on the comprehensive, coordinated and sustainable development, which is gradually formed and deepened in our Party's exploration of the laws of socialist modernization in accordance with the basic tenets of Marxism, is a necessity in our economic and social development. The classic Marxists believe that the ideal society in the future is one with highly developed social productive forces and spiritual life, where people live in harmony with each other and with nature. Since comprehensive, coordinated and sustainable development emphasize the connection and coordination not only among all aspects of economic and social development, but also between man and man, man and society, and man and nature, it conforms to the basic view of Marxism on the development of human society.

In addition, there are rich connotations in comprehensive, coordinated and sustainable development: "comprehensive" means that development should be comprehensive and integrate, including not only economic development, but also development in other aspects; "coordinated" means that development should be coordinated and balanced, with all aspects and links adapted to and beneficial to each other; "sustainable" means that the development should be lasting and continuous, ensuring not only current development, but also long-term one. To uphold comprehensive, coordinated and sustainable development, we should correctly handle the major relations in the construction of modernization such as that between economic and social development, between urban and rural development, among the development of the eastern, central and western regions, between the development of man and nature, between domestic development and opening up, and among reform, development and stability; coordinate and handle well the major issues in economic and social development such as consumption and investment, supply and demand, the speed, structure, quality and efficiency of development, the full play of the development of science and technology and advantages in human resources, the market mechanism, and macroeconomic regulation and control; and see economic, political, cultural, social and ecological civilization construction and the all-round development of human beings as an interconnected, mutually beneficial and indivisible process.

The 17th CPC National Congress emphasizes the comprehensive, coordinated and sustainable development, and regards them as the basic requirements of the scientific outlook on development, because they reflect the objective requirements of China's economic and social development at this stage. On the one hand, after the long-term development, we have accumulated a solid material and technological foundation and can make greater achievements in promoting comprehensive, coordinated and sustainable development. On the other hand, problems such as the uneven development of urban and rural areas, the uncoordinated economic and social development, and the incompatibility among economic development, population, resources and environment, have become more prominent. However, the basic requirements of the comprehensive, coordinated and sustainable development provide new ideas to solve the problems, and point out the right direction for China's economic and social development. Therefore, only by actively advancing comprehensive, coordinated and sustainable development, can we better release various constraints on the development of our country, promote the development and ensure the realization of the strategic goal of the development.

To achieve comprehensive, coordinated and sustainable development, we must, based on the overall layout of the socialist cause with Chinese characteristics, adhere to the economic construction as the center, constantly promote economic development and all-round social progress, and correctly understand that economic, political, cultural, social and ecological civilization, in the construction of socialism with Chinese characteristics, is a mutually reinforcing organic unity. Without economic construction, which provides the material basis for political, cultural and social construction, the construction in other fields will lack material foundations. Therefore, we should guarantee the central role of the economic construction, understand the strategic significance of accelerating economic development, and unswervingly promote the sound and rapid development of the national economy. Without political construction, which provides political security for economic, cultural and social construction, it will be impossible to fully arouse the enthusiasm, initiative and creativity of the masses, create an environment that is protected by a sound legal system, and guarantee the smooth construction in other fields.

We should stick to the socialist political development path with Chinese characteristics, uphold the organic unity of the leadership of the Party, people as the masters of the country and the rule of law, adhere to and perfect the fundamental systems of socialism with Chinese characteristics, deepen the reform of the political system, and constantly promote its self-improvement and development. Without cultural construction, which provides ideological guarantee, spiritual motivation, cultural environment and intellectual support for economic, political and social construction, there will be no common ideals and beliefs and moral norms, and the high-spirited and pioneering mainstream spirit will not be formed, providing no essential spiritual support for the construction in other fields. Therefore, we must consolidate the ideological guidance of Marxism, adhere to the development of an advanced socialist culture that is modern, international, advanced, national, scientific and popular, uphold the principle of "three closeness", strive to establish a socialist core value system, consolidate the mainstream opinions, promote reform and innovation of forms, methods and mechanisms, push forward the great prosperity and development of socialist culture, create a new upsurge of socialist cultural construction, and enhance the national soft power.

Without social construction, which provides favorable social conditions for economic, political and cultural construction, a favorable social environment for promoting the construction in other fields will not be formed. Therefore, we must speed up the social construction that focuses on improving people's livelihood, promote social fairness and justice, improve social management, stimulate social creation and build a more harmonious society. The ecological civilization construction, which is the foundation of the civilized system of socialism with Chinese characteristics, embodies the strategic concept of the all-round development of socialism, has inherent unity with socialism with Chinese characteristics, and makes its overall layout more systematic and better. Therefore, we must firmly establish the concept of ecological civilization, green economy and seeking development under strict constraints, make resource conservation the basic national policy, develop a recycling economy, and adhere to the path of civilized development featuring growing production, affluent life and sound ecological environment, so as to realize the unity of speed, structure and quality, and the coordination of economic growth, population, resources and environment, and to build a resource-saving and environment-friendly well-to-do society. In short, according to the requirements of the overall layout, we should take the socialist economic, political, cultural, social and ecological civilization construction as a unified task, a unified undertaking and a unified goal, develop socialist market economy, democracy, advanced culture, and harmonious society vigorously, and promote the cause of socialism with Chinese characteristics comprehensively.

CHAPTER FIVE

Main Ways of Developing Socialism with Chinese Characteristics

Section I

Reform is an important driving force of socialism in China

First, the socialist society is a constantly changing society

The development of human society is a constant process from low-level forms to the advanced forms. The basic force that drives this process is always the contradiction between productive forces and production relations, economic base and the superstructures. Pushed by these contradictions, human society is always in a movement of change. Constant change and development, advance links replacing the backward ones, is the general law of human social development.

Socialist society is one of the existing social forms of human beings. It is the result of the movement of the basic social contradiction. The basic force to decide and promote the development of socialist society is still the contradiction between productive forces and relations of production, and economic foundation and superstructure. Therefore, like any other societies, the socialist society is also a society that needs constant reform and follows the social development law that the advanced replaces the backward. It is of great importance for the leaders and builders of the socialist cause to recognize it. If we fail to realize it, regard socialism as a society that is constantly reformed and consciously replace the backward with the advanced, socialism may lose its vitality and vigor, its superiority may fail to be given a full play and it may even perish.

Deng Xiaoping is the chief designer of China's reform and opening up and socialist modernization. In the face of the austere problems including the slow development of social productive forces after the end of the "Cultural Revolution", the basic necessities of life, the backwardness of science and technology and education, the prevailing bureaucratism and patriarchal style, and the various doubts of the people on socialism, he made the earliest initiative of reform. After his return to leadership post for the third time, Deng Xiaoping made it clear that the realization of the four modernizations is "a great revolution in which China's economic and technological backwardness will be overcome and the dictatorship of the proletariat further consolidated. Since its goal is to transform the present backward state of our productive forces, it inevitably entails many changes in the relations of production, the superstructure and the forms of management in industrial and agricultural enterprises, as well as changes in the state administration over these enterprises so as to meet the needs of modern large-scale production… Therefore, it is essential to carry out major reforms in the various branches of the economy with respect to their structure and organization as well as to their technology. The long-term interests of the whole nation hinge on these reforms, without which we cannot overcome the present backwardness of our production technology and management."[1]

He also said: "Now the economic management work in China is overstaffing with overlapping levels, complex procedures, and extremely low efficiency, which are usually hided by the political empty talks. It shall not be attributed to any comrade's fault but our failure to propose the reform in the past. "However, if we do not carry out the reform now, our cause of modernization and the cause of socialism will be ruined."[2]

The experience gained during those 20 years–particularly the lessons of the "cultural revolution"—taught us that we could not proceed unless we carried out reform and formulated new political, economic and social policies.[3]

Since the 4th Plenary Session of the 13th Central Committee of the Party, Jiang Zemin further pointed out:

"Based on our national conditions, we have summed up our practical experiences and based on the realistic level of social productive forces in China and the objective requirements for further development of them, we should consciously adjust and reform the part of the socialist relations of

1   Selected Works of Deng Xiaoping, 2nd edition, Vol.2, pp.135-136 and https://archive.org/stream/SelectedWorksOfDengXiaopingVol.1/Deng02_djvu.txt.
2   Selected Works of Deng Xiaoping, 2nd edition, Vol.2, p.150 and https://archive.org/stream/SelectedWorksOfDengXiaopingVol.1/Deng02_djvu.txt.
3   Selected Works of Deng Xiaoping, 1st edition, Vol.3, p.266 and https://archive.org/stream/SelectedWorksOfDengXiaopingVol.3/Deng03_djvu.txt.

production that is incompatible with the demand of the development of the productive forces, and that of the socialist superstructure that is incompatible with the economic base. This is what we call the socialist reform. If we do not carry out such a reform, we will suffocate the inherent vitality of socialism and seriously hamper the superiority of socialism."[4]

Second, reform is the self-improvement and development of socialism

Socialism is a society of self-improvement and development. The requirements and impetus of socialist self-improvement and development are rooted in the inherent stipulation of socialism. The national system of people's being masters of the country, the relations of production based on public ownership, the value of realizing common prosperity and the social objective of obtaining all-round development of the people have fundamentally eliminated the possibility of class exploitation and class oppression and have ensured the equality of among all nationalities, all classes and all people. Moreover, they also determined that the ruling communist party has not sought for and does not seek for any special interests except the fundamental interests of the majority of the people. Thus, the communist party can transcend the historical limitations of all private classes and their political parties, and treat the self-improvement and development of socialism with the spirit of forging ahead with determination, the wide horizon of facing the future and the broad mind of accepting good advices; those which are better and more beneficial to the people will be selected; those which are outdated and against the people will be abandoned; those which are imperfect, immature will be perfected and improved with any methods. The ability to draw on advantages and avoid disadvantages and to exhale the old and inhale the new is a manifestation of the superiority of the socialist system, and also the inherent root for the socialist to maintain exuberant vitality.

Socialist society is the most progressive society in the history of China. Its establishment conforms to the objective law of historical development, represents the onward direction of social development and accords with the fundamental interests and aspirations of the overwhelming majority of the people. As a result, it has the strong support of the people. With the arduous exploration and unremitting efforts of the Party and the people of all ethnic groups in China for more than half a century, China has made great achievements widely appreciated in the world in the material, political, and spiritual civilization construction and all aspects of social life, bringing about great social changes and primarily demonstrating the superiority of the socialist system.

---

4   Selected Works of Jiang Zemin, Vol. 1, p. 68, Beijing, People's Publishing House, 2006.

However, compared with the development history of the capitalist society which is hundreds of years, the history of China's socialist construction which is only more than half a century is not long after all. Regardless of the fast development of China reflected in that there is significant increase in social productivity and comprehensive national strength and the people's life has reached the well-off level in general, there is still a long way to go in industrialization and modernization. In terms of economic system, management system, democratic legislative system and ideological and moral aspects, there is a considerable distance from the construction target that we should achieve. In the aspects including productivity development, science and technology progress and improvement of living standard, there is still a big gap from those of the western developed countries. China's socialism is still not fully developed, and is still in the primary stage of socialist development. It still needs constant self-improvement and development.

Reform is the fundamental way of the socialist self-improvement and development. In the stage of socialist development, there will be no way out in the face of the emerging new situations and new problems if we do not carry out reform and institutional innovation. Therefore, "in all historical stages of a socialist society, it is necessary to continue to promote the self-improvement and development of the socialist system in a timely manner through reforms in accordance with the requirements of economic and social development so that the socialist system will be full of vigor and vitality. All comrades in the entire Party absolutely must unify thoughts, raise understanding and firmly implement the policy of socialist reform and development."[5]

Third, the reform and opening is China's second revolution

Reform is not a tinkering and kind of minor improvement. The essence of the reform is to fundamentally change the various concrete systems that hinder the development of productive forces and social progress so as to meet the needs of socialist modernization. Deng Xiaoping made it clear that "reform is the second revolution in China."[6]

First of all, reform is the second revolution in China, as opposed to the new democratic revolution. The new democratic revolution led by the Party turned a semi-colonial and semi-feudal old China into a new socialist China. After winning the revolution, the socialist transformation of agriculture, handicrafts and capitalist industry and commerce was successfully realized, and the socialist economic foundation was established. It is the first great revolution of China in the real sense since modern times. The aim of the reform lead by the Party is to fundamentally change the specific system,

---

5   Selected Works of Jiang Zemin, Vol. 3, p.274.
6   Selected Works of Deng Xiaoping, 1st edition, Vol.3, p.113.

management methods and ideas that are not adapted to the development of productive forces and social progress, and turn a relatively backward socialist China into a prosperous, democratic and civilized socialist modern China. "The reform, like China's past revolutions, is also aimed at removing the obstacles to the development of social productive forces and lifting China out of poverty and backwardness."[7]

Secondly, reform is the second revolution in China, starting from liberating the productive forces and removing the obstacles to the development of productive forces. The so-called liberation of productive forces refers to the development of productive forces by relieving the shackles of productive forces. In the past, we had always believed that the revolution was the liberation of productivity. We also believed that there were only the problems of developing productive forces and there were no problems of liberating productive forces under the socialist conditions. All these are one-sided understanding. Revolution is to liberate the productive forces and reform is also to liberate the productive forces. In this sense, reform can also be called revolution.

Thirdly, reform is the second revolution in China, which is in the sense of the profundity and universality of reform. Seen from the scope of reform, China's reform is a comprehensive reform, including the economic basis and the superstructure, the economic system and the system of politics, culture and other aspects, the system level and the ideological level. From the depth of reform, it is the fundamental transformation of the old system and old ideas, the innovation of the system and the adjustment of the interests that lead to the profound changes of the society. In this sense, the reform leads to a new revolution.

More than 30 years of reform practice has proved that socialism with Chinese characteristics has always been advancing in the reform. The reform has not only liberated the productive forces, developed the productive forces, enhanced the overall national strength, improved the living standard of the people, promoted the diversification of economic elements, interests, distribution patterns, jobs and ideas, but also laid a solid foundation for the settlement of some major problems in current economic and social development of China, the sustainable economic and social development of China, and the long-term stability of China.

Fourth, the goals, tasks, principles (policies) and methods of reform

On the basis of summing up the historical experiences and lessons, Deng Xiaoping made a very clear exposition on the object, purpose, principle and method of the reform.

---

7 Selected Works of Deng Xiaoping, 1st edition, Volume 3, p. 135 and https://archive. org/stream/SelectedWorksOfDengXiaopingVol.3/Deng03_djvu.txt.

On the subject of reform, he pointed out that there are still many disadvantages in the existing concrete system of the Party and the state and in the various systems of China. Seen from the various systems of the state, there are disadvantages including the lack of clear-cut job responsibility among governments and enterprises, segmentation of trap and block, excessive control of the government on the enterprises, neglect of commodity production, value law and market function, equalitarianism, and communing pot; from the perspective of the leadership system and the cadre system of the Party and the state, the main drawbacks include bureaucracy, excessive centralization of power, patriarchal style, life tenure of leading cadres and various privileges. In addition, there are remaining patriarchal concepts and hierarchical concepts in social relations; some inequality of identity in leader-member relations and relations with the masses; the weak consciousness of civil rights and obligations; the autocratic style in the field of culture; the recognition of the great importance of science and education to socialism, the rigidity of thought, the serious influence of small producers.

These drawbacks "hinder or even seriously impede the development of the superiority of socialism, and if we fail to carry out serious reforms, we will hardly be able to meet the urgent needs of our modernization drive and we will have to deviate severely from the masses."[8]

However, Deng Xiaoping emphasized particularly: "The socialist system is one thing, and the specific way of building socialism another."[9]

The system reform is not to change the fundamental socialist system but to separate it from the various systems that manifest it.

Regarding the purpose of the reform, Deng Xiaoping pointed out: In the reform of the political structure, our general objectives are the following: (1) to consolidate the socialist system, (2) to develop the socialist productive forces and (3) to expand socialist democracy in order to bring the initiative of the people into full play. The chief purpose of mobilizing the people's initiative is to develop the productive forces and raise living standards. This in turn will help increase the strength of our socialist country and consolidate the socialist system. In short, "all our reforms have the same aim: to clear away the obstacles to the development of the productive forces."[10]

Jiang Zemin further pointed out that the fundamental purpose of the reform is to establish a more mature and stereotyped system adapted to the basic national conditions in the primary stage of socialism, make the production relations adapt to the development of the productive forces and promote the superstructure to adapt to the development of the economic

8   Selected Works of Deng Xiaoping, 2nd edition, Vol.2, p.327.
9   Selected Works of Deng Xiaoping, 2nd edition, Vol.2, p.327.
10   Selected Works of Deng Xiaoping, 1st edition, Vol.3, p.134.

foundation, thus making the socialism with Chinese characteristics full of vitality and vigor.

On the principle of reform, Deng Xiaoping pointed out that the reform was characteristic with the socialist nature. First of all, the reform should be carried out under the CPC's leadership, and the Party Central Committee should maintain its authority. Secondly, all reform measures should be carried out under the premise of adhering to socialism. The reform should adhere to two important principles: one is taking public ownership as the main body; the other is common prosperity. On the basis of summarizing the positive and negative experiences of the international and domestic socialist development, Jiang Zemin further emphasized two basic conclusions: first, the reform should adhere to socialism. Second, the reform should explore the socialist development path which is in accordance with the actual state.

On the method of reform, Deng Xiaoping pointed out that: first, the reform should be orderly carried out in steps. Being orderly is to be both bold and prudent. Moreover, experiences should be summed up timely and steady progress should be made. If there is no order, efforts will be made on various interferences encountered. And the reform will not be achieved as a result. Secondly, the reform should be carried out in all aspects in mutual coordination. "We will not carry out the reform of the economic structure without the reform of the political system."[11] The reform in other aspects should also be coordinated. Third, the theory should go before practice. There should be a blueprint before the reform is implemented. Deng Xiaoping's exposition on the object, purpose, principle and method of the reform provides scientific guiding ideology for the smooth implementation of the reform practice in China.

Fifth, reform should seek new breakthroughs

The essence of reform is making institutional innovations. After 30 years of reform and practice, we already have a good foundation for promoting the socialist system innovation. Meanwhile, China's institutional innovation has entered a crucial stage, which means continuing to promote the reform will be more difficult, and its tasks will be more complex. We must be bold and courageous to make great progress in institutional innovations.

First of all, we should continue to promote the reform of market orientation, constantly improve the socialist market economic system, fundamentally eliminate the institutional obstacles to the development of productive forces, and promote the self-improvement and development of the socialist economic system. According to the development requirements of advanced productive forces, we should deepen the understanding of the

133

---

11   Ibid., p. 177.

basic economic system with the public ownership as the main body and the common development of economy with different types of ownership, and accelerate the adjustment of the ownership structure; we should deepen the reform of state-owned enterprises, regulate the corporate governance structure, and form the operation and management mechanism with relatively matching incentive and restraint; we should accelerate the pace of rural reform, and promote the marketization of rural economy by urbanization; in accordance with the requirements of WTO's rules, we should effectively change government functions, regulate the market order and protect intellectual property rights.

Secondly, we should actively and steadily promote the reform of the political system, develop socialist democracy, build socialist political civilization and promote the self-improvement and development of the socialist political system. The reform of political system is an important part of the self-improvement and development of the socialist system. The development of socialist democracy and the construction of socialist political civilization are an important goal of socialist modernization and an important content of the self-improvement and development of the socialist political system. We should strengthen the system construction of socialist democratic politics, realize the institutionalization, standardization and sequencing of socialist democratic politics, consolidate and develop the political situation of democratic unity, liveliness, stability and harmony. To promote the reform of political system, we should start from our national conditions and follow our own political development path rather than completely copy the western political system model.

Thirdly, we should meet the requirements of the development of socialist market economy and promote the cultural system reform according to the characteristics and laws of socialist spiritual civilization construction. We should combine deepening reform with the adjustment of structure and the promotion of development, adjust the relationship between government and cultural enterprises, strengthen the construction of cultural and legal system and the macro management, deepen the internal reform of cultural enterprises and institutions, and gradually establish the cultural management system and operation mechanism used for mobilizing the enthusiasm of cultural workers and promoting cultural innovation to create more competitive works and cultivate more talents.

Finally, according to the request of the 17th CPC National Congress, in the process of deepening the reform, all the ideological concepts hindering development should be resolutely broken; all the practices and provisions restraining development should be resolutely changed; and all the institutional defects affecting development should be resolutely dismissed. We should carry through the spirit of reform and opening up in the whole process and every link of the administration of the country. We should start from the reality, obtain advancement on the whole, and make gradual and order progress and key breakthrough.

Sixth, correctly dealing the dialectical relationships between reform, development and stability

Reform, development and stability are an organic whole. Their mutual relationship runs through the whole process of socialist modernization, and thus should be attached with close attention and handled seriously.

Development is the goal, which is the concept should be established first-ly when dealing with the relationship among the three parts. "Development is the overriding issue". The key for China to solve all its problems is to rely on its own development. Only continuous development can overcome the difficulties encountered on the way forward; ensure the final realization of the peaceful reunification of China; gradually eliminate exploitation and polarization, and finally achieve common prosperity; give full play to the superiority of the socialist system and create strong material conditions for the final victory over capitalism and the transition to communism.

Reform is the driving force. To develop, we should carry out reform. Only through reform can we overcome the previous influence hindering the development of social productive forces and the improvement of people's living standard, solve the new problems in the process of the development of productive forces and open up a broad space for the development of pro-ductive forces. Reform is an indispensable driving force for development. In turn, only development can ensure that the reform is sustainable and deepening and will not be unfinished. Therefore, on the one hand, develop-ment cannot be achieved without reform because reform is the driving force of development; on the other hand, reform cannot be carried out without development because development is the purpose of reform. The two parts are interrelated and inseparable.

Stability is the prerequisite. Reform and development require a stable so-cial environment. Deng Xiaoping repeatedly pointed out that the key to the development of China is social stability. One is political stability and the other is policy stability. Political stability is a prerequisite and guarantee for the healthy implementation of reform and development. Without a stable political situation, the country will be always in turmoil. And it will be un-able to create favorable conditions for the development of productive forces from time and space and provide a stable environment for the improvement of the living standards of the people, As a result, any good wish will come to nothing and any good plans and programs will be unable to be imple-mented. However, the stable political situation only is not enough, and the current policy stability should also be achieved. If the policy changes frequently, the result will be the same as that caused by political instability. In view of that China had suffered a lot from the changes of policies in the past, Deng Xiaoping stressed that: in general, we have "four adherences", including the adherence to the Four Fundamental Principles, the adherence to the four modernizations, the adherence to two opening up and the adherence to the guideline of implementing reform. And he pointed out: "When we say the policy will not change, we mean the policy as a whole–that no aspect of it will change. If any aspect changes, the others will be affected."[12]

Therefore, in the context of reform and development, we should not only make changes, but also achieve stability. We should organically combine changes and stability and strive to combine depth, breadth and pace of reform with the stability, coordination and the degree of social acceptance of the reform and development programs to an extreme, thus promoting development through reform in a stable social environment.

The stable social environment is inseparable from the reform and development. Stability does not mean a stagnant pool of water or standstill. The true stability should be a situation with both centralism and democracy, both discipline and freedom, both unity of will and personal ease of mind and liveliness, just like what Mao Zedong said. In order to create this situation, we should carry out reform to coordinate and straighten out various social relations and achieve the best combination of various relations, various elements, and various components. At the same time, the stable social environment is realized on the basis of the increasing development of social productive forces and the constant improvement of the living standard of the people. It is impossible to obtain real stability on the basis of the slow development of social productive forces and the low living standard of the people. Therefore, to create and maintain a stable social situation, it is necessary to reform and develop. Only through carrying out reform, vigorously developing the social productive forces, enhancing the comprehensive national strength of the country and improving the living standard of the people can the cohesion of the whole society be formed and can the stability of the society be fundamentally guaranteed. Jiang Zemin pointed out that reform, development, stability are like three closely linked strategic moves on the checkerboard of China's modernization construction. The game will win only if the three moves are well done and mutually promoted; if any of them is not well down, the other two moves will be in trouble and the whole situation will face setback. We should unify the momentum of reform, the speed of development and the degree of social tolerance and take the constant improvement of people's life as an important integration point treating the relationship among reform, development and stability to

---

12 Deng Xiaoping Selected Works, 1st edition, Vol.3, p.218 and https://archive.org/stream/SelectedWorksOfDengXiaopingVol.3/Deng03_djvu.txt.

promote reform and development in social stability and promote social stability through reform and development.

It is of great significance to correctly understand and deal with the dialectical relationship between reform, development and stability. Whether the dialectical relationship among reform, development and stability can be successfully understood and handled is the key to the success of socialist reform; the correct understanding and handling of the dialectical relationship among reform, development and stability can make us better adhere to the direction of progress in practice, reduce mistakes and avoid detours; helps people to cultivate dialectical thinking and set up overall viewpoint; and helps people to establish strategic vision, enhance the ability to analyze things and grasp rules in the work.

Section II

Opening to the outside world is an external condition for the development of socialist society

First, the world today is an open world

To open to the outside world is a basic national policy of our country. Its formulation and implementation are the result of our party's keen observation and examination of the development trend in the current world. Deng Xiaoping pointed out: "The present world is an open world."[13]

No country can obtain development if it isolates itself and turns inward. This scientific judgment profoundly reveals the objective basis of China's opening to the outside world.

"The current world is an open world". With the promotion of the socialized production, world market, capital and science and technology, the relations among countries, regions and nations are increasingly closer and stronger, showing the trend of globalization and integration. The trend is mainly reflected in the following aspects:

Firstly, globalization of the environment, resources and population. In particular, ecological protection and environmental governance have broken through national boundaries and become a common concern of the world. Now, a country will be isolated and punished if it considers and solves ecological problems only from its own perspective without a global vision and a vision of future and without the intention of cooperation and collaboration.

---

13   Selected Works of Deng Xiaoping, 1st edition, Vol.3, p.64 and https://archive.org/ stream/SelectedWorksOfDengXiaopingVol.3/Deng03_djvu.txt.

Secondly, the globalization and integration of economic life. As early as the 1840s, Marx and Engels pointed out in The Communist Manifesto that the production and consumption of all countries became world-wide because the bourgeoisie developed the world market. The local and ethnic self-sufficiency and self-seclusion in the past were replaced by the interdependence of all ethnic groups. At present, this trend is more obvious: (1) Production and division of labor become more and more international. The socialized production develops into internationalized production; the division of labor goes beyond national boundaries and becomes international division of labor. (2) Capital and markets are becoming more and more internationalized. The domestic unified market develops into international unified market; the global capital flows have made the linkages between economies and markets of various countries unprecedentedly close. (3) With increasing size, capital, technology and strength, the transnational corporations and transnational groups play a leading role in the development of the world economy.

Thirdly, the internationalization of science and technology development and application. The rapid development of science and technology not only changes the way of human production and life, but also changes the research and application of science and technology. First, the transformation of new inventions and new technologies to the field of production and life becomes faster and faster. And once the transformation is realized, the technology will be immediately promoted and used in the world and becomes international technology. Second, the cooperation and collaboration of science and technology research becomes stronger, more socialized and more internationalized. Previously, a major technology invention could often be completed by one or several scientists in the laboratory. But now, things are changed. Major scientific and technological research projects, such as space exploration, ocean development, nuclear energy utilization and biological engineering, are difficult to undertake with huge investment and great risk. They cannot be completed by one, a few of or dozens of scientists, and even by the manpower, material and financial resources of one country. They require for worldwide cooperation and coordination. Only by using the human resources, material and financial resources of various countries in the world can something be gained and can certain progress be made.

Facts have shown that global interaction is becoming more and more obvious. For example, the impact of the Asian financial crisis on the global economy, the impact of the devaluation of Japan on Asia and the global economy, the impact of the Russian financial crisis on the global economy, the global financial crisis and economic crisis caused by American sub-prime crisis are all sufficient evidences proving that the global interaction becomes more and more obvious. Now, what we face is not the small country completely isolated with a small population, but is a picture of globalization that the countries, the regions and the nations are mutually communicated and mutually connected. In this picture, it is impossible for any country or any nation to isolate itself. Only by implementing policy of opening to the outside world can the country survive and develop itself. Although many countries and nations should also take economic protection policies conducive to state and national interests in their own development process, protection is not equal to self-seclusion. If the protection is turned into self-seclusion, there will be no future except lagging behind and being vulnerable to attacks.

Second, China's development is inseparable from the world

The present world is an open world, and "China cannot develop without the world."[14] This conclusion is not only the result of the keen observation of the world development trend, but also the result of the profound summary of the historical lessons of China's long stagnation and backwardness.

Before the establishment of capitalist production mode in western countries, China had been at the forefront of world civilization. However, after the western world entered into capitalism, China was gradually behind the times. Especially, after The Opium War, China was gradually reduced to a semi-colonial and semi-feudal country, suffering from the humiliation of being butchered. There are many reasons for China's transition from strong to weak. However, based on careful analysis, we can find that there is an important reason, namely the shift from opening to the outside world to self-seclusion. According to historical records, in the 15th century, China had been keeping a foothold in the world with the opening to the outside world. However, after the 15th century, especially the establishment of the Qing dynasty, the ruling class gradually closed the door to the outside world and stopped communication and contact with the outside world for maintaining the stability of the regime and for other reasons,.

However, under the condition that the capitalist mode of production has been established and the world market has been formed, self-seclusion becomes impossible. The force of socialized mass production, market and capital intrinsically demands outward expansion, and no boundaries and ethnic boundaries can limit it. If one country chooses self-seclusion rather than conforming to this power to actively open to the outside world, it will not only miss the good opportunity for great development, but also lag behind and be vulnerable to attacks. In this regard, "we suffered from isolation, and so did our forefathers. You might say it was an open policy of a sort when Zheng He was sent on voyages to the western oceans by Emperor Cheng Zu of the Ming Dynasty. But the Ming Dynasty began to

---

14   Selected Works of Deng Xiaoping, 1st edition, Vol.3, p.78.

decline with the death of Emperor Cheng Zu. The following Kang-Qian Flourishing Age of the Qing Dynasty cannot be regarded as open."

In the Qing Dynasty, during the reigns of Kang Xi and Qian Long, there was no open policy to speak of. China remained isolated for more than 300 years from the middle of the Ming Dynasty to the Opium War, or for nearly 200 years counting from the reign of Kang Xi. As a consequence, the country declined into poverty and ignorance.[15]

In short, "one of the important reasons why China lagged behind after the industrial revolution in western countries was that, it was closed to the outside world."[16]

Our forefathers suffered from isolation, and so did us. After the founding of new China, "we also want to expand the economic and technological exchanges between China and foreign countries, including the development of economic and trade relations with some capitalist countries and even the introduction of foreign capital, joint ventures and so on. But, there were no conditions at that time because an embargo was being imposed on China.

And later, the Gang of Four branded any attempt at economic relations with other countries as "worshipping things foreign and fawning on foreigners" or as "national betrayal", and so sealed China off from the outside world."[17]

"In particular, during the ten-year period when the world economy was developing rapidly, we closed our doors and engaged in the so-called "Cultural Revolution", the result of which has been a long-term stagnation and backwardness of the national economy.

"The experience of the past thirty or so years has demonstrated that a closed-door policy would hinder construction and inhibit development. There could be two kinds of exclusion: one would be directed against other countries; the other would be directed against China itself, with one region or department closing its doors to the others. Both kinds of exclusion would be harmful."[18]

The development of China is inseparable from the world.

With sharp observation of the world development trend and the profound summary of the historical lessons, Deng Xiaoping put forward the policy of opening to the outside world in time around 1979, and regarded it as a long-term basic national policy. Since then, he has repeatedly emphasized the necessity and significance of opening to the outside world and pointed out: "To expand the productive forces we must carry out reform and open

15   Ibid., p.90.
16   Selected Works of Deng Xiaoping, 1st edition, Vol.3, p.64.
17   Selected Works of Deng Xiaoping, Ed. 2, vol.2, p.127.
18   Selected Works of Deng Xiaoping, 1st edition, Vol.3, p.64-65.

to the outside world; there is no other way. We cannot continue to keep our doors closed as we did for more than twenty years. The closure of the past two decades must change."[19]

"Adhering to the reform and opening-up is a move which determines the fate of China."[20] The former General Secretary Hu Jintao pointed out in the report of the 17th CPC National Congress: "the most striking feature of the new era is reform and opening up". Without reform and opening up, there would be no socialism with Chinese characteristics. In the 21st century, China should expand its opening to the outside world to absorb and learn from all the advanced things, in order to obtain development, make progress and become prosperous and strong. Self-seclusion causes lagging behind and those who lag behind will be vulnerable to attacks.

Third, opening to the outside world is an indispensable condition for the realization of socialist modernization

We build socialism on the basis of a relatively backward economy and culture. For more than 60 years, although the socialist economic construction has made great achievements, it is still in the primary stage of socialism. Compared with the world's advanced level, there is still a considerable distance. In this way, the modernization construction will inevitably encounter many difficulties. Among them, there are several most prominent difficulties. One is that various systems, especially the economic system, cannot meet the requirements of modern construction. The second is the lack of funds, technology, management personnel and management experience necessary for modern construction. For the former difficulty, we can solve it through system reform. For the second difficulty, it can also be solved through system reform and tapping internal potential. However, it will be difficult to solve them completely depending on our own strength. If we depend on our strength only, our distance from the advanced level of the world will not be reduced, but will be extended because the world economy and science and technology develop by leaps and bounds. If we depend on ourselves only to slowly understand and solve the problems in the construction of modernization, we will never catch up with the pace of the world economy and technology. However, if we boldly use the approach adopted by the developed countries in the process of modernization, namely opening up to the outside world, we can both solve some of the major difficulties we face in the modernization construction and avoid taking the repeated path taken by other countries in many aspects. We will start at a higher starting point, narrowing the gap with the world's advanced level as soon as possible and striving to catch up and surpass the advanced world level in some areas. Because:

19   Ibid., p.265.
20   Ibid., p.368.

141

Firstly, the implementation of the opening to the outside world provides the necessary conditions for us to solve the serious shortage of funds in the modern construction. The modernization construction of China is a vast project. It is not only to achieve the goal of modernization, but also to cover the task of industrialization. There are a lot of things to do with great difficulty. Among them, the most prominent difficulty is the serious shortage of construction funds. The solution to this problem will undoubtedly depend on our own long-term accumulation. But we can also find solutions in the international capital market. This is not only necessary, but also possible because there have been a lot of hot money in the international capital market since the 1980s. The hot money looks for profitable investment places around the world. In developed countries, there are only a few of such investment places. However, in developing countries, they are everywhere. And the corresponding profits are also considerable. In particular, China, a developing country with a large population and a vast territory, is an attractive and profitable market. As long as we implement the opening up policy, we will attract a large number of foreign capitals. These funds, whether in the form of loans or in the form of sole proprietorship, joint ventures and cooperative ventures, can solve the meet the huge fund demand of China's construction.

Secondly, the implementation of the opening to the outside world provides us with the conditions for the introduction of advanced foreign technology and advanced equipment. China is a country with relatively backward science and technology, and there is a certain gap between China's scientific and technological level and the advanced level in the world. We should basically realize modernization in the middle of the 21st century, approaching or reaching the level of the developed countries in the world. The key is to develop our own science and technology. To develop science and technology, it is necessary to introduce advanced science and technology and production equipment in the world while relying on our own strength to carry out scientific research and technological innovation. To achieve the goal of catching up or surpassing the advanced level of the world through vigorously introducing the world advanced science and technology is an effective way proved by the postwar development achievements of Germany and Japan. China, as a developing country, should be so. In the past, although we intended to introduce foreign advanced technology and equipment, but there were no such conditions at that time because an embargo was being imposed on us. But now, things are different. We have a lot of good conditions in this respect. As long as we steadfastly follow the path of modernization and insist on opening to the outside world, many countries in the world are willing to engage in scientific and technological exchanges and cooperation with us and are willing to transfer technology and equipment to us, which is very conducive to our modernization.

Thirdly, the implementation of the opening to the outside world provides conditions for us to learn from and absorb advanced foreign management experience and management methods. Practice has proved that the availability of funds, technology and equipment does not mean that the expected productivity and economic benefits can be obtained. In addition to funds, technology and equipment, there also should be corresponding management experiences and management methods. In fact, the gap between China and the developed countries is reflected not only in the funds, technology and equipment, but also in the lack of management experience and management methods that meet the requirements of modern mass production. Therefore, in the opening to the outside world, we should not only pay attention to the introduction of foreign capital, technology and equipment, but also make great efforts on introducing foreign advanced management experience and management methods. There should be no ideological concern on this issue. The advanced management experience and management methods, which meet the requirements of modern production, have no class nature, just like the science and technology. They can be used by both the bourgeoisie and the proletariat. We should not reject them only because they were firstly used by the bourgeoisie.

Fourthly, opening to the outside world is an important condition for us to learn the world information and grasp the pulse of the world. We are now facing fierce international market competition in the information age. In addition to the competition of funds, technology and equipment, there is also information competition which is more important. In the situation of economic globalization, whoever has rich, accurate and timely information will be able to accurately judge the objective trend of world political and economic development and thus will be active in the development and remain invincible fierce market competition. On the contrary, those without rich, accurate and timely information will be eliminated.

Deng Xiaoping pointed out: "A closed-door policy would be greatly to our disadvantage; we would not even have quick access to information. People say that information is important, right? It certainly is. If an administrator has no access to information, it's as if he was purblind and hard of hearing and had a stuffed nose."[21]

Our experience shows that China cannot rebuild itself behind closed doors and that it cannot develop in isolation from the rest of the world; especially when world's technological revolution is booming.[22]

The implementation of the opening to the outside world allows us to understand and master the world information in a timely manner and thus catch up with the world.

21   Deng Xiaoping Selected Works, 1st edition, Vol.3, pp.306-307.
22   Ibid., p. 290.

Fifthly, the implementation of the opening to the outside world is also the necessary condition for us to carry out socialist market economy system construction. The socialist modernization construction is connected with the socialist market economy system. The experience of economic development in the past few decades has proved that there are many disadvantages in the planned economy system. These disadvantages are not conducive to economic development and modernization. Market economy system is the inevitable choice of history. It is conducive to the rational allocation of resources. But, the market economy also has its own flaws and failures. Therefore, how to give full play to the advantages of the market economy system and avoid the shortage of market economy is a problem that needs to be studied and solved in the process of the construction of socialist market economy system. We used to implement the planned economy system in the past for a long term. After the establishment of the socialist market economic system, there must be a variety of problems in its specific operation. To solve these problems, it is necessary to draw lessons from the experiences of western market economy construction, absorb the good experiences of using the market economic system to manage and develop the economy, and avoid the repeated emergence of the problems in the use of market economic system. In the face of problems, we can also draw lessons from the western countries to solve the problem, thus developing our economy and modernization more quickly and smoothly. To achieve this, we should carry out the opening to the outside world. At the same time, to meet the wave of world economic globalization, better carry out dialogue and exchange with other countries, win the increasingly fierce market competition in the world, develop ourselves and expand ourselves, it is necessary to integrate with the world in accordance with international customs and rules. That is to say, it is necessary to carry out the opening to the outside world.

As Deng Xiaoping said: "In short, if we want socialism to achieve superiority over capitalism, we should not hesitate to draw on the achievements of all cultures and to learn from other countries, including the developed capitalist countries, all advanced methods of operation and techniques of management that reflect the laws governing modern socialized production."[23]

Fourth, improve and develop an all-round, multi-tiered and wide-ranging opening-up pattern

Deng Xiaoping has repeatedly pointed out that invigorating the domestic economy and opening to the outside is not a short-term policy, but a long-term policy. The policy will not change within at least 50 to 70 years. In short, opening-up is necessary. We must continue to be open and become more open. Under the guidance of Deng Xiaoping, China's opening to the

---

23   Selected Works of Deng Xiaoping, 1st edition, Vol.3, p.373.

outside world starting from the establishment of special economic zone, the opening of the coastal cities, the establishment of Hainan Special Economic Zone to the opening of Shanghai Pudong new area has formed a comprehensive, multi-level and wide-ranging pattern of opening to the world.

First, the opening to the outside is the comprehensive opening to the outside world.

Deng Xiaoping once pointed out that: there are still some people who have not made clear the opening to the outside world. They think that our opening is only to the western developed countries. In fact, our opening is to three aspects. The first is the western developed countries from which we absorb foreign capital and introduce technology. The second is the Soviet Union and the eastern European countries. Even though state-to-state relations are not normal, exchanges can go on, for instance, in commercial transactions, technology and even in joint ventures and technical innovations, like innovations in the 156 projects. They have a part to play in all these respects. The third region is the developing countries of the Third World, each of which has its special characteristics and strengths and offers enormous potentialities. Hence, opening to the outside world involves three regions (One is the developed countries in the West, second Soviet Union and the East European countries, third developing countries), not just one region.[24]

145

Second, the opening to the outside world is multi-level and in steps.

China's opening to the outside world is carried out gradually in stages. The initial stage of China's opening to the outside world is marked by the establishment of special economic zones. In April 1979, Deng Xiaoping put forward at the Central Working Conference that: a piece of land could set aside as the special zone. However, he then said that kind of special zone was "the special economic zone", and was not a special political zone. In May 1980, the Party Central Committee and the State Council, on the initiative of Deng Xiaoping, formally named the special zone as "special economic zone", and then decided to set up four special economic zones including Shenzhen, Zhuhai, Shantou and Xiamen. On the basis of the initial success of the four special economic zones including Shenzhen, Zhuhai, Xiamen and Shantou, the central government has taken a series of important steps to make the opening up develop from point to line and from line to surface after carefully summarizing experiences and highly affirming achievements. In 1984, the Central Committee of the Party and the State Council decided, on the proposal of Deng Xiaoping, to open 14 coastal ports and make them fully play the role of central city in economic construction, so as to promote the economic construction of the mainland

---

24   See Deng Xiaoping anthology, 1st edition, Vol.3, p.98-99.

and thereby promote the economic construction of the whole country. In February 1985, the Central Government set up the economic opening area in the Yangtze River Delta, the Pearl River Delta, and the Southeast Fujian and the Circum-Bohai Sea Region. Then, the Jinan City in Shandong Province, the Shaoguan City, the Heyuan City and the Meizhou City in Guangdong Province were included into the economic open area. Basically, the policy of open coastal city is implemented in these areas. In April 1988, Hainan Province was set as special economic zone and became the largest special economic zone in China. In April 1990, the Central Committee of the Party and the State Council decided to develop the Pudong new area. In this way, the pattern of China's coastal opening to the outside world was preliminarily formed. In 1992, with Deng Xiaoping's Southern Talks and 14th CPC National Congress as an important symbol, China's opening to the outside world entered a comprehensive implementation stage. Since the beginning of 1992, the opening to the outside world expanded from the coast to the mainland, and has launched a series of new initiatives of opening-up along river, opening-up along border, and inland open. By the middle of December 1995, a multi-level, multi-form and multi-directional pattern of opening to the outside world was basically formed, including 1,194 cities and counties, 222 open ports and an area of more than 500,000 square kilometers. In 2007, China's total import and export trade amounted to $ 2.17 trillion, a 104-fold increase from the $ 20.64 billion in 1978, showing the great results of opening to the outside world.

Third, China's opening to the outside world is wide-ranging.

China's opening to the outside world is not only comprehensive and multi-level, but also wide-ranging. The so-called wide-ranging opening refers to that the opening covers fields including science and technology, culture, education, sports, health in addition to economic field. All countries of the world have their own advantages and advantages in these fields. Particularly, the western developed countries have accumulated a wealth of experience and achieved many historical results of civilization after hundreds of years of development. Thus, there are many things for us to draw lessons from and introduce in terms of socialist modernization and socialist market economy system construction. Among the wide-ranging opening to the outside world, the opening to the economic, technological and cultural fields is the focus.

Now, China has basically established its comprehensive, multi-level, wide-ranging and characteristic pattern of opening to the outside world, with remarkable results. The open economy of the coastal open zone develops rapidly, and the open cities along the Yangtze River have begun to drive the economic development of the Yangtze River basin. The economic development of the open cities and towns along the border has been accelerated obviously, and the inland open cities have promoted and driven the economic development of the hinterland. Through opening to the outside, China has absorbed and made use of a large number of foreign capital construction funds and introduced advanced technology and management experience. In this way, China has vigorously promoted the adjustment and upgrading of industrial structure, provided new jobs, increased the national financial income, and obtained rapid development of foreign economic and trade. In the process of opening to the outside world, the import and export trade expands unceasingly, and the flow and exchange of production factors increase gradually. And the service trade has further developed on the basis of strengthening international relations in the field of production and circulation. A variety of international economic and technical cooperation modes have been widely adopted, with rich successful experiences of international exchange and cooperation. Practice has proved that opening to the outside world has promoted the development of social productive forces, strengthened the comprehensive national strength and international competitiveness, and promoted the process of establishing the socialist market economy system in China.

Fifth, the new situation of the opening-up

After a long period of negotiation, China formally joined the World Trade Organization in December 2001. The accession to WTO is the need of China's economic development and reform and opening up. And it is also conducive to the development of the world economy at the same time. The accession to WTO will help expand China's opening to the outside world, win a better international environment for China, promote the strategic adjustment of economic system reform and economic structure, and enhance the vitality and international competitiveness of China's economy. Thus, it is in general accord with the fundamental interests and long-term interests of China. We must adapt to the new situation of economic globalization and accession to WTO, implement the method of combining "going out" and "brining in", participate in international economic and technological cooperation and competition in a larger scope, wider areas and at a higher level, make full use of the international market and the mainland market, optimize the allocation of resources, widen the space for development, and promote development and reform with opening to the outside world.

We should further expand the trade of goods and services. We should implement market diversification strategy, give play to our comparative advantage, consolidate the traditional market, expand the emerging market, and strive to expand exports. We should adhere to win through high quality and improve the competitiveness of export goods and services. We should optimize the import structure, and solemnly introduce advanced technology and key equipment. We should deepen the reform of economic and trade system, promote the diversification of foreign trade bodies, and improve the relevant tax system and trade financing mechanism.

We should further attract foreign direct investment and improve the quality and level of utilization of foreign capital. We implement the strategy of "bringing in" and "going out" to improve the level of opening to the outside world. "Brining in" is to gradually promote the opening of the service sector, use the medium and long-term foreign investment in a variety of ways, combine the use of foreign capital with the domestic economic structure adjustment and the reorganization and transformation of state-owned enterprises, and encourage transnational corporations to invest in agriculture, manufacturing and high-tech industries. We vigorously introduce overseas talents of all kinds, improve the investment environment, provide national treatment for foreign investment, and improve the transparency of laws and policies. "Going out" is to encourage and support the external investment of various enterprises with comparative advantages, promote the export of goods and services, form a group of competitive transnational corporations and famous brands, and actively participate in regional economic exchanges and cooperation.

The "bringing in" and the "going out" are the two closely linked and mutually reinforcing aspects of our guideline regarding opening to the outside world. Both are indispensable. Jiang Zemin vividly pointed out: "'bringing in' and 'going out' are the two wheels that drive opening to the outside world and must be turned at the same time."[25]

Sixth, correctly understand and deal with the relationship between opening to the outside world and independence and self-reliance

Independence and self-reliance are the important principles that the Party has always adhered to. The principle of independence refers to that China handles all domestic affairs independently and opposes any form of external interference; the principle of self-reliance refers to that China relies on its own strength to build, develop and strengthen itself. However, independence is not a self-seclusion and self-reliance is not blind exclusion. The emphasis on independence and self-reliance is not to advocate self-seclusion and isolated construction, but to raise the opening the outside world to a new and higher level. Therefore, in the process of socialist modernization and reform and opening up, there is always a problem, namely how to correctly deal with the relationship between opening to the outside world and independent and self-reliance.

How to correctly deal with the relationship between opening to the outside world and independent and self-reliance is how to correctly handle the relationship between internal and external factors. In the view of Marxist

25   Selected Works of Jiang Zemin, Vol. 3, p. 457.

philosophy, the development of anything has two kinds of factors: internal factor and external factor. Internal factor is the internal basis of the existence, change and development of things, and external cause is the external condition of the existence, change and development of things. The nature and development direction of things is mainly determined by the internal contradiction of things, namely internal factor. Although the external contradiction of things, namely external factor, plays a role in the nature and development direction of things, this role takes effect only with internal factor. Therefore, the internal factor is basis, and the external factor is the condition. The external factor acts through the internal factor. This is the dialectics of the existence, change and development of things, and is the correct way to deal with the internal and external relations in the development of things.

In the process of socialist modernization and reform and opening up, independence and self-reliance are internal factors and are the internal basis determining the nature and direction of socialist modernization. Opening to the outside world, absorbing and drawing lessons from all outstanding achievements and advanced experience from abroad is the external cause, and is an important external condition for the socialist modernization construction. The integration of independence, self-reliance and opening to the outside world is the correct way to deal with the relationship between them.

China is an eastern country with backward economy and culture. The socialist modernization carried out in such a big country should seek foreign aid and introduce foreign capital, science and technology, advanced management experiences and management methods, which is valuable experience obtained from the long-term historical development and is also common practice of many modernized countries. We must realize that the development and progress of China cannot be separated from the civilized achievements of various countries in the world. We should actively learn and apply civilization results created by any social system as long as they are progressive and excellent. However, we also should have a clear understanding that such learning and application must always be based on independence and self-reliance. The experience and lessons of more than one hundred years of the modern history of China proves that the ability to deal with national affairs independently is a major problem for the survival of the country and the nation. If the country's affairs are interfered by others or if the country needs to take its cue from other countries, the country and its nation will be unable to survive and develop. To develop, we must firstly rely on our own strength. It is unrealistic notion and extremely dangerous to rely on the assistance of others and expect others to help us. Particularly, if a big country like China develops on the basis of the assistance of other countries, it will be unable to develop itself. Moreover, it will even lose the right of independence, which will further threaten its survival and its nation. Therefore, Deng Xiaoping said: "China's affairs should be run according to China's specific conditions and by the Chinese people themselves. Independence and self-reliance have always been and will always be their basic stand."[26]

Deng Xiaoping pointed out: "However, it isn't easy to get funds and advanced technology from the developed countries. There are still some people around who are wedded to the ideas of the old-line colonialists; they are reluctant to see the poor countries develop, and attempt to throttle them. Therefore, while pursuing the policy of opening to the outside world, we must stick to the principle of relying mainly on our own efforts, a principle consistently advocated by Chairman Mao Zedong since the founding of our People's Republic. We must seek outside help on the basis of self-reliance, depending mainly on our own hard work."[27]

We need to be open to the outside world. We cherish our friendship and cooperation with other countries and peoples. However, we need the spirit of independence more deeply and value our hard-won independence more deeply. No foreign country should expect China to be its vassal or to accept anything that is damaging to China's own interests. In short, while adhering to the opening to the outside world, economic cooperation, the use of foreign capital and drawing lessons from foreign experiences, we must always keep a clear mind. We must not forget to put the sovereignty and security of the country in the first place. We must not abandon the protection of the rights and interests of the country and the people. We must not allow anything decadent and harmful to the people to spread freely.

Section III

Adhere to the idea of "Three Favorables"

First, the first proposal of the idea of "Three Favorables"

"Three Favorables", namely "whether it is conducive to the development of the productive forces of the socialist society, whether it is conducive to enhancing the comprehensive national strength of the socialist country and whether it is conducive to raising the standard of living of the people", is the standard for judging the gains and losses of our reform and various efforts. It clarifies the vague and wrong understanding of people in the practice of building socialism with Chinese characteristics, dispel the hesitation, concern and worry of people when they encounter different opinions

---

26 Deng Xiaoping Selected Works, 1st edition, Vol. 3, p.3.
27 Selected Works of Deng Xiaoping, 2nd edition, Vol.2, p.405-406 and https://archive.org/stream/SelectedWorksOfDengXiaopingVol.1/Deng02_djvu.txt.

and resistance, and provide a solid and reliable action basis for the bold discovery and trial of people, the acceleration of the reform and the striving for the further development of the national economy every few years.

"Three Favorables" is the outcome of Deng Xiaoping's insistence on emancipating the mind and seeking truth from facts in the practice of building socialism with Chinese characteristics, and is the result of the analysis and summary of various new problems, new situations and new experiences appearing in the course of socialist modernization construction and reform and opening up in a timely manner. It has experienced a three-step developing and deepening process starting from the establishment of practical standards to the establishment of productivity standards and to the establishment of the "Three Favorables" criterion. This process has always reflected the ideological line of emancipating the mind and seeking truth from facts of the Party, and embodies Marxism's epistemology principle of integrate subject with object, recognition and practice.

In 1978, the 3rd Plenary Session of the 17th Central Committee of the Party established the ideological line of the Party, resolutely suspended the wrong route "taking class struggle as the central task", realized the shift of the Party's work focus to economic construction; and established the fundamental task of realizing the four modernizations. To develop the productive forces and realize the four modernizations, the Central Committee formulated a series of policy measures, including reform and opening up. In the rural level, the household contract responsibility system which was initiated by farmers was affirmed, and popularized in the whole country. And the people's communes which had been implemented for several decades were abolished. In the city level, the previous form of ownership which was quite simple was changed, and the structure with public ownership as the main body and with the existence of individuals, private and " foreign-invested" enterprises and other economic elements was implemented to encourage the development of individual economy, private economy and "foreign-invested" enterprises together with state-owned and collective economy under fair competition; in the country level, open cities, economic development zones and special economic zones were set up from the coast to the border areas to serve as a window for absorbing foreign capital, technology, management experience and management talents. All these measures have achieved very obvious results in practice and are proved to be conducive to the cause of socialism and in line with the four basic principles. However, since the impact of traditional concepts and traditional thinking are hard to be eliminated immediately and reform is a new cause, it is inevitable to face certain problems and make mistakes. Moreover, since reform affects vested interests, some people did not understand some new things or new approaches in the reform, and always used the old thinking, old experience and old approaches to evaluate new situations and understand new problems. They feel concern about these new things and new approaches. Some people even used the past ultra-left approaches, traditional thinking and "dogmatic thinking" to blame the new things. Especially, whenever they met difficulties and setbacks in the reform, they would think that reform is not in line with Marxism and is wrong and unsuccessful practice. This puts forward a problem, namely what are the standards for judging the gains and losses of the reform. It is a major problem related to the smooth development of the reform. On this issue, the whole Party must reach a consensus and put forward a unified and objective standard, otherwise the people will be confused and in a dilemma due to lack of such standard. The lack of a unified and objective standard makes it difficult to take a bold step of reform and is bound to hinder the development of the productive forces and the realization of the four modernizations.

Faced with this situation, Deng Xiaoping called for bold and courageous attitudes and conduct to be assumed by the revolutionaries and cadres and he urged all the party and the people throughout the country to "liberate their minds and progress more steadily and even faster than before in carrying out the policies of reform and opening to the outside world."[28]

From this, he constantly stressed the importance of developing productivity and achieving the four modernizations, and repeatedly called for using the development of productivity and the realization of the four modernizations as the standard to weigh the gains and losses of our work.

In September 1978, Deng Xiaoping pointed out in his speech "Hold High The Banner of Mao Zedong Thought and Adhere To the Principle of Seeking Truth from Facts" " After all, from the historical materialist point of view correct political leadership should result in the growth of the productive forces and the improvement of the material and cultural life of the people."[29]

In October 1979, in his "Greetings address to the Fourth Congress of Chinese Literary and Art Workers", he further pointed out: "strive for the four modernizations. The basic standard for judging all our work is whether it helps or hinders our effort to modernize."[30]

In May 1980, when meeting with Duval, President of Guinea, he pointed out: "According to our experience, in order to build socialism we must first of all develop the productive forces, which is our main task. This is the only way to demonstrate the superiority of socialism. Whether the socialist economic policies we are pursuing are correct or not depends, in the final

28   Selected Works of Deng Xiaoping, 1st edition, Vol. 3, p.265.
29   Selected Works of Deng Xiaoping, 2nd edition, Vol.2, p.128.
30   Ibid., p.209.

analysis, on whether the productive forces develop and people's incomes increase. This is the most important criterion. We cannot build socialism with just empty talk. The people will not believe it."[31]

In short, our work in all fields should help to build socialism with Chinese characteristics, and it should be judged by the criterion of whether it contributes to the welfare and happiness of the people and to national prosperity.[32]

The statement in the report of the 17th CPC National Congress means that the whole party has reached a consensus on the understanding of what should be used as the standard for judging the gains and losses of the reform, and set productivity as the fundamental standard.

However, the development of things is not always smooth, so is reform as an unprecedented new cause. In China, the cause of reform encountered a severe test. Because some comrades, especially senior leaders, had an excessively one-sided understanding of the standard of productivity and neglected other aspects, especially the ideological education work for young students, a political turmoil occurred at the turn of the spring and summer of 1989. At the international level, the reforms of the Soviet Union and eastern European countries diverged from the socialist direction, leading to the collapse of the communist party and the failure of the socialist cause. The political turmoil in China, the drastic changes in Eastern Europe and the disintegration of the Soviet Union caused an uproar among Chinese people. Some people threw doubt upon and even denied the Party's line, principles and policies since the 3rd Plenary Session of the 11th Central Committee of the Chinese Communist Party. They put forward the question of whether the path was capitalist or socialist. Moreover, they rejected many approaches approved to be correct by many practices in the course of reform and opening up and regarded them as the bourgeois liberalization. They thought that it was necessary to make clear whether the path was capitalist or socialist before implementing and carrying through all measures, approaches and new things in the reform. In general, there is nothing wrong to make clear whether the path is capitalist or socialist in order to adhere to the right direction of the reform and carry out reform better and smoother. But some people's starting point is more than that. On the one hand, they put forward the question of whether the path was capitalist or socialist with the aim of criticizing and opposing the reform. They pinned political labels on the people, and regarded reform cause as capitalist cause and bourgeois liberalization frequently; on the other hand, their discussion on whether the path was is capitalist or socialist is completely separated from the development of productivity and is empty talk. They ignored the actual situation of

---

31 Ibid., p.314.
32 Selected Works of Deng Xiaoping, 1st edition, Vol.3, p.23.

China's social development, judged the real life with the abstract, rigid and distorted socialism principles, which was typical metaphysics and the reflection of the "left" thoughts in the past. If we cannot overcome and break through such "left" thoughts confining people's thought, it will be difficult to continue reform and opening up and the socialist modernization cause will be face the danger of being destroyed. For some time, these "left" thoughts were really threatening, making the society unstable. In this serious case, Deng Xiaoping published the famous Southern Talks, and made sharp criticism of the thoughts opposing reform. He pointed out sharply: Regarding reform and the open policy as means of introducing capitalism, and seeing the danger of peaceful evolution towards capitalism as coming chiefly from the economic sphere are "Left" tendencies."[33]

And he pointed out: "The reason why some people hesitate to carry out the reform and opening up policy and dare not break new ground is, in essence, that they're afraid it would mean introducing too many elements of capitalism and, indeed, taking the capitalist path. The crux of the matter is whether the path is capitalist or socialist. The chief standard for making that judgment should be whether it promotes the growth of the productive forces in a socialist society, increases the overall strength of the socialist state and raises living standards."

He also made a thought-provoking remark on the question of whether the special administrative region is "capitalist" or "socialist": "As for building special economic zones, some people disagreed with the idea right from the start, wondering whether it would not mean introducing capitalism. The achievements in the construction of Shenzhen have given these people a definite answer: special economic zones are socialist, not capitalist." Of course, as a new cause and a major test, the reform will inevitably encounter various risks and there will inevitably be different views and concerns on reform, which is normal. What should we do in this situation? Deng Xiaoping argued that it is necessary to emancipate the mind, seek truth from facts, and be bold and steady. Deng Xiaoping pointed out: "We should be bolder than before in conducting reform and opening to the outside and have the courage to experiment. We must not act like women with bound feet. Once we are sure that something should be done, we should dare to experiment and break a new path. That is the important lesson to be learned from Shenzhen. If we don't have the pioneering spirit, if we're afraid to take risks, if we have no energy and drive, we cannot break a new path, a good path, or accomplish anything new. Who dares claim that he is 100 per cent sure of success and that he is taking no risks? No one can ever be 100 per cent sure at the outset that what he is doing is correct. I've never been that sure…"[34]

33   Deng Xiaoping Selected Works , 1st edition, vol. 3, p.375.
34   Ibid., p.372 and https://archive.org/stream/SelectedWorksOfDengXiaopingVol.3/ Deng03_djvu.txt.

Deng Xiaoping also pointed out: "it is quite nature that we have different views on reform and opening up at the beginning... It was our policy to permit people to do that, which was much better than coercing them. In carrying out the line, principles and policies adopted since the 3rd Plenary Session of the 11th Central Committee, we did not resort to compulsion or mass movements. People were allowed to follow the line on a voluntary basis, doing as much or as little as they wished. In this way, others gradually followed suit. It was my idea to discourage contention, so as to have more time for action. Once disputes begin, they complicate matters and waste a lot of time. As a result, nothing is accomplished. Don't argue; try bold experiments and blaze new trails."[35]

Deng Xiaoping's speeches, like a giant cyclone, have blown away the worries and doubts of the people, strengthened their determination and confidence to carry out the reform, and provided a comprehensive scientific standard for the correct evaluation of the reform and the evaluation of the gains and losses of the reform.

According to Deng Xiaoping's thoughts, when discussing the fundamental task of socialism, the 14th CPC National Congress took "Three Favorables" standard put forward by Deng Xiaoping as the fundamental standard to judge the gains and losses of the work, and organically combined it with the essence of socialism, socialist basic task and the impetus of socialist development to form the basic guideline for the construction of socialism with Chinese characteristics. The 15th CPC National Congress further stressed the importance of "Three Favorables". Moreover, it promoted the standard to an important content of the ideological line of emancipating the mind and seeking truth, thus making it a weapon used by the Party and the people in the process of comprehensively pushing forward the cause of socialism with Chinese characteristics to the 21st Century.

Second, the most fundamental criteria to measure the success and failure of all our work

The "Three Favorables" criteria is the product of emancipating the mind and seeking truth from facts, and also a sharp weapon to further emancipate the mind, seek truth from facts and advance our work comprehensively. The correct understanding and grasp of the "Three Favorables" is of great importance for us to enhance confidence in reform and make bold attempts. To correctly understand and grasp the "Three Favorables", it is necessary to make clear:

---

35   Ibid., p.374 and https://archive.org/stream/SelectedWorksOfDengXiaopingVol.3/Deng03_djvu.txt.

First, the "Three Favorables" is objective standard rather than subjective standard. It is in the process of reform and opening up and in the process of socialist modernization construction. It generates and develops on the basis of summing up the experiences and lessons from the pros and cons and opposing the "left" erroneous tendency and right erroneous tendency. It is the product of emancipating the mind and seeking truth from facts.

Second, there is inherent and indivisible relationship between "Three Favorables" standard and socialism. The "Three Favorables" is the fundamental standard inevitably adopted under the essential requirement of the socialist for measuring the gains and losses of all work, and is the basic manifestation of the superiority of the socialist system. Therefore, when using this standard, we should think of the direction of socialism, the principle of socialism and how to give full play to the superiority of the socialist system at any moment. The "Three Favorables" will lose its original value and significance as long as it is separated from socialism and the play of the superiority of the socialist system.

Third, among the "Three Favorables", whether it is conducive to the development of the productive forces of the socialist society, namely the standard of productivity, is the core standard. This standard not only reflects the principle of historical materialism that productivity is the most basic decisive force in the development of human history, but also reflects the principle of Marxism that it is necessary to attach the greatest importance to the development of productive forces and socialism is the development of the productive forces. It is the basis of the other two standards. Without the development of productivity, it is impossible to obtain the enhancement of comprehensive national strength, let alone the improvement of the living standard of the people. We should never discuss other standards without the involvement of the standard of developing productivity.

Fourth, although the productivity standard is the most fundamental standard and the basis of "Three Favorables", it is not the only standard. The development of productive forces, the enhancement of comprehensive national strength and the improvement of the living standards of the people are closely linked. The enhancement of comprehensive national strength and the improvement of people's living standard cannot be separated from the development of productive forces. And the development of productive forces also should be reflected in the enhancement of comprehensive national strength and the improvement of the living standards of the people. Therefore, it is impossible to enhance the comprehensive national strength and improve the living standards of the people without developing productive forces, and it is impossible to develop productive forces without enhancing the overall national strength and improving the living standards of the people.

Fifth, among the "Three Favorables" standard, whether it is conducive to improve the standard of living of the people is the highest standard. The purpose of the communist party is to work for the welfare of the people. And the purpose of socialism and communism is to liberate all mankind, achieve the common prosperity and the free and comprehensive development of human beings. Therefore, in the process of developing the productive forces and enhancing the comprehensive national strength, we should never forget that our ultimate goal is to improve the living standard of the people and achieve common prosperity.

CHAPTER SIX

Ultimate Purpose of Socialism with Chinese Characteristics

Section I

People-oriented principle is the starting point and foothold of developing socialism with Chinese characteristics

First, scientific connotation of people-oriented principle and its concrete manifestations

1. The scientific connotation of people-oriented principle

Being "people-oriented", the fundamental concept of the Party and the state, is first put forward in *The Decisions of the Central Committee of the Communist Party of China on Improving the Socialist Market Economic System* adopted by the 3rd Plenary Session of the 16th Central Committee of the Communist Party of China, stressing the importance of adhering to the people-orientation, establishing a comprehensive, coordinated and sustainable development concept and promoting the all-round development of the economic society and people. *The Decision of the Central Committee of the Communist Party of China on the Construction of a Socialist Harmonious Society*, adopted by the 6th plenary session of the 16th Central Committee of the Communist Party of China, has comprehensively expounded the scientific connotation of "people-oriented", and pointed out that: "We must always regard the fundamental interests of the overwhelming majority of the people as the starting point and foundation of all the party and state work, realize, safeguard and develop the fundamental interests of the overwhelming majority of the people and continuously meet the people's growing material and cultural needs, we should achieve development for the people and by the people, and ensure that all the people share the fruits of development so as to promote all-round development of people."[1]

---

1 CPCCC Party Literature Research Office: "Selection of Important Literature since the 16th National Congress", Vol. II, p. 651, Beijing, Central Literature Publishing House, 2008.

The people-oriented concept we speak today has a specific meaning, which is fundamentally different from the people-oriented thought in our history and the humanistic trend of thought in modern western countries. In our country, the sages had long ago put forward the ideas of "People are the foundation of the country and the country will be safe if the foundation is firmed" and "From heaven to earth, nothing is more important than the people", arguing that "To a state, the people are the most important, the state comes second, while the ruler is the least important", stressing that "the prosperity of the political affairs lies in meeting people's common aspirations, while the failure of political affairs lies in countering them", and believing that to achieve long-term stability, we should help the people, enrich the people, nourish the people and benefit the people. The people-oriented thought in ancient China reflected the simple value of pay great attention to people and played the role of easing class contradiction and lightening the burden of the people in a certain degree. We emphasize the people-oriented value today, which inherits the positive factors of the ancient Chinese people-oriented thought, but differs essentially from it. "People" in the people-oriented thought was in contrast to" the emperor" and the rulers. Its essence was to maintain the ruling status of the feudal ruling class, to realize the "support from the people, preservation of the state, holding of the throne, and realization of the peace of the country", which were ways to "tame people" and "rule people", and the value orientation was essentially monarch-based and not people-oriented. The rise of humanism in the modern west was against superstition, advocating science, opposing autocracy, advocating freedom, opposing divinity and advocating human nature, which had played a positive role in opposing feudalism and promoting human liberation. However, the western humanism, which is individual-oriented, had the realization of the self-value as its basic pursuit, advocating the supremacy of individual interests in the relationships among people and the relationships between individuals and society. At the same time, if humanism departs from the specific historical conditions and the sociality of human beings, and interprets the social history with abstract and eternal human nature, its essence is for the bourgeoisie to obtain power and maintain its ruling status.

Marx sharply criticized the bourgeois humanism, revealed the essence of its idealism, and formed the theory of human from the perspective of historical materialism. While clarifying the law of human social development, Marxism also pointed out the law of the people's creation of history, emphasizing that the people are the creators of history and the decisive force that promoted social development. He continued to point out that the people, as the most active and the most revolutionary factor in the productive forces, had created the material wealth and spiritual wealth of the society. It was the first time that the people-oriented thought had been built on the scientific basis of historical materialism, and become an important ideological principle to guide the proletarian's remolding of the objective world and subjective world. Today, we emphasize the people-oriented thought, adhere to the basic position and basic views of historical materialism, reflecting the essential requirements of building the Party for the public and exercising state power for the people.

In today's China, "people" in "people-oriented" refers to the masses, which mainly include workers, farmers, intellectuals and other workers, and also include the overwhelming majority of the people who are Chinese characteristic socialist builders. "Orientation" in "people-oriented", is the source, the root, the starting point, the foothold and the fundamental interests of the majority of the people. The people-oriented thought regards the fundamental interests of the majority of the people as the starting point and foothold of all work and as the starting point and foothold of the development of socialism with Chinese characteristics. "People-oriented" not only advocates that human is the fundamental purpose of development, which answers why there should be development and "for whom" it develops, but also advocates that human is the fundamental motivation of development, which answers how to develop and on whom should we depend to develop. "For whom" and "depend on whom" are inseparable. Man is the fundamental purpose of development and the fundamental motivation of development. All is done for man and everything is dependent on man, both of which constitute the whole content of "people-oriented". Specifically speaking, "people-oriented" is to always adhere to the people's predominant status in the cause of socialism with Chinese characteristics, to respect the people's initiative and to give full play to their enthusiasm, initiative and creativity. "People-oriented" is to adhere to the fundamental interests of the people to seek development and promote development, constantly meeting the growing material and cultural needs of the people and constantly achieving, maintaining and developing the fundamental interests of the majority of the people. "People-oriented", adhering to the basic interests of all people, is to correctly reflect and balance the interests of different regions, different departments, different aspects of the interests of the masses and properly coordinate the interests of all aspects to achieve common prosperity. "People-oriented" is to ensure that the people enjoy various rights and interests in accordance with the law, to uphold social fairness and justice, to meet the development aspirations and diversity needs of the people, to care about the value, interests and freedom of the people, to pay attention to people's quality of life, development potential and happiness index, to reflect the humanitarian and humanistic care of socialism, and to promote the all-round development of people.

2. Sticking to the principle of serving the people wholeheartedly

People-oriented is not only the fundamental value of socialism with Chinese characteristics, but also the fundamental ruling concept of our Party. Therefore, we should adhere to the people-oriented thought, the first thing of which is to stick to serving the people wholeheartedly.

Serving the people wholeheartedly is the fundamental purpose of the Communist Party of China. This purpose is determined by the nature of our Party as the vanguard of the Chinese working class and the Chinese people and as the vanguard of the Chinese nation. Under the capitalist conditions, the working class is at the bottom of the society, and their own liberation cannot be solved through the individual struggle of the workers. The individual struggle of the working class can, at best, make a few individuals into the position of the ruling class, but the status of the working class as a whole cannot be changed. Only through the complete overthrow of the capitalist system and the liberation of the whole society can the working class finally obtain true liberation. As Marx and Engels pointed out, the proletariat could finally liberate itself only by liberating all mankind. Therefore, the working class is the most selfless class in the history of mankind, whose interest overlaps the development direction of human society and the fundamental interests of the masses. In order to realize its own interests, the working class must represent the interests of the overwhelming majority of the people at the same time. This law determines that the Communist Party, as the vanguard of the working class, whether as a revolutionary Party or as the Party in power to lead the socialist construction, must serve the interests of the working class at the same time and must serve the broad masses of the people. This is in sharp contrast to the bourgeois political parties. In the history, some bourgeois political parties, in the revolutionary period of overthrowing the feudal autocratic system, shared the same interests of the people to a certain degree and needed the support of the masses, thus, they could to a certain extent represent the interests of the people had played a certain role in promoting the development of history. But fundamentally, as the exploiting class, the bourgeoisie' interests are based on the exploitation and oppression of the proletariat and other working people, which is fundamentally opposed to the interests of the people. Once the bourgeoisie gets its ruling status, it will gradually come to the opposite of the people. This class limitation of the bourgeois political parties determine that their political parties can only serve the minority.

The Communist Party of China, adopting Marxism as the guide to action, makes its basic purpose wholeheartedly serving the people. It is the vanguard of the Chinese working class, the vanguard of the Chinese people and the Chinese nation, and a faithful representative of the interests of the working class and people of China. All the struggle and work of the Party is for the benefit of the people, and the Party always regards the achieving, maintaining and developing the fundamental interests of the majority of the people as the starting point and foothold of all the work of the Party and the state. Except for the interests of the working class and the masses of the people, the Communist Party of China has no special interests of its own. As early as they edited the *The Communist Manifesto*, Marx and Engels pointed out: "All previous movements were movements of minorities, or in the interests of minorities. The proletarian movement is the independent movement of the immense majority, in the interests of the immense majority."[2]

Therefore, the Communist Party is not the interest group on behalf of the minority or the narrow-minded. All its policies and practical activities must take the fundamental interests of the working class and the masses of the people as their starting point and foothold. The Communist Party of China has summarized this characteristic as "serving the people wholeheartedly" and regarded it as the fundamental purpose of our Party. As Mao Zedong pointed out: "These (army) battalions of ours are wholly dedicated to the liberation of the people and work entirely in the people's interests."[3]

If the fundamental purpose of serving the people wholeheartedly is lost, the Party will go bad. Serving the people wholeheartedly is not an empty slogan, but a practical action of the Party. It is not only reflected in the Party and state guiding principles and policies, but also in the innumerable outstanding Party members. Only by believing and relying on the masses of the people, serving the people wholeheartedly, and representing the interests of the people through its correct theory, route, guidelines and policies, can the Communist Party of China, guided by Marxism, win the great enthusiasm, initiative and creativity of the people in order to push forward the cause of socialism with Chinese characteristics.

163

Recalling the 90-year history of the Communist Party of China from the date of birth, we can easily see that the Communist Party of China in the smoky revolutionary era took up the positions of the fallen and rise to fight one after another to save the country so that it might survive; while in the bustling construction and reform era, the Communist Party of China exerted all its strength and wisdom for the country's prosperity and the well-being of the people. The Chinese Communist Party has led the Chinese people to achieve great achievements one after another. For more than 90 years, because of the changes in historical conditions, the work and the priority of the Party in different historical periods were not the same, but whether as a Party that leads the people's revolution, or as a Party that leads the socialist construction for the people, the political standpoint of the Chinese

2   Selected Works of Marx and Engels, 2nd Edition, Vol.1, p.283.
3   Selected Works of Mao Zedong, 2nd Edition, Vol.3, p.1004.

Communist Party, which is on behalf of the fundamental interests of the overwhelming majority of the Chinese people has never wavered, and the purpose of serving the people wholeheartedly has never changed. These history can be summed up by an important conclusion that the Chinese Communist Party has won the support of the people because it always represents the development requirements of China's advanced productive forces, the advance direction of China's advanced culture, the fundamental interests of the Chinese people at large in various historical periods of revolution, construction and reform, and unremittingly struggle for the realization of the fundamental interests of the state and the people through the formulation of correct policies and policies. The Communist Party of China has always been practicing for the purpose of serving the people. For the past 90 years, our Party has won the trust and love of the people and has gained the support from the people by its purpose and practice of serving the people.

3. The Party is built for the public and it exercises state power for the people

The basic embodiment of the "People-oriented" refers to that the Party is built for the public and it exercises state power for the people. Being built for the public and exercising state power for the people is the essential characteristic of the Communist Party of China, the consistent thought that our Party has always adhered to in the long-term revolution and construction and the practical embodiment of the fundamental purpose of the Communist Party of China's serving the people wholeheartedly. Being built for the public is the whole theory, program, route, policy and work of the Party, which should reflect the common interests of the state and the nation, and reflect the common wishes and demands of the whole people. Exercising state power for the people is to say that after the Party has obtained the political power, it will adhere to serving the people wholeheartedly, and use the state power to make the best interests for the people, so that the overwhelming majority of the people can fully enjoy the progress of social development and the achievements of modern civilization. Being built for the public shows that our Party is from the people, rooted in the people, serving the people and representing the interests of the people, and except for the interests of the people, the Party has no special interests of its own. Exercising state power for the people determines that the object of our Party's service can only be the largest masses of the people, and cannot be a part of the people or a minority.

The fact that the Party is built for the public and it exercises state power for the people is decided by people's historical principal status, the nature of the socialist state power, and also by the Communist Party of China's retaining the true qualities of the Marxist political parties. The Marxist political Party distinguishes itself from all other political parties in that it represents the interests of the vast majority of people, and takes realizing communism as its lofty ideals, therefore, all the theory and struggle of Marxist political parties are committed to realizing the fundamental interests of the majority of the people, which is also the most distinctive political position of Marxism. Marx and Engels have clearly pointed out at the very beginning of the establishment of scientific socialism: The Communists, they have no interests separate and apart from those of the proletariat as a whole.[4]

In this regard, the party's position has always been unwavering and consistent. Mao Zedong pointed out: "The Communist Party is a political party which works in the interests of the nation and people and which has absolutely no private ends to pursue."[5]

In the new historical period, Deng Xiaoping further pointed out: "The meaning or task of the Chinese communists, if to speak in broad terms, is only two sentences: serving the people wholeheartedly and taking the interests of the people as the highest standard for every party member."[6]

It is also required that the whole Party should take whether the people are supportive, approving, happy, and willing or not as the starting point and the purpose of formulating all policies. Jiang Zemin has repeatedly emphasized: We must always take what reflects the will and interests of the people as both our starting point and end point in all work we do; we must always take reliance on the wisdom and strength of the people as the basic line of work in promoting our cause.[7]

"Our party always upholds that the interests of the people are above everything. Apart from the interests of the overwhelming majority of the people, the party has no special interests of its own. All party work must be based on the fundamental interests of the overwhelming majority of the people, as its highest standard."[8]

Party General Secretary Hu Jintao also pointed out: "Who do we represent, who do we rely on, and who we are is the key, whether or not we always stand firmly on the position of the overwhelming majority of the people is the watershed between the concept of historical materialism and the idealist view of history, as well as the yardstick for judging Marxist political parties. As a Marxist ruling party, we should always uphold the principle that the Party was founded for the public good and that it exercises state power for the people. We must always make realizing, safeguarding

4   Selected Works of Marx and Engels, 2nd Edition, Vol.1, p.285.
5   Selected Works of Mao Zedong, 2nd Edition, Vol.3, p.809.
6   Selected Works of Deng Xiaoping, 2nd Edition, Vol.1, p.257, Beijing, People's Publishing House, 1994.
7   Jiang Zemin: On the Three Represents, p.152, Beijing, Central Literature Publishing House, 2001.
8   Ibid., p.162.

and developing the fundamental interests of the overwhelming majority of the people the starting point and goal of all the work of the Party and country, and to give full play to the enthusiasm of all the people in developing advanced productive forces and advanced socialist culture."[9]

For this reason, the Communist Party of China has always regarded the people's cause as the most important. Whether in the revolutionary years or in the construction and reform era, the Communist Party of China has always with the noble character of selfless led the people to strive for the rejuvenation of the Chinese nation and the lofty ideals of communism. At present, the Chinese nation is committed to the great cause of building socialism with Chinese characteristics. The fundamental task of socialist construction in our country is to further emancipate the productive forces, develop productive forces, and gradually realize socialist modernization, and to this end, reform the aspects and segments in the production relations and superstructure that are not adapted to the development of productive forces. Therefore, the Communist Party of China has established the development as the first task of the Party in governing and rejuvenating the country. Whether it is conducive to the development of the productive forces of the socialist society, whether it is conducive to the enhancement of the comprehensive national strength of the socialist country, and whether it is conducive to raising the standard of the living standards of the people have become the inspection standard of the Party's work. The Party has led the national people to build socialism with Chinese characteristics, that is, to strive for the unity of the lofty ideal and the interests of the most people, to adhere to the consistency of the work of the Party and the realization of the interests of the people, and to maintain the consistency of safeguarding the people's rights and interests and promoting the all-round development of the people, so as to achieve that the development is for the people, the development relies on the people, and development results are shared by the people.

The Communist Party of China upholds the Marxist view of the masses, adheres to the purpose of serving the people wholeheartedly, and always takes the realization and maintenance of the fundamental interests of the vast majority of the people as the fundamental basis of the Party's theory, route, guideline, policy and all work. The Communist Party of China is always deeply rooted in the people, and unremittingly struggle for the fundamental interests of the Chinese people and the Chinese nation. The new democratic revolution, the socialist revolution and construction, and the Reform and Opening up were all done in order to conform to the people's will and realize the interests of the people. In the practice of building

---

9   CPCCC Party Literature Research Office: "Selection of Important Literature since the 16th National Congress" (Vol. I), p.369, Central Literature Publishing House, 2008.

socialism with Chinese characteristics, the Party and the state propose such major tasks as adhering to People-Oriented, realizing scientific development, building a socialist harmonious society, building new socialist countryside, and building a new and innovative country, in order to conform with the wishes of the people and realize the interests of the people. Except for the fundamental interests of the overwhelming majority of the people, the Communist Party of China has no special interests of its own, and the whole task and responsibility of the Party is to lead the broad masses to realize their own interests. All the work of the Party, after all, is done in order to achieve, maintain and develop the fundamental interests of the majority of the people. Adhering to the principle of "people-oriented", we should uphold that the Party is built for the public and it exercises state power for the people, always make it a reality that the government must function by the mandate of the people, empathize with the feelings of the people, and work for the well-being of the people, always regard the fundamental interests of the vast majority of the people as the highest standard of all work, as the basic starting point and the foothold for the development of socialism with Chinese characteristics.

4. The development is for the people and dependent on the people, and the development results are shared by the people

That the development is for the people and dependent on the people, and the development results are shared by the people is the most fundamental requirements and principles of "People-oriented". In the report of the 17th National Congress of the Communist Party of China, When Hu Jintao spoke of "People-oriented", he stressed that we should always take achieving, maintaining and developing the fundamental interests of the people at large as the starting point and goal of all the work of the Party and the state. "Development for the people, development depending on the people and the development results shared by the people" is a perfect interpretation of the starting point and the foothold of the "People-oriented" development of socialism with Chinese characteristics, which reflects directly and vividly the realistic requirements of the Party and the state to lead the national people to build socialism with Chinese characteristics.

Adhering to "People-oriented" is to put solving the people's vital interests in the first place. Therefore, in the process of administering the country, the Party should fully reflect and represent the wishes of the people, adhere to the principle that the development is for the people and dependent on the people, and the development results are shared by the people, and constantly let the people get real benefits in the socialist development, and make the whole people move steadily towards common prosperity.

Adhering to the principle that the development is for the people is to make achieving, maintaining and developing the fundamental interests of the people at large as the fundamental starting point and purpose of all the guidelines and policies of the Party and the state, to measure all decisions with whether the people are supportive or not, approving or not, pleased or not and agree or not, to achieve the purpose of development by meeting the needs of the people, achieving the interests of the people and improving the living standards of the people. This requires the Party and the state to fully reflect and safeguard the interests of the people in all aspects of economic and social development and in all its work. Economic construction should focus on creating more rich social material wealth, constantly improving people's life and improving the living standards of the people. Political construction should focus on safeguarding the rights and legitimate rights and interests of the people, and constantly developing socialist democracy and improving the socialist legal system. Cultural construction should focus on satisfying the spiritual and cultural needs of the people, improving the quality of spiritual life of the people, enriching people's spiritual world and enhancing the spiritual strength of people. Social construction should focus on coordinating the interests of all parties, enhancing the creative vitality of the whole society, and constantly building a harmonious society, in which all the people could do their best and each is in a proper place.

Adhering to that the development relies on the people is to respect the subjective status and initiative of the people, closely contact the masses, always believe in the masses, firmly rely on the masses, and fully mobilize the enthusiasm, initiative and creativity of the people, to maximize the wisdom and strength of the whole society, to mobilize and organize the hundreds of millions of people into the great cause of socialism with Chinese characteristics. Socialism is an unprecedented great cause, and it is obviously rather difficult to carry out the construction of socialism in a country with more than 1.3 billion people and relatively backward productivity. The cause of socialism with Chinese characteristics can only be achieved with the wholehearted support of the people. The various policy and work plans of the Party and the state can be effectively implemented only with the sincere support of the people. We should give full play to the great wisdom and creativity contained in the people, in this way, the reform and construction of our country will obtain the most widely and reliable mass foundation and the most profound source of strength. We should also arouse and mobilize the enthusiasm of all sectors, unite people of all sectors of the society who contribute prosperity and strength to the motherland, encourage their entrepreneurial spirit, protect their legitimate rights and interests, commend the outstanding ones, bring the will, wisdom and strength of the whole nation into the great cause, and make it an inexhaustible force for the continuous development of the socialist cause with Chinese characteristics.

In the revolutionary era, the Communist Party of China firmly relied on the people, and achieved the victory of the revolution, and the mass line was the magic weapon of the Party's victory. In the period of socialist construction and Reform and Opening-up, the Party still needs to adhere to the mass line of coming from the masses and going to the masses, to firmly establish the views that the people are the creators of history, we should learn from the people with an open mind, serve the interests of the vast majority of the people, and we should also keep in mind that the power of the cadres is the given by the people, and the responsibility for the Party is consistent with responsibility for the people. We should effectively change the way of thinking and work style, constantly go down deeply to the grassroots, go deep among the masses, go deep into the realities of life, conscientiously do the investigation and research, timely discover and summarize the fresh experience created by the people, and resolutely prevent and overcome formalism and bureaucratism. We should conscientiously improve the Party's leadership and methods of leadership, adhere to and improve the system of linking the masses and other various systems, broaden the channels to reflect the social conditions and public opinion, and guarantee the rights of the people to be masters of their own affairs.

Adhering to the principle that the development results are shared by the people is to have the achievement of all aspects of the reform and development reflected in the continuous improvement of people's quality of life and health, reflected in the continuous improvement of the ideological and moral quality and scientific and cultural quality of the people, reflected in the full protection of the economic, political, cultural, social and other aspects of the rights and interests of the people, so that the fruits of economic and social development benefits all the people. Adhering to the principle that the development results are shared by the people is the concrete embodiment and ultimate purpose of developing for the people and relying on the people. If the fruits of development are not or are rarely enjoyed by the vast majority of the people, developing for the people will come to naught, and development relying on the people will be without foundation. Throughout the process of Reform and Opening up and modernization, people must benefit from the noticeable and visible material benefits, which grow with the development of the economy, and we should make efforts to make workers, farmers, intellectuals and other people enjoy the fruits of economic and social development. We should strive to achieve common prosperity, not the other way round, which is the essence of socialism.

Since the 3rd Plenary Session of the 11th Central Committee of the Party, China has achieved fruitful results in the Reform and Opening up, the people's livelihood in general has reached a well-off level, the income of urban and rural residents has steadily increased, the mass living quality of the people has been continuously improved, the spiritual and cultural life has become more and more colorful, various rights and interests have been protected by law, and the enthusiasm of the masses of people to join the Reform and Opening up and modernization drive has greatly improved. At the same time, it should be soberly noticed that with the in-depth development of socialist market economy and the profound changes of social structure, different regions and departments, different groups and individuals differ in the enjoyment of the fruits of economic and social development, the degree of improvement of material and cultural life is also different. Employment, income distribution, social security, medical treatment, children's schooling, ecological environment protection, safe production, social security and other issues have become hot issues for the broad masses of the people. If the people's livelihood problems are not solved effectively, they will not be conducive to the maximum stimulation and mobilization of the enthusiasm of the masses of the people, and will affect the economic and social development, and finally affect the overall stability and unity. This requires the Party and the state to start with the most concerned, direct and realistic interests of the people, effectively expand employment and improve social security, do everything possible to increase employment opportunities and speed up the improvement of the social security system commensurate with the level of economic development, and constantly expand its coverage. Vigorously develop the education, conscientiously do the work of

ensuring compulsory education, increase the investment in rural compulsory education, resolutely rectify the phenomenon of arbitrary charges in the field of education, and effectively reduce the burden of education of the masses. Earnestly improve the public health service, actively promote the new rural cooperative medical system, promote the development of urban community medical treatment, and gradually solve the problem of difficult and expensive medical treatment of the masses. Vigorously strengthen the construction of social security prevention and control system, combat various criminal activities according to the law, resolutely safeguard social stability, and effectively guarantee the safety of people's lives and property. Earnestly do the work of safety production, strictly implement the safety production responsibility system, strengthen the supervision over food, medicine, catering hygiene and traffic safety, and reverse the frequent occurrence of accidents as soon as possible. Further improve the animal epidemic prevention and control system, and effectively guarantee the life and health safety of the people. Correctly handle the contradictions among the people and resolutely safeguard the legitimate rights and interests of the masses. Implement reasonable demands of the people without discount, and when the objective conditions are not available, make clear and thorough persuasion and education to guide the masses to correctly understand the relationship between individual interests and collective interests, local interests and the interests of the whole, as well as the current interests and the long-term interests.

Second, adhering to the principal status of the people

1. People are the main body of building socialism with Chinese characteristics

Adhering to People-oriented, is to uphold and respect the main status of the people. In contemporary China, the people are the main body of building socialism with Chinese characteristics, and socialism with Chinese characteristics is the cause of the people. Only by adhering to People-Oriented, fully giving play to the role of the people in building socialism with Chinese characteristics, can the cause of socialism with Chinese characteristics flourish.

The practical activity of the people is the real motive force of the historical development, and it is the material wealth and spiritual wealth created by the people that provide the motive power for the constant change and progress of the society. From the beginning, Marxism believed that all human history should start from the individual with life, the production of consumption goods is the "first historical activity" of human being, and the "basic condition" of all history. Only from the production practice can we solve the fog of social development, and the main body of production practice-people, is the main body of social development. The development direction of social history represents the intention and wishes of the overwhelming majority of the people, and only the social historical activities that represent the interests of the masses can be successful. Marxism has always emphasized and fully affirmed the dominant position of the people. Marx has pointed out clearly in his book *The Holy Family*: "history is nothing but the activity of man pursuing his aims... Together with the thoroughness of the historical action, the size of the mass whose action it is, will therefore increase."[10]

Lenin also repeatedly stressed: "It is the majority of the people who decide the historical outcome,"[11] "the great majority, whose energy and initiative plays crucial role in creating socialism."[12]

The theory and practice of scientific socialism have fully proved that the victory of the revolution and construction can only be achieved by adhering to people's principal status in them.

171

---

10   Complete Works of Marx and Engels, First Chinese edition, Volume 2, p.104, Beijing, People's Publishing House, 1957.
11   Complete Works of Lenin, 2nd Chinese Edition, Vol.43, p.92, Beijing, People's Publishing House, 1987.
12   Complete Works of Lenin, 2nd Chinese Edition, Vol.33, p.53, Beijing, People's Publishing House, 1985.

The Communist Party of China has always believed in the decisive role of the people, and the leaders of the past dynasties also have unique insights and explanation on the subject of the people. The first generation of the central leadership of the Party with Mao Zedong as the core not only inherited the traditional Marxist writers' attention to the people, but also made a penetrating interpretation of the role of the people in the Chinese revolution and construction based on the reality of the Chinese revolution and construction. Mao Zedong once vividly compared the image of the people to "God" in the Seventh Party Congress's closing speech, "The Foolish Old Man", saying that people was the "root" of the Chinese revolution, stressing that without the decisive role of the people, China could not have won the war of resistance against Japan, and the struggle against Kuomintang reactionaries and could not have won the new-democratic revolution either. That was true. Because all the revolutionary struggles led by the Chinese Communist Party is in line with the wishes of the people and conform to the trend of the historical development of China, we can organize and arouse the people, fully exert their principal status, and make the socialist new China finally stand in the east of the world.

After the 3rd Plenary Session of the 11th Central Committee of the Party, China has entered a new period of new Reform and Opening up and a new period of the construction of socialist modernization. Under the new historical conditions, our Party has further practiced and enriched the thought of the principal status of the people. Our Party put forward that the people is not only the practice subject of building socialism, but also the main body to enjoy the development results, its principal status is all-round. In the previous process of building socialism and during the period of "Cultural Revolution", we did not respect the masses and guide the people to exercise the main role in promoting social progress, as a result, we violated the will of the people and deviated from the socialist track. The people had not received any tangible benefits and tangible interests, and the status of their socialist ownership was not reflected at all. After the implementation of the socialist market economy, the people can fully demonstrate their own potential and ability, and can better contribute to the socialist construction under the correct economic operation mechanism, at the same time, they will feel and experience the enormous improvement and wealth of their life brought by the development of socialist market economy. Therefore, Deng Xiaoping advocated that the people, subject of socialism, inject permanent vitality into the socialist market economy, and we should respect knowledge, respect talent, respect labor, respect the masses, closely combine the "Three Favorables" with the aspirations and demands of the people, and take "whether people are supportive or not", "whether people agree or not", "whether people are happy or not", and "whether people say yes or no" as the starting point and destination to consider all problems, and fully embody the principal status of the people in the new stage of the development of socialism with Chinese characteristics.

The third generation of the central leadership of the Party, with Jiang Zemin as the core, deepened and expanded the theory of Marxism on the principal status of the people, standing at the new historical height and endowing the people with more distinctive characteristics of the times and more profound ideological connotation. We should organically combine the historical materialism view of the people's principal status with the Party's construction theory, scientifically recognize the internal relations between the principal status of the people and the fundamental purpose of the Party, constantly strengthen and improve the Party's construction, improve the Party's ability of ant-corrosion and risk- resisting, ensure the effectiveness, direction and correctness of the Party leadership, and lay a solid leadership foundation for the people to gain more and better interests after devoting themselves to the cause of the socialist construction with Chinese characteristics. As Jiang Zemin said: "Our party must always represent the fundamental interests of the overwhelming majority of the Chinese people, means that in its theory, line, program, principles, policies and all its work, it must persevere in taking the fundamental interests of the people as its starting point and objective, give full expression to the people's enthusiasm, initiative and creativity, and enable the people to constantly obtain tangible economic, political and cultural benefits on the basis of social development and progress."[13]

This has developed Deng Xiaoping's theory of the socialist goal of "achieving common prosperity finally". With the improvement of the overall quality of the people and the relatively comprehensive development, the people can play their main role and accelerate the realization of socialist modernization in China. Attaching importance to the combination of the principal status of the people and the promotion of the quality of the people and the all-round development of the people illustrates our Party's precise grasp and profound understanding of the people's principal status, and endows the people with a more comprehensive connotation under the new historical conditions.

The report of the Seventeenth National Congress of the Communist Party of China clearly pointed out that only by resolutely safeguarding the principal status of the people, can we thoroughly carry out the scientific outlook on development and achieve a new victory in building a well-off society in an all-round way. The people are the main body of the development of socialist market economy, the main body of advancing the advanced socialist culture, the main body of accelerating the social construction, the main

13   Selected Works of Jiang Zemin, Vol.3, p.279.

body of improving the socialist democratic politics, and also the strong backing and main support of our complete motherland unification and the new great project of building the Party. We must adhere to the people-oriented, firmly carry out the basic purpose of serving the people wholeheartedly, and contribute all the struggle and work to the people finally.

In a word, socialism with Chinese characteristics is the cause of all Chinese people, and it is an unprecedented huge historical project. The Communist Party of China has achieved the great victory of the socialist cause with Chinese characteristics precisely because of its giving full play to the main role of the people. Adhering to the principal status of the people is the fundamental guarantee of the continuous development of socialism with Chinese characteristics.

2. Give full play to the people's initiative

To adhere to the people-oriented and respect the main status of the people, the most fundamental is to give full play to the people's initiative, which is the primary condition for building socialism with Chinese characteristics. The report of the Seventeenth National Congress of the Communist Party of China stressed that we should respect the status of the people and give full play to the people's initiative. On the one hand, all the Party's struggle and work are for the benefit of the people, and at any time and in any circumstance, the fundamental interests of the overwhelming majority of the people should be put at the top priority, and we should adhere to the principle of developing for the people and by the people, and the development results are shared by the people; On the other hand, the tasks proposed by our Party depend on the hard work of the masses. This requires that we closely contact the masses, fully mobilize the enthusiasm, initiative and creativity of the people, maximize the wisdom and strength of the whole society, mobilize and organize the millions of people into the great cause of socialism with Chinese characteristics.

Social development is dependent on the people. It is the wisdom and creation of millions of people fighting in their posts that has made varieties of civilization in human history. History is not the creation of some or some heroic characters, but the product of the life practice of the people. The Communist Party of China deeply understands the essence of historical materialism, and always believes that the fundamental task of socialism is to develop, that the development is for the people, that development needs people's initiative spirit, and that give full play to people's initiative in the great practice of Reform and Opening up and socialist modernization. In the construction of the great cause of socialism with Chinese characteristics, the leadership of the Party and the play of the people's initiative are closely related and inseparable. While constantly mobilizing the initiative and enthusiasm of the people to build socialism with Chinese characteristics, the Party should also pay comprehensive attention to fostering, supporting the social development of our country, guiding and encouraging the people to play their creativity, which is the general guiding principle of the Party in the work of giving full play to the people's initiative. Therefore, respecting the status of the people and giving full play to the people's initiative have made a high demand for the leadership and organizational capacity of the Party itself. Therefore, we must comprehensively promote the new great project of building the Party with the spirit of reform and innovation, arm the whole Party with the latest achievements of Marxism in China, strengthen the Party's construction at the grass-roots level, do well in the Party's democratic construction, strengthen the Party's ruling ability, conscientiously better the Party's style of work and improve the Party cadres' sense of self-discipline and corruption-resisting. Only in this way, can we guarantee the full play of the people's initiative.

In short, to give full play to the people's initiative is the inevitable requirement of the great cause of building socialism with Chinese characteristics. It is not only the objective basis and strength source of our economic, political, cultural and social construction, but also the experience of our development for many years. From the perspective of summing up experience, there are two basic reasons for the success of our Reform and Opening up: one is that the masses of the people fully play the role of the principal status, and the other is that the Party has fully played a leading role. The correct leadership of the Party and the practice of the people together determine the economic and social development and the progress of political culture in our country for the past 30 years. The series of guidelines and policies formulated by our Party since the 3rd Plenary Session of the 11th Central Committee of the Communist Party of China have been proved correct, but this series of correct guidelines and policies are not created out of thin air, but are formed by our Party's insistence on combining the basic tenets of Marxism with the practice of hundreds of millions of people, and the insistence on respecting the initiative of the masses and scientifically summing up the practical experience of the people. Deng Xiaoping repeatedly mentioned this point. He said: "It was the peasants who invented the household contract responsibility system with remuneration linked to output. Many of the good ideas in rural reform came from people at the grass roots. We processed them and raised them to the level of guidelines for the whole country."[14]

---

14 Selected Works of Deng Xiaoping, 1st edition, Vol.3, p.382

"If the Central Committee made any contribution in this respect, it was only by laying down the correct policy of invigorating the domestic economy."[15]

Summing up the experience of Reform and Opening up, we should not only see the role of the Party, but also the role of the people. The report of the 17th National Congress of the Communist Party of China (CPC) took the respect for the people's initiative spirit and strengthening and improving the leadership of the Party as the successful experience of the Reform and Opening up, which was a deep revelation of the successful experience of the Reform and Opening up in our country.

In the new period, fully mobilizing the masses of the people to give full play to their pioneering spirit should be reflected in various fields.

First of all, we should combine respecting the people's initiative with the leadership of the Party, which should be reflected in the construction of socialist democratic politics. We should realize the new ideological emancipation, continue to focus on improving the Party's style of work and promote the reform of the political system. To strengthen and improve the Party's style of work and to ensure the flesh and blood relationship between the Party and the people is the necessary requirement to respect and bring into play the initiative of the people. Since the 3rd Plenary Session of the 11th Central Committee of the Party, the Party's style of work has been generally good through our strengthening our own construction. At the same time, we should clearly see that there are still some negative phenomena and problems affecting the relations between the Party and the masses in the Party. For some Party organizations and Party cadres, they have some severe problems in the form of formalism and bureaucracy, falsification, exaggeration, autocratic, slack attitude and so on. If these problems exist and develop, the leading cadres of our Party members will not be able to hear the voices of the masses and respect the practice and creation of the masses, which will certainly undermine the relationship between the Party the masses and the relationship between the masses and the carders, dampening the enthusiasm of the people to join the reform and construction, not to mention respecting the people's initiative. In the new historical starting point, if our Party is to seize the new victory of Reform and Opening up and socialist modernization, we must insist on building the Party for the public, govern for the people, widely spread truth and pragmatism, learn from the masses with an open mind, understand the wishes of the masses in depth, widely collect the wisdom of the masses, make decisions and work for the demands of the reality and the masses, not from the books or from our own head; We should unswervingly develop socialist democratic politics, effectively guarantee the right of the people to be the masters of

15 Selected Works of Deng Xiaoping, 1st edition, Vol.3, p.238.

their own affairs, maximize the enthusiasm of the masses to innovate, make full release of the creativity of the whole society, and make the innovation achievements constantly emerge, so as to make socialism with Chinese characteristics more colorful, attractive and appealing.

Secondly, we should combine respecting people's initiative with the Party's leadership in the construction of socialist market economy, and continue to establish and improve the exploration and implementation of socialist market economic system. The socialist market economy system, as a major innovation of the Party on Marxism, its establishment and development itself embodies the unity of the people's initiative spirit and the leadership of the Party, and its further improvement depends on our combining respecting the people's initiative with strengthening and improving the Party's leadership. The "Decision of the CPC Central Committee and the Central Government on Several Issues Concerning the Establishment of a Socialist Market Economy" passed by the 3rd Plenary Session of the 14th Central Committee of the Party in 1993, explicitly stated: "we must respect the pioneering spirit of the masses and attach importance to the vital interests of the masses. We must sum up the new experiences created by the masses, respect the will of the masses, guide the enthusiasm of the masses well, so that they can play their role."[16]

While respecting the principal status of the people and giving full play to their pioneering spirit, we must attach great importance to the advanced nature of the Communist Party members, give full play to the exemplary role of the Communist Party members, strengthen the correct guidance over the masses, and achieve the unity of advanced nature and mass character of the party.

Only by ensuring that the Party can correctly combine maintaining the correctness of its leadership and the people's initiative through the Party building, can socialist market economy system be continuously full of vitality in the combined force of the people's initiative and the Party's vanguard role.

Thirdly, we should combine respecting the people's initiative with the leadership of the Party in the construction of socialist advanced culture, adhere to the "Double Hundred" policy, form a good environment to encourage innovation and encourage exploration, and create good conditions for respecting and giving full play to the people's initiative. The "Double Hundred" policy, the basic guideline of our Party's guiding scientific and cultural development, embodies the Party's ideological line of emancipating the mind and seeking truth from facts. Its essence is to effectively protect people's freedom of academic exploration and artistic creation, and

16   CPCCC Party Literature Research Office: "Selection of Important Literature since the 16th National Congress" (Vol. I), p.522.

embody the law of socialist cultural development, which is consistent with respecting and developing the people's initiative spirit. Since the 3rd Plenary Session of the 11th Central Committee of the Party, our Party has corrected the "left" mistakes, restored and developed the "Double Hundred" policy, and greatly promoted the development of the socialist culture with Chinese characteristics. With the development of our society, the trend of social consciousness diversification constantly presents itself, and the development of modern communication science and technology, especially the emergence of the internet, makes the diversity of social consciousness quickly and conveniently expressed and disseminated. Under the guidance of Marxism, we must conform to the historical trend of building socialism with Chinese characteristics, more consciously and actively carrying out the "Double Hundred" policy and promoting the ideological emancipation, cultural development and academic prosperity.

Finally, we should combine respecting the people's initiative with the leadership of the Party in the construction of a socialist harmonious society, thoroughly implement the scientific concept of development and promote the development of a harmonious society as soon as possible. Since the Reform and Opening up, China's society has developed diversification development trends in economic composition, organization form, employment mode, interest subject and distribution pattern, which is not only in line with the objective law of economic and social development, but also brings challenges to social harmony. Especially in the key stage of China's reform and development, because of the deepening of reform and the adjustment of interest pattern, our social contradictions will further highlight itself, therefore, how to promote social harmony has become an urgent problem to be solved. The promotion of social harmony is not to negate the diversification of interests, but to balance the various interests, so that all the people can do their best and play their proper roles. We should adhere to combining respecting people's initiative with the leadership of the Party, so that all the creative desire for social progress can be respected, the creative energy can be supported, the creative ability can be exerted, the creation achievements could be affirmed, and all aspects of the initiative can be mobilized to the maximum extent, so that all the people can do their best and play their proper roles, which has important significance for the realization of social integration and the promotion of social harmony.

In conclusion, to promote the construction of a well-off society in a comprehensive way and realize the sound development of economy, society, politics and culture, we must fully give play to the initiative spirit of the people under the premise of strengthening the Party's leadership and construction, and guarantee a steady flow of vitality and vigor for the smooth conduct of the socialist cause with Chinese characteristics.

3. To achieve, maintain and develop the fundamental interests of the majority of the people

The Communist Party of China comes from the people and roots in the people, and all the struggle and work of the Party is for the benefit of the people. Achieving, maintaining and developing the fundamental interests of the majority of the people is the starting point and ultimate goal of all the work of the Party and the state, the fundamental purpose of building socialism with Chinese characteristics, and the fundamental requirement of People-oriented.

The interests of the most people are decisive factors for the development of the Party and the national cause. Serving the people wholeheartedly, establishing the Party for the public and ruling for the people is the fundamental difference between our Party and all the exploiting class parties. The Communist Party of China leads the people's revolution, construction and reform in order to liberate and develop the productive forces. The Party platform adopted by the First National Congress of the Party affirms that our Party strives for the complete liberation of all mankind. The Seventh National Congress of the Party explicitly included "serving the Chinese people wholeheartedly" into the Party constitution and made it to the height of "the Party's sole purpose". Since then, the Party constitution adopted by the various congresses of the Party has adhered to this purpose, and stipulated that the Communist Party of China is a faithful representative of the interests of the Chinese people of all ethnic groups. Such words as "representing the fundamental interests of the overwhelming majority of the Chinese people" and "representing the fundamental interests of the overwhelming majority of the Chinese people" are not only written in the Party constitution of the Chinese Communist Party, but also in the practice of the Party for decades. All the struggle of the Communist Party of China is in the final analysis for the fundamental interests of the overwhelming majority of the people. Therefore, all the work of the Party must be based on the fundamental interests of the overwhelming majority of the people. At any time, we must adhere to the unity of respect for the law of social development and respect for the historical principal status of the people, adhere to the unity of striving for the lofty ideal and the seeking the interests of the majority of the people, and adhere to the unity of all the work of the Party and the realization of the interests of the people. In the process of the construction of the great socialist cause with Chinese characteristics, the interests of the majority of the people are always related to the overall situation of the Communist Party of China, to the overall development of the national economic and political culture, and always related to the unity of the people of all ethnic groups and the overall social stability of the whole country. Only by truly taking the interests of the most people fully into account, can we win the hearts of the people, withstand trials, overcome difficulties, and achieve the ultimate victory of socialist construction.

In contemporary China, with the deepening of Reform and Opening up and the development of socialist market economy, there inevitably appeared a diversity of the material interests and different requirements of interests. How to deal with the interests of all aspects of the people and solve the various interest conflicts of the society is the fundamental task for the Communist Party of China to face in the long run. In the practice of dealing with social interests and contradictions, our Party has summed up and adhered to the following basic principles:

First, the fundamental standpoint is the fundamental interests of the overwhelming majority of the Chinese people. This is the inevitable requirement of the Party to serve the basic purpose of serving the people under the condition of being in power. In order to truly represent the fundamental interests of the overwhelming majority of the people, our Party must focus on dealing with three relationships. The first is to correctly handle the relationship between the diversification of interests and the fundamental interest. In the formulation and implementation of the Party's policy, the basic focus is to represent the fundamental interests of the overwhelming majority of the people, correctly reflect and balance the interests of different classes and different aspects of the interests of the masses, so that the entire people are in the direction of common prosperity. The second is to correctly handle the relationship between local and global interests, consciously give greater importance to the overall situation, and the local obeys to the whole. The third is to correctly handle the relationship between the current interests and long-term interests. Reforms have benefited the vast majority of people, but have also temporarily affected certain groups' interests, which is difficult to avoid. Therefore, in the process of reform, we should pay attention to the sufferings of the masses of the people, help them overcome the temporary difficulties, combine caring for the masses with the correct understanding of the reform, correctly unify and combine the current interests with the long-term interests, and promote the reform unswervingly.

Second, properly handle and balance the interests of different classes and different aspects of the interests of the masses. At present, China is in the critical period of reform and the key period of the development of modernization, the social economic components, the diversification of economic interests, the diversification of people's way of life and the diversification of employment positions and forms of employment make the various interests and contradictions complicated. As the ruling Party, the policy of the Communist Party of China should fully reflect and manifest the interests of various aspects, and win the support of the masses of the society to the maximum extent, so as to better strengthen the ruling social foundation and consolidate the ruling position. The Party should attach great importance to and safeguard the most realistic, most important and immediate interests of the people, so as to enable workers, peasants, intellectuals and other people to enjoy the fruits of economic and social development. The Party should resolutely safeguard the ownership of the working class, and seriously consider and take into account the interests of other strata and parties.

Third, to effectively solve the practical problems of the interests of the people. Caring for the masses and representing the interests of the masses is by no means an empty slogan and must be implemented very concretely to solve the practical problems of mass production and life. The Party demands that cadres at all levels must treat and deal with the issues put forward or reported by the people with enthusiasm, and must not be indifferent to the masses or even treat the masses harshly. We should go to the most difficult places, go to the place where the masses have the most opinions and go to places where the work is needed to be done to work hard with the cadres and the masses there to solve problems, resolve contradictions and get the ball rolling. Besides, we should care for the masses, especially the sufferings of the difficult masses, seek benefit for the overwhelming majority of the people, especially for the difficult people, because they are the most difficult at present and need help most. Furthermore, attention should be paid to those who have encountered difficulties temporarily in their work and life, putting their affairs on the agenda and focusing our attention on the solutions to ensure that their basic livelihood is guaranteed. In particular, the practical problems encountered by such people as laid-off workers, the rural poor and the urban poor must be effectively addressed.

Section II

Promoting the comprehensive development of people

First, promoting the comprehensive development of humans is the essence of Marxism in the construction of a new socialist society

1. Achieving the overall and comprehensive development of men is the most fundamental and highest social ideal and value goal of Marxism

The understanding of Marxism on socialism and communist society has always been the fundamental improvement and progress made by the development of man himself. The realization of all-round development of man is the essential feature that distinguishes communism and socialism from other social forms. In Marx's early works, communism is a movement, whose remarkable characteristic is the "return" to the human essence, positively sublating the private property, and striving for complete and comprehensive development of men in the new social system. In *Capital*, Marx once again demonstrated the importance of rebuilding the individual ownership on the basis of abolishing the bourgeois private ownership, and pointed out that the social system after capitalism would bring great space and realistic conditions to human development. Marx and Engels' vision and outlook for the future communist society also showed their great concern on the issue of human development, and believed that communist society was a combo of the free people, in which "the free development of everyone is the condition for the free development of all human beings". There, the class has completely disappeared, there are no three differences, labor is not to maintain the livelihood, but the first need of life, and people in the free and conscious labor process also developed themselves. Compared with capitalism, communism makes people no longer dependent on the matter, but emancipated from the shackles of the private ownership of the productive materials. People are able to obtain freedom under the social system of the productive materials, to work for the development and freedom, to carry out production and to live. All the characteristics of the communist society show the ultimate concern for human beings, whether the highly developed productive forces, the abnormal advanced economic, political, social system, or the prosperity and diversity of cultural life, are for the ultimate value goal of "human". In this sense, the realization of all-round development of man is the most fundamental and highest social ideal and value goal of Marxism.

2. Promoting the all-round development of people is the fundamental value goal of socialism with Chinese characteristics

For decades, whether in the revolutionary years or in the construction and reform era, generations of the members of Communist Party of China have kept taking up the work of the former generation in pursuit of the ultimate realization of great material wealth, huge improvement of the spiritual realm and the lofty communist ideal of the free and comprehensive development of everyone. But the realization of communism is a very long historical process and only on the basis of full and highly development of the socialist society can it be achieved. Socialist society is the primary form of communism, and China is still and for a long time will still be in the primary stage of socialism. Therefore, we should base ourselves on the reality that our country is and will be in the early stage of socialism, and unremittingly struggle to realize the basic program of the Party at the present stage. The all-round development of human beings is not only a historical process with different levels of realization in different stages of development, but also a value goal that should be pursued in the socialist society and finally realized in the communist society. Therefore, in the process of developing socialism with Chinese characteristics, we should always promote the all-round development of people as the fundamental value goal of building socialism with Chinese characteristics.

As early as 1978, Deng Xiaoping made it clear that our schools in China "are places for the training of competent personnel for socialist construction. Are there qualitative standards for such training? Yes, there are. They were stated by Comrade Mao Zedong: We should enable everyone who receives an education to develop morally, intellectually and physically and become a worker possessed of both socialist consciousness and a general education."[17]

Since then, new generations of people with lofty ideals, moral integrity, good education and a strong sense of discipline have become the basic standard for the Party and the state to cultivate comprehensively-developed socialist new generations. When we entered the 21st century, Jiang Zemin solemnly proclaimed in his speech to celebrate the 80th anniversary of the founding of the Communist Party of China, "We firmly believe in the basic principle of Marxism concerning the inevitability of human society towards communism."Communism can only be achieved on the basis of fully developed and highly developed socialist society. Communism will be a society in which material wealth is greatly enriched and abundant, the spiritual realm of the people is greatly enhanced, and everyone will enjoy all-round free and full development."[18]

"All undertakings to build socialism with Chinese characteristics, and in fact, everything that we do should aim not just at meeting people's immediate material and cultural needs, but also at improving the qualities of the people or achieving their all-round development. This is the essential requirement of Marxism regarding the building of a new socialist society. We will constantly advance the all-round development of human beings based on a higher level of the material and spiritual civilization of the socialist society."[19]

Shortly thereafter, in the report of the 16th National Congress of the Communist Party of China, the comprehensive development of human beings was identified as one of the important goals of building a well-off society in an all-round way. In October 2007, on the 17th National Congress of the Party, Hu Jintao again stressed the need to promote the all-round development of people in his expounding of the scientific development concept. Man is the decisive force in the productive forces. in the great process of building socialism with Chinese characteristics, we constantly improve the quality and ability of all aspects of the people, and promote the all-round development of people, which is the meaning of emancipating the productive forces and developing productive forces. Eliminating exploitation and polarization is to achieve the ultimate common prosperity, while liberating

---

17   Selected Works of Deng Xiaoping, 2nd edition, Vol. 2, p.103.
18   Selected Works of Jiang Zemin, Vol.3, p.293.
19   Ibid., p.294 and http://www.china.org.cn/e-speech/a.htm.

people from various social shackles is to create the necessary social conditions for the comprehensive development of human beings. Repeated emphasis and putting the promotion the comprehensive development of the people to the Communist Party of China's programmatic document for many times highlight the Party leaders' fundamental value of building socialism with Chinese characteristics.

Second, to achieve the comprehensive development of people is a long-term gradual process

1. The ultimate purpose and mission of socialism is to create social conditions for the realization of men's all-round comprehensive development

Today, the development of socialism is far beyond the original ideas made by the founders of Marxism. However, no matter how the concrete realization of socialism changes, the fundamental purpose and mission of socialism will not change, with the fundamental purpose of socialism being the realization the comprehensive development of man and the fundamental purpose and mission of socialist system to create social conditions for the all-round development of man. Because of our past serious mistakes in the understanding of the fundamental purpose and mission of socialism, the superiority of socialism cannot be truly reflected. Before the Reform and Opening up, because of the neglect of the development of productive forces, China deviated from the fundamental task of socialism, and made socialism in our country a poor socialism, which was unable to reflect the superiority of socialism. The Soviet Union attached great importance to the development of productivity and developed into a superpower next to the United States, but the superiority of its socialist system was not reflected either, and ultimately failed. This prompts people to ask the following questions: What are the fundamental purpose and mission of socialism? And what does socialism really rely on to show the world that it is more advanced and superior than capitalism?

With the deepening of our Party's understanding of the nature of socialism, the understanding of the fundamental purpose and mission of socialism is also becoming clear and scientific. We recognize not only that the essence of socialism is to liberate the productive forces, develop productive forces, eradicate exploitation, eliminate polarization, and ultimately achieve common prosperity, but also that the development of productive forces and the enhancement of the common prosperity are creating social conditions for the all-round development of people, because in the process of liberating and developing productive forces and gradually going towards the common prosperity, people will gradually get more free and more comprehensive development. This is the essential requirement of the new socialist society and the most fundamental superiority of socialism. With the deepening of the understanding of socialism, we also clearly see that one of the root causes of the failure of the Soviet socialist system is "only productive forces but no men's development", which means they only attached importance to the development of the productive forces and the economy, but neglect the interests of the people and the realization of their richness, and they ignored and even denied that man is the ultimate purpose of the socialist society. They put the emphasis on man as the" bourgeois human nature", which made it difficult for the people to feel the superiority of socialism and made it difficult to get the true support of the people. Because of this, our Party especially emphasizes and advocates that on the basis of the development of socialist material civilization and spiritual civilization, we should constantly promote the all-round development of people. The indicators used to measure the effectiveness of socialist construction include not only economic, political, cultural and social factors, but also the human development factors, but also the human development factors, thus and socialism should fully display its fundamental superiority over capitalism, that is, a socialist society is a real people-oriented society. Attaching great importance to the all-round development of people is the essential requirement of socialism with Chinese characteristics. Both relying on the people as the main body of socialist construction, and highlighting the importance of improving the comprehensive quality of the people are the basic experience and root that allow the construction of socialism with Chinese characteristics to continuously achieve success.

185

On the basis of summarizing the historical and practical experience of socialist construction, we realize that the fundamental purpose and mission of the construction of socialism with Chinese characteristics is to create social conditions for the all-round development of human beings. This requires us to resolutely carry out the Scientific Outlook on Development, work hard to build socialist market economy, socialist democratic politics, socialist advanced culture and harmonious socialist society, at the same time to vigorously promote material civilization, political civilization, spiritual civilization, ecological civilization and improve people's livelihood. We should insist on that everything is relied on the people and everything is for the people, achieving the mutual promotion of social development and human development, and creating the conditions for the realization of human freedom and comprehensive development. If we ignore or deny that the fundamental purpose and mission of socialism is to create conditions for the all-round development of human beings, we will deviate from the essential requirements of Marxism on the construction of a new socialist society and cannot truly and fully display the superiority of socialism.

2. Creating the social conditions for the all-round development of human beings is a historical process

The realization of the all-round development of man is a long-term and gradual process, which will be bound by the conditions of social economy, politics and culture, and cannot go beyond the specific stage of economic and social development. The level of economic, political and cultural development is a historical process that improves gradually, so the creation of the social conditions for all-round development is a historical process that progresses step by step, and the degree of human's all-round development is also a historical process that improves gradually. Under the leadership of the Communist Party of China, the Chinese people are committed to the great cause of building socialism with Chinese characteristics. In this great historical process, we need to create conditions of all aspects and strive to promote the all-round development of people.

First of all, we should provide a solid material foundation for the comprehensive development of human through the construction of socialist material civilization. Material production is the basic condition to realize the comprehensive development of man. Only through the development of social productive forces can the talents and potentials of human beings be brought into full play to create a comprehensive and rich relationship between man and the object world, to realize the universal possession of the natural and social relations by the members of the society, and to make mankind move from the realm of necessity to the realm of freedom. Achieving common prosperity is the essential requirement of socialism, and satisfying the growing material and cultural needs of the people is the fundamental goal of social and economic development. we should enable the whole nation to live a well-off life and move forward to a higher level constantly by means of economic construction. With the deepening and development of the Reform and Opening up and the modernization construction, we are to provide the society with increasingly rich material products and more and more perfect material facilities, to constantly improve people's conditions of eating, wearing, living, traveling, using and medical and health, and to constantly improve the quality of people's life. We should establish and improve the social security system to ensure that the people live and work in peace and contentment, and get social assistance when they are in trouble.

Secondly, the construction of socialist political civilization provides a strong political guarantee for the comprehensive development of human. The construction of democratic legal system is not only an important condition and guarantee for developing economy, building socialist spiritual civilization and realizing socialist modernization, but also an important content of socialist modernization construction. The fact that people are the masters of their own is the essential feature of socialism. Under the leadership of the Communist Party of China, we should continue to promote the reform of the political system, further expand the socialist democracy, improve the socialist legal system, and build socialist democratic politics with Chinese characteristics, constantly enhancing the vitality and vigor of the Party and the state. We should adhere to the general plan of ruling the country by law, maintain and safeguard the democratic rights of the people in accordance with the law, and constantly improve the ability and level of people's participation in political affairs. We should adhere to the regular, lasting and vivid publicity and education of observing the rules and the law, constantly improve the consciousness of all citizens to abide by the rules and the law, oppose the acts of extreme democratization and anarchy, and dare to combat the phenomenon of the violation of the Party discipline and the state laws in order to maintain the normal social order and good social environment, and ensure the smooth progress of the Reform and Opening up and the modernization construction. What's more, we ought to give full play to the subjective initiative and great creative spirit of the people to ensure that the people manage their own affairs in accordance with the law and realize their own wishes and interests. We must ensure that the people fully exercise their democratic elections, democratic decision-making, democratic management and democratic supervision, so that the people can really be the masters with power and status, and can be in a good mood and in high spirits. In this way, people's senses of mastership and pride are boosted and they could better devote themselves to the great cause of Reform and Opening up and modernization in our country.

Thirdly, the construction of socialist spiritual civilization provides intellectual guarantee and spiritual motivation for the comprehensive development of human. The superiority of socialism not only lies in that it can greatly liberate and develop the social productive forces, create a high material civilization, but also in that it can create a high spiritual civilization and ensure the all-round progress of society. Under the guidance of Marxism, we should vigorously strengthen the construction of socialist spiritual civilization, actively absorb the outstanding achievements of human civilization and the essence of our traditional culture, and with rich spiritual civilization construction results, we are to constantly meet people's growing demand for spiritual and cultural life, and to realize the comprehensive development of people's ideological and spiritual life. Through the construction of socialist core value system and the construction of civic morality, the ideological and moral quality of the people is constantly improved, providing a strong spiritual impetus for the socialist construction and the all-round development of our country. Through the implementation of the strategy of rejuvenating the country through science and education, the scientific and cultural qualities of the people are constantly enhanced, providing a strong intellectual support for the socialist construction and the all-round development of the people in our country.

Finally, to promote the all-round development of human beings, we must also strive to achieve harmony between people and the natural world, and strive to build ecological civilization. Man comes from nature, and is the product of the evolution of the material world. Man not only confirms himself in the transformation of nature, but also develops himself in the transformation of nature. Human development is inseparable from the nature, only in harmony with the nature can human society continue to develop, otherwise, the failure to respect the natural must result in natural retaliation. Therefore, we should firmly adhere to the guidance of the Scientific Outlook on Development, adhere to the path of production development, subsistence and ecological civilization, build a resource-efficient and environment-friendly society, achieve the unification of the speed, structural quality and benefits and the coordination of economic development with the population resource environment, enable the people to work and live in a good ecological environment, and achieve sustainable economic and social development.

CHAPTER SEVEN

Economic System of Socialism with Chinese Characteristics

Section I

Establishment and perfection of the socialist market economic system

First, establishing the socialist market economic system

At a certain stage of social and economic development, resources would always become scarce compared to people's needs which requires the scientific and rational allocation of limited and relatively scarce resources, and the production of the most suitable products and services so as to gain maximum benefits with the least resource consumption. Under the conditions of socialized large-scale production, there are mainly two modes of resource allocation: planned allocation and market allocation. The market economy, where resources are allocated through the market, first appears in the era of free-competition capitalism, based on the private ownership of the means of production, and the resources are allocated entirely by the "invisible hand", that is, the spontaneous regulation of the market, resulting in the anarchy of the entire social production as well as the promotion of economic development. Marx and Engels criticize this mode of allocation and points out that social labor and means of production are not reasonably arranged and effectively utilized, and serious economic crisis may occur. For this reason, Marx and Engels have elucidated on the inevitability of the market economy being replaced by a planned one.

After the October Revolution, military communism was practiced and the commodity-currency relations were canceled in Russia, which seriously weakened the economy of the country. Then Lenin realized that it was a policy mistake and resolutely suspended the practice. Instead, he implemented a new economic policy and resumed the exchange of commodities. After his death, the Soviet Union gradually established a highly centralized planned economic system, which played an active role under the historical conditions. For example, it enabled the Soviet Union to rapidly realize socialist industrialization and secured the country from the economic crisis in the 1930s. The socialist countries later concluded that planned economy, which was superior to the market economy, conformed to Marxism to the largest extent, and followed the example of the Soviet Union one after another.

After completing the socialist transformation, our country also gradually established a highly centralized planned economic system, drawing on the Soviet experience in many ways. But more importantly, we found it useful to solve the severe political and economic problems confronting the founding of New China to adopt such an economic system. Firstly, despite the low level of productive forces, the weak national economic strength and few modern industries in our country, the implementation of this system facilitated the direct participation of the state in economy and the expansion of the public economy, which further consolidated the regime. Secondly, in the context of the domestic economic dislocation and the big gap between us and the developed countries in the west, it was an effective way to stabilize the economy and maximize the industrial accumulation. Thirdly, this system was suitable for coordinating the various social problems that occurred in the macro-economy, because it could integrate resource allocation and social coordination, which would maintaina high level of employment, and satisfy the most basic living needs of the people, as well as maximize the accumulation and concentration of funds for the industrialization.

The highly centralized planned economy we adopted played an important positive role at the time: by centralizing manpower, material and financial resources, the construction of key national projects was guaranteed and the material foundation of socialism was established rapidly. However, with the completion of the initial tasks of socialism, the continuous expansion of the economy, and the increasingly complicated economic relations, the drawbacks of this economic system gradually became evident. In order to promote the development of the socialist economy, all the socialist countries, including China, had carried out economic reforms since the middle of the 20th century and explored the relationship between the plan and the market. In the late 1950s and early 1960s, based on the reality of the backward production of commodities in our country, Mao Zedong clearly pointed out that it was necessary to develop commodity production and make use of the rule and the law of value, which laid the foundation for the formation of our theory of socialist market economy. However, at that time, we failed to break through the traditional concept, and considered the economic system as the institutional attributes closely linked with the social system. Therefore, instead of breaking through the general framework of the planned economy, we merely strengthened the market regulation theoretically and practically, but failed to achieve desired results.

After the 3rd Plenary Session of the 11th Central Committee of the Communist Party of China, Deng Xiaoping led the Chinese Communist Party to sum up historic experiences. He pointed out that China must develop while adhering to the basic socialist system and must make fundamental changes to the original economic system. He said: "To develop the productive forces, the reform of the economic system is the only way forward."[1]

As a result, after 1978, China entered a new period of reform and opening up, with the market regulation mechanism playing a greater role, the price control over most commodities being gradually relaxed, the range under direct management of the plan gradually narrowed and the scope of market regulation continuously expanded. The practice of reform and opening up proved that when the market played a more important role, the economic vitality would be stronger and the development more rapid. The progress and achievements of the economic reform provided a practical basis for the formation and development of the socialist market economic theory. By summing up practical experience in the continuous exploration since the reform and opening up, Deng Xiaoping creatively put forward the theory of the socialist market economy and achieved major innovations in the socialist economic theory, which point out the direction for China's economic reform, and laid the foundation for our transformation from a highly centralized planned economy to the socialist market economy, and the establishment of a socialist market economic system.

The setting up of the socialist market economic system and Deng Xiaoping's theory on the development of the socialist market economy went through four stages.

The first stage: from 1978 to 1983, the thought of planned economy supplemented by the market regulation was put forward. After the 3rd Plenary Session of the 11th CPC Central Committee, more and more scholars in the theoretical circles agreed that there was an objective monetary commodity relationship in the socialist economy, and the law of value played a role not only in circulation but also in the production. In 1979, Deng Xiaoping clearly pointed out: "It is wrong to maintain that a market economy exists only in capitalist society and that there is only "capitalist" market economy. Why can't we develop a market economy under socialism? Developing a market economy does not mean practising capitalism. While maintaining a planned economy as the mainstay of our economic system, we are also

---

1   Selected Works of Deng Xiaoping, 1st edition, Vol. 3, p. 138.

introducing a market economy. But it is a socialist market economy... We cannot say that market economy exists only under capitalism... We can surely develop it under socialism."[2]

This realization broke the traditional rigid concept that only planned economy can be practiced in socialism, and actually linked the market economy with socialism. The Resolution on Some Historical Issues of the Party Since the Founding of the PRC passed in 1981 by the 6th Plenary Session of the 11th CPC Central Committee formally proposed the system of "planned economy supplemented by market regulation", which was also affirmed by the 12th CPC National Congress. Although this proposal still insisted that the overall framework of the planned economy remain unchanged and the market regulation is only supplementary, it provided a realistic basis for the market to play a regulatory role and opened the way for the development of the socialist market economy.

The second stage: from 1984 to 1987, a planned commodity economic theory was proposed. In the Decisions on the Economic System Reform of the CPC Central Committee passed in the 3rd Plenary Session of the 12th CPC Central Committee in 1984, the Party made it clear that the socialist economy was a planned commodity economy based on public ownership. From practical experience, we gradually realized that the commodity economy was an insurmountable stage of the socialist economy, the planned economy and the commodity economy were compatible, and the planning and market could be combined. Under the guidance of the theory of planned commodity economy, from the end of 1984, we have begun to shift the focus of economic restructuring from rural areas to cities with obvious market orientation, such as reducing the proportion of mandatory plans, expanding the scope of market regulation, increasing the autonomy of enterprises, and implementing double-track price system. Based on the practice of reform, Deng Xiaoping further elaborated his view on the relationship between planning and market. In the meeting with a delegation of US entrepreneurs in 1985, he pointed out: "There is no fundamental contradiction between socialism and a market economy. The problem is how to develop the productive forces more effectively. We used to have a planned economy, but our experience over the years has proved that having a totally planned economy hampers the development of the productive forces to a certain extent. If we combine a planned economy with a market economy, we shall be in a better position to liberate the productive forces and speed up economic growth."[3]

---

2   Selected Works of Deng Xiaoping, 2nd Edition, Vol. 2, p.236.
3   Selected Works of Deng Xiaoping, 1st Edition, Vol. 3, pp. 148-149.

Before the convening of the 13th CPC National Congress in 1987, Deng Xiaoping conducted a more in-depth discussion on the relationship between planning and market. He pointed out: "Planning and market are both means of developing the productive forces. So long as they serve that purpose, we should make use of them. If they serve socialism they are socialist; if they serve capitalism they are capitalist."[4]

Therefore, the 13th CPC National Congress defined the new system of socialist planned commodity economy as one of internal unity between planning and market, emphasizing that both of them were new economic operating mechanisms that covered the whole society, with the market controlled by the state and business guided by the market in general, which was close to the idea of a market economy under state's macro-economic regulation.

The third stage: from 1987 to 1992, the theory of socialist commodity economy was put forward. The 13th CPC National Congress held in 1987 further developed the theory of a planned commodity economy. It clearly pointed out that the difference between the socialist and capitalist commodity economy lay not in the number of markets and planning. Instead, the socialist commodity economy should be an internal unified system of planning and market, which should cover the whole society, with the organic integration of them. The socialist market system included not only the commodity market, but also factor markets such as capital and labor market. Therefore, in order to carry out the economic system reform, it was necessary to establish the economic operation mode of "market controlled by the state, and the business guided by the market". During this period, Deng Xiaoping further elaborated on the relationship between socialism and the market economy. In December 1990, Deng Xiaoping proposed: "We must understand theoretically that the difference between capitalism and socialism is not a market economy as opposed to a planned economy. Socialism has regulation by market forces, and capitalism has control through planning."[5] In early 1991, Deng Xiaoping further pointed out: "Don't think that any planned economy is socialist and any market economy is capitalist. That's not the way things are. In fact, planning and regulation by the market are both means of controlling economic activity, and the market can also serve socialism."[6]

These assertions of Deng Xiaoping clearly defined the attributes of the market economy, thus lifting the bondage between socialism and the market economy and laying the theoretical foundation for the ultimate goal of establishing a socialist market economic system in China.

4   Ibid., p.203.
5   Anthology of Deng Xiaoping, 1st edition, Vol.3, p.364.
6   Ibid., p.367.

The fourth stage: Since 1992, the theory of socialist market economy has been formally put forward, which fundamentally broke away from the ideological shackles of regarding the planned economy and the market economy as the product of the social system, and the establishment of the socialist market economy was set as the reform goal. During his Southern Talks in the spring of 1992 Deng Xiaoping clearly pointed out that "the proportion of planning to market forces is not the essential difference between socialism and capitalism. A planned economy is not equivalent to socialism, because there is planning under capitalism too; a market economy is not capitalism, because there are markets under socialism too. Planning and market forces are both means of controlling economic activity."[7]

This argument fundamentally negated the traditional concept of setting socialism and the market economy in opposition. The 14th CPC National Congress made it clear that the goal of China's economic restructuring is to establish a socialist market economy. Therefore, it was necessary to guarantee the market's fundamental regulatory role in the allocation of resources under macroeconomic control, so that economic activities would follow the law of value and adapt to changes in the supply-demand relationship. In 1994, the 3rd Plenary Session of the 14th CPC Central Committee made the Decisions on Several Issues Concerning the Establishment of a Socialist Market Economic System by the CPC Central Committee, which comprehensively and systematically expounded the basic framework and strategic plan for establishing a socialist market economy. In 1997, the 15th CPC National Congress further confirmed that "to build a socialist economy with Chinese characteristics means to develop a market economy under the conditions of socialism and continuously liberate and develop the productive forces." In 2002, the 16th CPC National Congress reiterated: "to adhere to the reform direction of the socialist market economy and to enable the market to play a fundamental role in the allocation of resources under the macro-control of the state." In order to further improve the socialist market economic system, the 3rd Plenary Session of the 16th CPC Central Committee held in 2003 discussed some major issues concerning the improvement of the socialist market economic system and made the Decisions on Several Issues Concerning the Perfection of the Socialist Market Economic System. In 2007, to reach the goal of economic development in the new historical period, the 17th CPC National Congress proposed the major progress to be made in perfecting the socialist market economic system.

---

7   Ibid., p.373.

Second, the basic characteristics of the socialist market economic system

Although both planning and market are means of economic regulation, which do not belong to either "socialism" or "capitalism" in essence, they can play different regulatory roles in different social systems. Capitalist market economy refers to the market economy under the capitalist system, while socialist market economy refers to one under the socialist system. The latter, first of all, has the general characteristics of market economy, such as enterprises with clear ownership rights and strict budget constraints operating independently and assuming sole responsibility for their own profits and losses; free and fair market competition; prices determined by market supply and demand being flexible; the market being open; the and government mainly using economic instruments to regulate the economy; otherwise it cannot be called a market economy. In terms of the operational rules, there is no substantive difference between the socialist and the capitalist market economy. As Deng Xiaoping said, the socialist market economy is similar to a capitalist one in method.[8]

Therefore, we can absolutely learn the experience of market operation and management from developed countries in the world in order to develop our market economy.

In the theoretical innovation of the socialist market economy, Deng Xiaoping separates market economy from the capitalist system, and regards it as a means and mode of resource allocation on the one hand; on the other hand, he emphasizes that we must integrate the market economy with the basic socialist system, by pointing out that: "It is right to implement the policy of opening up, to combine the planned economy with the market economy, and to carry out a series of structural reforms.

Does this run counter to the principles of socialism? No, because in the course of reform we shall make sure of two things: one is that the public sector of the economy is always predominant; the other is that in developing the economy we seek common prosperity, always trying to avoid polarization."[9]

In other words, apart from the general features of the market economy, socialist market economy also has its own features.

Firstly, in terms of the ownership structure, we adopt the basic economic system that takes public ownership as primary with other ownership forms developing in tandem. All forms of ownership in conformity with the "Three Favorables" can and should be used to serve socialism; enterprises of different ownership can also voluntarily practice various forms of

---

8   See, Selected Works of Deng Xiaoping, 2nd Edition, Volume 2, p. 236.
9   Selected Works of Deng Xiaoping, 1st Edition, Vol.3, p.149.

joint operation; the market is open to all kinds of enterprises, and the state-owned economy plays a leading role in market competition.

Secondly, in terms of the distribution system, we must adhere to the system of distribution according to work being the main form with the coexistence of multiple ways of distribution. We should combine distribution according to work with that according to productive factors, and use various regulatory means to encourage the excellent, to improve the efficiency, to rationalize the income gap, to prevent polarization and to gradually realize common prosperity.

Thirdly, in terms of the macro-control, it can combine the current interests with the long-term ones of the people, and the partial interests with the overall ones, and give better play to the strengths of both planning and market. In other words, the socialist market economy is able to combine the advantages of the basic socialist economic system with that of the market economy, giving full play to the fundamental role of the market economy in the allocation of resources. Meanwhile, through macro-control, it can overcome the blindness, spontaneity and other weaknesses and negative aspects of the market economy, so that the superiority of the socialist system can be brought into full play, which is also the particularity of the socialist market economy. As Jiang Zemin said, the term "socialist" in the socialist market economy is the "finishing touch," and "the so-called 'crucial' point is to clarify the nature of our market economy... Our market economy is carried out under the socialist system...Our creativity and characteristics are also reflected here."[10]

The socialist market economic theory that the Party has gradually formed and developed during the new period of reform and opening up is very important and innovative. It enriches and develops the basic tenets of Marxism and opens the way for opening up new horizons of development for Marxist economic theory.

Third, the improvement efforts to perfect the socialist market economic system

Since the 14th CPC National Congress, which set the goal of the socialist market economic system reform, significant progress has been made in the reform in theory and in practice. The socialist market economic system has been initially established, the basic economic system that takes public ownership as primary with diverse other ownership forms developing in tandem has been established, and the pattern of opening up from all dimensions, at various levels and in broad fields has basically taken shape. The continuous deepening of the reform has greatly promoted the improvement of social

10   CPCCC Party Literature Research Office: "Jiang Zemin on Socialism with Chinese Characteristics (Special Editorial)", p.69, Beijing, Central Party Literature Press, 2002.

productive forces, overall national strength and people's living standards, enabling us to survive the international economic and financial turmoil, severe domestic natural disasters and major epidemics. However, at the same time, some problems also emerge such as unreasonable economic structure, unbalanced distribution relations, slow growth of peasants' incomes, prominent employment conflicts, increasing pressure on resources and the environment, and generally weak economic competitiveness, which are mainly caused by the fact that our country is in the primary stage of socialism, with an imperfect economic system and many institutional obstacles in the development of productive forces. In order to adapt to the international environment of economic globalization and the accelerating development of science and technology, and the new situation of building a moderately prosperous society in all respects, and to build a sound socialist market economic system, the 16th CPC National Congress made a series of major decisions on deepening reform, further opening up and the continuous improvement of the socialist market economic system.

In order to implement the strategic plan of building a sound socialist market economy and a more dynamic and open economy as proposed by the 16th CPC National Congress, and to deepen the economic system reform and promote the all-round economic and social development, the 3rd Plenary Session of the 16th CPC Central Committee made the *Decisions on Several Issues Concerning the Perfection of the Socialist Market Economic System* by the CPC Central Committee, pointing out the direction for the further perfection of the socialist market economic system.

The goal of perfecting the socialist market economic system is: to meet the requirements of the balanced urban and rural development, balanced economic and social development, the harmonious development of man and nature, and the overall planning for domestic development and opening up; and to give more play to the market's role in resource allocation, enhance the vitality and competitiveness of enterprises, improve the macro-control, perfect the government's social management and public service functions, and provide a strong institutional guarantee for building an overall well-to-do society. The main tasks include: to improve the basic economic system that takes public ownership as primary with diverse other ownership forms developing in tandem; to establish a system conducive to the gradual change of the dual economic structure in urban and rural areas; to form a mechanism for the coordinated development of regional economy; to establish a unified, open modern market system with orderly competition; to improve the macro-control, administrative management and economic legal system; to perfect the employment, income distribution and social security system; and to establish a mechanism to promote sustainable economic and social development.

Guided by Deng Xiaoping Theory and the important thought of Three Represents, we must follow the Party's basic line, basic program and basic experience, fully implement the spirit of the 16th CPC National Congress, emancipate the mind, seek truth from facts, and advance with the times. We should also adhere to the socialist market economic reform, focus on system construction and innovation, adhere to the respect for the pioneering spirit of the masses, and arouse the enthusiasm of both the central and local authorities. In addition, we must continue to handle the relations of reform, development and stability correctly, promote the reform with a focus and step by step, adhere to overall planning, coordinate various interests in the reform, stick to the people-oriented principle, establish a comprehensive, coordinated and sustainable development concept, and promote the all-round development of the economy, society and the people.

The 17th CPC National Congress further emphasized: to achieve the goal of economic development in the future, we must make major progress in accelerating the transformation of the mode of economic development and improving the socialist market economic system. We should vigorously promote the strategic restructuring of the economy, pay more attention to improving independent innovation, raising the level of energy conservation and environmental protection, and improving the overall economic quality and international competitiveness, deepen our understanding of the laws governing the socialist market economy, give better play to the basic role of the market in resource allocation, and form a macro-control system conducive to scientific development.

Section II

Adjustment and perfection of the ownership structure

First, The basic economic system that takes public ownership as primary with diverse other ownership forms developing in tandem

The basic economic system at the initial stage of socialism is, in essence, a matter of ownership. The 3rd Plenary Session of the 11th CPC Central Committee proposed to reform the production relations and superstructures incompatible with the development of the productive forces, according to the real situation of our socialist construction, and point out that the non-public economy was a necessary complement to the socialist economy. In addition, the 3rd Plenary Session of the 14th CPC Central Committee in 1993 further point out that we must adhere to the principle of taking the public ownership economy as primary with various economic sectors developing in tandem. In 1997, the 15th National Congress of the CPC comprehensively expounded the basic line and basic program of the primary stage of social-ism and clearly put forward the following: "The public ownership as the subject and the diversified ownership economy develop jointly is the basic economic system in the primary stage of our socialism. The establishment of this system is determined by the nature of socialism and the national conditions at the primary stage: First, as China is a socialist country, it must adhere to the public ownership as the foundation of the socialist economic system. Second, as China is in the primary stage of socialism, we need to develop a diversified ownership economy under the conditions of public ownership as the main body; third, all forms of ownership that conform to the 'Three Favorables' can and should be used to serve socialism."[11]

In the report of 16th CPC National Congress, Jiang Zemin made it clear that, in order to solve the contradictions and problems in deepening the economic system reform, we should adhere to and perfect the basic eco-nomic system of taking public ownership as primary with diverse other ownership forms developing in tandem, in accordance with the require-ments of liberating and developing the productive forces. The 17th CPC National Congress also emphasized that it was necessary to uphold and improve the basic economic system, unswervingly consolidate and develop the public economy, encourage, support and guide the development of non-public economy, and adhere to the equal protection of property rights, so as to form a new pattern of fair competition among and the promotion of various ownership economy.

Socialist public ownership, in which all or part of the workers possess the means of production under the conditions of socialism, adapts to social-ized mass production, and thus fundamentally eliminates the basic contra-dictions of capitalism and makes way for the further development of social productive forces. In fact, the primary role of socialist public ownership is determined by the nature of public ownership and its role in the national economy, or to be specific, the reason lies in: firstly, the socialist public economy is compatible with socialized mass production and in line with the direction of social development; secondly, the public economy is the fundamental feature of the socialist system and the economic foundation of socialist society. Only by relying on the power of the public economy that plays a primary role, will the socialist countries have sufficient economic means to guide the development of the individual, private and foreign in-vestment economy toward the direction conducive to socialism; thirdly, the public economy, being the mainstay of the construction of socialist mod-ernization, the main source of state revenue and the major material basis for the state's macro-control, controls the lifeline of the national economy,

---

11   CPCCC Party Literature Research Office: "Selection of Important Literature since the 15th National Congress" (Vol.I), p.20.

possesses modern material and technology, and controls the production and circulation; fourthly, the means of production of socialist public ownership are no longer means of exploitation. Instead, they are used to develop production continuously and to meet the growing material and cultural needs of the people. Besides, it is not only the economic basis for implementing the principle of distribution according to work, but also the indispensable material guarantee for the realization of the master position of the working people economically and politically, and the common prosperity of all members of society. In short, upholding the primary role of public ownership, and consolidating and expanding the socialist public economy is an unshakable fundamental principle of Marxism, the basic premise and the fundamental starting point for our ownership restructuring, and the basic symbol of our socialist market economy.

However, only when public ownership meets the demand of the development of productive forces, can its status be reflected and its role be brought into effective play. Therefore, we cannot demonstrate the superiority of public ownership without referring to the productive forces, neither can we blindly seek to expand the scope and increase the degree of public ownership regardless of the level and requirements of the development of productive forces. It is known to all that socialism in China is born out of a semi-colonial and semi-feudal society, with very backward productive forces (modern industry accounting for only about 10%, while scattered and backward agriculture and handicrafts accounting for 90%). Since the founding of New China, especially after the reform and opening up, although we have entered a new era of building a moderately prosperous society in all respects, having made remarkable achievements in economic construction, on the whole, our level of productive forces and socialization of production was not high, with very low per capita gross national product and generally low level of education and science and technology, most of the industrial and agricultural production was far from modernization, with backward management and means of economy, and imbalances and multilevel development still existed among regions and industries. Therefore, besides ensuring the primary position of public ownership, we should develop non-public economy in the long run. The 15th CPC National Congress incorporated the non-public economy into the basic economic system of the primary stage of socialism, making it clear that it was an important part of China's socialist market economy, due to its important role in meeting people's diverse needs, increasing employment and promoting the development of the national economy, which deepened the understanding of the primary stage of socialism.

The ownership form of the means of production cannot be evaluated by referring to the level of social public ownership, but by judging whether it meets the requirements of the development of productive forces, whether it promotes the development of productive forces, and whether it is beneficial to all-round social progress. All forms of ownership, not only the public ownership, regardless of the level of public ownership, are irreplaceable within the range of productivity they can accommodate, and all those consistent with the "Three Favorables" can and should be used to serve socialism. By adopting the basic economic system that takes public ownership as primary with diverse other ownership forms developing in tandem, we can meet the requirements of the development of the productive forces, give full play to the enthusiasm, initiative and creativity of the working people; make full use of manpower, material and financial resources and make rational use of means of production; increase employment and raise people's living standards; improve technology and management level; improve social division of labor and develop specialized production; enliven the economy and promote the development of a market economy; and accelerate the prosperity of the country and the happiness of the people. In conclusion, in the course of the practice, we must, through systematic investigations and studies, take necessary measures to gradually rationalize the proportions and ranges of various economic components in the entire national economy.

Since the 3rd Plenary Session of the 11th CPC Central Committee, China has been actively pursuing the development of a diversified economy while maintaining the dominant position of public ownership, with declines in the proportion of the public economy and a rapid development of non-socialist economy. However, on the whole, the primary role of the public economy has not been changed, in tandem with considerable room allocated for the development of the non-public sectors of the economy.

Second, unswervingly consolidate and develop the public economy

Public ownership, the foundation of the socialist economic system, which is guided by the state, is the basic force to promote economic and social development and an important guarantee for the realization of the fundamental interests and the common prosperity of the people. Maintaining the dominant position of public ownership, and making sure that the state-owned economy controls the lifeline of the national economy and plays a leading role in economic development, is crucial to giving full play to the superiority of the socialist system, strengthening economic strength, national defense strength and national cohesion, and enhancing China's international status. Therefore, both the 16th and the 17th CPC National Congress emphasize that we must unswervingly consolidate and develop the public economy.

The report of the 15th CPC National Congress clearly pointed out that it was necessary to fully understand the meaning of public economy, which included not only the state-owned and collective economy, but also the state-owned and collective components of the mixed-ownership economy. It cleared the misunderstanding that the public economy merely referred to state-owned and collective economy and that state-owned economy, rather than the public ownership, played a primary role, which broadened the path for the development of a mixed ownership economy. With the deepening of the reform of the economic system, the development of the socialist market economy, the diversification of sources of investment and the organizational forms, various forms of mixed ownership economy would continue to develop. Having state-owned and collective components, the mixed ownership enterprises, whose capital and income belonged to the state and the collective, definitely belonged to the public-ownership economy, and those controlled by the state and the collective were public-owned more obviously. This mode of ownership helped expand the control of the public economy, and enhance the dominant role of public ownership. With the deepening of reform and the establishment of a modern enterprise system, in the future, the mixed ownership economy would become increasingly important with the share of its public components in the entire public economy increasing.

In addition, the 15th CPC National Congress also made a clearer definition of the dominant position of public ownership, which mainly lied in that: public assets dominated the total assets of the society; the state-owned economy controlled the lifeline of the national economy and played a leading role in economic development, which was true for the whole country, but situations in some places or industries could vary. Besides, public assets were dominant in the total social assets not simply in quantity and proportion, but mainly in "quality", that is, in industrial properties, technological composition, technological content, economies of scale, the proliferation of assets, the competitiveness of the market and etc.

In order to consolidate and develop the public economy unswervingly, we must give full play to the leading role of the state-owned economy, i.e. socialist economy under ownership by the whole people, which refers to the public ownership of the means of production by the whole people, because it is compatible with the higher productive forces, with a higher degree of public ownership and the basic realization of the equality of laborers in the ownership of means of production and the direct union of laborers and means of production. In other words, the means of production owned by the whole people are no longer means of exploitation, but a means to achieve the well-being of all people, which makes it possible to maintain the coordinated development of the national economy in the whole society. At the present stage, the means of production in our country are owned by the state on behalf of all the people, in the form of state ownership, so the system is called state-owned economy.

In the public economy, the state-owned economy controls the lifeline of the national economy and plays a leading role in economic development, which is manifested in its ability to control the development direction of the national economy and economic system, the overall trend of the economic operation and important scarce resources. In the past, due to a lack of understanding of the initial stage of socialism, the scope and proportion of the state-owned economy is so large that it exceeds the level of productive forces and economic socialization. As a result, since the reform and opening up, due to the gradual marketization of the economy and some historical and social reasons, a considerable amount of the state-owned economy have lost competitiveness in the market economy. Some state-owned enterprises have high debt-to-asset ratios, and even become insolvent, gaining low returns and suffering serious losses. If the situation remains unchanged, the state-owned economy will not be able to play its leading role no matter how high the proportion is. Therefore, the dominance and competitiveness of the state-owned economy should be enhanced, the quality of the public economy should be improved so that people can understand the status and role of the public economy and emphasize its quality rather than quantity and unify the two, instead of simply focusing on its share in the national economy, which provides the theoretical basis and points out the direction for restructuring of the state-owned economy strategically.

In order to give full play to the leading role of the state-owned economy and enhance its control over the economy, we should strategically readjust the layout of the state-owned economy and adhere to the principle of "being flexible and having dos and don'ts". "having dos and don'ts" means that, on the one hand, the state-owned economy should control a few key areas that determine the lifeline of the national economy and national security, and dominate national defense, natural monopoly industries, and the public-benefit industries providing public goods and services; in some important competitive areas, the state-owned economy should control or hold the shares, so as to control and affect more social capital through a small amount of state-owned capital; on the other hand, state-owned capital should gradually be withdrawn from the general competitive industries, allowing the participation of more social investment entities, so that various economic components can help solve problems in social and economic development facing current China. Meanwhile, we should strategically adjust the layout of the state-owned economy, making sure that it occupies the dominant position in key industries and key areas that determine the lifeline of the national economy. In order to enhance the control and competitiveness of the state-owned economy, we must also actively promote the reform of state-owned enterprises towards the goal of establishing a modern enterprise system, change the management mechanism of enterprises, and enhance the vitality of enterprises. Meanwhile, we should also strengthen the supervision and administration of state-owned assets, prevent the loss of state-owned assets and ensure the preservation and appreciation of them. However, we should never develop state-owned economy by negating or excluding other economic components. Instead, we can rely on reform, its participation in market competition, transformation of operational mechanisms, enhancement of its vitality, and the development of its own potential and advantages.

In order to consolidate and develop the public economy unswervingly, we must also vigorously support and promote the development of the collective economy, that is, the socialist collective economy, which refers to the public ownership of the means of production by some working people. As a cooperative economic sector organized by the working masses based on the principle of free will and mutual benefit, it operates independently and assumes sole responsibility for its own profits and losses. In a socialist society, it belongs to socialist economy, because it realizes the equality of the laborers in terms of the ownership of means of production in the scope of the collective economy, and the direct combination of laborers and means of production. Besides, it is free from exploitation, with the equal cooperative relations among laborers. Being a flexible economic form compatible to a large scope of productive forces, collective economy is realized in different forms determined by the development level of productive forces and other economic conditions, but instead of having a fixed pattern, it may differ in different economic regions, production categories and economic conditions, and vary according to different degrees of socialization, modes of distribution, and contents and ways of cooperation.

The collective economy, being an important part of the socialist public economy, plays an extremely crucial role in our national economy. Besides being the main economic form in the rural areas, it also occupies a large proportion in the industrial, transportation and commercial areas of cities and towns. It can embody the principle of common prosperity, being able to absorb the idle funds in the society widely, and plays an extremely important role in the development of production, improving people's livelihood , creating a thriving market, stabilizing prices, increasing employment, expanding commodity exports, increasing public accumulation and national tax revenue, encouraging and helping the development of various forms of collective economy in urban and rural areas, giving play to the dominant role of the public economy, consolidating the alliance of workers and peasants, and strengthening the people's democratic dictatorship.

At present and in the years to come, in the deepening of rural reform, we will continue to focus on stabilizing the "Household Responsibility Contract System", and perfecting the two-tier operation system with the combination of centralization and decentralization, promoting the integration of trade-industry-agriculture, developing social service system in various forms actively, gradually improving the strength of collective economy and promoting rural economic development. Since in a few economically developed areas, with the growth of the collective economy, especially the development of township and village enterprises, most of the labor force in the rural areas has turned to non-agricultural industries, and the objective conditions for land scale operation have been in place, based on the voluntary and mutually beneficial principle, we should encourage and promote various forms of cooperation and alliance, adopt different forms and carry out moderate-scale management according to the local conditions, so as to meet the needs of scientific farming and socialization of production, to modernize agricultural production, and to gradually achieve the second leap.

Third, the diversification of public ownership

There are connections and differences between the concept of ownership and the realization of ownership. The former refers to the relations among people in the possession of means of production in the course of production, which includes a wide range of economic relations in people's ownership, possession, dominance and use of means of production, while the latter is the concrete form in which these economic relations are realized, mainly referring to the organization form and mode of operation of assets or capital. In the socialist market economy, the realization of public ownership can and should be diversified. All the management modes and organizational forms that reflect the law of production should be made fully use of, and efforts should be made to find a realization form of public ownership that can greatly promote the development of productive forces. Public economy can take the form of wholly-owned enterprises, share-holding enterprises, cooperatives, joint-stock cooperative companies and etc., and the modes of operation such as public-owned public-operated, public-owned private-operated, leasing and contract operation. With the deepening of reforms in state-owned and collective economy, the development of a diversified ownership economy and the diversification of investors, the realization of public ownership will certainly be more diversified. In fact, the search and development of diversified realization forms according to the nature and size of the public-owned enterprises is beneficial to raising and expanding capital funds, strengthening the restriction of property rights, arousing the enthusiasm of the workers, improving the operation efficiency of enterprises and capital, and promoting the development of productivity.

Although the shareholding system, a realization form of public owner-ship, is derived from and has emerged and developed in the capitalist so-ciety, it is a form of capital organization of the modern enterprise that is conducive to the separation of ownership and management rights, and the improvement of the operational efficiency of enterprises and capital, and can be used both in capitalist and socialist societies. In effect, we should learn all the advanced organizational forms and management methods of enterprises that reflect the law of socialized production from countries all over the world, including the capitalist developed countries. Actually, the shareholding system is neither exclusive to "socialism" nor "capitalism", for the nature of a shareholding enterprise is determined by its ownership. If it is owned by the state and the collective, it is obviously public-owned and is conducive to expanding the range of the public economy and enhancing the dominant position of public ownership. If it is implemented in state-owned enterprises, the enterprises can independently use and operate the capital of all the investors, which will benefit the separation of government and enterprises, as well as the separation of ownership and management; it can make sure that enterprises operate in accordance with the laws of the market economy, so that self-discipline and self-motivation mechanism can be enhanced, and the operational efficiency of enterprises and capital can be improved; it can also raise funds through the issuance of stocks, which will help solve the problem of insufficient accumulation of capital and can pave the way for establishment of large trans-regional, trans-industrial, multi-ownership and trans-national enterprise types.

Joint stock cooperative system, a form of public ownership that combines the characteristics of joint stock and cooperative system, belongs to collec-tive economy which is featured by and based on the union of labor and the union of the capital of the laborers. In this system, besides getting paid according to work, laborers also receive corresponding rewards according to the shares they hold, which makes it different from the shareholding and the cooperative system. What's more, employees in joint-stock cooperative enterprises are not only laborers but also investors, since they share the risks and benefits, and the interests of the laborers and enterprises become one, which can fully arouse the initiatives of the laborers. Therefore, we must support and encourage the development of the joint stock cooperative system, strengthen the guidance and constantly draw on the experience to gradually improve it.

The 3rd Plenary Session of the 16th CPC Central Committee pointed out that in order to promote the development of the public economy, we must practice various effective realization forms of public ownership, adhere to the dominant position of public ownership; give play to the leading role of state-owned economy, actively promote various effective realization forms of public ownership, and speed up the restructuring of state-owned economy. In order to adapt to the continuous development of the marketization of economy, we should further enhance the vitality of the public economy, vigorously develop the mixed-ownership economy invested by state-owned, collective and non-public capital, realize the diversification of the investors and make the shareholding system the main form of public ownership. We can choose to implement absolute control or relative control over enterprises needed to be controlled by state-owned capital according to different situations. We should also improve the mechanism for the flexible and proper flow of the state-owned capital, further invest it in key industries and key areas that affect the lifeline of national security and the national economy, enhance the dominant position of the state-owned economy, and make sure that state-owned enterprises in other industries and fields are able to survive in the fair competition in the market, through reorganization of assets and structural adjustment. In addition, we are supposed to develop large enterprise groups with international competitiveness, continue to invigorate the state-owned small and medium-sized enterprises, deepen the reform on collective enterprises by focusing on clear property rights, and develop various forms of collective economy. The report of the 17th CPC National Congress further proposed that we should deepen the shareholding system reform of state-owned enterprises, perfect the modern enterprise system, optimize the layout and structure of state-owned economy, enhance the vitality, control and influence of the state-owned economy, deepen the reform on monopoly industries should, introduce competition mechanisms, strengthen government supervision and social supervision, accelerate the construction of a state-owned capital management budget system, perfect all kinds of state-owned assets management system, promote collective enterprise reform and develop various forms of collective economy and cooperative economy.

Fourth, the non-public economy as an important component part of the socialist market economy

The non-public economy in the primary stage of socialism mainly includes individual economy, private economy, foreign investment economy, and Hong Kong, Macao and Taiwan investment economy.

The individual economy is a kind of small private economy in which the individual laborer owns the means of production based on the work of the individual (including family members) and the income generated. It is featured by small size, simple tools, convenient operation and flexible management. In general, it adapts to scattered productive force but can also be linked with socialized mass production. In our country, since the development level of social productive forces is generally not high, for quite a long period of time, the individual economy sector will still exist to make up for the insufficient development of modern large-scale production.

The private economy is based on the private ownership of the means of production and the wage-labor, with obtaining profits being the purpose of production and operation. In the socialist market economy, the private economy has a dual nature: on the one hand, it has the general characteristics of capitalist private ownership, that is, private ownership and domination of means of production, and the reliance on wage labor for production and operation; on the other hand, it is produced and developed under the condition of the dominant position of the socialist public ownership, with a close link between its production and operation activities and the public economy, so it must be carried out within the scope prescribed by the laws of the socialist countries. Meanwhile, its employees, whose basic economic and political rights are protected by relevant state laws, are the masters of the socialist countries. Since the reform and opening up, in our country, private economy has grown from nothing to become an important force in the socialist market economy.

Foreign investment economy and Hong Kong, Macao and Taiwan investment economy refers to the foreign investment and Hong Kong, Macao and Taiwan investment in the sole proprietors, joint ventures and cooperative enterprises established by foreign investors and those from Hong Kong, Macao and Taiwan in accordance with Chinese laws and regulations, most of which are invested by enterprises in capitalist countries and regions. There is no doubt that the capital invested by foreign and overseas capitalists is capitalist in nature. However, the enterprises, operated under the management and regulation of the socialist countries, are closely linked with the socialist economy. They must abide by the laws of our country and accept the guidance, management and supervision of our government. Therefore, the foreign investment economy and Hong Kong, Macao and Taiwan investment economy in our country do not belong to general capitalism, but "the capitalism that we can control, the scope of whose activities we can define." What's more, the joint-venture and cooperative enterprises, some of which are even controlled by the state and the collective, may also contain the elements of socialist public economy, so they obviously belong to public ownership.

Before the reform and opening up, under the guidance of the thought of "keeping large in size and collective in nature", we always held a restraint and exclusive attitude toward the non-public economy. However, after the reform and opening up, Deng Xiaoping, after summing up historical experience and analyzing the development stage of socialism in China scientifically, made it clear that non-public economy should be developed under the conditions of guaranteeing the dominant position of public ownership, and that all kinds of ownership should be developed jointly. In practice, we also restored and continuously developed non-public economy after a process of understanding it status and role. For example, the 12th CPC National Congress proposed that the individual economy was a necessary complement to the public economy. The 13th CPC National Congress regarded the private economy, foreign investment economy and individual economy together as a necessary and beneficial supplement to the public economy. The 14th CPC National Congress put forward the long-term development of various ownership systems and further emphasized that this was not an expedient measure, but a long-term policy. The 15th CPC National Congress not only established a basic economic system that took the public ownership economy as primary with diverse other ownership forms developing in tandem but also made it clear that "non-public economy is an important part of China's socialist market economy." The changes in the Party's understanding of the status and role of the non-public economy reflect the continuous deepening of its understanding of China's national conditions and the theory of ownership of Marxism, and show that, with an attitude of seeking truth from facts, it has scientifically summed up the practice since the reform and opening up.

In the primary stage of socialism, adhering to the principle of taking public economy as the primary and developing non-public economy, which is fundamentally determined by the low-level, multi-level and unbalanced development of productive forces in the initial stage, meets the demands of developing the socialist market economy and easing various contradictions in the modernization of our country. Firstly, the development of non-public economy plays an important role in building the microscopic subjects of the socialist market economy, since the precondition for the development of market economy is the diversification of the market subjects and the decentralization of decision-making, while the single form of public economy is inconsistent with the development of a market economy, because non-public economy can compete with the public economy, which will promote the latter's development. Secondly, the development of non-public economy, especially the introduction of foreign investment economy, can provide not only reference for exploring the realization form of public economy, but also space and opportunities for the development of various realization forms. Thirdly, as a developing country, China will face many difficulties and contradictions in its process of modernization, among which the shortage of funds and the employment pressure will be sticky problems. On the one hand, China needs a huge capital investment in its modernization, which cannot be provided solely by state's financial capacity; on the other hand, a large number of private capital subjects afford the needed ideal high value-adding investment; on the one hand, our country is the most populous country in the world with a large unemployed population and the rapid growth of it; on the other hand, the arrangement and absorption capacity of the government and the public economy is limited, with an enormous employment pressure and the long-standing and prominent contradiction in the oversupply of labor resources. Therefore, according to the reality of our country, developing non-public economy will be conducive to arousing initiatives of the people, making full use of social funds, introducing foreign funds, and making up for lack of funds for construction. In addition, it is also an effective way to increase employment through multiple channels and ease employment pressure.

The 16th CPC National Congress once again made it clear that various forms of non-public economy such as the private and the individual sectors were important parts of the socialist market economy, and played an important role in fully arousing the initiatives of people from all walks of life and speeding up the development of the productive forces. Therefore, we must unswervingly encourage, support and guide the development of the non-public economy. The 3rd Plenary Session of the 16th CPC Central Committee further proposed measures to be taken to vigorously develop and actively guide the development of the non-public economy: to clear up and revise laws, regulations and policies that restrict the development of the non-public economy and eliminate institutional obstacles; to relax control over market access and allow non-public capital to be invested in infrastructure, public utilities and other industries and fields not prohibited by laws and regulations; to make sure that non-public enterprises receive equal treatment as other enterprises in terms of investment and financing, taxation, land use and foreign trade; to support the development of non-public small and medium-sized enterprises and encourage qualified enterprises to expand; to require non-public enterprises to operate according to law, pay taxes according to regulations, and protect the legitimate rights and interests of workers; to improve the service and supervision of non-public enterprises. The report of the 17th CPC National Congress further put forward the promotion of fair access to the market, improvement of financing conditions and breaking institutional barriers to promote the development of individual and private economy and small and medium-sized enterprises. Besides, based on the modern property rights system, we should develop a mixed-ownership economy and further set a clear direction for the development of public economy.

Section III

Reform and perfection of the distribution system of the primary stage of socialism

First, adhering to the distribution according to work as the primary, and a variety of distribution modes in tandem

In the primary stage of socialism, in terms of personal income distribution, we must adhere to distribution according to work as the primary, and a variety of distribution modes in tandem, which is determined by the nature of socialism and our national conditions of being at the initial stage. Marxists hold that the mode of production determines that of distribution, and the distribution of consumption data is the result of that of production conditions. In the primary stage of socialism, the implementation of the basic economic system that takes public ownership as primary with diverse other ownership forms developing in tandem determines that we must adhere to distribution according to work as the primary, and a variety of distribution modes in tandem. In the socialist distribution system, we can neither negate the coexistence and development of multiple modes of distribution due to our emphasis on the dominant position of distribution according to work, nor can we topple the dominant position of distribution according to work due to the coexistence of a variety of distribution modes.

In the socialist society, distributing personal income according to work, as a basic principle of Marxism, means that: all those who have the ability to work should serve the society, receive the corresponding rewards according to their work, and get corresponding personal consumer goods according to the amount and quality of the labor, with more pay for more work and vice versa.

The principle of distributing individual consumer goods according to work is determined by the objective economic conditions. First of all, the public ownership of means of production in socialism is a prerequisite for the implementation of the distribution according to work, because it ensures the equality of the laborers in terms of the means of production, which eliminates the possibility of possessing the labor results of others unpaid through the possession of means of production, and provides the precondition for the principle of distribution according to work. Secondly, in the socialist society, the old mode of division of labor has not yet disappeared, and there are major differences in the division of labor. As a means of making a living, labor, is the direct reason for the principle of distribution according to work, because besides recognizing the differences in labor, we should also distribute personal consumer goods according to work, so as to fully arouse the enthusiasm of workers and promote the development of socialist production by closely linking labor contributions with labor reward. Finally, the development level of the socialist productive forces is the material condition for the distribution according to work. As the development level of productive forces is not high, social products are not abundant, and consumer goods cannot fully meet people's various needs in current China, it is impossible to implement distribution according to demand. Therefore, it is obvious that it is necessary for socialist societies to adhere to distribution according to work, which is an objective economic law that is independent of people's will.

Second, the distribution according to factors of production is one important distribution principle of the socialist market economy

There is no fundamental incompatibility between distribution according to work, the distribution principle of socialism, and other modes of distribution. Instead, they can work together towards the objective of promoting the development of productive forces and realizing common prosperity. The 15th CPC National Congress, explicitly pointed out to: "adhere to the principle of distribution according to work as the primary, and a variety of distribution modes in tandem, and combine the distribution according to work and the distribution according to factors of production…allow and encourage to take into consideration factors of production such as capital and technology in the distribution." It classified a variety of distribution modes into "distribution according to factors of production", and put forward "the combination of distribution according to work and the distribution according to factors of production", which was a major development of the theory of socialist distribution that the 15th CPC National Congress achieved. The 16th CPC National Congress further emphasized: "the principle of distributing according to the contribution of labor, capital, technology and management, and the perfection of the distribution system of distribution according to work as the primary, and a variety of distribution modes in tandem."

The essence of considering factors of production in income distribution is to realize the ownership of the factors of production economically, since all the production process is the interaction of various factors of production, and both value creation and use value creation are done on the premise of the participation and consumption of factors of production. For the owner of the factors of production, any input of the factors will generate the right to claim the benefit. Therefore, considering factors of production in income distribution follows the development law of market economy.

Distribution according to factors of production in the market economy, which involves factor owners and can improve resource allocation efficiency, is a distribution mode that can be realized through market mechanisms. The realization of the claim for the benefit in regard to the production factors depends on whether and to what extent the factors are recognized by the society. For the owners of the factors, the only way to guarantee the realization of their claim is to improve the quality of the factors and to adjust their supply according to the market needs. Therefore, the realization process of distribution according to the factors of production can be streamlined is motivated by releasing the ownership benefits from these production factors, by recognizing the contribution of the production factors, and by aiming the optimal allocation of—human and technology other—resources.

However, recognizing the rationality of distribution according to the factors of production does not mean that the factors—alone—are the sources of value. Actually, the creation of value and the distribution of value are two different issues, because the only source of value is the laborer's work. It must be acknowledged that the economic basis for the distribution according to factors of production does not lie in its participation in the creation of value, but in the way value created by labor is distributed, otherwise, the Marxist theory of labor value and surplus value would be negated. In fact, capital, land and other factors of production do not create value, and distribution according to the factors of production is a matter of distribution of the value created by labor, which fundamentally speaking, should meet the needs of production and development, and should be conducive to promoting the development of social productive forces. By recognizing the legitimacy of the distribution according to the factors of production, we can improve the efficiency of using the factors, because only by acknowledging its legitimacy and allowing the owners of the factors to invest directly or indirectly and gain a certain amount of income from the value created by labor, can the production factors—human and technology other—be used effectively and rationally, which will alleviate the shortage of these production factors of production and improve its efficiency.

213

In the socialist market economy, combining distribution according to work and distribution according to factors of production will be conducive to implementing the principle of the priority of efficiency with due consideration to fairness, and beneficial to encouraging a part of the people and a part of the regions to get rich first and eventually achieve common prosperity. In the further development of the socialist market economy, with the adjustment and perfection of the ownership structure and the development of the mixed ownership economy and the factors market, distribution according to factors of production will become more and more important. Therefore, under the precondition that distribution according to work plays the main role, it is necessary to combine distribution according to work and distribution according to factors of production in order to the develop the socialist market economy, which is a major breakthrough in the Marxist socialist distribution theory.

Third, allow a part of the people and a part of the regions get rich first, and ultimately achieve common prosperity

In the past, the biggest problem of the original distribution system in our country was egalitarianism such as all eating from the same "big pot", "iron rice bowl" and the practice of same treatment for those who do different amounts of work. In 1978, Deng Xiaoping put forward the new policy of putting an end to egalitarianism, i.e. the practice of "eating from the same big pot", allowing and encouraging some people and some areas to get rich first which can influence and promote the development of the entire national economy. He emphasized: "In economic policy, I think we should allow some regions and enterprises and some workers and peasants to earn more and enjoy more benefits sooner than others, in accordance with their hard work and greater contributions to society."[12]

Later, he pointed out again: "I have consistently maintained that some people and some regions should be allowed to prosper before others, always with the goal of common prosperity."[13]

To realize common prosperity is the objective and the most important manifestation of the nature of socialism, because the fundamental task of socialism is to develop social productive forces, continually meet the needs of the people's growing material and cultural life, and realize the common prosperity of all. However, common prosperity is not equal to averaging and synchronic affluence. In the past, under the guidance of egalitarianism, common prosperity was often understood as realizing an average affluence at the same rate, and people preferred to be all poor rather than differ in affluence. This kind of thinking of "not worrying about poverty, but rather one-sided focusing to the uneven distribution of income and wealth" would surely lead to the common backwardness and poverty and the bad reputation of the socialist system.

Our distribution policy should not only make sure that enterprises that legitimately run their businesses and those who work honestly get rich first, and the income gap is widened rationally, but also prevent disparity between the rich and the poor, and stick to the objective of common prosperity. Allowing and encouraging some people and some regions to get rich first through honest labor and legal business, and asking those who get rich, first should help others get rich is in line with the objective economic conditions in the primary stage of socialism.

In the primary stage of socialism, the policy of allowing a part of the people and a part of the regions to get rich first and differences in the level of wealth on the path to common prosperity is implemented, because at

12   Selected Works of Deng Xiaoping, 2nd Edition, Vol.2, p.152.
13   Selected Works of Deng Xiaoping, 1st Edition, Vol.3, p.166.

214

a certain period, we must recognize and allow differences in the level of wealth, which is determined by the economy. Firstly, it is the inevitable result of distribution according to work. Though distribution according to work does not involve any class difference, it recognizes differences in personal talent and work ability. Due to differences in physical strength, intelligence and diligence, workers receive different labor rewards. Even if they receive the same rewards, differences in the level of wealth will still occur due to different degrees of family burdens. Secondly, it is the inevitable result of the implementation of various forms of ownership and multiple modes of distribution, which will also result in greater differences in income among different members of the society. Thirdly, it is also the inevitable result of developing the socialist commodity economy, in which the existence of the law of value and competition will inevitably lead to the survival of the fittest, which is independent of people's will. Fourthly, it is in full compliance with the law of development. In the development process of all things, imbalance is always definite, while balance is relative. Therefore, on the path to realizing common prosperity, uneven development is inevitable, and it is impossible to realize the same level of prosperity simultaneously for all. Allowing some areas, some enterprises and individuals to get rich first through legitimate business and honest work will set an example that will affect their neighbors, and people in other regions and other units will follow suit. In this way, the entire national economy will continue to develop in a wavy manner and people of all nationalities in the country can get rich fast.

However, it must be noted that the difference in the level of wealth caused by allowing and encouraging a part of the people and a part of the regions to get rich first is fundamentally different from that between the rich and the poor caused by polarization and the brutal exploitation in the class society. Firstly, polarization is the product of private ownership and the commodity economy based on private ownership. In the class society, some people get wealthy and become exploiters, while others lose their means of production and have to be exploited, which will result in poverty and bankruptcy. While in the socialist society, encouraging some people and some areas to get rich first is a major policy aimed at eliminating egalitarianism on the premise of guaranteeing the primary role of public ownership, and realizing common prosperity is a matter of time, unrelated to class differentiation. Secondly, the purpose of implementing this policy is to achieve common prosperity. Getting rich through hard work and abiding by law is allowed and encouraged, while people who illegally infringe the interests of others and make huge profits by illegal means will be punished severely. Thirdly, the state will adopt effective measures to regulate excessive personal income obtained through legitimate activities in order to prevent great disparities in personal income. Fourthly, various effective measures will be taken to carry out anti-poverty work, so that people who get rich first can help the poverty-stricken areas to shake off poverty and individuals to get rid of poverty as soon as possible, and embark on the path of common prosperity.

While encouraging some people and some regions to prosper first, it should be paid attention to preventing polarization. Deng Xiaoping once pointed out that socialism can prevent polarization. He said: "The aim of socialism is to make all our people prosperous, not to create polarization. If our policies led to polarization, it would mean that we had failed; if a new bourgeoisie emerged, it would mean that we had strayed from the right path."[14] "So long as the public sector plays a predominant role in China's economy, polarization can be avoided.[15]

Fourth, the establishment of multi-level social security system

Social security refers to the system of distribution and redistribution of national income by the state and society through legislation, which guarantees the basic living rights of all members of society, especially those who have special difficulties in life. Aiming at guaranteeing the reproduction of labor force, it is also the precondition of the smooth progress of social reproduction. Social security is a huge system, mainly composed of social relief, social insurance, social welfare, social care and social assistance.

As the product of the development of the commodity economy at a certain stage, social security plays a very important role in economic development and social progress. Firstly, it can maintain and improve the quality of workers by relieving them from worries over their health, aging, sickness, death, disability and unemployment, and providing necessary conditions for their and their children's education and vocational training, so that they can continuously improve their labor skills and scientific and cultural level. Secondly, it can regulate the social and economic relations by raising funds from the society and its members, and distributing them to those who have difficulties in maintaining basic livelihood, which will narrow the gap between the rich and the poor and regulate economic relations. Thirdly, it can maintain social stability by guaranteeing the basic livelihood of all members of society and adjusting economic relations, which will eliminate the possible destabilizing factors that may arise in this regard. Fourthly, it is necessary to reform and perfect the social security system in order to promote economic restructuring, transform the operating mechanism of state-owned enterprises and establish a socialist market economic system.

---

14   Selected Works of Deng Xiaoping, 1st edition, Vol.3, p.110-111.
15   Ibid., p.149.

After the founding of New China, our government attached great importance to the social security work and was devoted to the establishment and development of a social security system that included social relief, social insurance, social welfare and social care. After more than 50 years of unremitting efforts, we have made tremendous achievements in the work, including safeguarding people's basic livelihood, stabilizing social order and ensuring the smooth progress of economic construction.

At present, we are confronted with five major challenges in the social security work: firstly, the coverage of urban social security is still not wide enough, with a large number of workers from collective, private and foreign investment enterprises, free-lancers, individual businesses and migrant workers uncovered; secondly, there are difficulties in raising social security funds; evasion and delay in the payment of premiums is rampant; the adjustment of local fiscal expenditure structure is inadequate, with great dependence on the central government; and some channels for supplementing social security funds have not yet been opened up; thirdly, with the aging of population, requirements on pension and medical insurance become higher, but capital accumulation and safeguarding services are far from satisfactory; fourthly, with the acceleration of structural adjustment and the accession to the WTO, some industries in our country are impacted, resulting in increasing unemployment, which exerts unprecedented pressure on unemployment insurance; fifthly, since we have just begun to explore the social security in rural areas and small towns, the development of the system in most of the areas is still in its infancy.

To build an overall well-to-do society and develop a socialist market economy, we should establish and perfect the social security system that fits in with the level of economic development, which is also a fundamental plan for maintaining social stability and long-term peace and stability of the country. Based on the actual conditions in different places, we should try to realize the "independence of enterprises and institutions, diversified funding sources, standardization of the guarantee system and socialization of management services", by adhering to the principle of broad coverage, appropriate standards, and the combination of basic insurance and supplementary programs, so as to establish and perfect the social security system with Chinese characteristics.

The 3rd Plenary Session of the 16th CPC Central Committee put forward some specific measures to speed up the construction of a social security system that fits in with the level of economic development: to improve the basic pension insurance system for enterprise employees through integrating social pooling and individual accounts, and gradually funding the individual account; to include urban workers into the basic pension insurance; to establish and improve the provincial pension insurance funds; after improving the municipal coordination, to gradual implement provincial coordination; when conditions permit, to implement national coordination on the basic parts of the pension; to perfect the unemployment insurance system and merge the basic livelihood guarantee for laid-off workers in state-owned enterprises with unemployment insurance; to continuously improve the basic medical insurance system for urban workers, carry out the synchronous reform on health care and drug production and circulation system, expand the coverage of basic medical insurance, and improve social medical assistance and multilevel medical security system; to continuously implement worker's injury and maternity insurance; to actively explore the reform of social security system of government departments and public institutions; to perfect the minimum living allowance system for urban residents and determine the standards and methods of the insurance; to take a variety of ways including the transfer of part of state-owned assets according to law to enrich the social security fund; to strengthen the collection of social insurance funds, and expand the coverage of the collection; to regulate the supervision of the funds in order to ensure the safety of them; to encourage qualified enterprises to set up supplementary insurance programs and actively develop commercial pension and medical insurance; to combine the primary pension security in rural areas on family basis with community protection and state relief; and to explore the establishment of a system of minimum living allowance in rural areas where conditions permit. The 17th CPC National Congress further pointed out that it was necessary to speed up the establishment of a social security system covering both urban and rural residents, and to ensure people's basic livelihood, based on social insurance, social assistance and social welfare, with a focus on basic pension, basic medical care and minimum living allowance system, and supplemented by charity and commercial insurance, to accelerate the development of the social security system, and to further fulfill the basic tasks of establishing the social security system.

CHAPTER EIGHT

Building Socialist Democratic Politics with Chinese Characteristics

Section I

Exploration of the correct path for socialist political construction in China

First, there is no democracy without socialism and no socialism without democracy.

The term "democracy" first appeared in the book The Histories of Herodotus, an ancient Greek historian. It's combination of the words "people" and "power," meaning the power of the people, also known as "rule of the majority" or "the will of the majority." In societies in which classes and state exist, democracy manifests itself primarily as a form of state, a state formation. As Lenin said: "Democracy in Greek literally means the power of the people."[1]

In the long process of history, there had been the city-state, slave-owners' democracy of the Greece and Rome, other forms of political civilization forms, city parliaments of the autonomous cities in the feudal age, which have evolved to parliamentarian monarchies and finally evolved to democratic republics as the democracy of the western bourgeois democracy in capitalist societies. However, evaluating the issue from the aspect of class essence of democracy, these democracies in history were the democracies that could only be enjoyed by the minority exploiting classes, namely the ruling class, and the masses of working people are in the position of being oppressed and exploited. When analyzing the "democracy" in the Republic of Athens, Engels pointed out profoundly that there were about 455,000

---

[1]   Selected Works of Lenin, 3rd Edition, Vol. 4, p. 32.

inhabitants of Athens at that time, of whom only 90,000, the slave-owners and free men have enjoyed democratic rights. But the total number of 365,000 slaves were only production tools and property of others, i.e. talking machines. "The slaves also belong to the population: as against the 365,000 slaves, the 90,000 Athenian citizens constitute only a privileged class."[2]

Since the bourgeois revolution in modern times, the capitalist democracy has replaced the feudal autocracy, which is a great progress of human democracy. But the modern capitalist democracy, in essence, is only the bourgeois democracy and the state system of the bourgeois dictatorship, and it actually maintains the ruling and political interests of the bourgeoisie. The basic contradiction of capitalist society is the contradiction between the socialization of production and the private possession of production means. In the democratic system, the contradiction is reflected as the contradiction between the social nature of democracy itself and the monopoly of democratic rights by the minority. With the development of capitalism, the inherent hypocrisy and one-sidedness of the capitalism democracy becomes more and more obvious. Facts have proved that human society has never experienced the people's democracy ruled by the majority of people in the real sense under the exploitation system based on private ownership.

With the proletariat, which represents the advanced productive force, appearing on the historical stage, the replacement of capitalist democracy by a new democratic system, namely socialist democracy, has become the inevitable development of history. Socialist democracy is the first national democracy under non-exploitation system since the human society entered the class society. It enables the workers, peasants and intellectuals who make up the majority of the people to enjoy the most extensive democracy. Its essence exactly is people being the masters of the country. This is also the most fundamental political objective of the proletarian revolution. As Marx and Engels pointed out in the Manifesto of the Communist Party: "We have seen above, that the first step in the revolution by the working class is to raise the proletariat to the position of ruling class to win the battle of democracy."[3]

Therefore, democracy is always an important goal assiduously pursued by socialism, and an important and essential means to consolidate and develop socialism. For the socialism, "people's democracy is the life of socialism", as pointed out by Hu Jintao in the report of the CPC's 17th National Congress. It mainly includes the following two aspects:

---

2   Selected Works of Marx and Engels, 2nd Edition, Vol. 4, p.171.
3   Selected Works of Marx and Engels, https://www.marxists.org/archive/marx/works/1848/communist-manifesto/ch02.htm.

First, democracy is the essential requirement of socialism. There would be no socialism without democracy. It is stressed again in the report of CPC's 17th National Congress that "the more developed the socialist is, the more developed the democracy is". The socialist system, as a new type of social form which replaces the system of exploitation with the non-exploitation system for the first time in human history, implements the public ownership of the production means and distribution according to work. This kind of social economic foundation inevitably determines the implementation of the social system of people being the masters of the country in terms of superstructure. On the eve of the October Revolution, Lenin pointed out profoundly: "socialism is impossible without democracy because: (1) the proletariat cannot perform the socialist revolution unless it prepares for it by the struggle for democracy; (2) victorious socialism cannot consolidate its victory and bring humanity to the withering away of the state without implementing full democracy."[4]

After the 3rd Plenary Session of the 11th Central Committee of the CPC, the CPC has also become more aware of the correctness of this assertion. Deng Xiaoping once again emphasized in 1979: "There is no socialism without democracy and no socialist modernization."[5]

In 1980, he further pointed out: "We should continue to develop socialist democracy and improve the socialist legal system. This is a basic, consistent policy that has been carried out by the Central Committee ever since its 3rd Plenary Session, and there must be no wavering in its enforcement in future."[6]

Jiang Zemin brilliantly summed up this indivisible relationship between socialism and democracy as follows: "Socialism is the cause of the people, the cause of the people masses' conscious participation and the realization of their own interests. People are the masters of our society and the masters of the socialist cause. People's democracy is the essential requirement of socialism."[7]

Hu Jintao proposed more vividly in the report of the CPC's 17th National Congress: "People's democracy is the life of socialism".

Second, democracy is the objective need for the construction of the cause of socialist modernization, and there would be no socialist modernization without democracy. Reviewing the development course of international socialism, there is a general and extremely important historical experience.

---

4   Complete Works of Lenin, Vol. 28, p. 168, Beijing, People's Publishing House, 1990.

5   Selected Works of Deng Xiaoping, 2nd edition, Vol.2, p.168.

6   Ibid., p. 359.

7   CPCCC Party Literature Research Office: "Selection of Important Literature since the 14th National Congress" (Vol. I), p. 622f.

Namely, if the socialist country is not fully democratic or if the democracy is destroyed, the order of the socialist country will be in chaos. The state power will be in face of turbulence and crisis, and the economic construction will suffer major setbacks. In the new historical period, on the basis of summing up the historical experience and lessons, Chinese Communist Party fully affirms the status and role of democracy, and regards the development of socialist democracy as an extremely important strategic task and goal of building socialism with Chinese characteristics. In essence, the ruling of the communist party is to lead and support people to master the power of administering the country; ensure that the people exercise democratic elections, democratic decision-making, democratic management and democratic supervision, and enjoy extensive rights and freedoms in accordance with the law; respect and guarantee human rights. The construction of socialist modernization is not only economic construction, but also democratic political construction and spiritual civilization construction. Only full development of democracy can totally mobilize and play the enthusiasm, initiative and creativity of the masses of the people, and promote the development of socialist modernization; only full development of democracy can make the lines, guidelines and policies formulated by Chinese Communist Party truly accord with the will, interests and needs of the masses of the people and conform to the basic national conditions and objective laws of China, thus achieving the grand goal of building a "strong, democratic, civilized and harmonious socialist modernization country".

222

Second, the historical development of socialist democratic politics with Chinese characteristics

Chinese Communist Party is the vanguard of the Chinese working class and the vanguard of the Chinese people and the Chinese nation. Since its establishment in 1921, the Chinese Communist Party has always been responsible for the realization and development of the people's democracy. Therefore, in the long-term revolutionary struggle, the Chinese Communist Party has thoroughly affirmed the status of people for pushing history forward, mobilized the people for the people's revolution, and gone on a path of wholeheartedly representing and realizing the fundamental interests of the Chinese people and a path truly pursing and implementing democracy.

During the new democratic revolution, the Chinese Communist Party had creatively combined the universal truth of Marxism with the concrete reality of the Chinese revolution, put forward democratic concepts such as "workers and peasants democracy", "people's democracy", "new democracy", constantly enriched and developed the democratic political theory of Marxism, and successively created the realization forms of democratic politics which are suitable for Chinese actual conditions and can ensure people being the masters of the country, such as striking workers' congresses, peasant associations, workers, peasants and soldiers' representative soviet, councils, people's representative conference, and other practices and organizations. These claims and practices were in sharp contrast to the Kuomintang's dictatorial regime at that time, which reflected the people's wishes and won the support of the people. In July 1945, Mao Zedong, in a conversation with the famous patriotic democratic people Huang Yanpei and others, particularly pointed out that Chinese Communist Party had found a new path in the course of leading the people's revolution.

"This new path is democracy. It is only by letting the people supervise the government that the government cannot afford to relax. Only when everyone is responsible for it will there be no political death."[8]

In September 1949, on the eve of the founding of the new China, the Chinese Communist Party and the democratic parties, the people's groups and democratic personages without party, under the call of the Chinese Communist Party for democratic government building, jointly held the first plenary session of the Chinese People's Political Consultative Conference to discuss the plan for the establishment of a people's Republic and establish new China's national system and organizational form of the regime in accordance with the principle of democracy. The Common Program of the Chinese People's Political Consultative Conference, which was adopted at the meeting, stipulates clearly that: "The People's Republic of China is a state of new democracy, namely a state of people's democracy, and implementing the people's democratic dictatorship under the leadership of the working class, based on the alliance of workers and peasants, and in unity with the democratic classes and the peoples of the country"; "the state power of the People's Republic of China belongs to the people. The organs of the people exercising state power shall be the people's congresses at all levels and the people's governments at all levels". On October 1, 1949, the People's Republic of China was founded. This marked a fundamental change in the political status of the Chinese people, and led to the realization of the great leap of changing from the feudal autocracy with a history of more than 2,000 years and the failure of copying the western democratic political model in modern times to the construction of a new type of people's democracy with Chinese characteristics.

In 1953, the first universal suffrage with unprecedented scale was held countrywide. The people, through the election of their own representatives, exercised their right to be the masters of their own affairs, and convened the people's congresses at a higher level. In September 1954, the holding of the first meeting of the First National People's Congress and the launch of the first Constitution of the People's Republic of China marked the formal

8 Feng Xianzhi, Jin Chong (editors in chief): "Mao Zedong Biography: 1949-1976", p. 746, Beijing, Central Party Literature Press.

establishment of the system of the people's congress in the whole country. On this basis, China has gradually established the system of the people's congress, the system of multi-party cooperation and political consultation led by Chinese Communist Party, and the system of regional ethnic autonomy, forming the basic institutional framework of the socialist democratic politics with Chinese characteristics. The Chinese people have truly become the masters of their own affairs and the masters of the country, society and their own destiny.

The socialist democratic politics with Chinese characteristics is the unprecedented creation in the development history of democratic politics. It has no ready-made experiences for references, nor smooth development. From the late 1950s, because of the disturbance and influence of the "left" thought, the construction of democracy in China had experienced ups and downs. In particular, the 10-year "Cultural Revolution" caused detours to China's democratic politics. The so-called "Great Democracy" implemented during that period seriously undermined the socialist legal system, weakened the leadership of the Party and brought disasters to the Party, the country and the people. In December 1978, the Party held the 3rd Plenary Session of the 11th Central Committee to bring order out of chaos and correct the mistake of the "Cultural Revolution", which opened a new historical period of implementing reform and opening policy. Under the leadership of Deng Xiaoping, the Chinese communists and the Chinese people began a new exploration of building socialist democracy with Chinese characteristics. Under the support and promotion of Deng Xiaoping, the reform of the Party and the state leadership system was carried out, and the life tenure of the leading posts was gradually abolished. The Constitution of the People's Republic of China revised in 1982 summarizes the experience of democratic political construction since the founding of new China, and makes clear stipulations on the basic principles and basic system of socialist democratic politics in the form of constitution, which greatly promotes the course of the construction of socialist democratic politics in China.

After the 4th Plenary Session of the 13th Central Committee, the third generation of central leading collective of the Party, with Jiang Zemin as its core, further explored and promoted the socialist democratic political construction under the new historical conditions including reform and opening up and the development of socialist market economy. The construction of Chinese democratic politics entered a new stage as a result. On the basis of summing up the history and practical experience of China's socialist democratic politics, the 16th National Congress of the Party proposed: "To develop socialist democratic politics, the most fundamental is to adhere to the Party's leadership, people being masters of the country and the rule of law organically". This conclusion reveals the basic law of building the socialist democratic politics with Chinese characteristics, and raises the theory of democratic political construction in China to a new realm.

Since the 16th National Congress of the Party, the Party Central Committee, with Hu Jintao as the General Secretary, continuously promoted the self-improvement and development of the socialist political system through deepening reform and institutional innovation, further improved the democratic system, enriched the forms of democracy, widened the channels for democracy, and expanded and safeguarded the exercise of democratic rights by the people. In recent years, the Party and the government have established and improved the democratic supervision mechanism for the power operation from the aspects including the inner-party supervision, the supervision of the National People's Congress, the administration supervision, the judicial supervision and the public opinion supervision. The system of people's congresses at all levels in China is further improved. The speed of legislation is accelerated. The legislation quality is improved and the legislation process is open. The role of the representatives of the people's congress is further played; the system of multi-party cooperation and political consultation led by Chinese Communist Party has been strengthened, which has promoted the development of deliberative democracy in China; the construction of ethnic regional autonomous system is further promoted, and the law of ethnic regional autonomous has been further implemented; great progress has been made in the construction of grass-roots democracy. At the same time, the Party's inner-party democracy has expanded further: the central Committee of the Party sets an example. The Political Bureau of the Central Committee reports to the Central Committee. The major decisions of the central government are consulted in a broader context, and the experimental reform of the Party's internal democracy, such as the permanent system of the party representative congress has been carried out. In 2011, China solemnly declared to the world that: the socialist legal system with Chinese characteristics has been formed. This marks a new stage of China's overall implementation of the basic strategy of governing the country by law; at the same time, it is also a solemn declaration: China unswervingly implements the basic strategy of ruling the country according to law, and builds a socialist country ruled by law.

Third, the distinctive characteristics of socialist democratic political construction in China

The over 90 years history of the Chinese Communist Party has fully proved that the realization and development of people's democracy is the unswerving goal of the Chinese communists. The history since the founding of new China, especially since the reform and opening up, has shown that the Chinese people have successfully taken a development path of socialist democratic politics with Chinese characteristics under the leadership of Chinese Communist Party. This path has distinctive Chinese characteristics and institutional advantages.

China's democracy is the people's democracy led by Chinese Communist Party. Without Chinese Communist Party, there would be no new China and there would be no people's democracy, which is an objective fact proved by history. The Chinese people become the masters of their own affairs under the leadership of Chinese Communist Party through extremely hard and bitter struggling. China's democratic political system is founded by the Chinese people under the leadership of Chinese Communist Party. The development and improvement of the democratic political system in China is carried out under the leadership of Chinese Communist Party. The leadership of Chinese Communist Party has fundamentally guaranteed people being masters of the country.

Democracy in China is the democracy that the most people are the masters of the country. People being the masters of the country is the essence of socialist democracy in China. In China, the public ownership economy is the economic foundation of the socialist system. In the primary stage of socialism, the country adheres to the basic economic system with public ownership as the pillar and all forms of ownership developing together, and insists on the distribution system with distribution according to work as the main body and coexistence of various modes of distribution. This has decided, from the economic foundation, that China's democracy is not under the manipulation of capital and is not the democracy of the minority, but is the democracy of the majority of the people. In China, the scope of people enjoying democratic rights includes all those who are not deprived of political rights by law. The people's representatives and CPPCC (Chinese People's Political Consultative Conference) members in China have an extensive mass basis. They include not only the representatives of workers, farmers and cadres, but also the representatives of the democratic parties and the new social classes. Representatives and members participate in the political affairs and discuss the national affairs under the unified leadership of the Party, so as to absorb the public opinion in the widest sense.

China's democracy is a democracy with the people's democratic dictatorship as a reliable guarantee. The people's democratic dictatorship, on the one hand, requires the implementation of the broadest democracy among the people, respect for and guarantee of human rights, and ensure that state power is in the hands of the people and serves the people; on the other hand, it requires to use sanctions of dictatorship against various criminal acts, such as the destruction of the socialist system, endangering national security and public security, infringement of the personal and democratic rights of citizens, corruption, bribery and dereliction of duty, so as to protect the fundamental interests of the overwhelming majority of the people.

China's democracy is the democracy with democratic centralism as the fundamental organization principle and the mode of activity. The democratic centralism is the fundamental organization principle and the leadership principle of the Chinese state power. The implementation of democratic centralism requires the full development of democracy, collective deliberation, and the full expression and reflection of the will and demands of the people. On this basis, the correct views are collected and collective decisions are made to implement and meet the wills and requirements of the people. The implementation of democratic centralism also requires "respect for the majority and protection of the minority" and opposes to the "great democracy" of anarchism and the supremacy of the will of the individuals over the collective.

The current democratic system in China can provide effective political system guarantee for the reform and opening up and modernization construction of China. Under the premise of adhering to the socialist fundamental political system, we reform and improve the specific system of socialism. We creatively combine the control means of market economy with the basic system of socialism, and realize the transformation from the single planned economy system to the establishment of the socialist market economy system; based on the reality of the primary stage of socialism in China, we have established the basic economic system of keeping public ownership as the mainstay of the economy and allowing diverse forms of ownership to develop side by side; we actively participate in international competition, join in a series of important international organizations such as the World Trade Organization (WTO), and actively respond to various risks and challenges from the international community; we are vigilant against all kinds of decadent cultural erosion and at the same time absorb all the positive achievements of civilization including capitalism with broad mind and self-confidence to maintain the vitality of socialism.

Of course, China's democracy also requires constant development and improvement. Serving as a national system, democracy should go through a long, arduous and gradual process of historical development before attaining perfection. This is because democracy, as a kind of social superstructure, is bound to be restricted by certain social and economic foundation. For China, which is a socialist country based on backward economy and culture, there is still a considerable gap between the theoretical superiority of socialist democracy and the concrete practice of socialist democracy in reality due to the remnants of the old society and various historical conditions. Therefore, on the one hand, the socialist democracy is the highest form of human democracy development so far. On the other hand, socialist democracy should go through a long term of continuous construction and improvement before truly achieving the theoretical height in practice.

Section II

Socialist democratic political system with Chinese characteristics

First, the system of people's democratic dictatorship

On the eve of the founding of New China, in his article "On the People's Democratic Dictatorship", Mao Zedong pointed out clearly: "The combination of these two aspects, democracy for the people and dictatorship over the reactionaries, is the people's democratic dictatorship."[9]

This is the basic state system of China. The so-called state system in essence is the class essence of the state, namely which class or alliance of classes, lead and control the state power. The Constitution of the People's Republic of China clearly stipulates that China is a socialist country under the people's democratic dictatorship. It is led by the working class and is based on the alliance of workers and peasants. This is the fundamental nature of the state in China.

The people's democratic dictatorship is first and foremost a broad democracy for the majority of the people. Under current historical conditions of China, the scope of people's democracy has expanded unprecedentedly. In addition to the original classes of people in China, which included workers, peasants, cadres and intellectuals, there emerged the new social classes, such as the entrepreneurs and technicians of private science and technology enterprises, the management technicians employed by foreign enterprises, the entrepreneurs of private enterprises, the employees in intermediary organizations, the free and self-employed professionals, and so on. They are all the builders of the socialist cause with Chinese characteristics, namely a part of the people as a political category. Therefore, the people's democratic dictatorship of China has a broad class basis and gives the people broad democratic rights. The people not only have the right to administer state affairs, but also have the right to manage the economy and science, cultural and educational undertakings and the right to manage the social organization and social life of the grassroots. On the other hand, the people's democratic dictatorship has made clear that it is necessary to exercise dictatorship over the handful of bad elements and hostile forces opposing socialism and social revolution, who are hostile to and attempt to undermine socialist construction, so as to protect the socialist democratic system.

The people's democratic dictatorship has distinctive Chinese characteristics: firstly, evaluating from the class structure and the goals of the dictatorship, in the new democratic period and the transition to socialism, the

9   Selected Works of Mao Zedong, 2nd Edition, Vol. 4, p. 1475, Beijing, People's Publishing House, 1991.

classes participating in state power include not only working class, peasantry class and urban petty bourgeoisie, but also the national bourgeoisie in certain historical period. After entering socialism in 1956, national bourgeoisie inherited from the old China was dis-propertied by fair compensation, thus eliminated. And the vast majorityof them had been transformed into self-supported workers and participated in the state power as a member of the people. The object of dictatorship only targeted a very small number of hostile elements. Secondly, from the perspective of the relationship between the parties, multi-party cooperation led by the communist party is adopted. Under the leadership of Chinese Communist Party, the implementation of multi-party cooperation is a characteristic and advantage of China's political system. Third, from the concept of expression, the people's democratic dictatorship is in line with the national conditions of China and has its outstanding advantages. The formulation of the people's democratic dictatorship more comprehensively and clearly expresses the two interrelated aspects, namely the people's democracy and the people's dictatorship.

Second, the people's congresses system

The state system determines the form of government, and the system of government reflects the state system and adapts to the state system. The so-called system of government is the organizational form of the state power. Chinese Communist Party led the Chinese people to victory through the long-term struggles of the new-democratic revolution, and finally established the system of government that was adapted to the people's democratic dictatorship, namely the people's congress system. This system is the basic political system of the Chinese people being the masters of the country.

The system of the people's congress is the most distinctive feature of the socialist democratic politics in China, and is embodied in the following aspects:

First, all power of the state belongs to the people, which is the political basis, fundamental principle and core content of the system of the people's congress of China. The Constitution of the People's Republic of China stipulates: "all power of the People's Republic of China belongs to the people" and "the organs for the people to exercise state power are the National People's Congress and the local people's congresses at all levels". Under the system of the people's congress, all people, in accordance with the principle of democratic centralism, regularly elect the people's representatives through democratic elections to constitute the people's congresses at all levels as the organs of state power; the people's representatives shall elect other organs of state power through the people's congress to realize the administration of the affairs of the people; the people's representatives, through the people's congress, represent the will of the people to determine all major national and local affairs. The National People's Congress is the highest organ of state power, and its permanent organ is the Standing Committee of the National People's Congress.

Second, the system of the people's congress of China is the political system "combining legislative and executive powers". It is conducive to safeguarding the unity of national sovereignty, protecting the fundamental interests of the people, and maintaining efficient operation of the national machinery. "Combination of legislative and executive powers" is an important principle of the proletarian state power organization proposed by Marx based on the experience of Paris Commune. It is distinguished from the "three rights separation" system of the bourgeoisie. The principle of "combining legislative and executive powers" of the people's congress system is specifically embodied in that the National People's Congress is both the highest legislative organ and the highest organ of power with the supremacy and full authority of power. This mode of operation is conducive to the maintenance of the unity of national sovereignty and the maintenance of the fundamental interests of the people, and is beneficial to the efficient operation of the national machinery. Deng Xiaoping pointed out: "We have a unicameral legislature, the National People's Congress, which best conforms to China's realities. As long as it keeps to the right policies and direction, such a legislative body helps greatly to make the country prosper and to avoid much wrangling."[10]

Third, the National People's Congress is both the supreme legislative organ and the supreme organ of power. It mainly administers the country through the exercise of legislative power, power of decision, power of appointment and removal, and supervision power. Legislative power means that the formulation of national laws shall be fully discussed and democratically adopted by the people's congress, and then be promulgated and implemented. The power of decision refers to that some important matters of the state, such as the national economic and social development plan, the national budget, and the national administrative regional settings, shall be considered by the National People's Congress and its standing Committee. The power of appointment and dismissal refers to that the people's congresses at all levels have the power to elect, appoint the personnel of administrative and judicial organs at the same level, and the power to supervise and remove such personnel. Supervision power refers to legal supervision and work supervision: the so-called legal supervision refers to the power for the National People's Congress and its standing Committee to supervise the implementation of the constitution and laws; the so-called work supervision means that the work of the state administrative organs, trial and procuratorial organs must report to the people's congresses for supervision. At the same time, the people also have the right to supervise the work of the

10   Selected Works of Deng Xiaoping, 1st edition, Vol. 3, p.220.

people's congresses and the right to require representatives to perform their duties and dismiss incompetent representatives and personnel from state organs, thus ensuring that the people's congresses can focus on the will of the people, reflect the demands of the people and represent the interests of the people.

Fourth, China's people's congress system is the people's democratic system led by the CPC. But this kind of leadership is mainly political leadership. Namely, it is to ensure that the Party's lines, policies and guidelines are effectively implemented in the people's representative organs and other state organs, so that the state power is mastered by the people. At the same time, the leadership of the Party is also reflected in that the Party not only leads the people to set up the state power, but also leads and supports the organs of the political powers to fully play their functions to realize the will of the people.

The system of the people's congress of China is the best form of government suited to the state system of the people's democratic dictatorship in China. To make this kind of government fully realize the utility of people's democracy, it is necessary to constantly improve the system of the people's congress. The 17th Congress of the Party proposed to further strengthen and improve the system of the people's congress, ensure that the people's congresses and its standing committees perform their functions in accordance with the law and legislation and decision-making can better reflect the will of the people, gradually implement the election of deputies to the National People's Congresses according to the proportion of the same population in urban and rural areas, and optimize the knowledge structure and age structure of the members of the Standing Committee of the National People's Congress. This points out the direction for strengthening and perfecting the system of the people's congress of China.

Third, multi-party cooperation and political consultation system under the leadership of the CPC

The system of multi-party cooperation and political consultation under the leadership of Chinese Communist Party is a basic political system in China. It is the product of the combination of Marxist party theory and the United Front theory with the concrete reality of China, and is an important form of the socialist democratic political system in China.

The system of multi-party cooperation and political consultation led by Chinese Communist Party includes Chinese Communist Party and eight democratic parties. The eight democratic parties are: the Revolutionary Committee of the Chinese Kuomintang, the Chinese Democratic Alliance, the China Democratic National Construction Association, the Chinese Democratic Promotion Association, the Chinese Peasants' and Workers'

Democratic Party, the China Zhi Gong Dang, Jiusan Society and Taiwan Democratic Self-Government League.

The system of multi-party cooperation and political consultation under the leadership of Chinese Communist Party is formed in the revolutionary struggle of the Chinese people against imperialism, feudalism and bureaucrat-capitalism, and is the common choice of Chinese Communist Party and the democratic parties and the democratic personages from all walks of life. In the long-term revolutionary struggle, on the basis of common political demands, Chinese Communist Party and the democratic parties have gradually established close cooperation and have always stood together regardless of situation. After the 3rd Plenary Session of the 11th Central Committee of the Party, the system of multi-party cooperation and political consultation led by Chinese Communist Party has entered a new historical period. According to the general task of the new period and the present situation of the democratic parties, the 16-character guideline of "long-term coexistence, mutual supervision, sincere treatment with each other and the sharing of weal or woe" was put forward by the 12th Congress of the CPC in 1982 as the basic principle of the cooperation between Chinese Communist Party and the democratic parties in the new period.

The practice has proved that the system of multi-party cooperation and political consultation led by Chinese Communist Party is a political party system adapted to the state system of the people's democratic dictatorship of China. It helps to expand orderly political participation of people from all walks of life, helps to keep the development of interests in line with the overall development direction of the whole society, and helps to realize the fundamental interests of the most people. Therefore, this system is one of the democratic political systems with Chinese characteristics and in accordance with China's national conditions. It has great superiority and strong vitality.

The main ways of multi-party cooperation in China are: the democratic parties and non-party democrats participate in the National People's Congress and the CPPCC and participate in the administration of the country and the administration and discussion of state affairs; the communist party and the democratic parties carry out political consultation and democratic supervision through various channels; the outstanding talents from the democratic parties and non-party democrats are appointed to take leadership positions in the state organs. Multiple parties work together to realize multi-party cooperation.

The system of multi-party cooperation and political consultation under the leadership of Chinese Communist Party is a new socialist political party system, fundamentally different from the two-party system or the multi-party system of capitalist countries. First, in the political party system of China, the Chinese Communist Party is the ruling party. The democratic parties accept the leadership of the Chinese Communist Party. They are the close friends of the Chinese Communist Party, working together with the Chinese Communist Party on the socialist cause. They are the participatory parties rather than the parties out of power, let alone the opposition parties. Second, adhering to the leadership of Chinese Communist Party and adhering to the four cardinal principles are the political basis for multi-party cooperation. Third, all democratic parties participate in the state power, the administration of state affairs, the national policy and leadership candidates consultation, and the formulation of national guidelines, policies, laws and regulations. Fourth, Chinese Communist Party and the democratic parties all take the constitution as the basic criterion of activity. All democratic parties are protected by the constitution and enjoy political freedom, organizational independence and legal equality within the scope of the constitution.

Fourth, the system of ethnic regional autonomy

The ethnic regional autonomy system is third basic political system in China. It refers to the system of regional autonomy, the establishment of autonomous organs and the exercise of the right of autonomy under the unified leadership of the central government in minority enclaves. The core of ethnic regional autonomous is to protect the rights of ethnic minorities to take charge of their own affairs and to manage their own affairs. The implementation of such a system reflects China's adherence to the principles of equality, solidarity and common prosperity of all peoples.

China is a unified multi-ethnic country. Among the 56 ethnic groups, the Han nationality has the largest population, and the other 55 ethnic minorities having relatively few population are customarily referred to as ethnic minorities. At present, the Chinese government has established 155 ethnic autonomous areas, including five autonomous regions (the Inner Mongolia Autonomous Region established in 1947, the Xinjiang Uygur Autonomous Region established in 1955, the Guangxi Zhuang Autonomous Region established in 1958, and the Tibet Autonomous Region established in 1965), 30 autonomous prefectures and 120 autonomous counties (banner). The minority population of the autonomous region accounts for 71% of the total population of the minority nationalities, and the area of national autonomous areas accounts for about 64% of the total area of China.

The implementation of the system of ethnic regional autonomous is the basic policy for Chinese Communist Party to use Marxist national theory to solve the ethnic problems in China. It is determined by the actual conditions of China. First, China has been a unified multi-ethnic country since ancient times. Especially since the modern times, the people of all ethnic groups in

China have formed the relationship of going through thick and thin together in the long-term struggle against imperialism and feudalism and a unified multi-ethnic country composed of 56 nationalities has been founded. Therefore, the establishment of a unitary multi-ethnic unified country is the common requirement of all ethnic groups in China. Second, the development of ethnic groups in China is intertwined in the region. There are close connection economic life and extensive cultural exchange among ethnic groups. Thus, it is suitable for the implementation of ethnic regional autonomous within the united country. Third, China's socialist modernization should be realized in a unified multi-ethnic country where the ethnic groups support and help each other to obtain complementary advantages and common prosperity.

According to the provisions of the constitution of China and the law of ethnic regional autonomous, the organs of self-government of various ethnic autonomous areas in China enjoy broad autonomy. The first is to independently manage the internal affairs of the nation and the region; the second is to enjoy the right to make autonomous regulations and specific regulations; the third is to enjoy the freedom of religious belief; the fourth is to enjoy the right and freedom to use and develop the ethnic language, live and carry out social activities in accordance with traditional customs and customs. In addition, there are also rights to arrange, manage, develop economic construction and independently develop other undertakings such as education, science and technology, culture and so on.

The system of ethnic regional autonomous in China has the following two distinctive features: first, the regional autonomy of the Chinese nation is the autonomy under the unified leadership of the state. The national autonomous areas are the inseparable part of the People's Republic of China. The organs of self-government of all ethnic autonomous areas are the local political power under the leadership of the central government, and must obey the leadership of the centralized unity of the central government. The implementation of ethnic should not only benefit the national unity, social stability and national unity, but also facilitate the development and progress of the autonomous ethnic groups, and benefit the construction of the country. Any act that undermines the unity of the nation and creates the division of the nation is prohibited. Second, China's ethnic regional autonomous is not only the simple national autonomy or local autonomy, but is the combination of national factors and regional factors and the combination of political factors and economic factors. The main body of ethnic regional autonomy is still the people of ethnic minorities, and regional autonomy of the ethnic minority is the concrete embodiment of the people's democratic dictatorship in minority areas. In China, all ethnic autonomous areas must abide by the general principles stipulated in the constitution, firmly accept the leadership of Chinese Communist Party, take the socialist path, implement the national policies and decrees and fulfill their obligations under the constitution.

The regional autonomy of our nationalities "organically combines the centralization and unification of our country with the regional autonomy in the regions where the ethnic minorities live in compact communities and organically combines the political and economic factors. It is the basic system for resolving ethnic issues that is completely suited to our own national conditions. It is the great undertaking by the party and people of all nationalities."[11]

The implementation of ethnic regional autonomy both reflects the respect for the power of national minorities to govern their affairs and the management of their affairs and maintain the single form of state structure in China, thereby developing the ethnic relations of socialism and consolidating the state power of the unification of the motherland and the people's democratic dictatorship. In the twelfth five-year plan of China's national economic and social development, the central government clearly proposed that we should continue to thoroughly implement the ethnic policy of the Party and the state, guarantee the legitimate rights and interests of ethnic minorities, carry out publicity, education and creation activities of ethnic unity, consolidate and develop equal, unified and harmonious ethnic relationships.

Fifth, the grassroots democracy system by mass organizations

Grass-roots democracy is a democratic right which is directly exercised by workers, peasants, intellectuals and people from all walks of life in urban and rural grassroots political power organs, enterprises and institutions, including democratic rights in fields of politics, economy, culture and education. It permeates in all aspects of social life, with the characteristics of broad and direct participation of all citizens. It is not only a grass-roots democratic self-government system by mass organizations, but also a widespread and profound practice of socialist democracy as the embodiment of the people's democracy state system.

For the first time, the 17th Congress of the CPC included the system of community level self-governance into the basic category of the socialist democratic political system with Chinese characteristics, and proposed that the construction of the grassroots democratic self-government system should be promoted as the basic project of the development of socialist democratic politics. This is because: first, the development of grass-roots democracy is the basic work of the development of socialist democracy. China is the socialist country where the people are the masters of the

---

11 CPCCC Party Literature Research Office: "Selection of Important Literature since the 13th National Congress" (Vol.II), p. 1834.

country. To ensure that the working class and the broad masses of working people exercise the right to administer the state and manage economic and social affairs, it is necessary to ensure that they are masters of their economic, political, cultural and other social affairs at the grassroots level. Socialist democracy should also be achieved through the development of grass-roots democracy. Second, the grass-roots democracy, as the most extensive practice of socialist democracy, has the broadest mass and sociality. The development of direct democracy at the grass-roots level is conducive to improving the democratic quality of the whole people and their ability to exercise democratic rights, which creates conditions for the further development of socialist democracy.

After the 3rd Plenary Session of the 11th Central Committee of Chinese Communist Party, Deng Xiaoping, with strategically insight, initiated a series of major political activities, such as criticizing "Two Whatevers" and discussing the standard of truth, encouraging and supporting the people's active participation in social and political life and actively absorbing the political opinions of the people. Jiang Zemin pointed out clearly in the Party's 15th National Congress that: "It is the most extensive practice of socialist democracy to expand grassroots democracy, ensure people's direct exercise of democratic rights, manage their own affairs according to law, and create their own happy life". Since the 16th National Congress of the Party, the

Party Central Committee, with Hu Jintao as its general secretary, adhered to the principle of "establishing the party for the public and running the power for the people", and made efforts to promote the social atmosphere of abiding by and upholding the constitution, which further expanded and strengthened democracy at the grassroots level.

In the rural areas, the construction of the villagers' committees is the main way and result of the democratic political construction in the rural areas. Its basic content is to implement the villagers' autonomy. Namely, the broad masses of farmers directly exercise their democratic rights, elect villagers' committees, and implement self-management, self-education, and self-service. Democratic election, democratic decision-making, democratic management and democratic supervision are the main contents of the villagers' autonomy, and have become an effective way to expand the grassroots democracy and improve the level of rural governance in rural China.

In the cities, the central government of China mainly implements the community democratic political construction with urban residents' committee construction as the basic content. Urban residents' committee is a grassroots mass autonomous organization for Chinese urban residents to achieve self-management, self-education and self-service and is an important form of direct democracy at the urban grassroots level. At present, the urban community construction is advancing from point to face, from big cities to small and medium-sized cities, and from the eastern region to the western region, so as to improve urban residents' autonomy. The national activities of building the new community with order management, complete services, beautiful environment, civilization and peace are being carried out throughout the country.

In enterprises and public institutions, China implements the system "of conferences of workers and staff in enterprises" which is the basic system ensuring employees' democratic self-government of enterprises and public institutions. The laws and regulations of China, such as Constitution, Law of the PRC of Industrial Enterprises Owned by the Whole People, Labor Law, Trade Union Law and The Regulations of Workers and Staff's Congress of Industrial Enterprises Owned by the Whole People, have made corresponding stipulations on the system of workers' congresses: the democratic rights enjoyed by the employees in the enterprises and public institutions are realized mainly through the system of the workers and staff's congress. The workers and staff's congresses play an irreplaceable positive role in the implementation of democratic management in enterprises and public institutions, coordination of labor relations, safeguarding and protecting the legitimate rights and interests of employees, and promoting the reform, development and stability of enterprises and institutions.

Section III

Governing the country according to law and building a socialist country under the rule of law

First, the basic strategy that CPC represents and leads the people to control and run the state power

The implementation of the rule of law and the construction of a socialist state governed according to law is the basic strategy of the Party to lead the people to govern the country, the objective need to develop the socialist market economy, and which is an important symbol of the progress of social civilization, and an important guarantee for the long-term stability of the country.

The so-called governance of state according to law refers to the fundamental principle of governing the country. In September 1997, for the first time in Jiang Zemin's report to the 15th CPC National Congress, Jiang Zemin solemnly outlined the principle of governing the state according to law as the basic governance strategy of the party and the state. He pointed out: "This is a scientific definition of the rule of law, and also clearly shows that the rule of law proposed by the 15th National Congress of the Party is the rule of law with Chinese characteristics and is the rule of law integrating the adherence to the Party's leadership, the development of democracy, and the strict accordance with the law. Subsequently, in the constitutional amendment adopted at the second session of the 9th National People's Congress, the content of "the rule of law and building a socialist country ruled by law" was formally written."[12]

Second, the basic connotations and important significance of governing the country according to law

The rule of law is to carry out administration by law. The rule of law is to carry out governance by law. The rule of law certainly sublates the rule of man. Its core is to handle affairs according to law and govern the country according to law. In the history of the Party and Chinese socialism, proposing the policy of "the rule of law and building a socialist country ruled by law" and taking the rule of law as the basic strategy for the Party to guide the people to administer the country is a significant innovation of the theory and practice of socialist democracy construction with profound connotation.

First, the rule of law is the dialectical unity of developing socialist democracy and strengthening socialist legal system. Democratic politics and the rule of law are closely linked and interdependent. Only under democratic political system can the rule of law find the soil for survival and development. And the historical experiences have repeatedly proved that if people's democratic rights cannot be turned into institutions and laws and if such systems and laws are not stable, continuous and authoritative, the people's democratic rights will not be guaranteed.

Second, the subject of governing the country according to law are the masses under the leadership of the party. Who will rule the country according to law has a fundamental bearing on the nature of the legal system. Jiang Zemin pointed out: "Our socialist democracy is the most extensive democracy enjoyed by the people of all ethnic groups across the country. Its essence is that the people should be the masters of the country."[13]

This is exactly is the basic feature of socialist democracy. If the people are taken as the object of the rule of law and the minority national public officials to replace the law by personal views and govern the people by power, the socialist rule of law cannot be true.

Third, the objects of the rule of law include state affairs, economic and cultural undertakings and social affairs. Therefore, we must attach importance to the rule of law. The report of the CPC's 17th National Congress points out that power must be exercised in public in order to ensure that the power is exercised properly. We should improve the organization laws

---

12   Selected Works of Jiang Zemin, Vol.2, p.28-29.
13   Ibid., p.257.

and procedural rules and ensure that the state organs exercise their powers and perform their duties in accordance with the statutory powers and procedures. We should prevent the abuse of power by government or government workers at all levels, and punish law breaking while in charge of their enforcement and corruption through misuse of law.

Fourth, the rule of law and the leadership of the Party are mutually reinforcing relations. We should not replace government with the Party, nor replace government with the law. The rule of law serves as the basic strategy for the Party to lead people to govern the country, showing that the Party is the advocate of the rule of law. The Party guides people to make laws and carry out activities within the scope of the constitution and the law. The rule of law and the leadership of the Party are basically the same. However, in practice, we should realize the harmonious unification of the two parts. We should also constantly explore the basic mode and basic method of the Party's leadership in governing the country according to law, and formulate the legal principle of the relationship among the ruling party, the National People's Congress and the government.

Fifth, the core of the rule of law is to uphold the authority of the constitution and the laws, and govern the country based on the constitution and the laws. The national people, state organs staff and social organizations, enterprises and institutions must strictly follow the socialist legal system with the constitution as the core. Everyone should be equal before the law. No one and no organization should have the privilege of overcoming the constitution and the laws. And administrative regulations and rules cannot be inconsistent with the constitution and the laws.

The rule of law and building a socialist country ruled by law has great practical significance and historical significance: first, the rule of law is the basic guarantee of building socialist democracy, and is an important symbol of the progress of social civilization. Secondly, the rule of law is the objective need of developing socialist market economy. The essence of the socialist market economy determines that it must be rule-of-law economy. Only by the rule of law and building a socialist country ruled by law can we give full play to the advantages of the socialist market economy. Moreover, the rule of law is an important guarantee for the maintenance of social stability and the long-term stability of the country. Finally, the rule of law is an important symbol of the progress of social civilization. The construction of socialist spiritual civilization and the development of socialist culture must be guaranteed by the legal system. The rule of law is the basic strategy for the Party to lead the people to govern the country, the need of developing the socialist market economy, and an important guarantee of the country's long-term stability and stability. The strategic goal of the rule of law is to build a socialist country ruled by law.

Third, strengthening the socialist legal system

The socialist legal system is the legal system and the law enforcement mechanisms and principles established by the people according to their own will. It is the basic method for the people to be the masters of the country and to govern the country. The legal system is the premise and foundation of governing the country according to law. We should strengthen the socialist legal system construction while promoting the development of social and economic culture.

The basic requirement of strengthening the socialist legal system construction is "establishing legal basis, abiding by the laws, strict law enforcement and prosecuting violations of law". These four aspects are interrelated and mutually restricted. Establishing legal basis is the premise. Abiding by the laws is the core. Strict law enforcement is the key. And prosecuting violations of law is the guarantee.

"Establishing legal basis" is the basic premise to strengthen the socialist legal system. Therefore, we must first build the socialist legal system with Chinese characteristics, namely establishing a unified, complete and scientific legal system. In this regard, the 16th National Congress of the Party proposed a clear task which includes adapting to the new situation of comprehensive progress of socialist market economy and society and accession to the new situation of WTO, strengthening legislative work and improving the quality of legislation. After a long period of unremitting efforts, the socialist legal system with Chinese characteristics had been formed by 2010. This is a great achievement of the construction of socialist democratic politics in China, showing that we have established a complete social legal department, made basic principal laws in each legal department, and achieved harmony and scientific unification within each legal department. The socialist legal system with Chinese characteristic enables China to take a solid step towards the construction of the modern country and the construction of the rule of law. Of course, the socialist legal system with Chinese characteristics is an open and dynamic legal system advancing with the times and requiring timely modification and improvement.

In addition to "establishing legal basis, there also should be "abiding by the laws" which is to strengthen the core of socialist legal system. Experience has proved that the complete laws only are not the rule of law. The most important and the most fundamental is to strictly comply with the laws. Citizens, regardless of nationality, race, sex, occupation, family origin, religious belief, level of education, property status and duration of residence, must abide by the constitution, laws and other regulations on an equal footing, and no organization or individual shall be allowed to have privileges that exceed the constitution and the law.

"Strict law enforcement" is the key to strengthen the socialist legal system. It is to ensure the judicial organs to exercise the judicial power and procuratorial power independently and impartially according to law. In addition, while improving the socialist legal system, the law enforcement should be strengthened and the legal operation mechanism should be improved to ensure strict and impartial law enforcement and judicature. In accordance with the requirements of fair justice and civilized law enforcement, the institutional settings, functional division and management system of judicial organs should be improved to form the judicial system and work mechanism with clear powers and responsibilities, mutual coordination, mutual restriction and efficient operation to safeguard judicial authority, the legitimate rights and interests of citizens, legal persons and other organizations, social fairness and justice.

"Prosecuting violations of law" is the guarantee of strengthening the socialist legal system. It refers to that all illegal and criminal acts should be punished according to the principle of "taking facts as the basis and taking the law as the criterion". To uphold equality before the law, no organization or individual should have the privilege to go beyond the constitution and the law.

The construction of a country under the rule of law is a long-term historical process with gradual development, and it cannot be achieved overnight. It needs the development of economic, social, political, cultural and other objective conditions, and also needs the development of subjective conditions such as the development of thought. This requires us to start from our national conditions, actively explore in practice, gradually establish and improve the socialist legal system, and constantly advance the historical process of the rule of law.

Section IV

Building socialist political civilization and deepening political reform

First, the great significance of building socialist political civilization

From the 12th CPC National Congress to the 15th CPC National Congress, the Party has always stressed that the construction of both socialist material civilization and socialist spiritual civilization in tandem "should be adhered to with great importance"; on this basis, the 16th National Congress of the Party proposed the concept of "building socialist political civilization" for the first time. The report of the 17th National Congress of Chinese Communist Party further put forward the concept of "building ecological civilization". The four goals of—material, spiritual, political and ecological—civilization are interrelated, permeate, coordinate and interact with each other

First, it is of great theoretical significance to put forward "building socialist political civilization". As an organic social system, the socialist society contains four basic levels including economic construction, political construction, cultural construction and social construction. Based on this, the "four-in-one" overall arrangement of the construction of the socialist cause with Chinese characteristics is formed. The goal of economic construction is to create a highly advanced material civilization; the goal of political construction is to create a highly advanced political civilization; the goal of cultural construction is to create a highly advanced civilization; the goal of social construction is to build a socialist harmonious society. Political civilization is an important part of human civilization. Material civilization forms the basis of human civilization, and political civilization and spiritual civilization constitute the superstructure of human civilization. In the different historical stages of the development of human civilization, political civilization and spiritual civilization are based on the material civilization in a certain historical stage. Among it, the political civilization reflects the development status and progress of the political legal system in that historical stage, and provides the basic guarantee of political operation and political system for material civilization, spiritual civilization and ecological civilization. The 16th National Congress of the Party put forward "socialist political civilization" as a separate concept to emphasize it. It is an innovative formulation in the history of the Party, further improving the theory of human civilization development. It also enriches and develops the Marxist theory, and is a remark of the further development of the Party.

Second, it is of great practical significance to put forward "building socialist political civilization". The construction of "two civilizations" is inseparable from the construction of political civilization. In fact, since the 3rd Plenary Session of the 11th Central Committee of the Party, the Party has done a lot in the construction of socialist political civilization, such as the reform of the Party and state leadership system, the reform of the judicial system and the reform of the government institutions. All of these are the concrete embodiment of political civilization. But we must fully realize that there are still many problems in the construction of socialist political civilization in reality. For example, we are not democratic enough in many aspects of state affairs. And bureaucratism, corruption, and the lack of the rule of law are still common and even serious in certain places. From the historical perspective, since China is in and will be in the initial stage of socialism for a long term, the effects of the remnants of feudalism and capitalism from the feudal society with a history of more than 2,000 years and from the semi-colonial and semi-feudal society with a history of more than 100 years will still exist for a long time. Therefore, China's socialist democratic political construction has both considerable urgency and long-term difficulty.

Third, it is of profound historic significance to put forward "building socialist political civilization". Through the joint efforts of the whole Party and the people of the whole country, China has successfully achieved the first and the second strategic objectives of modernization. The people in general have achieved a well-off life, and are moving towards a more comprehensive, high-level and balanced well-off society. Moreover, the democratic consciousness, democratic demands and aspirations of the people are also significantly improved. Putting the socialist political civilization in the position as important as that of the socialist material civilization, spiritual civilization and ecological civilization is the objective demand of the social progress in China. It will undoubtedly make a historical breakthrough in the socialist democratic political construction and promote more comprehensive development of the socialist cause with Chinese characteristics.

Second, fundamental requirements of building a socialist political civilization

Seen from its basic connotation, civilization is a concept opposite to savagery and ignorance. Thus, generally speaking, civilization refers to a state of human progress and refers to all positive results created by human beings in material production and spiritual and cultural activities. Socialist political civilization is a high-level form of the development of human political civilization. It is the sum of the positive results created and accumulated by the socialist countries in their democratic political construction and all political activities. It is not only the accumulation of the achievements of civilization, but also the creation of civilization. Therefore, the socialist political civilization has both the connotation at the system level and the connotation at the practice level. Namely, the forms of the civilized social political system of socialism, including the state system and the political system of socialism and other civilized political systems of socialism (the judicial system), are an important content of building the socialist political civilization; and the political practice of socialism, namely the political activities of the socialist countries such as the decision-making process, the judicial process and the supervision process of the communist party and the state, should be realized and developed in accordance with the requirements and methods of civilization, which is the inevitable requirement of socialist political civilization.

To develop socialist democratic politics and build socialist political civilization, the most fundamental requirement is to organically unify the Party's leadership, people being masters of the country and the rule of law. This is the basic policy that we must follow to promote the construction of political civilization, and is also the essential feature distinguishing the socialist political civilization in China from the capitalist political civilization. First, the leadership of the Party is the fundamental guarantee of people being masters of the country and the rule of law. It is under the leadership of the communist party that people being masters of the country and the rule of law is carried out. Chinese Communist Party, as a ruling party of the socialist country with more than 1.3 billion people, is in an absolute leadership position in the political life of the country, which makes the Party leadership decisive for the realization of people being masters of the country and the rule of law. The most fundamental mission of the Party is to represent the fundamental interests of the vast majority of the Chinese people, establish the party for the public and run the power for the people, lead and support the people to be the masters of the country through the formulation of correct guidelines, guidelines, policies and theoretical platforms, which is the greatest advantage of the socialist democratic political construction in China. Second, people being masters of the country is the essential requirement of socialist democracy. The people of all ethnic groups in the country are the main body of building the cause of socialism with Chinese characteristics. Whether the people can really be the masters of the country, and whether the enthusiasm and creativity of the people can be given full play is the fundamental standard for inspecting the leadership and ruling ability of the Party, and the fundamental standard for verifying the realization degree of socialist democracy; only if the Party can truly achieve the public opinion, seek the benefit of the people and win the hearts and minds of the people, can it be supported and advocated by the people and never be invincible. Third, the rule of law is the basic ruling strategy of the Party and the country. In current historical conditions, the will of the Party and the people will be fixed mainly through the laws. The Party's leadership and people being masters of the country will be realized in the legal system through the rule of law. In modern society, the power of the ruling party must pass through certain legal transformation procedures before turning into the social public power of ruling the country. The constitution and the laws are the embodiment of the will of the people, and the embodiment of the Party's claims. To ensure that the Party represents the fundamental interests of the people, the Party's leadership and ruling way should conform to the principles of the rule of law. In this way, the Party's administration activities will strictly be within the scope of the constitution and the laws.

Third, actively and steadily promote the political system reform under the premise of adhering to the fundamental system of socialism

Political system refers to the concrete manifestation and the realization form of the political system. The political system in China refers to the specific leadership system, organizational system and work system which conforms with the fundamental system of the state.

After the founding, China established the fundamental system, namely people's democratic dictatorship, and established the specific political system adapted to the state system at the same time. However, since the founding of new China, China had not been completely freed from the backward economic culture. In addition to, there were also complicate factors such as the influence of the Soviet model. As a result, the Party and the country had made mistakes in the specific leadership system, organizational forms and working methods, such as excessive concentration of power, lack of supervision and other defects, and even made serious mistakes such as the "Cultural Revolution". In order to build China into a strong and prosperous, democratic and harmonious socialist modern power, it is necessary to carry out the reform of the political system. In 1980, Deng Xiaoping put forward in *The Reform of the Party and State Leadership System*, the programmatic document of the political system reform in China, that we should reform the parts of our specific system which are not adapted to the socialist requirements and which are not completely conform to the socialist requirements, so as to fundamentally eradicate the disasters like the Cultural Revolution", promote the development of social productive forces and the construction of socialist democracy, and ensure the long-term stability of the country.

How to promote the reform of the political system? In general, we must follow the report of the 17th National Congress of the Communist Party of China: "We must adhere to the correct political orientation, regard the people as the masters of their own affairs, and aim to increase the vitality of the party and the state and mobilize the enthusiasm of the people. We should extend socialist democracy, build a socialist country under the rule of law and develop a socialist political civilization."[14]

Specifically, the following principles should be adhered to:

First, to adhere to the correct political direction, the first is to ensure the effective governance of the country by the people under the leadership of the Party. The adherence to the leadership of the Party is the key to achieve the stability and development of China and the key to realize socialist modernization. In the 21st century which is full of opportunities and

14   CPCCC Party Literature Research Office: "Selection of Important Literature since the 17th National Congress" (Vol.II), p.22.

challenges and in contemporary China, there is no political party having gathered Chinese elites as much as those collected by Chinese Communist Party. There is no party deeply aware of the history and conditions of China like Chinese Communist Party. And there is no party having accumulated so many strategies and experience in governing the country like Chinese Communist Party. It is under the leadership of Chinese Communist Party that the people really become the masters of the country. In order to ensure the effective governance of the people under the leadership of the country, the Party leaders should be good at turning the Party's ideas into law, administering the state by relying on the law, and managing the society, so that all the work of the country can run under the rule of law.

Second, the political system reform involves political thought, political system, administrative management, legal construction and many other aspects. It is a complex and long-term system engineering with extensive contents. Each measure involves the interests of thousands of people, and should be in steps, guided and orderly. The policy of reform should be firm, but the method should be fine and steady. We should pay great attention to and conscientiously do the work of maintaining social stability, and always maintain the social and political situation of stability and unity, and promote the reform of the political system in an orderly manner in a harmonious and stable environment. Looking at the general law of human democracy development, we usually have experienced such evolution trend: one is the development of economy and education; the second is the construction of civil society and the rule of law society; and the third is the orderly expansion of the political and democratic rights of citizens. If the order is wrong, the society often will have to pay a heavy price.

Third, to promote the reform of the political system, we must unswervingly follow our own path of political development. To evaluate the correctness of the political system, political structure and policy of a country, there are three key points: first, whether the political situation of the country is stable; second, whether the unity of the people and the lives of the people can be improved; third, whether the productive forces can be continuously developed. The current democratic system in China can maintain the long-term stable development of the country and benefit the long-term stability of the country. Under the socialist democracy with Chinese characteristics, the state power has a high stability, and the national policy has obvious continuity, which is the first condition of the sustainable development of the economy and society. Since the 1990s, many countries have blindly introduced the western "democracy" system and the results have stimulated more chaos and conflict. The most conservative number of deaths in the Bosnia War in Yugoslav is more than 100,000 according to estimation. And the Bosnia War becomes the war with the largest number of deaths after the Second World

War in Europe. Take Iraq, which was forced to accept the Bush government's "democratic gift" in the form of war, as an example. Several years after the war, the people in Baghdad described their tragic situation as "hell on earth". While, under the current political system in China, we have maintained social stability and economic development for long term. The Chinese people live and work in peace and contentment, and the country is increasingly prosperous and prosperous. Of course, it does not mean that China's political system reform cannot and do not need to absorb and draw lessons from the positive results of western political civilization. The western political civilization contains the common civilized achievements of human society. Therefore, we can draw lessons from some of its thoughts, forms and methods. However, the learning and absorbing should be analyzed and criticized. The history and reality of China are very different from the western countries. We are completely different from capitalist countries in terms of ideology, value concept and economic foundation. The political and economic system in the western world cannot be copied by China. It is not only because of various concepts and theories from the western system which are significantly different from Chinese reality, but also because of the irreconcilable conflicts under several basic premises of both parties. The system suitable for the western developed capitalist countries is not necessarily suitable for the developing socialist countries in the east. Based on the reality of China, if the three powers, if the separation of three powers and the multi-party rotation of the ruling party is implemented in China, there will be chaos of the national social and political life and there will be no peace in the country and the society.

In the current and future period, the main task of China's political system reform includes: first, to improve the democratic rights protection system, implement democratic election, democratic decision-making, democratic management, democratic supervision, improve the system of democracy, enrich democratic forms, realize the institutionalization, standardization and sequencing of socialist democracy politics, and consolidate the political status of people being the masters of the country. Second, to improve the legal system, uphold the unity and dignity of the socialist legal system, and establish the authority of socialist legal system. Third, to improve the judicial system mechanism, adhere to the judicature for the people, carry out fair justice, promote the reform of the judicial system and work mechanism, build a just, efficient and authoritative socialist judicial system, and play the role of judicature in maintaining fairness and justice. Fourth, to build a service-oriented government, deepen the reform of administrative management system, optimize institutional settings, pay more attention to the performance of social management and public service functions, and strengthen the social management and public service functions in accordance with the requirements of changing functions, integration of power and responsibility, strengthening service, improving management and increasing efficiency. Fifth, to deepen the construction of the Party conduct and of an honest and clean government and fight against corruption, adhere to the strategic guideline of combating corruption and upholding integrity including party administering by the party itself, strengthening Party self-discipline, carrying out treatment of both symptoms and root causes and comprehensive treatment, simultaneously promoting punishment and prevention and paying attention to prevention. In addition, it is also necessary to promote the punishment integrating education, system and supervision and establish the system of corruption prevention.

CHAPTER NINE

Building A Socialist Culture with Chinese Characteristics

Section I

Strategic status of socialist cultural construction with Chinese characteristics

First, the connotation and characteristics of socialist culture with Chinese characteristics

Culture is a realm with very rich content and can be comprehended in broad and narrow senses. Broadly speaking, culture refers to the sum of material wealth and spiritual wealth created by human in the process of transforming nature and society; narrowly speaking, culture includes the ideological concepts, in line with economy and politics, in the fields of humans' social life including social thought trends, morals and manners, literature and art, education and science and other spiritual/intellectual creations. In the present era, culture is increasingly becoming an important source of national cohesion and creativity, a vital element of comprehensive national strength of countries which contest among themselves. It has become the ardent aspiration of Chinese people to enrich their spiritual and cultural lives. Culture as a powerful source comprehensively fuses nation's vitality, creativity and cohesion.

The Chinese Communist Party has always attached great importance to cultural construction. As early as during the period of the new-democratic revolution, Mao Zedong put forward: "We want not only to change a politically oppressed and economically exploited China into a politically free and economically prosperous China, but also to change a China which has been ignorant and backward under the rule of the old culture into a China that will be enlightened and progressive under the rule of a new culture."[1]

---

1   Selected Works of Mao Zedong, 2nd Edition, Vol.2, p.663.

He put forward a series of views on cultural construction in many works during the democratic revolution and after the founding of new China, emphasizing the construction of a national, scientific and popular new democratic culture led by proletarian cultural thought. Literature and art should serve the public, absorb the essence of national culture, excluding its feudal dross, promote a hundred flowers blossom and a hundred schools of thought contend, make the past serve the present, make foreign things serve China etc., these have become important guidelines for the construction of our culture.

Since the 3rd Plenary Session of the 11th Central Committee of CPC, Deng Xiaoping has made a constructive exposition of the thought on the construction of socialist spiritual civilization while vigorously promoting the construction of economic and democracy and legal system in the process of leading the development and construction of the socialist path with Chinese characteristics. He pointed out that the socialist spiritual civilization is the key feature of the socialist society. "While working for a socialist civilization which is materially advanced, we should build one which is culturally and ideologically advanced by raising the scientific and cultural level of the whole nation and promoting a rich and diversified cultural life inspired by high ideals."[2]

To "grasp both links at the same time and attach sufficient importance to both" material civilization and spiritual civilization, the perfection of both civilizations is a veritable socialism with Chinese characteristics. To improve the ideological and moral quality and scientific and cultural quality of the whole nation, cultivate a new socialist generation with ideals, morality, culture and discipline. Under the guidance of this idea, the 6th Plenary Session of the 12th Central Committee of CPC passed the "Resolution of the CPC Central Committee on the Guiding Principles for Building a Socialist Society with an Advanced Level of Culture and Ideology" in 1986, and in 1996 the 6th Plenary Session of the 14th Central Committee of CPC passed the "The Resolution of CPC Central Committee on Several Important Issues about Strengthening the Construction of Socialist Spiritual Civilization".

Along with the progress of the practice of building socialism with Chinese characteristics, the Party has been constantly deepening its understanding of spiritual civilization construction and cultural construction. The 15th National Congress of the Party put forward the concept of "socialist culture with Chinese characteristics", which was brought into the fundamental principles of the primary stage of socialism together with building socialist economy & politics with Chinese characteristics. The 16th National Congress of the Party regards cultural construction as an important aspect

---

2   Selected Works of Deng Xiaoping, 2nd edition, Vol.2, p.208.

of building a well-off society in an all-round way. Jiang Zemin pointed out that the Chinese Communist Party should always represent the direction of China's advanced culture, insist on arming people with scientific theory, guiding people with correct public opinion, remolding people with lofty ideals, and inspiring people with excellent works; The socialist culture with Chinese characteristics is a significant symbol of comprehensive national strength and to construct a socialist culture with Chinese characteristics is to cultivate citizens with lofty ideals, moral integrity, better education and good sense of discipline, guided by Marxism, and to foster a national, scientific and public socialist culture marching towards modernization, embracing the world and future; We should highlight the themes of the times and encourage diversification in a unified manner, closely band together the rule of law and the rule of virtue; etc. These important ideas point out the direction of cultural construction.

Since the 16th National Congress of the Communist Party of China (CPC), the Party Central Committee with Hu Jintao as General Secretary put cultural construction in a more prominent position, emphasizing the need to firmly grasp the direction of the advanced socialist culture, to build a socialist core value system and develop a harmonious culture. Hu Jintao pointed out that the socialist core value system is the essence embodied in the socialist ideology, and we must build a socialist core value system, enhance the attraction and cohesion of socialist ideology. Harmonious culture is the important spiritual support of all people's unity and progress, we need to build a harmonious culture, cultivate a civilized prevailing custom. Chinese culture is the inexhaustible driving force of the Chinese nation to keep its unity and make progress from generation to generation, we need to carry forward Chinese culture and construct the common spiritual home for the Chinese nation. The liberation and development of cultural productive forces is the definite path to prosper the culture, we need to promote cultural innovation and enhance the vitality of cultural development. The 17th National Congress of the Party put forward the strategic task of enhancing the soft power of the national culture and made a comprehensive plan for the rise of the new upsurge of the socialist cultural construction and the great development and prosperity of the socialist culture. The 6th Plenary Session of the 17th Central Committee of CPC passed the "Decision of the Central Committee of the Communist Party of China on Several Important Issues in Deepening the Reform of the Cultural System and Promoting the Great Development and Prosperity of the Socialist Culture". The guiding ideology, important principles and objectives and tasks of advancing the cultural reform and development are specifically stated, calling for effort for the construction of a socialist powerful cultural country.

In the long-term cultural construction practice, the Communist Party of China combined Marxism with the reality of our country's cultural construction, formed a series of important theoretical achievements on cultural construction, and creatively enriched and developed the Marxist cultural theory. The socialist culture with Chinese characteristics, in terms of its main content, is consistent with the socialist spiritual civilization that has always been advocated since reform and opening up. In contemporary China, developing an advanced socialist culture and building a harmonious culture means building a socialist culture with Chinese characteristics. To realize the grand goal of socialist modernization and the great rejuvenation of the Chinese nation, we must firmly grasp the direction of the advanced culture of socialism and strive to build a socialist culture with Chinese characteristics.

The socialism culture with Chinese characteristics has the following distinctive features: first, Scientificity. The socialism culture with Chinese characteristics is guided by the scientific world outlook and methodology, which embodies the advancing direction of the advanced culture and reflects the requirements of human development and progress. It can greatly inspire the enthusiasm, initiative and creativity of the masses and transform the spiritual power into the material strength for the common struggle of the masses, and is the advanced culture that can materially lead the development and progress of contemporary China. Second, Contemporaneity. Socialism with Chinese characteristics focuses on the development and changes and requirements of the present era, grasp the pulse of the times, reflect the trend of the times, and is always up-to-date. It not only originated from more than five thousand years of civilization of the Chinese nation, but also is rooted in the practice of socialism with Chinese characteristics. It reflects the basic characteristics of economy and politics in the primary stage of socialism in China, and has played a huge role in promoting economic and political development. Third, Nationality. The socialist culture with Chinese characteristics inherits and carries forward all the outstanding ideology, morality and cultural achievements in the history of our nation, and forms a new culture organically combining socialism contents with form of the Chinese nation. It conforms to the national psychology, reflects the national characteristics, embodies the national character, binds the fundamental interests of our people of all nationalities together, expresses the common aspiration of the broad masses of the people and obtains the broad acceptance of the people of all ethnic groups. Fourth, Openness. The socialism culture with Chinese characteristics is closely integrated with the basic system of socialism in China, and it has the character of advancing with the times and the grace of openness and tolerance. It promotes the themes of the times, advocates diversification, and is good at absorbing the excellent ideology and culture achievements created by mankind, and always maintain the vigor and vitality of socialist culture by organically integrating persistence with development, dominance with inclusiveness, carrying forward tradition with standing on the basis of contemporary society.

Second, the great significance of building socialist culture with Chinese characteristics

Cultural construction possesses a very important strategic position in the overall layout of the cause of socialism with Chinese characteristics. The construction of socialist culture with Chinese characteristics and the development of advanced socialist culture is of great significance to reform, opening up and modernization.

First, vigorously strengthen the construction of socialist culture with Chinese characteristics is of great significance to promote the all-round development of the cause of socialism with Chinese characteristics and is an inevitable requirement for the current comprehensive construction of a well-off society. The socialist society is a full scale development and all-round progress society. Neither material poverty nor spiritual emptiness is socialism. A certain culture is a reflection of politics and economy, at the same time, it has a tremendous impact on certain politics and economy. Therefore, both material and spiritual civilization should be grasped and both hands hardened. "Material progress will suffer delays and setbacks unless we promote cultural and ethical progress as well. We can never succeed in revolution and construction if we rely on material conditions alone."[3]

To achieve the grand goal of socialist modernization, what's necessary is to have not only a prosperous economy, a sound democratic politics, but also a prosperous culture. Only the organic combination and coordinated development of these three aspects, can successfully promote the cause of socialism with Chinese characteristics, and achieve the goal of socialist modernization.

After the founding of new China, especially since the reform and opening up the unremitting efforts have brought rapid development to China's economic society, the people's material and cultural life has been greatly improved, but the cultural construction is still inadequate, not suited to the requirements of the overall construction of a well-off society, as well as to the people's growing spiritual and cultural needs. Accelerate the cultural construction, and constantly meet the people's growing multi-level spiritual and cultural needs, is what is required of the full implementation of the national development strategy, and the achievement of the goal of building a well-off society in an all-round way.

---

3   Selected Works of Deng Xiaoping, 1st edition, Vol.3, p.144.

Second, vigorously strengthen the construction of socialist culture with Chinese characteristics to provide spiritual power, intellectual support and ideological guarantee for the reform and opening up and modernization. The construction of socialist culture with Chinese characteristics and the development of advanced socialist culture can improve the scientific and cultural quality of laborers, create talents to meet the needs of modernization, provide labor force with high scientific and cultural knowledge and mastery of labor skills and offer a strong scientific support and intellectual support to smoothly achieve modernization strategic objectives; it can enable people, on the basis of common interests, to form common ideals and moral standards, to improve people's ideological and moral qualities, to stimulate and inspire people to fight for modernization; to guide people to identify and accept the socialist basic economic system and political system, to put into a comprehensive, dialectical and developmental perspective on the developing socialism, to establish a correct world outlook, outlook on life and values, to firm belief in socialism, to enhance national self-esteem, self-confidence and pride, so as to provide a strong ideological guarantee for reform and opening up and modernization construction.

Third, it is of great significance to greatly strengthen the construction of socialist culture with Chinese characteristics, to improve the soft power of the national culture and to enhance the international competitiveness. Socialist culture with Chinese characteristics is an important symbol of comprehensive national strength. With the further development of the world multi-polarization, the economic globalization and the ever-increasing progress of science and technology, the degree of integration of culture and economy and politics has been deepened, the combination of culture with science and technology has been more closely, the cultural content of the economy has been increasingly improved, the economic function of culture is getting stronger and stronger, culture has become an important factor in the country's core competitiveness. The country that occupies the commanding heights of cultural development, that has a strong cultural soft power, will be able to win initiative in the fierce international competition. The role of culture has become increasingly prominent, not only the economic and social development are more and more dependent on cultural support, cultural products and services directly become an important part of international trade and international competition, but also cultural fields have become the main battlefield of the international political struggles and international ideological contests. More and more countries are taking the improvement of the cultural soft power as an important development strategy. China is a developing socialist country, in order to stand in an invincible position in the new international competition, effectively resist the Western ideological and cultural infiltration, safeguard national development interests and cultural security, we must uphold our own cultural ideals, and form cultural advantages adapting to China's economic and social development and international status, enhance the national cultural soft power, promote Chinese culture, and strive to build a socialist country with a powerful culture.

Third, the fundamental tasks of building socialist culture with Chinese characteristics

The basic task of building socialist culture with Chinese characteristics is to meet the needs of reform and opening up and the socialist modernization construction, cultivate socialist citizens with ideals, morality, culture and discipline, and improve the ideological and moral quality and scientific and cultural quality of the whole nation. Improving the ideological and moral quality and scientific and cultural quality of the whole nation is not only the starting point of the construction of socialism with Chinese characteristics, but also its foothold. Nowadays, when science and technology are developing rapidly and cultural contests collision among the nations have become intensive, if people's ideological and moral qualities and scientific and cultural quality are not fundamentally improved, the realization of the goal of socialist modernization can only be empty talk.

To cultivate socialist citizens with ideals, morality, culture and discipline is also the need to promote the all-round development of human beings. The construction of a socialist modern country and the advancement of the socialist society in its entirety, in the final analysis, are for the all-round development of human beings, which is the ultimate goal of the socialist society and the communist society. To achieve the comprehensive development of man is a long-term process, to cultivate citizens with four qualifications points out the direction of the goal to promote the all-round development of human beings. At the present stage, it is necessary to guide people, educate people and train people in accordance with the requirements of "four qualifications", and gradually make all citizens establish noble ideals and beliefs, lofty moral feelings, conscious discipline and high cultural quality, give full play to the spirit of creation, greatly improve the spiritual realm, continuously move the overall level of all-round development of human beings toward a higher level.

As early as the initial period of the founding of the new China, Mao Zedong raised the idea that "the majority of youth should keep fit, study well and work hard" and required that they should take the life path of becoming "red and professional." He treated moral, intellectual and physical all-round development as an important standard for training socialism successors. After the 3rd Plenary Session of the 11th Central Committee of CPC, in the face of the arduous task of reform and opening up and socialist modernization construction, Deng Xiaoping put forward the goal of nurturing idealistic, moral, well-educated and disciplined new socialist people. In the practice of promoting the cause of socialism with Chinese characteristics, Jiang Zemin further put forward that we should strive to improve the ideological and moral qualities and the scientific and cultural quality of the whole nation, and provide a strong spiritual and intellectual support for economic development and overall social progress and cultivate citizens with lofty ideals, moral integrity, better education and good sense of discipline generation after generation who can meet the requirements of socialist modernization . At the new stage of the new century, Hu Jintao stressed the need to focus on improving the quality of people, promote the comprehensive development of human beings, strengthen ideological and moral construction, develop scientific education and culture, cultivate socialist citizens with ideals, morality, culture and discipline, which is the requirement of building a well-off society in an all-round way and accelerating the socialist modernization.

Ideals, morality, culture and discipline is an organic unity, and is the comprehensive requirements of socialist modernization construction on the quality of people. While ideals, morality and discipline are the ideological and moral requirements on citizens; culture is the requirement on scientific and cultural quality of citizens. Ideological and moral quality and scientific and cultural quality can complement each other, promote each other and develop in a harmonious way. In the "four qualifications", ideal is the core and spiritual pillar, morality is the norms of behavior and the embodiment of ideals, discipline is the important guarantee to achieve ideals and maintain morality, culture is the foundation and the essential condition to form ideals and beliefs, moral sentiments and discipline. These four aspects constitute the overall standard of cultivating socialist citizens. To build socialist culture with Chinese characteristics and to develop socialist advanced culture, we must keep cultivating talents in accordance with the overall standard of "four qualifications" to improve the overall quality of the people and provide intellectual support and talent support for reform and opening up and modernization construction.

Fourth, the basic principles (policies) of socialist cultural construction with Chinese characteristics

To build socialist culture with Chinese characteristics requires proper guidelines to develop and prosper. We should hold high the great banner of socialism with Chinese characteristics, take Marxism-Leninism, Mao Zedong Thought and the theoretical system of socialism with Chinese characteristics as the guide, thoroughly implement the scientific concept of development, adhere to the direction of socialist advanced culture, take scientific development as the theme, take building socialism core value system as the fundamental task, so as to meet the people's spiritual and cultural needs as the starting point and the foothold, to reform and innovate as the driving force, develop national, scientific, and public socialist culture marching towards modernization, embracing the world and future, cultivate high cultural awareness and cultural confidence, improve the civilization quality of the whole nation, enhance the national cultural soft power, promote Chinese culture, and strive to build a socialist powerful cultural country.

We must adhere to the "two serve", that is, serve the people and serve the direction of socialism. Vigorously develop the advanced culture, support healthy and beneficial culture, and strive to transform backward culture, resolutely resist the decadent culture. Strongly advocate all ideas and spirit that are conducive to the development of patriotism, collectivism and socialism, and vigorously promote all ideas and spirit that are conducive to reform, opening up and modernization construction, and vigorously promote all ideas and spirit that are conducive to national unity, social progress and people's happiness, and strongly advocate all ideas and spirit that are conducive to striving for a better life through honest work. Insist on occupying ideological positions by use of advanced culture, and constantly improve the quality of cultural product and the level of cultural appreciation of the masses, never allow products which may poison the people, pollute the society and are anti-socialism to spread unchecked. We must strive to transform the backward culture, resolutely prevent the decadent culture to erode the people, gradually reduce and eliminate the breeding ground for them, and strive to form a positive, civilized and healthy way of life in the whole society.

We should strive to carry out the "Double Hundred" policy, i.e., letting a hundred flowers blossom and a hundred schools of thought contend, and strive to create a lively, pragmatic and good atmosphere within the scope stipulated by the Constitution, fully carry forward the academic democracy and artistic democracy, advocate different views and schools to freely discuss on academic issues, promote different artistic styles and schools to contend and learn from each other in the creation of art, promote the healthy and reasoning criticism and counter-criticism. Highlight the themes of the times, promote diversity, and fully mobilize the enthusiasm and creativity of the broad masses of literary and art workers, and promote the prosperity of academic research and artistic creation. Adhere to the "Three Close", i.e. close to reality, close to life and close to the masses, respond to and solve practical problems, reflect the nature of life, meet the cultural needs of the masses. We should continue to promote the innovation of cultural ideas, contents, forms, institutional mechanisms and means of communication, and enhance the attractiveness and appeal of the socialist culture with Chinese characteristics.

We must base on the contemporary era and inherit our national outstanding cultural traditions, we should base on our country and fully absorb the world's outstanding ideological and cultural achievements. Only by deeply rooted in the national soil and inheriting excellent traditional culture, can we maintain the Chinese characteristics; only by learning from foreign outstanding cultural achievements, can we better face the world and maintain the vitality of advanced cultural development. We should stand on the practice of reform, opening up and modernization construction, focus on the forefront of world cultural development, carry forward the excellent tradition of domestic national culture and learn from the strengths of all nations of the world. Strengthen external cultural exchanges and enhance the international influence of Chinese culture.

Grasp prosperity in one hand, and management in the other hand. Adhere to the emphasis on construction, keep on advancing, promote the great development and great prosperity of socialist cultural, rise a new upsurge of socialist cultural construction. We must adhere to scientific management, management according to law, and promote the legalization, standardization and institutionalization of cultural management. Actively promote the cultural system reform, liberate and develop cultural productive forces, improve the national cultural soft power, and constantly enhance the international competitiveness of China's culture. Always insist on putting the social benefits in the first place, and strive to achieve the coincidence of economic and social benefits.

Section II

Building the socialist core value system

First, the main content of the socialist core value system

The construction of the socialist core value system proposed by the 6th Plenary Session of the 16th Central Committee of CPC is a major theoretical innovation and major strategic task of ideological and cultural construction of the Party. The socialist core values are the theme of rejuvenating the nation, the essence of the socialist advanced culture, and determines the direction of the development of socialism with Chinese characteristics.

The 17th National Congress of the Party pointed out: "The socialist core value system is a reflection of the essence of the socialist ideology." This is the intrinsic stipulation of the socialist system in the value level, and the inner spirit of the socialist system. It includes the Marxist guiding ideology, the common ideal of socialism with Chinese characteristics, the patriotism as the core of the national spirit and the reform and innovation as the core of the spirit of the times, the socialist concept of honor and disgrace. The socialist core value system clearly answers the question of what kind of spiritual banner we will use in the new historical conditions to unite and lead the whole people to advance, and the major question of what kind of spirit the Chinese nation will hold to stand firm among the nations of the world. Building a socialist core value system is of great practical significance and far historical significance to consolidate the guiding position of Marxism, to consolidate the common ideal of socialism with Chinese characteristics, to consolidate the common ideological foundation of the unity and struggle of the Party and people of all ethnic groups throughout the country, and to comprehensively promote the great cause of socialism with Chinese characteristics.

The four components of the socialist core value system have their own functions and foci, they are interrelated and inseparable, constituting an organic unity. Marxist guiding ideology as the soul of the socialist core value system, solves the problem of what banner is to be held, which is the theoretical basis of socialist core value system, and occupies the dominant position. It is necessary to adhere to Marxism as the guiding ideology to foster the common ideal of socialism with Chinese characteristics, to carry forward and cultivate national spirit and the spirit of the times and establish the socialist concept of honor and disgrace. The common ideal of socialism with Chinese characteristics as the theme of the socialist core value system solves the problem of what path to take and what goal to achieve. Adhere to the Marxist guiding ideology, carry forward and cultivate national spirit and the spirit of the times, establish the socialist concept of honor and disgrace, are all to guide and inspire the whole people to achieve the common ideal of socialism with Chinese characteristics. National spirit and the spirit of the times as the essence of the socialist core value system, solves the problem of what kind of mental state and spiritual appearance to have. It is the spiritual condition for adhering to the Marxist guiding ideology, establishing the common ideal of socialism with Chinese characteristics and carrying forward the socialist concept of honor and disgrace. The socialist concept of honor and disgrace, which mainly consists of "Eight Honors and Eight Disgraces", is the basis of the socialist core value system, and solves the problem of people's behavioral norms. It covers the contents of the other three aspects of the socialist core value system in the form of basic code of conduct, so that the socialist core value system can be put into practice, and people have behavioral norms to refer to. The socialist core value system answers the fundamental question in the ideological field of our country, embodies the fundamental interests of the overwhelming majority of our people, and is a scientific system with complete structure and logical meticulosity. It is the common foundation of the unity and struggle of the people of all ethnic groups within the whole party and across the country, and is the driving force for realizing scientific development and social harmony. It is also the core content of the national cultural soft power.

Second, adhere to Marxism as the guiding ideology

Marxism is the soul of the socialist core value system, it is the fundamental guiding ideology of our Party and our state. In building the socialist core value system, the first is to adhere to the guiding position of Marxism.

Marxism is established as the fundamental guiding ideology of our Party and our country, which is the choice of history and the people. In modern China, in the face of an unprecedented national crisis and social crisis, the Chinese people carried out an indomitable struggle and countless people with lofty ideals had been exploring the truth of saving the nation and people. All kinds of doctrines and propositions came into being and then shattered; all kinds of organizations and political parties were on stage, and also quit. Only after the Chinese people had found the scientific theory of Marxism, had it fundamentally solved the problem of the future and destiny of China. Since the establishment of the Communist Party of China, it has insisted on combining the basic principles of Marxism with China's reality and continuously made the theoretical achievements of localization of Marxism in China and guided the Chinese revolution, construction and reform to march from victory to victory. The glorious history of the Chinese revolution, construction and reform has fully demonstrated the powerful strength of Marxism and fully proved the correctness of the Chinese people's choice of Marxism.

While in the late 1980s and early 1990s, drastic changes happened in Eastern Europe, the Soviet Union disintegrated and the world socialist movement suffered serious setbacks, some people in the West claimed that "Marxism has died". However, this has not shaken the Chinese people's belief in Marxism. Deng Xiaoping pointed out: "I am convinced that more and more people will come to believe in Marxism, because it is a science."[4]

In the face of international changes and serious political turmoil in China, China has always adhered to the guiding position of Marxism and the leadership of the Communist Party of China. It has not only succeeded in stabilizing the political situation, but also has achieved sustained and rapid development, greatly improved the people's living standard and the overall national strength. Socialism and Marxism have shown vigor and vitality in the land of China. The facts eloquently proves that history and people have chosen Marxism and developed Marxism by reform and opening up. Marxism is the foundation of our Party and our country, as well as the basic principle for rule of the Party and the country, the guiding position of Marxism cannot be shaken at any time.

4　Anthology of Deng Xiaoping, 1st edition, Vol.3, p.382.

We should insist on Marxism and adhere to its the constant development of it. Only by ongoing constant development of Marxism in order to arm the whole party and educate the people, can we make Marxism truly play its role of powerful ideological weapon to understand and transform the world, can it truly become our guide to action. We should adhere to Marxism during its development, and develop Marxism during the insistence of it, and consciously obey the "two insistence, no ambiguity": adhere to the Marxist stand, point of view, methods, adhere to the basic principles of Marxism, which should be firm and unshakable and not vague; we should carry out the ideological line of emancipating the mind and seeking truth from facts, persist in the revolutionary spirit of bravely pursuing and exploring the truth, which should also be firm and unambiguous.

The system of theories of socialism with Chinese characteristics, adhere to and developed the Marxist-Leninism and Mao Zedong Thought, which embodied the wisdom and painstaking effort from hard work of practice by generations of people led by Chinese Communists, and is the latest achievement of Marxism in China and the most valuable political and spiritual wealth, the common ideological foundation of the unity and struggle of the people of all nationalities, and the scientific socialism rooted in contemporary China. In contemporary China, adhering to the theoretical system of socialism with Chinese characteristics, is to truly adhere to Marxism.

We must always insist on using the system of theories of socialism with Chinese characteristics to arm the whole party, to educate the people, and to constantly improve the level of Marxist theory of the whole party, so that the theoretical system of socialism with Chinese characteristics can enjoy more popular support and play a better guiding role.

It is necessary to constantly add to Chinese Marxism, virgule the distinctive characteristics of practice, national characteristics and characteristics of the times, and constantly promote the popularization of Marxism in contemporary China if we are to use the system of theories of socialism with Chinese characteristics to arm the mind and guide the practice. Popularization is the inherent requirement of Marxism. We should adhere to the reality, be close to life, concern the masses, use welcomed forms and lively words to explain the issues of common concern in a simple but profound manner, enhance people's political, ideological, value, and emotional identity on the theoretical system of socialism with Chinese characteristics, so that the theory can better be accessible to the masses, and the masses can better grasp the theory. Practice is constantly evolving, and people's understanding is always deepening. In China's reform and opening up and the process of socialist modernization, there will be new practical topics which need to be studied and answered, the new practical experience needs to be summed up and refined, the new hot and difficult topics need to be explained and interpreted. We should take promoting the popularization of contemporary Chinese Marxism as a long-term task, and constantly expand the content and form, means and channels of theoretical propaganda, strive to enhance the relevance and persuasiveness of theoretical education to make the theory play a greater role in guiding practice and promoting work with better results.

It is necessary to extensively carry out the propaganda and popularization activities of the theoretical system of socialism with Chinese characteristics in order to arm our mind and guide the practice with the theoretical system of socialism with Chinese characteristics. Guide the broad cadres and the masses to thoroughly study and understand the theoretical system of socialism with Chinese characteristics, master the Marxist standpoint, viewpoint and method, and consciously use this theoretical system to guide the transformation of the subjective world and the objective world. Be profoundly aware that in contemporary China, only the banner of socialism with Chinese characteristics rather than other banners can maximize the unity and cohesion of different social stratum, the wisdom and strength of different interest groups. Only the path of socialism with Chinese characteristics and rather than other path can guide the great rejuvenation of the Chinese nation. Only the theoretical system of socialism with Chinese characteristics rather than anything else can lead China's development and progress. Always hold high the great banner of socialism with Chinese characteristics unswervingly, stick to the path of socialism with Chinese characteristics unswervingly, and adhere to the theoretical system of socialism with Chinese characteristics unwaveringly.

Third, establishing the common ideal of socialism with Chinese characteristics

The common ideal of socialism with Chinese characteristics is the theme of the socialist core value system. Common ideal as the common value pursuit and goal of all members of society is the banner of a political party to govern the country, and the guide for a nation to struggle forward. Only by establishing a firm and common ideal can we gather all the wisdom and strength from all stratum of the society and mobilize all the potentials of the whole county and nation to form a unified pace and a strong fighting capacity.

Under the leadership of the Communist Party of China, taking the path of socialism with Chinese characteristics and realizing the great rejuvenation of the Chinese nation is the common ideal of the people of all ethnic groups at present. This common ideal is the inevitable choice of history and reality. Getting rid of poverty and backwardness, building a prosperous , democratic , civilized and harmonious country, and achieving the great rejuvenation of the Chinese nation are the dreams and pursuits of the Chinese people from generation to generation. The history since the Opium War has fully proved that the leadership of the Communist Party of China and the path of socialism with Chinese characteristics is the choice of history and the people. By adhering to this path, we can achieve the great rejuvenation of the Chinese nation. Since the founding of new China, especially since the reform and opening up, China's economic and social development has made great achievements, which is an irrefutable proof of this point. More than 30 years have past since the reform and opening up, the Communist Party of China and the Chinese people have been unswervingly following the path of socialism with Chinese characteristics and courageously marching forward, with indomitable spirit and magnificent innovative practice, we have written the new magnificent poems of the Chinese nation's self-improvement and tenacious forging ahead, and the socialist economic construction, political construction, cultural construction, social construction of our country have made remarkable achievements. China's development not only made the Chinese people steadily embarked on the path of prosperity and well-being, but also made a significant contribution to the development of the world economy and the progress of human civilization. The glorious achievements of socialist modernization in our country have fully demonstrated the unparalleled superiority of socialism with Chinese characteristics and the vitality of the Chinese institutional pattern, breaking the myth long agitated by the capitalist countries that without copying the Western model, it would be impossible to make the country powerful and the people well-off. The facts eloquently proved that only socialism can save China and only socialism with Chinese characteristics can develop China and realize the great rejuvenation of the Chinese nation. In contemporary China, adhering to the path of socialism with Chinese characteristics, is to truly adhere to socialism.

The common ideal of socialism with Chinese characteristics embodies the fundamental interests and common aspirations of our country's workers, peasants, intellectuals and other socialist workers, builders of socialist cause, and patriots who support socialism and the reunification of the motherland. This common ideal depicts the blueprint for a better life, shows the glorious future of the motherland, demonstrates the prospect of the revival of the Chinese nation brings to all the Chinese people great motivation and encouragement. This common ideal has convincing necessity, universality and inclusiveness, has a strong appeal, affinity and cohesion, is an important link to ensure that all people are united in one political ideology and work together to create a better future. Regardless of people from which social class, which interest group, they all should and are able to agree with this common ideal which is inseparable from their own interests, and strive for it.

The Communist Party of China's highest ideal and ultimate goal is to achieve communism. The common ideal of socialism with Chinese characteristics is the realistic embodiment of communism, the highest ideal, in the primary stage of socialism in our country and the necessary stage for realizing the supreme ideal of communism. Without the guide of common ideal, there will be no common ideals to be established and adhered to. Without the achievement of common ideal, there will be no realistic basis for the highest ideal. In the journey of realizing the great rejuvenation of the Chinese nation, we must always adhere to the unity of lofty ideals and realistic struggle. We should not only establish the lofty ideal of communism and strengthen our conviction, demand and spur ourselves with noble thought and morality, but also start from the reality of the primary stage of socialism, make unremitting efforts in a down-to-earth manner to realize the Party's basic program for the current stage.

Building and developing socialism with Chinese characteristics is the cause of hundreds of millions of people. Only after the broad masses of the people have actively engaged in the great cause of socialism with Chinese characteristics, can the common aspiration of the whole nation be achieved. It must be profoundly understood by the broad cadres and masses that the CPC always represent the requirements of the development trend of China's advanced productive forces; the orientation of China's advanced culture and the fundamental interests of the overwhelming majority of the Chinese people. Only the Communist Party of China can lead the people of all ethnic groups in the country to continue to seize the new victory of socialism with Chinese characteristics; it must be deeply realized that socialism with Chinese characteristics not only adheres to the basic principles of scientific socialism, but also bases on distinctive Chinese characteristics given by China's reality and characteristics of the times, is the banner of contemporary China's development and progress, is the whole The people of the whole country can stand the banner of unity and struggle, and only take the path of socialism with Chinese characteristics to realize the prosperity of the country and the happiness of the people. It must be deeply understood that the decision to begin reform and opening up is vital to the destiny of contemporary China, that reform and opening up are the only way of developing socialism with Chinese characteristics and rejuvenating the Chinese nation, only with reform and opening can we develop China, develop socialism, and develop Marxism. We should educate the broad masses of the people to consciously incorporate their personal ideals into the common struggle of the realization of socialist modernization, and to achieve their own ideal of life in the realization of national prosperity and rejuvenation, people's well-being and social harmony.

Fourth, carrying forward the long cherished national spirit and the spirit of the times

National spirit and the spirit of the times, is the strong spiritual support for the self-improvement, development and rejuvenation of the Chinese nation, is the endless spiritual power for us to continue to open up new journey and start new future, is the essence of the socialist core value system.

The national spirit is formed of the nation's long years of living together and common social practice. it is the ideological character, value orientation and moral norms recognized and accepted by the majority of members of the nation, is a comprehensive reflection of national psychological characteristics, cultural traditions, thoughts and emotions, is the most essential and concentrated expression of national culture. During the long history of more than five thousand years, the Chinese nation formed a great national spirit of unity, peace-loving, diligence and courage and self-reliance, with patriotism as the core. This national spirit is the spiritual pillar of millions of Chinese people who have made great efforts and been undaunted by repeated setbacks through the ages, and is the strong spiritual motivation for Chinese Nation's vigorousness and development.

Patriotism is the core of the spirit of the Chinese nation, unity, peace-loving, diligence and courage and self-reliance are the concrete manifestation of the spirit of the Chinese nation. Patriotism is the deepest, purest, noblest and most sacred emotion of the Chinese people to their motherland. The Chinese nation is a great nation with a patriotic tradition. Patriotism runs through the whole process of the formation and development of the Chinese national spirit, penetrates into all areas of the Chinese national spirit, and is embodied in all aspects of the Chinese national spirit. Patriotism is a historical category, in different periods and stages of social development, it has different content. In contemporary China, patriotism is manifested mainly by dedication to the great cause of socialism with Chinese characteristics, the great cause of peaceful reunification of the motherland. Patriotism and socialism are identical in essence. The establishment of the socialist system and the development of the path of socialism with Chinese characteristics has created a prosperous and powerful China, to love China is to love the socialist China. Safeguarding reunification of the motherland is the core interest of the Chinese nation, which means patriotism is bound to manifest itself in safeguarding the reunification of the motherland. Any attempt to create a national secession and to undermine national sovereignty and territorial integrity will be strongly opposed by all Chinese at home and abroad.

The spirit of the Chinese nation is like a long river, which continues to enrich and sublimate itself in the course of history, and always nourishes the Chinese nation. The Communist Party of China is the successor, promoter and nurturer of the Chinese national spirit. In the practice of leading the people of all nationalities to carry out revolution, construction and reform, the Party has formed its own fine tradition and cultivated Jinggangshan Spirit, the Spirit of the Long March, Yan'an Spirit, the Spirit of Anti-fascist, Xibaipo spirit, Lei Feng spirit, the Spirit of "Two Missiles and One Satellite", Daqing Spirit, Flood Fighting Spirit, the Spirit of the Fight against SARS, the Spirit of Manned Space Flight, Earthquake Relief Spirit, Beijing Olympic Spirit, and so on. These spirits inherited and carried forward the fine tradition of the Chinese nation, intensively reflected the high-spirited and vigorous, indomitable and hard-working spirit outlook of the Chinese people under the leadership of the Communist Party of China, which unprecedentedly carried forward the Chinese national spirit to a new stage of development. No matter in the past, at present or in the future, the national spirit will always be a powerful force, calling the Chinese people to make unremitting efforts to unite wholeheartedly, and work together to achieve the great rejuvenation of the Chinese nation.

In the new historical period, using one theoretical character of Marxism, i.e, keeping in step with the times—and by depending on the enterprising character and morals of the Chinese nation—we have achieved breakthroughs in the practice of reform and opening up and socialist modernization, and we have also created the (concept of) spirit of the times centered on reform and innovation, as well as the spirit of advancing with the times, spirit of pioneering, spirit of being realistic and pragmatic. These spirits of the times reflect the development direction of contemporary Chinese social progress and leads the trend of the progress of the times. It is the view and concept, value orientation and behavioral pattern of the members of the whole society, which reflects the new spirit of contemporary Chinese society. In the organic unity of the spirit of the times, reform and innovation occupies the key status. The spirit of reform and innovation is manifested as the idea of breaking through stereotypes, bold exploration and courage to create, manifested as the sense of responsibility and mission to not lag behind, strive for the first and pursue progress, manifested as the mental state of perseverance, self-improvement and forging ahead. The spirit of reform and innovation inherits the tradition of getting rid of the stale and taking in the fresh of the Chinese nation, embodies the requirements of contemporary China's development and progress, runs through all the practice of reform and opening up and all aspects of the spirit of the times. Over the past 30 years, reform and innovation has become the strongest voice of the times and become the trend of social development. Practice has proved that reform and innovation is the source of vitality of our Party and the state's development and progress, and is an inexhaustible motive force for the development of socialism with Chinese characteristics.

National spirit and the spirit of the times complement each other and bring out the best in each other. If national spirit is apart from the spirit of the times, it cannot timely absorb fresh power from the practice, and thus will lose its value of the times, and to carry forward and cultivate the national spirit would be impossible; if the spirit of the times is apart from the national spirit, the carrier of the nation would fade away, and the national characteristics would be lost, and to carry forward and cultivate the spirit of the times would be also be impossible. National spirit and the spirit of the times blend and unite with each other and are deeply cast in the nation's vitality, creativity and cohesion, together they constitute the spirit of self-reliance of the Chinese nation, and become the spiritual power to promote the great rejuvenation of the Chinese nation.

The great cause needs and produces a lofty spirit, the lofty spiritual support and promote the great cause. Since the reform and opening up, the Communist Party of China has led the people of the whole country to blaze new trails, strive for progress, and has overcome various risks and tests, painted a magnificent historical scroll of reform and opening up, endowed a new and vigorous vitality for the nation's rejuvenation, what we relied on is the great national spirit that we been carrying forward and what we cast is the spirit of the times. Today, in order to build a well-off society in an all-round way, accelerate the socialist modernization and realize the great rejuvenation of the Chinese nation, we must further vigorously carry forward this national spirit and the spirit of the times so that all the people will maintain a high-spirited state and fully boost the creative spirit and creative vitality of the whole nation.

Fifth, establishing a socialist concept of honor and disgrace

The socialist concept of honor and disgrace with "Eight Honors and Eight Disgraces" as the main content, intensively summarizes the most basic values and codes of conduct in contemporary China and is the basis of the socialist core value system.

The concept of honor and disgrace is the fundamental view and attitude towards honor and stigma. It is the sum of the concept of honor and disgrace which is gradually formed in people's activities of self-evaluation and social evaluation based on certain ideological and moral standards. It is the rational distillation of individual and fragmented concept of honor and disgrace. The concept of honor and disgrace has a distinct class nature, different societies and different stages have different standards for commendatory or derogatory and different concept of honor and disgrace. The socialist concept of honor and disgrace refers to the moral code used to guide and standardize the ideology and behavior of party members and the people in the struggle for building socialism with Chinese characteristics. When Hu Jintao visited the

Standing Committee members of the 4th Plenary Session of the 10th CPPCC, in response to the changes in international situation, and also in view of the actual situation of China's economic and social development and change, according to the basic experience of our socialist revolution and construction, and according to the value orientation of the socialist society, he put forward a comprehensive discussion of the socialist concept of honors and disgraces with the "Eight Honors and Eight Disgraces" as the main content for the first time in the history of the Communist Party of China. This is: Love, do not harm the motherland; Serve, don't disserve the people; Uphold science; don't be ignorant and unenlightened; work hard; don't be lazy and hate work; be united and help each other; don't gain benefits at the expense of others. Be honest and trustworthy, not profit-mongering at the expense of your values. Be disciplined and law-abiding instead of chaotic and lawless. Know plain living and hard struggle; do not wallow in luxuries and pleasures.

The socialist concept of honor and disgrace with the "Eight Honors and Eight Disgraces" as the main content, is the summarization of the socialist ideological and moral system in line with the socialist market economy, in harmony with the socialist legal norms, in succession of the traditional virtues of the Chinese nation, and in combination with the outstanding achievements of the world's moral civilization. It is clearly pointed out what is true and the beauty, what is false and evil, what should be insisted, what to oppose, what to promote, and what to resist in our society, providing basic norms to judge the behavior gains and losses and clear the value orientation under the Conditions of the Socialist Marketing Economy for all ethnic groups, all walks of life and different interest groups of people, it is the starting point and the foothold of socialist core value system. Love, do not harm the motherland; Serve, don't disserve the people; Uphold science; don't be ignorant and unenlightened; Work hard; don't be lazy and hate work; These "Four Honors and Four Disgraces" embody the spirit of the Chinese nation with patriotism as the core, embody the life view of serving the people, and are the basic requirements of the "five love" of the socialist morality based on the principle of collectivism, as well as the legal duties of every citizen. Be united and help each other; Don't gain benefits at the expense of others; Be honest and trustworthy, not profit-mongering at the expense of your values; Be disciplined and law-abiding instead of chaotic and lawless; Know plain living and hard struggle; do not wallow in luxuries and pleasures; These "Four Honors and Four Disgraces" reflect the most basic code for family life, professional life, social and public life that the citizens should follow. The socialist concept of honor and disgrace with the "Eight Honors and Eight Disgraces" as the main content, runs through patriotism, collectivism and socialist ideology, and embodies the correct world outlook, outlook on life, values and morals, reflects the of fundamental requirements the of spirit of the Chinese nation and the times of the spirit, it marks that the

Party's theoretical summarization on how to foster the socialist ideology and morality has reached a new height, since it embodies the contemporaneity, and more deeply grasps its laws, and also innovative.

Section III

Raising the ideological and moral standards as well as scientific and cultural education

First, strengthening ideological and moral construction

The main contents of the construction of socialist culture with Chinese characteristics include ideological and moral construction and education, science and culture construction. Ideological and moral construction is to solve the problems of the spiritual pillar and the spiritual power of the entire Chinese nation. Strengthening the ideological and moral construction of socialism is an important content and central link of the socialist cultural construction with Chinese characteristics. Ideological and moral construction mainly includes ideal construction and moral construction.

Construction of ideals is the core and primary task of ideal and moral construction. Deng Xiaoping attaches great importance to the ideal education. In "Four Haves", what he emphasizes above all is the ideal. He pointed out: "Today in China we are urging people to have lofty ideals and moral integrity, to become better educated and to cultivate a strong sense of discipline. Of these, the most important is to have lofty ideals."[5]

To have ideal is to have belief, ideal and belief are combined together. If there is no firm belief in the correctness, justice and inevitability of fulfillment of one's ideals, his or her ideal is not a true ideal. Likewise, belief or faith is empty if they are not concentrated on an ideal goal.

Ideal and belief is a powerful spiritual force. It is a powerful spiritual power that drives and inspires people to move forward, and is a strong spiritual pillar that supports people to overcome difficulties and withstand the severe test. Deng Xiaoping pointed out that ideal and faith is the strong cohesive force to unite the Party and the people of the country. Whether it be revolution or construction, "unity is of prime importance and that to achieve unity people must have common ideals and firm convictions. Over the past several decades we have united the people on the basis of firm convictions that enabled them to struggle for their own interests. Without such convictions, there would have been no cohesion among the people, and we could have accomplished nothing."[6]

5　Selected Works of Deng Xiaoping, 1st edition, vol.3, p.190.
6　Ibid., p.190.

Ideal is what people are long for and hope for the future, is the embodiment of people's political stance, world outlook, values and outlook on life on objective of the struggle. The construction of socialism with Chinese characteristics, turning our country into a prosperous, democratic, civilized and harmonious socialist modernization country, and realizing the great rejuvenation of the Chinese nation is the common ideal of the people of all nationalities at the present stage. This common ideal, starting from the basic national conditions of the primary stage of socialism, concentrates the interests and aspirations of our workers, peasants, intellectuals and other laborers, patriots, and is the powerful ideological weapon to ensure that all people are politically, morally and mentally consistent and can overcome all the difficulties and strive for victory.

To establish the common ideal of building socialism with Chinese characteristics, we must establish a correct world outlook, outlook on life and values. To establish a correct view of the world, the core is to adhere to the viewpoint of perseverance in the reality, and pursuing the truth on the basis of fact. The outlook on life is the fundamental view on the purpose, attitude and choice of the road and direction of people's life. It is the value judgment of the meaning of life, and the answer to the vital questions of life such as the meaning of life. To establish the correct outlook on life, is to establish an outlook on life in line with the law of social development and to promote the historical progress, establish the point of view that the meaning of life is to sacrifice for the society and others. Values are the positions, opinions and attitudes that people hold on the question of universal value. The socialist core value system is a rich ideological system, including the specific content and level of many aspects. We must closely focus on the construction of the socialist core value system, in accordance with the requirements of the development of advanced culture and the construction of harmonious culture, and persevere in the use of the theoretical system of socialism with Chinese characteristics to arm the whole party and educate the masses and guide the whole society to firmly establish the common ideals of building socialism with Chinese characteristics, Advocate the national spirit with patriotism as the core and the spirit of the times with reform and innovation as the core, advocate patriotism, collectivism, socialist ideology, advocate socialist concept of honor and disgrace with the "Eight Honors and Eight Disgraces" as the main content, and constantly consolidate the common ideological foundation of the unity and struggle of the whole Party and the people throughout the country.

Moral construction is the main content of ideological and moral construction. Morality is a code of conduct that regulates the relationship between people and the relationship between individuals and society. The construction of socialist morality should focus on serving the people, take collectivism as the principle, and take loving one's motherland, loving people, loving science, and loving socialism as the basic requirement, vigorously advocate social morality, professional ethics, family virtue and personal character. In accordance with the requirements to adapt the socialist market economy, we should further cultivate the socialist ideology and morality, and gradually establish a moral system which can increasingly perfect itself, reflect the requirements of different levels and different professions, and have strong leading-force and normative force to promote the healthy development of socialist market economy; in accordance with the requirements of coordination with the socialist legal norms, we should further combine the rule of law with the rule of virtue, so that the law and moral complement each other, promote each other; in accordance with the requirement to inherit traditional Chinese virtues, we should further carry forward good traditions of the Chinese nation, so that the socialist ideology and morality not only has national characteristics, but also has distinctive characteristics of the times.

Serving the people is the purpose of the Communist Party of China, it's the revolutionary spirit and morality formed by the Chinese Communists in the long-term revolution and construction practice. The idea of serving the people is linked to the socialist system and has been universally accepted by the broad masses of the people and has become the core content and concentrated expression of the socialist morality. Under the conditions of the socialist market economy, it is necessary to promote the spirit of serving the people in the whole people, to advocate respecting people, caring for people, loving public welfare, aiding the poor, and doing good things for the people and the society, to oppose money worship, hedonism and egoism, so as to be conducive to the healthy development of the socialist market economy.

The principle of collectivism is the objective requirement of the basic system of socialism. The basic system of socialism fully protects the individual interests of the members of society, and at the same time, decides that the members of society have a common interest and will inevitably require the members of society to adhere to the principle of collectivism. In socialist society, national interests, collective interests and personal interests are fundamentally consistent. Therefore, on the one hand, the state and the collective should attach importance to and legally protect the legitimate interests of the individual; On the other hand, when personal interests and national interests, collective interests are in conflict, the individual should take into account the overall situation, give priority to the national and collective interests, subject the personal interests to national interests and collective interests.

We should strive to cultivate civilization and morals, and actively advocate patriotism, dedication, integrity, friendliness and other moral norms, strengthen the construction of social morality, professional ethics and family virtues to promote interpersonal harmony. Vigorously advocate such socialist moral principles as social courtesy, helpfulness, care for public property, environmental protection, and law-abiding; strongly promote professional ethics of dedication, honesty and being trustworthy, fair and just in handling affairs, serving the masses, and commitment to society, strongly promote the family virtues of respecting the old and loving the young, the equality between men and women, harmony between the husband and wife, managing the house thriftily and accord among neighbors, carry forward the socialist humanitarian spirit, so as to form interpersonal relationships of solidarity, equality and friendship, and onward together in the whole society. We should pay attention to humanistic care and psychological counseling, strengthen mental health education, and promote people's psychological harmony. We should guide people to firmly establish the awareness of saving resources, protecting the environment, scientific development, and promote harmony between man and nature. We should extensively carry out activities of creating harmonious society, guide people to understand things with harmonious thinking, treat things with a harmonious attitude, deal with contradictions in a harmonious way, create a social mentality of self-esteem and self-confidence, ideal and peace, and being positive, cultivate good social trends of recognizing honor and disgrace, practicing integrity, and promoting harmony.

To succeed in the construction of socialist morality, we should strengthen the education of democracy and legal system. Moral and legal norms belong to the superstructure of community, and are both codes of conduct to adjust human relations, they are interrelated, complement each other, and are important means to maintain the social order. In our legal system, every legal norm embodies the norms and requirements of the socialist morality, thus effectively guarantee the implementation of the socialist moral norms, and promote the formation, consolidation and development of the socialist moral prevailing custom. Therefore, to strengthen moral education and to strengthen legal education is complementary and indispensable. The combination of moral education and legal education is of great significance to improve the moral quality of our citizens.

To succeed in the construction of socialist morality, we must adhere to starting from the reality, combine the requirement of advanced nature with the requirement of universality to guide people to comply with the basic ideology and ethics, on which basis to constantly pursue a higher level of ideological and moral goal. At the primary stage of socialism, we must encourage and support all the ideologies and moralities which are conducive to the liberation and development of socialist social productive forces, all the ideologies and moralities which are conducive to national unity, ethnic solidarity and social progress; all the ideologies and moralities which are conducive to the pursuit of truth and beauty, the resistance of false and evil, and the promotion of righteousness; all the ideologies and moralities which are conducive to the implementation of civil rights and obligations, the quest for a better life with honest labor. We have to unite and guide hundreds of millions of people to positively, progressively and constantly improve the ideological and moral level of the whole nation.

Second, development through science and education

Education and science are the important contents of the construction of socialist culture with Chinese characteristics and play an important role in improving the quality of the nation, uplifting the degree of social civilization, and promoting economic development and social progress.

As the primary productive force, science and technology are decisive for the present and future development of a country and a nation. Deng Xiaoping pointed out: "The key to the four modernizations is the modernization of science and technology. Without modern science and technology, it is impossible to build modern agriculture, modern industry or modern national defence. Without the rapid development of science and technology, there can be no rapid development of the economy."[7]

273

In the 21st century, the rapid progress in science and technology is increasingly becoming the decisive factor in economic and social development. The growth of national wealth and the improvement of human life are more and more dependent on the accumulation and innovation of knowledge. The competition in science and technology has become the focus of international competition in comprehensive national strength. We must focus on improving the ability of independent innovation, building an innovative country, which is the core of national development strategy, and the key to improve the overall national strength. We must adhere to the path of independent innovation with Chinese characteristics and carry out the enhancement of the ability of independent innovation to all aspects of modernization. Earnestly implement the national medium and long term scientific and technological development plan, increase investment in independent innovation, make every effort to break through the constraints of key technologies on economic and social development. Speed up the construction of national innovation system, support basic research, cutting-edge research, and technological research for public welfare. Speed up the establishment of the technological innovation system, in which enterprises play the leading role, the market points the way, and enterprises, universities

---

7   Selected Works of Deng Xiaoping, 2nd edition, Vol.2, p.86.

and research institutes work together. Guide and support the pooling of factors of innovation into enterprises, promote transformation of technological achievements into practical productive forces. We will deepen the reform of the science and technology management system, optimize the allocation of science and technology resources, and improve the legal guarantee, policy system, incentive mechanism and market environment that encourage technological innovation and industrialization of scientific and technological achievements. We will implement the strategy for intellectual property rights. We will make the best use of international resources of science and technology. Insisted on putting people first, give full play to the enthusiasm of the broad masses of scientific and technological personnel, cast the new brilliance of China's science and technology cause. Strengthen popularization of sciences and improve the scientific quality of the whole society.

Philosophy and social science is an important tool for people to understand the world and transform the world. It is an important force to promote historical development and social progress. In the process of recognizing and transforming the world, philosophy and social sciences are as important as the natural sciences; cultivating high levels of philosophical social scientists is as important as cultivating high levels of natural scientists; improving the quality of the philosophy and society of the whole nation is equally important as improving the quality of natural science of the whole nation; employing and giving full play to the role of philosophical and social science talents is equally important as employing and giving full play to the role of natural science talents. Base on the national conditions, base on the contemporary perspective, take major practical problems as our top priority, promote theoretical innovation and knowledge innovation; study and answer the overall, strategic, and forward-looking questions which are vital for the development of the Party and the Country; study and answer the urgent problem of building a well-off society in an all-around way, study and answer the widespread deep ideological understanding problems of the cadres and the masses; give full play to the role of understanding of the world, heritage of civilization, innovation of theory, education of people, and service to society, and strive to form philosophy and social science disciplines and teaching materials system which embody the latest achievements of Marxism in China with Chinese characteristics, Chinese style, and Chinese manner. Promote innovation in academic disciplines, academic viewpoints and research methods, promote the flourishing of philosophy and the social sciences, encourage the community of philosophy and social science to play the role of thinking bank for the cause of the Party and the people, to promote China's outstanding achievements and talents of philosophy and social science to go to the world.

Education is the cornerstone of national rejuvenation. We should make education a strategic priority and a major policy in long-term insisted by the Party and the state to promote the comprehensive, coordinated and sustainable development of our educational undertaking and cultivate hundreds of millions of high-quality laborers, millions of professionals and a large number of top-notch innovative talents, turn China into a human resources powerful nation, provide a strong talent and human resources guarantee for the comprehensive building of a well-off society in an all-round way and the achievement of the great rejuvenation of the Chinese nation. We should fully implement the Party's education policy, adhere to the people-centered education, moral education first principle, carry on quality education, improve the modernization level of education, train builders of and successors to the socialist cause who develop morally, intellectually, physically and aesthetically, run education to the satisfaction of the people. Optimize the educational structure, promote the balanced development of compulsory education, accelerate the popularization of high school education, vigorously develop vocational education, improve the quality of higher education. Pay attention to pre-primary education and care for special education. Update the educational concept, deepen the reforms in teaching content and method, examination enrollment system, quality evaluation system and so on to reduce the burden of primary and secondary school students and improve the overall quality of students. Adhere to the nonprofit nature of education, increase financial investment in education, standardize education fees, support education in poverty-stricken areas and ethnic areas, improve student funding system to guarantee the equal access of the families with economic difficulties and of migrant workers to compulsory education. Strengthen the construction of teaching staff, focusing on improving the quality of rural teachers. We will encourage and regulate educational programs run by nongovernmental sectors. Develop distance education and continuing education. Construct a learning society featured in universal learning and lifelong learning.

Third, advance the reform of cultural system, vigorously develop the cultural causes and cultural industry

The development of socialist advanced culture and the construction of a harmonious culture calls for vigorous development of cultural undertakings and cultural industries and promotion of the prosperity of socialist culture.

Since the reform and opening up, China's cultural construction has flourished and the cultural life of the masses has become increasingly colorful. But it should also be noted that with the development of the socialist market economy and the expansion of the opening to the outside world, the economic basis, the institutional environment and the social conditions for the survival and development of culture have undergone profound changes.

China's cultural construction is far from being able to meet the requirements of the development of the times, far from being able to meet the people's growing multi-level spiritual and cultural needs. Therefore, it is necessary to deepen the cultural system reform, further carry on the liberation and development of cultural productive forces.

In order to deepen the reform of the cultural system, we must insist on taking development as the theme, taking reform as the driving force, taking institutional innovation as the focus, taking creating more and better spiritual and cultural products to meet the needs of the people as the goal, to promote the comprehensive cultural prosperity and the rapid development of cultural industries. We must firmly establish the new concept of cultural development, further enhance the consciousness and firmness of deepening the reform, resolutely break through all the ideas that hinder the development of culture, and resolutely change all the practices and regulations that bind the cultural development, and resolutely remove all the institutional defects that affect the cultural development.

In order to deepen the reform of the cultural system, we must insist on putting the social interests in the first place, as well as the unity of social and economic benefits. Grasp the non-profit cultural undertakings in one hand, and grasp the operative culture industry in the other hand. The non-profit cultural undertakings and the operative culture industry are the carriers of cultural construction and development in China. The non-profit cultural undertakings and the operative culture industry are both different from each other and promotive to each other, they are unified in the great cause of prospering the advanced socialist culture. The basic task of the non-profit cultural undertakings is to provide the basic public cultural services for the masses of the people, to build a relatively complete public cultural service system covering the whole society, and to continuously meet the basic cultural needs of the people; the fundamental task of the operative culture industry is to prosper the cultural market, meet the people's many-sided, multi-level, and diverse spiritual and cultural needs. In order to develop the non-profit cultural undertakings, we must let government play the leading role, encourage social participation, and effectively improve the government's ability and level of service to the masses. In order to develop the operative culture industry, we must give full play to the basic role of allocation of resources by market, we must adhere to market-orientation, develop and grow in the market competition. Therefore, on the one hand, we must insist on the development of non-profit cultural undertakings as the main way to protect the basic cultural rights of the people, increase investment, strengthen the construction of community and rural cultural facilities. On the other hand, we should vigorously develop the operative culture industry, implement the major culture industry, implement the major policy of accelerating the development of the cultural industries, promoting the cultural industries to become a pillar industry in the national economy, also promote regional cultural industries, prosper cultural markets, enhance international competitive power in the cultural industry.

The great rejuvenation of the Chinese nation will definitely be accompanied by the thriving of Chinese culture. We should give full play to the main role of the people in cultural construction, mobilize the enthusiasm of the broad masses of cultural workers, be more conscious and more proactive in promoting the great development and prosperity of culture, and enhance cultural creation and production to promote the great practice of socialism with Chinese characteristics and see that people share the fruits of cultural development.

CHAPTER TEN

Socialism with Chinese Characteristics and What Kind of A Society To Build?

Section I

Scientific meaning and significance of constructing socialist harmonious society

First, the construction of a harmonious socialist society

To achieve social harmony and build a better society has always been a social ideal that mankind is diligently striving after. There are quite a number of ideas on social harmony in the history of Chinese ancient thoughts. Confucius said "harmony and peacefulness are prized"; Mozi put forward an ideal social plan of "Universal Loving" and "loving all uniformly"; Mencius portrayed the social status of "expend the respect of the aged in one's family to that of other families; expend the love of the young ones in one's family to that of other families"; etc. Utopian socialists of the early 19th century even more clearly set the goal of building a "harmonious and free" society. In 1803, French utopian socialist Fourier published the article "Universal Harmony", pointing out that the existing capitalist system is unreasonable and will inevitably be replaced by the "harmonious institution". In 1824, British utopian socialist Owen conducted an utopian socialist experiment called "New Harmony", a Communist Commune in Indiana, the United States. In 1842, the German utopian communist Weitling stated that the socialist society is "harmonious and free" in his book Guarantees of Harmony and Freedom and pointed out that the "harmony" of the new society will be "harmony of all".

However, the historical concept of harmony, including the ideology of the utopian socialists, mostly stays at the level of a social ethic or moral pursuit without forming a complete theoretical system nor a practical basis for practice. Utopian socialists failed to recognize the internal contradictions of capitalist society and failed to find the correct way to achieve social transformation. The result was only fantasy. Under the old system of class exploitation and oppression, both the experiment of peasant uprising in China with the hope to "average the poor and the rich, and search for a great harmonic universe" and the experiment of "New Harmony" of British utopian socialist Owen ended with failure.

However, it is undeniable that these treatises on harmony in human thoughts are still the precious wealth with glorious light of civilization in the long history. In the first "complete and comprehensive program" of proletarian parties throughout the world, the "Communist Manifesto," Marx and Engels fully affirmed the utopian socialists' ideal of the "abolition of the distinction between town and country ... and proclamation of social harmony"[1] taking it as "most valuable materials for the enlightenment of the working class" and is a "positive proposition." The profound criticism of Marxism on capitalism means the all-round development of communist society "in place of the old bourgeois society, with its classes and class antagonisms"[2], which clearly shows that the pursuit of social harmony should be the proper meaning of socialism.

The establishment of the socialist system eliminated the institutional roots that led to the antagonism of classes and social disharmony, opening up a wide path for social harmony. Since the founding of new China, our hard exploration of socialism over the past half century or more, especially the great practice of the Party and the people in carrying out the reform and opening up as well as the socialist modernization made our Party profoundly realize that socialism, as an entirely new category of social formation in human society, not only should but also is able to achieve the fundamental social harmony.

At the beginning of the founding of new China, the Chinese Communists with Mao Zedong as the main representative paid great attention to the coordination of various social relations while exploring the laws governing the construction of socialism with Chinese characteristics. He stressed that all positive factors at home and abroad should be mobilized to serve the cause of socialism. From 1956 to 1957, Mao Zedong successively published the famous influential works such as On the Ten Major Relations and On the Correct Handling of Contradictions among the People. He made appropriate

---

1   Selected Works of Marx and Engels, https://www.marxists.org/archive/marx/works/1848/communist-manifesto/ch03.htm.
2   Ibid.

and comprehensive arrangements in all aspects including economy, politics and culture, put forward the "double hundred" principle, namely, "letting a hundred flowers blossom and a hundred schools of thought contend", he also proposed the need to learn to use democratic methods to solve the contradictions among the people, which pointed out the basic direction for the all-round development of socialism in our country.

After the 3rd Plenary Session of the 11th Central Committee of CPC, the Chinese Communists with Deng Xiaoping as the main representative put forward the basic line of the Party, namely "one center and two basic points" on the basis of scientifically summing up the positive and negative experiences of socialist movement both at home and abroad; put forward major theoretical viewpoints of the coordinated development of socialist construction such as "doing two jobs at once and attaching equal importance to each" (grasping material civilization with one hand and spiritual civilization with the other hand). Further laid a solid foundation for the all-round and coordinated development of socialism with Chinese characteristics.

After the 4th Plenary Session of the 13th National Congress of the Party, the Chinese Communists with Jiang Zemin as the main representative inherited and developed Mao Zedong and Deng Xiaoping's thinking and placed greater emphasis on the coordinated development of economy and society based on the new reality of China's socialist modernization and reform and opening up. He clearly put forward that development should be taken as the most important task for the Party in governing and rejuvenating the country. At the same time, the socialist material civilization, political civilization and spiritual civilization must be coordinated in the development. He proposed that we should correctly handle the relations between reform, development, and stability, take development as the goal, reform as the driving force and stability as the basis, promote the healthy development of all social undertakings and make the society more harmonious. He proposed that development should focus on efforts to promote the all-round development of the people, stressed that the all-round development of the people and the social development are the prerequisite and basis for each other, He proposed that we should have new ideas for development and take the way of new industrialization, change the dual economic structure between urban and rural areas, speed up urbanization and promote the coordinated economic development of the eastern, central and western regions. These proposals further enriched and developed our Party's theory on the building of socialist society.

After the 16th CPC National Congress, the Party Central Committee with Hu Jintao as the General Secretary further deepened the understanding on social harmony on the basis of in-depth understanding of the law governing the development of socialism, profoundly summarizing the development experience of our country and accurately analyzing the stage characteristics of China's economic and social development. He took making society more harmonious as an important goal of building a moderately prosperous society in an all-round way and made it clear that social construction constitutes a "Four in One" strategic position along with economic construction, political construction and cultural construction in the general layout of the cause of socialism with Chinese characteristics. For the first time, the 4th Plenary Session of the 16th CPC Central Committee in 2004 clearly put forward the important concept of "constructing a socialist harmonious society", which was taken as a fundamental task of strengthening the building of the Party's governing capability. It emphasized that a society putting talents to full use with harmony is the social foundation for the Party to strengthen its ruling power, as well as the inevitable requirement for the Party's ruling to realize its historical task. In October 2006, the 6th Plenary Session of the 16th Central Committee of the Party examined and approved the Decision of the CPC Central Committee on Several Major Issues concerning Building a Harmonious Socialist Society, which comprehensively and profoundly clarified the nature and positioning of a harmonious socialist society, clearly pointed out the guiding ideology, goal and task, working principle and major deployment of the construction of a socialist harmonious society. In October 2007, the report of the 17th National Congress of the Communist Party of China further proposed that on the basis of economic development, we should pay more attention to social construction, strive to guarantee and improve people's lives, promote social system reform, expand public services, enhance social management and uplift social fairness and justice, so that all people can enjoy their rights to education, employment, medical care, pension, and housing, and promote the building of a harmonious society.

Second, the scientific meaning of building a socialist harmonious society

In *Modern Chinese Dictionary* (5th edition), "harmony" is explained as "be in harmonious proportion". Thus it can be seen that the essence of "harmony" is the coordination of the relations among different things. In general, a harmonious society is the harmonious, unified and coordinated development of man and nature, man and society, and between man and man. It is the harmonious unity and coordinated development between the productive forces and the relations of production, the economic foundation and the superstructure. The harmonious society is a description of the ideal conditions for the development of human society and an ideal of all people who pursue civilization and progress.

As for the scientific meaning of a harmonious socialist society, Hu Jintao made an incisive summary in an important speech delivered at a seminar on enhancing the ability of major leading cadres at the provincial and ministerial levels in building the socialist harmonious society in February 2005: the harmonious socialist society we want to build should be a society with democracy and rule of law, fairness and justice, honesty and fraternity, vitality, stability and order, and harmony between man and nature.

Democracy and the rule of law means that socialist democracy is fully developed, the basic strategy of governing the country according to law is effectively implemented, and positive factors in all aspects are widely mobilized.

Fairness and justice means that the interests of all sectors of society are properly coordinated, the contradictions among the people and other social conflicts are properly handled, and social fairness and justice are effectively maintained and realized.

Honesty and fraternity, that is, the whole society helps each other, be honest and trustworthy, the whole people are equal and friendly and get along well with each other.

Vitality means being able to respect all the creative aspirations that are conducive to social progress, supporting creative activities, giving play to creative talent, and creating results being affirmed.

Stability and order, that is, a sound social organization mechanism, perfect social management, good social order, the people live and work in peace, social stability and unity.

Harmony between man and nature is the development of production, affluent life and sound ecological environment.

The above six aspects of a socialist harmonious society are interrelated and interactive. These six aspects include not only the harmony of social relations but also the harmony between man and nature, embodying the unity of democracy and the rule of law, the unity of fairness and efficiency, the unity of vitality and order, the unity of science and humanity, the unity of man and nature. These six aspects are extremely rich in content. They not only depict a beautiful blueprint for a harmonious socialist society for us, but also give to us specific requirements for the sound construction of a harmonious socialist society. Together, they reveal the essential connotation of a socialist harmonious society and is the general requirement for us in building the harmonious socialist society. Its core is to deal with the relationship between people, between people and society and between man and nature.

Harmony between people. Under the conditions of socialism, the fundamental interests of each member of society are identical, but there are still contradictions and differences when it comes to specific interests. Especially with the deepening of reform and opening up and the development of the socialist market economy, the relations between social interests are becoming more complicated. Therefore, pursuing and realizing the harmony among people is an important task and the necessary condition for building a harmonious socialist society. In a certain sense, the process of building a harmonious socialist society is the process to realize the harmony between people. In order to realize the true harmony between people, we must pay attention to fairness and justice, rely on democracy and rule of law, and promote honesty and fraternity.

Harmony among the people and society. In our country, socialism has created the institutional foundation for the harmony between individuals and society, but plenty of contradictions still inevitably arise between individuals and society. The development and progress of socialist society should ultimately be embodied and implemented in the development and improvement of each member of the society. Only by continuously giving more consideration to each member of society and respecting the individual's position, value and dignity in the process of social development, can the society itself continuously develop and improve. To build a harmonious socialist society, we must strive to create a stable and orderly social environment, we must create a vibrant social atmosphere, and constantly promote the harmony between individuals and the society.

Harmony between man and nature. The harmony between man and nature is the most basic part of social harmony. The problems of environmental pollution, ecological fragility and energy crisis are the problems that the entire human society, including the socialist society, would inevitably encounter in the development process. If the endless recourse and conquest of nature are taken, it will lead to a serious shortage of resources, deterioration of the environment and the catastrophic consequences of the survival crisis for mankind. Therefore, the pursuit of harmony between man and nature is one of the important features of the socialist harmonious society. The proposition of "building ecological civilization" put forward in the report of the 17th National Congress of the CPC refers to the objective law that mankind must follow the harmonious development of man, nature and society. In the process of transforming the objective world, we can not only consider satisfying human needs, but should actively improve the relationship between man and nature, build an orderly ecological operation mechanism and create a good ecological environment. Ecological civilization is the higher form of human civilization after agricultural civilization and industrial civilization.

To accurately grasp the scientific meaning of a harmonious socialist society, we still have to pay special attention to grasp from the following four aspects:

First, the socialist harmonious society is not the social coordination and harmony advertised by any other social form in history, but a harmonious society with socialist nature. Under the new historical conditions, our Party not only fully absorbs the ideological nourishment of social harmony from human civilization, but also upholds the Marxist socialist value and adapts itself to profound social changes, combine "socialism" with "harmonious society" and clearly put forward the idea of "building a socialist harmonious society." It is different from the "Great Harmonic Universe" that some thinkers in history have been long admired and also differs from the "Utopia" portrayed by utopian socialists, but rather a product of combining Marxist thinking on social harmony with the reality of contemporary China. As pointed out by the 6th Plenary Session of the 16th CPC Central Committee, the socialist harmonious society we want to build is a harmonious society built and shared by all Chinese people along the path of socialism with Chinese characteristics and under the leadership of the CPC. This conclusion clearly reveals the core of leadership, the path of development, the subject of practice and the fundamental purpose of building a socialist harmonious society.

Second, the building of a socialist harmonious society is an organic, integral and inseparable part of the socialist economic, political and cultural construction. Under the new requirements of our country's economic and social development in the new phase of the new century, our Party has reviewed the current situation and, under the guidance of the scientific concept of development, clearly defined "building a socialist harmonious society" as our goal of development, which marked the overall layout of building a socialist cause with Chinese characteristics has been transformed from the "Three in One" of economic construction, political construction and cultural construction into the "Four in One" of economic construction, political construction, cultural construction and social construction. We must continuously enhance the material basis for the construction of a harmonious society through the development of socialist economic construction and continuously strengthen the political guarantee for the construction of a harmonious society through the development of socialist political construction and constantly consolidate the spiritual support for the construction of a harmonious society through the development of socialist cultural construction. At the same time, we should create favorable social conditions for the socialist economic, political and cultural development through the development of social construction.

Third, building a socialist harmonious society and building a well-off society in an all-round way both belong to a large category of building socialism with Chinese characteristics. The two complement each other and promote each other. The construction of a socialist harmonious society is a long-term historical task throughout the entire course of undertaking the cause of socialism with Chinese characteristics and an important content in building an overall well-off society. It is also a vital condition for building an overall well-off society. The proposal of building a moderately prosperous society in an all-round way as proposed by the 16th National Congress of the Party, which contains the requirement of " a more harmonious society". Building a socialist harmonious society further expands and enriches this requirement. In the phase of building the well-off society in an all-round way, building a socialist harmonious society is a major and realistic task. At the same time, building a socialist harmonious society is also a long-term process. After achieving the grand goal of building an overall well-off society, we must continue to strive for a higher level of harmonious society. According to the advanced point of view of dialectical materialism, harmony is always relative in the development and evolvement of things, and the absolute and static harmony does not exist. The same is true for social development. To build a socialist harmonious society is the process of continuously eliminating the factors of disharmony and increasing the factors of harmony so as to continuously raise the level of social harmony. This process is dynamic and never-ending.

Fourth, improving the ability to build a socialist harmonious society is an important part of strengthening the Party's ability to govern and the major task of the Party's governance. Domestically, building a socialist harmonious society and making every effort to achieve an all-round and coordinated development of the "Four in One" and trying to eliminate all kinds of disharmony in our society is an inevitable requirement for us to grasp and properly use the period of strategic opportunity in the first two decades of the 21st century and realize the grand goal of building an overall well-off society. Internationally, building a socialist harmonious society first deals with the domestic issues, striving to achieve social harmony and always maintaining the situation of national reunification, national unity and social stability is the inevitable requirements for us to grasp the complex and changeful international situation and effectively cope with the challenges arising from the international challenges and risks. Looking from the mission shouldered by our Party, building a socialist harmonious society, always adhering to the people-centered principle and taking the fundamental interests of the overwhelming majority of the people as the fundamental starting point and the foothold of our Party and our country's work, truly realizing, safeguarding and developing the interests of the broadest masses of people, and fully mobilizing all positive factors are the necessary requirements for us to consolidate the social foundation of the Party's governance and realize the historic mission of the Party's governance.

Third, the significance of building a socialist harmonious society

The construction of a socialist harmonious society is the fundamental principle of scientific socialism that the Communist Party of China adheres to, the Party absorbs the positive thoughts created regarding social harmony in human civilization, closely integrates the national conditions with the reality of China, and takes Marxism-Leninism, Mao Zedong Thought, socialism with Chinese characteristics and the Important Thought of "Three Represents" as its guide and comprehensively implement the scientific concept of development. The major strategic tasks proposed from the overall layout of the cause of socialism with Chinese characteristics and the overall situation of building a well-off society in an all-round way reflect the inherent requirements of building a prosperous, democratic, civilized and harmonious modern country, embody the common aspirations of the whole Party and the people of all ethnic groups throughout the country. Fundamentally speaking, taking "building a socialist harmonious society" as a clear goal of development is an innovative summary of the objective system for the development of socialism; it is deepening our understanding of what kind of socialism we should build and how to build socialism. It is also a major innovation in the theory of socialist construction, which is of great theoretical and practical significance.

First, building a socialist harmonious society is a deepening of our understanding of the laws governing the development of human society, the law of socialist construction and the law of the governing of the communist party. The development of human society has always been a historical process which forms a continuous development trend constantly changing, advancing, rising and perfecting in the contradictory movements from low level to high level, from part to whole, from simplicity to complexity. Putting forward the building of a socialist harmonious society is a practical process of unifying social forces, constantly eliminating the factors of discord in social conflicts, increasing the factors of harmony, and achieving social progress in full compliance with the requirements of the law governing the development of mankind, which is the enrichment and development of the Marxist theory on the construction of a socialist society by our Party. At the same time, our Party places great emphasis on the institutional foundation of a harmonious society, that is, this harmonious society is founded on the basis of adhering to the path of building socialism with Chinese characteristics and reveals that "social harmony is the essential attribute of socialism with Chinese characteristics", which sums up the general layout of socialist modernization of our country as the "Four in One" of economic construction, political construction, cultural construction and social construction, reflecting our Party's new understanding and development of the nature of socialism and further enriching and innovating socialism with Chinese characteristics, which deepens the understanding of the law of socialist construction. It is proposed to build a socialist harmonious society and to give more prominence to the ruling philosophy of "Party for the public and government for the people" and "exercising power for the people, showing concern for them and working for their interests", it is emphasized that only by building a socialist harmonious society, arousing the enthusiasm of all parties in a broad manner, properly coordinating the relations of interests between various social stratum, effectively safeguarding and realizing social fairness and justice, enabling all the people to be equally fraternal and harmonious, living in harmony with the, can our Party's purpose and requirements of governing for the people be more fully reflected, reflecting our Party's new understanding of the ruling law and governing strategy as the ruling party.

Second, building a socialist harmonious society is an inevitable requirement for building an overall well-off society and realizing socialist modernization. Over the past 30 years since the reform and opening up, all our undertakings including social construction have made great progress.

The Republic has been seeing unprecedented prosperity with magnificent achievements: we have successfully completed the first two steps of our "three-step" development strategy, The GDP per capita has exceeded 4,000 U.S. dollars, marking our entry into the ranks of the middle-income countries in the world. The socialist market economic system has been perfected day by day, which has greatly promoted the rapid development of the national economy which is the second largest in the world. Shenzhou VI spacecraft, Qinghai-Tibet Railway, the West-East electricity transmission project, West to East Power Transmission, South-to-North Water Diversion and other major projects have been reported with success. The radio and television "to every village" projects benefits the vast rural areas. Infrastructure such as airports, ports and highways was increasingly improved. The agricultural tax exemption for hundreds of millions of peasants in our country completely bid farewell to the history of "paying imperial-cereals" for thousands of years so that ordinary people get real benefits. The overall environment for economic and social development in our country is stable and people's creative vitality is being liberated. The socialist China is vibrant and our socialist society is an overall harmonious society. At the same time, we must also be soberly aware that despite the tremendous historical progress China has made, but our basic national conditions that the country is still in and will remain in the initial stage of socialism for a long time has not changed. The gap between the ever-growing material and cultural needs of the people and the low level of social production has not changed, nor has China's international position as the largest developing country in the world changed. In particular, it should be noted that with the deepening of reform and opening up, under the background of profound changes in the economic structure, profound changes in social structure, profound adjustments in the pattern of interests, and profound changes in ideological concepts, there are still many deep-seated contradictions in the rapid development of our country. There actually have emerged many discordant factors and phenomena. They are mainly manifested as the continuing expansion of the urban-rural gap, the regional gap, and the income gap, the increase of employment and social security pressures, the lag in education, health, culture and other social undertakings, the aggravated contradictions between population growth, economic development and ecological environment and natural resources, the backward mode of economic growth, that there is no fundamental change in the extensive economic growth, and the overall low quality of the economy and the lack of competitiveness, etc. We still face many difficulties and problems on the road forward and are at a stage of "contradiction protruding period" which is particularly apt to trigger various economic and social conflicts. These new developments and changes have set new demands on our Party: we must actively maintain social stability, promote social harmony, adjust social relations, maximize the creativity and enthusiasm of the whole society, resolve all kinds of contradictions and problems, and strive to realize the goal of coordinated development of economy and society as well as the coordinated development of man and nature of our country which are the necessary requirements of the social development in China today. "Building a socialist harmonious society" means that our Party should keep a clear head, be prepared for danger in times of peace, have a profound understanding of the stage characteristics of our country's development, scientifically analyze the contradictions and problems that have an impact on social harmony and their causes, impose pressure on ourselves and proactively make major strategic goals. Its basic spirit is to realistically and actively face the contradiction and resolve the contradiction, maximize the factors of harmony, minimize the factors of disharmony and promote social harmony on the basis of overall harmony of the actual socialist system.

Third, building a socialist harmonious society embodies the unification of the development process and goals of socialism with Chinese characteristics. In each specific stage of social development, social harmony always has specific and historical tasks and standards. The historical process of our socialism is a process of continuously promoting the harmonious development and continuously raising the standard of harmony. Through the founding of New China and the overthrow of the old system of exploitation, we have initially established a socialist productive relationship that is compatible and coordinated with the development of our productive forces, which is an embodiment of harmony. In the new era of reform and opening up, we have explored a socialist path of building socialism with Chinese characteristics, put forward the goal of building a prosperous, democratic and civilized socialist modern country, promoted the coordinated development of material civilization, political civilization and spiritual civilization, which is the further development of social harmony. On the basis of the tremendous achievements made in the past, our Party, in a new phase of the new century, further proposed that socialism is a society in which economic, political, cultural and social development are developing in an all-round way. It is also a society in which material civilization, political civilization, spiritual civilization and ecological civilization are organically unified. Building a harmonious society is a more in-depth, more specific and higher-standard plan for the goal of harmony. It is also a continuation of our historical process of pursuing a harmonious society. The 17th CPC National Congress proposed that scientific development and social harmony are the basic requirements for the development of socialism with Chinese characteristics. Building a well-off society in an all-round way is the goal for the Party and the state by 2020 and the fundamental interest of the people of all nationalities in the country. By the middle of the 21st century, we must basically realize modernization and build our country into a prosperous, strong, democratic, civilized and harmonious socialist modern country. This is our Party's immediate goal of struggle and a common ideal of the entire society. Therefore, the pursuit of social harmony is not only a concrete process of struggle, but also an objective of the struggle. It is not only an ideal of governing the country, but also a strategy of governing the country and a mechanism of governing the country, as well as the result of governing the country.

Section II

The guiding ideology, basic principles and tasks and requirements of building a socialist harmonious society

First, the guiding ideology and basic principles of building a socialist harmonious society

The 6th Plenary Session of the 16th CPC Central Committee has explicitly put forward the guiding ideology of building a socialist harmonious society: The guidance of Marxism, Leninism, Mao Zedong Thought and Deng Xiaoping Theory and the important thought of "Three Represents" shall be persisted, the Party's basic line, program and experience must upheld, using the scientific development concept to lead the overall economic and social development must be insisted on and in accordance with the general requirements of democracy, the rule of law, fairness and justice, honesty and fraternity, vitality, stability and order, harmony between man and nature, the Party should focus on solving the most practical problems of the utmost and immediate concern to the people, make every effort to develop social undertakings, promote social fairness and justice, build a harmonious culture, improve social management, enhance social vitality, take the path of common prosperity, and promote the coordinated development between social construction and economic, political and cultural construction.

While putting forward the major task of building a socialist harmonious society, the CPC Central Committee has also clearly proposed the basic principles that must be followed in advancing the construction of a harmonious society and pointed out the direction for actively and steadily promoting the building of a harmonious society in practice.

First, adhering to the people-oriented principle is the fundamental starting point and the ultimate goal of building a socialist harmonious society. To build a socialist harmonious society, we must implement people-oriented principle, take the realization of the fundamental interests of the overwhelming majority of the people as the highest standard of all the work of our Party and state. We should uphold the principle that development is for the people, by the people and with the people, and that people should share fruits and that we should promote the comprehensive development of men.

Second, upholding the scientific development is the guideline for building a socialist harmonious society. In order to build a socialist harmonious society, we must firmly establish and comprehensively implement the scientific concept of development, earnestly focus on development, which is the top priority for the Party in governing and rejuvenating the country, make overall plans for the harmonious development of urban and rural areas, regions, economy and society and between man and nature, make overall plans for domestic development and opening to the outside world, so as to achieve comprehensive, coordinated and sustainable development of economy and society.

Third, upholding reform and opening up is the driving force for building a socialist harmonious society. To build a socialist harmonious society, we must uphold the reform direction of the socialist market economy, adapt to the requirements of social development, promote reforms and innovations in the economic, political, cultural and social systems, and further expand the opening to the outside world.

Fourth, adhering to democracy and the rule of law is the work guarantee for building a socialist harmonious society. To build a socialist harmonious society, we must strengthen socialist democratic politics, develop socialist democracy, implement the basic strategy of governing the country according to law, and promote social fairness and justice through democracy and the rule of law.

Fifth, upholding the correct handling of the relations between reform, development and stability is the working condition for building a socialist harmonious society. In order to build a socialist harmonious society, we must unify the intensity of reform, the speed of development and the degree of social affordability, maintain social stability and unity, promote harmony through reform, consolidate harmony through development, ensure harmony through stability, so that people can live and work in peace and contentment, achieve social stability and order and the long-term peace and stability of the state.

Sixth, upholding the common building of the entire society under the leadership of the Party is the core of the leadership and the strength to build a socialist harmonious society. In order to build a socialist harmonious society, we must strengthen and improve the Party's leadership and give play to the leadership of the Party. At the same time, we must safeguard the dominant position of the masses and unite all forces that can be united to mobilize all positive factors and foster a dynamic environment in which everyone contributes to social harmony and benefits from a harmonious society.

The above-mentioned six basic principles constitute an organic whole containing rich contents and profoundly embody the fundamental requirement of building a socialist harmonious society. From different perspectives, they answered the question of for whom to build, who to build and how to build a socialist harmonious society, pointing out what thoughts we should follow to build a harmonious socialist society, coordinating the overall situation on the basis of what principle, advancing development on the basis of what requirements, what method is used to ensure harmony, and a relatively systematic guiding ideology and basic principle for building a socialist harmonious society has been formed.

Second, the main objectives and tasks of building a harmonious socialist society

According to the grand goal of building a well-off society established by the Party's 16th CPC National Congress and in accordance with the general requirements for building a socialist harmonious society, the 6th Plenary Session of the 16th CPC Central Committee has set the goal and major tasks for building a socialist harmonious society by 2020: (1) The socialist democracy and legal system would have been further improved and the basic strategy of governing the country according to law would have been fully implemented, and people's rights and interests would have been effectively respected and guaranteed; (2) the trend of widening the gap between urban and rural areas and regions would have been gradually reversed, and a rational and orderly pattern of income distribution has basically taken shape, and the people would could live a more wealthy life; (3) The social employment would be more adequate and the social security system covering urban and rural residents basically established; (4) The basic public service system would be more complete and the level of government administration and service greater improved; (5) The ideological and ethical standards of the whole nation, the scientific and cultural qualities and health qualifications would have been significantly improved, and good ethics and harmonious interpersonal relationships would have been further formed; (6) the vitality of the whole society would have been significantly enhanced and the innovative countries basically completed; (7) there would be a more complete social management system and a good social order; (8) there would be a marked improvement in the efficiency of resource utilization and in the ecological environment; (9) the goal of building a well-off society in a higher standard that will benefit billions of people in all aspects would be achieved, and all the people would do their best and get along well with each other in harmony. These nine goals and major tasks respectively reflect all aspects of the general requirements of democracy, the rule of law, fairness and justice, honesty and fraternity, vitality, stability and order, and the harmonious coexistence of man and nature, and supplement and enrich the content of building an overall well-off society.

In order to accomplish the above goals and tasks, the Party Central Committee made a comprehensive plan for the building of a socialist harmonious society and put forward a series of major initiatives, which include not only specific policies for solving problems, but also basic ideas and way of efforts to further solve the problems.

First, insist on coordinated development and strengthen the building of social undertakings. In order to build a socialist harmonious society, we must always adhere to the basic idea of using development to solve the problems in progress. According to the actual situation of our country, which is still and will remain in the initial stage of socialism for a long time, the CPC Central Committee has proposed specific measures such as to promote the building of a new socialist countryside, promote the coordinated development of urban and rural areas, implement the overall regional development strategy, promote the coordinated development of the region, implement a proactive employment policy and development harmonious labor relations, adhere to the priority of education, promote education fairness, strengthen medical and health services, improve people's health level, accelerate the development of cultural undertakings and cultural industries, meet people's cultural needs, strengthen the environmental governance and promote the harmony between man and nature.

Second, strengthen the institutional construction and ensure social fairness and justice. Social fairness and justice are the basic conditions for social harmony, and institution is the fundamental guarantee for social fairness and justice. We must make every effort to build a system that plays an important role in safeguarding social fairness and justice, safeguard people's rights and interests in the political, economic, cultural and social fields, and guide citizens to exercise their rights and fulfill their obligations in accordance with the law. Only by improving the institutional mechanisms that promote social fairness and justice can we provide institutional guarantees for building a socialist harmonious society. These concrete measures are: perfecting the system of guaranteeing the democratic rights, consolidating the political status of the people as the masters of the country; perfecting the legal system and consolidating the foundation of the rule of law for social harmony; perfecting the judicial system and mechanisms and strengthening the judicial guarantee of social harmony; improving the public financial system and gradually realizing equalization of basic public services; improving the income distribution system, standardizing the order of income distribution; improving the social security system to protect the basic livelihood of the masses.

Third, build a harmonious culture and consolidate the ideological and ethical foundation for social harmony. In order to truly achieve social harmony, we must uphold the correct orientation and create a positive and healthy atmosphere of public thinking and opinion. We should actively build a harmonious culture, advocate the concept of harmony, and cultivate a harmonious spirit. This is both a cultural premise for building a socialist harmonious society and an important task of building a harmonious society itself. To build a harmonious culture, the most fundamental thing is to establish the socialist core value system in our society with the Marxism guiding ideology and building socialism with Chinese characteristics as the common ideal, the national spirit with patriotism as the core of and the spirit of the times with reform and innovation as the core, as well as the concept of honor and disgrace of socialism as the basic content, further form the common ideals and beliefs and moral norms of the whole society and lay a solid ideological and ethical foundation for the unity and struggle of the people of all nationalities throughout the country. On this basis, we should conduct a wide range of activities for creating harmony, combine the building of a socialist harmonious society with the creation of a harmonious community, as well as a harmonious family and other mass spiritual civilization building activities and a harmonious, and create an atmosphere of "one for all, all for one".

Fourth, improve social management and maintain social stability and order. Strengthening social management and maintaining social stability are the necessary requirements for building a harmonious socialist society. We should focus our efforts on a series of important work such as building a service-oriented government, strengthening social management and public service functions, promoting community building, improving basic service and management networks; improving social organizations and enhancing social services; coordinating the interests of all parties and properly handling social conflicts; improving institutional mechanisms of emergency management to effectively deal with various risks; strengthening the comprehensive management of public security and enhancing people's sense of security; strengthening national security and national defense construction, safeguarding the stability and security of the state to provide a good social and political environment for the building of a harmonious socialist society.

Fifth, stimulate social vitality and enhance social solidarity. Socialist harmonious society is not only a dynamic society, but also a united and harmonious society. We must stimulate social vitality to the utmost and promote the harmony of relations between political parties, ethnic relations, religious relations, class relations, relations between compatriots at home and abroad, consolidate the great unity of the people of all ethnic groups across the country and consolidate the great unity of the Chinese people at home and abroad. We must stick to the path of peaceful development and create a favorable international environment. Only by fully mobilizing all the patriotic forces at home and abroad, inside and outside the country, and by enhancing social solidarity and vitality, can we provide a broad range of forces for the construction of a harmonious socialist society and lay a solid social foundation.

Sixth, correctly handle social conflicts. Social contradiction movements are the basic force to promote social development. We must abide by the laws governing social development, face up to the contradictions proactively, properly handle contradictions among the people and other social contradictions, continue to cultivate material bases for reducing and resolving conflicts, enhance the spiritual strength, improve policy measure and strengthen institutional security to maximize social vitality, maximize the harmonious factors and minimize the discordant factors. We should strengthen and innovate social management, perfect the social management pattern in which the Party committee leads, the government takes charge, the society coordinates and the public participate, and establish a socialist social management system with Chinese characteristics to comprehensively improve the level of scientific management of social administration and ensure people's livelihood and social harmony and stability.

The 17th CPC National Congress has made a new comprehensive plan for building a harmonious socialist society and building a well-off society in all respects. It further proposes that it is necessary to enhance coordination in development, make effort to achieve sound and rapid economic development, and create a solid material foundation for building a harmonious socialist society; it is necessary to unswervingly develop socialist democracy and ensure that the people be the masters of the country, accelerate the reform of the administrative system to build a service-oriented government; It is necessary to improve the mechanism of restraint and oversight and ensure that power entrusted by the people is always exercised in their interests; It is necessary to enhance cultural construction, build a harmonious culture and cultivate civilized prevailing custom; It is necessary to carry forward Chinese culture and build a common spiritual home for the Chinese nation; It is necessary to speed up the development of social undertakings and comprehensively improve people's lives. The report of the 17th National Congress of the Party also stressed in particular the need to speed up the social construction that focuses on improving people's livelihood, put forward the development strategy of prioritizing education, building a country rich in human resources and implementing employment expansion, promote employment through entrepreneurship and deepen reform of the income distribution system and increase the income of urban and rural residents, accelerate the establishment of a social security system covering both urban and rural residents and guarantee their basic living conditions, establish a basic medical and health system, improve the whole people's health level, improve social management, and maintain social stability and unity and other key initiatives to promote the building of a harmonious society. In the *Outline of the Twelfth-Five Year Plan*, which was implemented in 2011, it also sets forth an important proposition for strengthening and innovating social management. Take improving the scientific level of social management, innovating social management concepts and methods, and improving the scientific and effective policy formulation as the main goal of strengthening social management. We must take improving social management as an important task to improve people's lives and promote social harmony. First, promote reform and innovation in social management system. Second, properly handle contradictions among the people. Third, pay attention to the construction and management of social organizations. Fourth, strengthen safety management and supervision. Fifth, improve the social order prevention and control system.

"The ancient and modern prosperities are all based on reality, great undertakings all have small beginnings". The construction of a harmonious socialist society is not only a long-term historic task throughout the whole course of undertaking the cause of socialism with Chinese characteristics, but also an important and realistic subject in building an overall well-off society in the new phase of the new century. It must be well linked with the goal of building a well-off society in all respects and our strategic goal of fundamentally realizing modernization, based on the current, take a long-term perspective, do what one can do, do our best, march forward in priority areas and in phases. A harmonious and beautiful society requires hard work in a down-to-earth manner and joint efforts of all people.

CHAPTER ELEVEN

The Basic Forces in Developing Socialism with Chinese characteristics

Section I

Building socialism with Chinese characteristics is the common cause of the people of all ethnic groups in China

First, workers, peasants and intellectuals are the basic forces of the cause of building socialism with Chinese characteristics

To build socialism with Chinese characteristics is the common cause of the people of all nationalities and people of all walks of life in the country and requires the concerted efforts and hard work of all people of all nationalities and people of all walks of life across the country. In contemporary China, all the classes, strata and social forces who advocate, support and participate in the construction of socialism with Chinese characteristics are the we depend in promoting the cause of socialism with Chinese characteristics. The working class and the vast majority of peasants, including intellectuals, have always been the fundamental forces in promoting the development of our country's advanced productive forces and advanced culture and all-round social progress.

1. The working class is the leading class and main force in building socialism with Chinese characteristics

The working class is the leading class in our country and the fundamental force for promoting the development of our country's advanced productive forces and all-round social progress. It is the most solid and reliable class foundation for the Communist Party of China and the main force for building socialism with Chinese characteristics. To build socialism with Chinese characteristics, we must wholeheartedly rely on the working class.

The status and role of the working class in the cause of building social-ism with Chinese characteristics are determined by its own characteristics and social and historical status and by the nature of the People's Republic of China and the nature of the Communist Party of China. First of all, the working class in China is a product of the development of society, espe-cially the development of socialized mass production in China in recent years. Since it is linked with the modern mode of production, it has always been able to keep pace with the times, stand at the forefront of the times and continuously promote the development of advanced productive forces and advanced productive relations. It is the representative of the advanced productive forces and advanced productive relations in China. Secondly, China is a socialist country and the working class is the leading class of the country, which is expressly stipulated in the Constitution of the People's Republic of China. In China, the leadership of the working class is achieved through the Communist Party of China. The Communist Party of China is the vanguard of the Chinese working class. The advanced nature of the Party stems from the advanced nature of the working class. The working class, which is linked to socialized mass production, is therefore the most far-sighted, the most broad-minded in its breadth and the most disciplined in organization and is capable of leading the modern economic, political and social progress. The Chinese revolution met with success under the leadership of the Chinese working class. China's socialist construction has also made great achievements under the leadership of the working class. Therefore, the Party must rely firmly on the working class in its entire practice of leading revolutions, construction and reform and throughout the entire process, which is the fundamental guarantee for the victory of our cause. Thirdly, the working class is the basic driving force for reform, opening up and modernization. The working class, concentrated in the ad-vanced or more advanced modern enterprises in our national economy, has created the largest part of social wealth and is the major productive force that plays a decisive role in the national economy and the leading force in the socialist modernization drive. The leading position of the working class in the modernization construction and the characteristics of concentration and unification of working methods play a crucial role in safeguarding the stability, unity and social stability of the country, which are a powerful force for the stability of the country and society. To carry out moderniza-tion construction, implement reform and opening up, and build socialism with Chinese characteristics are in the fundamental interest of the working class, therefore, the working class is also the most basic motive force for reform, opening up and modernization construction. Since the reform and opening up, the workers' masses are mindful of the overall interests of the country, boldness in innovation, thriftiness and hard work, and have made great contributions to the socialist modernization and the socialist market economy. They are not only leaders in the cause of reform and opening up and the modernization drive, but also the practitioners, the backbone of promoting the cause of reform, opening up and modernization.

With the continuous advancement of the cause of socialism with Chinese characteristics, the ranks of the working class in our country have undergone significant changes and many new features have emerged. The major ones are summarized as follows: First, the working class have rapidly expanded. Since the reform and opening up, with the development of the secondary and tertiary industries in our country, with the acceleration of industrialization and urbanization, the proportion of Chinese agriculture practitioners has dropped significantly and the working class has been rapidly growing. Second, job mobility accelerated. The "iron rice bowl" under the planned economic system has been broken. The two-way choice between enterprises and institutions and the employees is a foregone conclusion. The dependency of staff and workers on the work units is greatly weakened and their autonomy is greatly enhanced. Third, significant changes have taken place in the internal structure. The proportion of intellectuals in the working class has greatly increased, and their quality of science, technology and culture and ideological and moral qualifications have remarkably improved. The peasants who have entered the cities for jobs have become an important part of China's industrial workers and are becoming an important driving force for industrialization, urbanization and modernization. The forms of ownership of economic organizations on which the workers depend are increasingly diversified, and the number of workers employed in various non-public economic organizations accounts for about half of the total workforce. All in all, the working-class in our country has grown in strength, its quality has been continuously improved and its advanced nature has been constantly enhanced. It has become a unified whole of all laborers consisting of all kinds of enterprises, various organs, institutions, and new economic organizations and new social organizations, including a large number of migrant workers.

The new changes that have taken place in the ranks of the working class in China have not changed the position of the working class as the masters of the country. The working class is still the major builder of socialist modernization, the major creator of social wealth, the representative of advanced productive forces and the leading class in the state of the people's democratic dictatorship. The most fundamental manifestation of the advanced nature of the working class is that it represents the advanced productive forces and is the precursor to the promotion of social development in China.

The Party Central Committee has always attached great importance to the working class. Deng Xiaoping once made it clear that one of the most important characteristics of the working class in China is that it is linked to the socialization of mass production. Therefore, it has the highest awareness and the strongest sense of discipline, and can play a leading role in economic progress and social progress. In elaborating the important thinking of the 'Three Represents', Jiang Zemin repeatedly stressed that all the activities and the entire process of the reform and socialist modernization led by our Party must wholeheartedly rely on the working class, which cannot shake at any time and in any case. Since the 16th CPC National Congress, the Party Central Committee with Hu Jintao as the General Secretary has reiterated that the working class should remain unshakable as the leading class in the country. Its role as the main force for reform, opening up and socialist modernization cannot be weakened, and the fundamental guidelines which the Party must wholeheartedly rely upon the working class cannot be changed.

To depend on the working class wholeheartedly and to bring the leading role of the working class into full play in the socialist modernization drive, we must safeguard the legitimate rights and interests of all workers, including migrant workers, and consolidate the master's position of the working class. In the process of deepening the reform, establishing a modern enterprise system and promoting urbanization, the Party and government must earnestly safeguard the workers' democratic rights through political, economic, legal, public opinions and administrative measures and implement the workers' rights of information, participation, expression and supervision, so as to maintain the rights and interests of the masses of workers. We must care for and arrange the lives of job-waiting and unemployed workers, broaden employment opportunities, promote reemployment projects and improve the social security system. We must continue to meet the ever-increasing spiritual and cultural needs of our workers and staff, and actively organize employees to participate in social affairs management. At the same time, the masses of workers and staff should further recognize their glorious mission, enhance their sense of responsibility, carry forward the fine tradition of knowing the general situation and taking overall plans into consideration, and correctly understand and handle the adjustment of the interest relations and the pattern of interests in the process of reform and development, particularly cherish the unity and maintain the stability of enterprises and society, and contribute to the promotion of scientific development and social harmony.

2. Peasants are the basic force to rely on when building socialism with Chinese characteristics

The problems concerning agriculture, rural areas and peasants are related to the overall development of the cause of socialism with Chinese characteristics. Agriculture is the foundation of our national economy. Agriculture is not only directly related to the basic subsistence conditions such as eating and dressing of over 1.3 billion of China's population, but also guarantees and supports the operation and stable development of the entire national economy. Without the solid foundation and modernization of agriculture, it will be impossible to have the independence and modernization of the entire country. Without the stability and overall progress in the countryside, it will be impossible for the stability and overall progress of the entire society. Without the "well-off" of the peasants, there will be no "well-off" of the people across the country.

In all historical periods of revolution, construction and reform in China, the CPC has consistently adhered to combining the basic tenets of Marxism with the concrete reality of China and has always attached great importance to, taken seriously and try really hard to solve the problems of agriculture, the rural areas and peasants and successfully opened up a victory path for new-democratic revolution and the path to the development of socialism. Mao Zedong once pointed out: "The people's democratic dictatorship is based on the alliance of the working class, the peasantry and the urban petty bourgeoisie, and mainly on the coalition of workers and peasants, because these two classes comprise 80 to 90 per cent of China's population. These two classes are the main force in overthrowing imperialism and the Kuomintang reactionaries. The transition from New Democracy to socialism also depends mainly upon their alliance."[1]

China's national conditions have determined that the vast majority of peasants are not only the main force of the new-democratic revolution in our country, but also the largest population and most basic force of reliance in our country's socialist modernization and reform and opening up.

The reform of contemporary China started from the countryside. In 1978, the 3rd Plenary Session of the 11th Central Committee of the Party made a historic decision to shift the work center of the Party and the state to economic construction and implement the historic policy of reform and opening up. Against this backdrop, the majority of peasants, proceeding from the strong desire to change their own poverty and backwardness, have the courage to explore and innovate boldly and gradually establish a double-tier agricultural production and operation system that combines unified and separate operations, which is mainly based on the household contract responsibility system, and drive the entire reform and construction. The rural reform greatly mobilized the enthusiasm of hundreds of millions of peasants, greatly liberated and developed the social productive forces in rural areas and greatly improved the material and cultural life of the broad masses of peasants. More importantly, the great practice of rural reform and development has creatively explored the establishment and improvement of the basic economic system and the socialist market economic system

---

1   Selected Works of Mao Zedong, 2nd Edition, Vol.4, pp.1478-1497.

in the initial stage of our socialism, and has made tremendous contributions to the historic leap forward in realizing the people's livelihood from inadequate basic living necessities to overall well-off society, laid a solid foundation for overcoming all kinds of difficulties and risks and maintaining the overall social stability, and accumulated valuable experience in successfully opening up the path of socialism with Chinese characteristics and forming the theoretical system of socialism with Chinese characteristics. In addition, the township and village enterprises that have been continuously developing and expanding during the rural reform have not only prospered the rural economy, but have also led to the transformation of a considerable number of rural laborers to the working class. In short, reform, opening up and modernization not only serve the peasants' fundamental interests but also enable them to receive benefits at the earliest stage. The vast number of peasants wholeheartedly support the line, principles and policies of building socialism with Chinese characteristics and become an important relying force of the cause of reform and opening up as well as the modernization drive.

Relying on the broad masses of peasants and mobilizing the enthusiasm and creativity of peasants has a bearing on the overall development of the country. Deng Xiaoping once pointed out that if the peasants are not motivated, the country cannot develop. Therefore, during the process of building a well-off society in all respects and realizing the great rejuvenation of the Chinese nation, we must constantly raise our awareness of the extreme importance of agriculture, rural areas and peasants, and earnestly safeguard the legitimate rights and democratic rights of peasants. We must always make realizing, safeguarding and developing the fundamental interests of the overwhelming majority of the peasants the starting point and foothold of all the rural work. Adhere to the people-oriented principle, respect the wishes of peasants, and strive to solve the most concerned, most immediate and most realistic interests of the peasants, improve the overall quality of peasants and promote the all-round development of peasants, give full play to the main role and pioneering spirit of peasants, firmly rely on hundreds of millions of peasants to build a new socialist countryside.

3. Intellectuals are the important reliance of building socialism with Chinese characteristics

As a part of the working class in China that mainly has scientific and cultural knowledge, intellectuals are mainly engaged in mental work. As the pioneer of advanced productive forces and the basic force of educational and cultural work, the intellectuals play an irreplaceable role in the process of reform and opening up as well as in the modernization drive. They take major social and historical responsibilities and are an important strength to rely on in building socialism. Mao Zedong pointed out: "Our country's formidable and arduous task of constructing socialism needs the service of as many intellectuals as possible."[2] Deng Xiaoping pointed out: As part of the working class, the vast majority of our intellectuals are "trying to serve the cause of socialism consciously."[3] Jiang Zemin further pointed out: "Without knowledge and intellectuals, it is impossible to build socialism."[4]

In today's world, science and technology are advancing by leaps and bounds. The competition among countries is mainly manifested in the competition of comprehensive national strength, whose core is the competition in science and technology. Without the rapid development of science and technology, there will be no rapid development of the national economy, which is an indisputable fact. As the primary productive force, science and technology have become increasingly prominent as the concentrated reflection and main symbol of advanced productive forces. This important position of science and technology determines the special important role of intellectuals in economic development and social progress. Intellectuals, as important creators, successors and disseminators of human scientific and cultural knowledge, are the new force in promoting scientific and technological progress and economic development in our country. They are the pioneers of advanced productive forces and the backbone and core force in the construction of socialist spiritual civilization. Without intellectuals, progress in science and technology and knowledge innovation, the development of culture and education, the improvement of ideological and moral standards, and the cultivation of citizens with four qualifications will be nothing but empty talk. At the same time, the intellectuals are also playing an important role in strengthening theoretical studies on democratic construction, formulating laws and regulations in all aspects, publicizing and popularizing democratic knowledge and legal knowledge, raising the democratic awareness of the entire nation and the concept of legal system, advancing the building of socialist democracy and the rule of law, and ensuring the scientificity in decision-making on construction and reform.

305

Relying on intellectuals to promote science and technology, economic development and social progress has become a key factor in the development of China's reform and opening up as well as in the cause of socialist modernization. In order to rely on intellectuals and give play to the role of intellectuals, we must strive to create a favorable environment that is more conducive for intellectuals to exert their wisdom and intelligence and further develop a good prevailing custom of "respecting knowledge and respecting talents" in the whole society. We must formulate relevant policies

2   Mao Zedong Collected Works, Vol.7, p.225, Beijing, People's Publishing House, 1999.
3   Selected Works of Deng Xiaoping, 2nd edition, Vol.2, p.186.
4   CPCCC Party Literature Research Office: "Selection of Important Literature since the 13th National Congress" (Vol.II), p.622f.

and measures and actively improve the working, studying and living conditions of intellectuals, give rewards to those intellectuals with outstanding contributions, and form a standardized system of rewards; we must fully trust the intellectuals in politics and at the same time actively guide and strictly require them to carry forward the spirit of "love the motherland, seek truth and innovation, work hard and sacrifice, and unite and cooperate with each other" to better assume the historic mission of the working class, play a greater role in the great cause of building socialism with Chinese characteristics, and truly become the "Nation's elites" and the "backbones of socialist modernization".

Second, the new social strata as the builders of the cause of socialism with Chinese characteristics

Since the reform and opening up, there have been new changes in the composition of social classes in China. There have emerged entrepreneurs and technicians in private science and technology enterprises, management and technical personnel employed by foreign-funded enterprises, practitioners in intermediary organizations, freelance professionals, private entrepreneurs, self-employed and other new social strata. Moreover, many people frequently move between different ownership systems, industries and regions, and their occupations and identities change frequently. These new social strata emerged in the process of China's reform and opening up and existed and developed in the overall situation of socialist public ownership and the superstructure of socialism leading the country's political and economic life. Most of them are laborers, differentiated from the ranks of workers, peasants, intellectuals and cadres. Under the guidance of the Party's principles and policies, they are the builders of socialism with Chinese characteristics through honest labor and work, through lawful operation, and contribute to the development of socialist productive forces and other undertakings. Some of them are private entrepreneurs, they possess means of production and employ workers, and they play an active role in boosting and promoting national economy and social development. They are also builders of the cause of socialism with Chinese characteristics. The Communist Party of China must unite with all social strata who are contributing to the prosperity of the motherland and encourage their entrepreneurial spirit, protect their legitimate rights and interests and commend outstanding persons among them so that the whole people do their best, find their proper places in society and live in harmony.

The formation of new social strata in China conforms to the requirements of the national conditions and the development of social productive forces in the initial stage of socialism. First of all, we should gradually establish and improve the socialist market economy in the primary stage of socialism, establish a basic economic system with public ownership as the mainstay and various ownership economy developing side by side. We should implement a distribution system under which distribution according to work is dominant and a variety of modes of distribution coexist and the basic state policy of opening up to the outside world, which will inevitably lead to the emergence of new social strata, the emergence of a large number of self-employed entrepreneurs, workers of private-owned and foreign enterprises, or freelancers. Institutional innovation in the economic field is a prerequisite for the emergence of new social classes. Second, the development of productive forces and changes in economic structure have made the division of labor in the society increasingly sophisticated, providing working conditions for the emergence of new classes. Finally, changes in the industrial structure contributed to changes in the employment structure and social class structure. Since the reform and opening up, with the continuous acceleration of the process of China's modernization, the proportion of the primary industry in the gross national product has declined, while the proportion of the secondary and tertiary industries has risen. A large number of diverted personnel from the primary industry have been transferred to the second and tertiary industries, some of whom become private entrepreneurs or self-employed.

Generally speaking, the broad masses of personnel in the new social strata uphold the leadership of the Communist Party and the socialist system, uphold the Party's line, principles and policies, abide by state laws and love the motherland. They have the courage to blaze new trails and dare to take risks and have come out of a path of entrepreneurship and hard work to get rich. The cause of building socialism with Chinese characteristics needs the outstanding persons in all aspects of society, who are loyal to the motherland and socialism. Taking the broad masses of personnel in the new social strata as builders of the cause of socialism with Chinese characteristics is a scientific conclusion drawn from reality, seeking truth from facts, respecting practice and respecting the masses.

Third, the respect for labor, knowledge, talented human resources and creativity

Respect for labor, respect for knowledge, respect for talent, and respect for creation is a major principle of the Party and the state. The purpose is to create an appropriate ideology and entrepreneurial mechanism that is compatible with the basic economic system at the primary stage of socialism, create a social atmosphere that encourages people to run their business and support people to accomplish their undertakings, so as to unleash all the vitality contained in work, knowledge, technology, management and capital and give full play to all sources of social wealth for the benefit of the people.

Labor, knowledge, talent, creation, these four elements are a unified whole with inner connection. Labor is at the core and basic position. Labor is the most basic and important social practice of mankind, is the fundamental premise of the survival and development of human society. Labor has created the world and mankind itself. Knowledge is an important resource for wealth creation, but it can form actual wealth only through workers and means of labor. Talent is the carrier of knowledge resources, the essence of talent lies in creativity. Only through labor to create enormous material and spiritual wealth for the society, can the values of talents be reflected. Creation itself is a kind of labor, and the process of creation is the process in which workers maximize their talents. Since the reform and opening up, Deng Xiaoping and Jiang Zemin had respectively put forward the views of "respecting knowledge and talents", "respecting labor, respecting talents", "respecting creativity and respecting innovation". The 16th National Congress of the Party systematized these together and clearly put forward that "We must respect labor, respect knowledge, respect talent, and respect creativity. This must be seriously implemented in society as a major principle of the Party and the state." Taking the "Four Respects" as a major guideline, reflects the Party's emphasis on the Marxist labor and labor theory of value, who attaches great importance to the historical status and social role of knowledge and intellectuals. Talents and talent resources are highly valued under the condition of socialism, and the creative spirit and creative work conducive to the prosperity of the motherland and the happiness of the people are also highly valued.

The principle of conscientiously implementing the "Four Respects" in the entire society is a new demand put forward by the times for the work of the Party and the state. In today's era, with the rapid development of science and technology with information technology as its core, the knowledge-based economy based on hi-tech and its industries has rapidly risen. The driving force behind the development of world economy has shifted to relying mainly on human capital, creation has become an important form of labor. Talents have become the most precious and important resource, and the status and role of mental labor in the form of labor are becoming more and more prominent. The "Four Respects" is a positive response made by the Party on the basis of profoundly understanding and grasping the essential characteristics of contemporary economic development and its influence, fully reflecting the spirit of the times and having great practical significance.

The principle of "four respects" must be conscientiously implemented throughout the whole society with the aim of mobilizing all positive factors in a most extensive and sufficient manner to gain inexhaustible sources of strength for the cause of socialism with Chinese characteristics. Only by establishing a new socialist labor concept, correctly viewing various forms of labor and acknowledging the legitimate rights and interests of workers, can we mobilize all positive factors to the fullest extent possible and promote the development of the cause of socialism with Chinese characteristics. Everything that benefits the people and society, both manual and intellectual, whether simple or complicated, are all the labors that contribute to the socialist modernization in our country, and are honorable and deserve recognition and respect. All legal labor income and legal non-labor income should be protected. "It is improper to judge whether people are politically progressive or backward simply by whether they own property or how much property they own. But rather, we should judge them mainly by their political awareness, state of mind and performance, by how they have acquired and used their property, and by how they have contributed to the cause of building socialism with Chinese characteristics through their work."[5]

Only by mobilizing all the positive factors of both the materialized dead labor and living labor and by giving full play to the positive functions of labor, knowledge, technology and management, can various types of labor and the enthusiasm of all kinds of workers of the whole society and the whole nation be widely and creatively mobilized.

The enthusiasm and creativity of the entire society and the entire nation have always been the most decisive factor in the development of the cause of the Party and our country. To this end, we must first give full play to and respect the pioneering spirit of the people, bring about the full release of creative energy for the entire society, continuously bring forth innovations and vigorously launch entrepreneurial activities. Second, we must continuously deepen the reform and strive to create an equally competitive social environment. Through deepening the reform, an effective mechanism for equal competition in the whole society was established. By regulatory and institutional constraints, power interference in the normal competitive order of the society was excluded and a social environment conducive to the implementation of the "Four Respects" was formed. Finally, we must continue to improve the relevant laws and regulations and strictly enforce the law, protect the rights and interests of workers according to the law. We must politically affirm all the work that is beneficial to the people and society and give protection to the legitimate rights and interests of workers.

The principle of conscientiously implementing the "Four Respects" is a concrete manifestation that the CPC represents the development requirement of China's advanced productive forces. Labor, knowledge, talent and creation are the four basic elements that promote the development of the

5   CPCCC Party Literature Research Office: "Selection of Important Literature since the 16th National Congress" (Vol.II), p.622f.

productive forces. By seizing these basic elements, we have seized the key to the development of advanced productive forces.

Fourth, consolidate and develop the unity and cooperation among all ethnic groups

China is a multi-ethnic country. Apart from the Han people, there are 55 ethnic minorities who sum up to a population of nearly 100 million. The areas of national autonomous areas add up to 64% of the total area of the country. During the long process of historical development, due to the interdependent economic and cultural ties among all ethnic groups, especially the relations of solidarity and common ground formed in the course of resisting foreign invasions and protracted revolutionary struggles in the modern history, all ethnic groups begin to breathe the same air and share the same fate, forming a Chinese nation with strong cohesion. The establishment of the socialist system has laid a fundamental political and economic foundation for the unity, progress and prosperity of all our ethnic groups and established a new type of ethnic relations of equality, unity and mutual assistance among all ethnic groups. National unity and ethnic solidarity are the necessary prerequisites for the rejuvenation of the Chinese nation. To build socialism with Chinese characteristics, we must rely on the unity of the people of all ethnic groups and give full play to the enthusiasm and creativity of all ethnic groups.

To consolidate and develop the unity and cooperation among all ethnic groups and realize the common prosperity of all ethnic groups is a major issue concerning the future and destiny of our country and the fundamental interests of our country, nation and people. To consolidate and develop the unity and cooperation among all ethnic groups is an important condition for consolidating and developing the people's democratic dictatorship and a stable and unified political situation. To consolidate and develop the unity and cooperation among all ethnic groups is related to the unification of the country and the consolidation of the frontier. Most of the ethnic minorities in our country are concentrated in the frontier areas of southwest, northwest and northeast China. To consolidate and develop the unity and cooperation among all ethnic groups is of great significance for safeguarding national unity, safeguarding the security of the country's frontier and developing friendly relations with its neighbors. To consolidate and develop the unity and cooperation among all ethnic groups has a bearing on the success or failure of the socialist modernization drive and the development of the various ethnic areas themselves. The ethnic minority areas are rich in resources but sparsely populated with poor economy and culture. The Han population has a large population and is relatively highly involved in the developed economy, science and culture. Combining the advantages of the two can not only promote the development and prosperity of ethnic minority areas, but also be of great strategic significance for promoting the modernization of the entire country.

To consolidate and develop the unity and cooperation among all ethnic groups and to continuously promote economic and social progress in ethnic minority areas is an important goal of China's socialist modernization and an inevitable requirement for enhancing the cohesion of the Chinese nation and realizing the great rejuvenation of the Chinese nation. For this reason:

First of all, we must integrate the Marxist concept of nation with the concrete reality of the Chinese nation and recognize the issue of nationalities in the light of the historical materialism. Under the system of exploitation, the essence of the ethnic issue is the issue of class and class struggle. In socialist society, the essence of the ethnic issue has become the issue of vigorously developing the productive forces in all ethnic areas and trying to meet the ever-increasing material and cultural needs of people of all nationalities. Under the premise of upholding the leadership of the Communist Party of China and persistently building socialism with Chinese characteristics, the basic principle of our country in resolving the ethnic issue is: To uphold national equality, ethnic solidarity and common prosperity of all ethnic groups.

Second, upholding and improving the system of regional ethnic autonomy is the correct way to strengthen ethnic unity and solve ethnic issues. The system of regional ethnic autonomy organically integrates ethnic and regional factors, political and economic factors, the centralization and unity of the country, and the autonomy of ethnic minority areas. Practice has proved that it is perfectly suited to China's national conditions.

Finally, speeding up the economic and social development in ethnic minority areas and promoting the common prosperity of all ethnic groups are the fundamental tasks of strengthening ethnic unity and resolving ethnic issues. the Party's basic line in the primary stage of socialism emphasizes that all work should center on economic construction and that ethnic work must also focus on the center of economic construction. The core issue of doing a good job in ethnic work and enhancing national unity is to actively create the conditions for accelerating the economic and cultural development and all-round social progress in ethnic and ethnic minority areas. Only by developing the ethnic areas can they be stable and only by development can they be united and stable.

Section II

Consolidate and develop the patriotic united front

First, the united front is an important magic weapon for building socialism with Chinese characteristics

The historical experience of China's revolution and construction proves that, under the leadership of the Communist Party of China, uniting all forces that can be united, mobilizing all positive factors and forming the broadest possible united front are important guarantees for the Chinese people in triumphing over difficulties and winning revolution and construction victories, and are a great political advantage of the Communist Party of China. During the period of the New Democratic Revolution, the Communist Party of China, exactly on the basis of the alliance of the working class with the peasant class, the alliance of the urban petty bourgeoisie and the national bourgeoisie, formed a broad anti-imperialist and anti-feudal revolutionary united front, and completed the historic mission of the national independence and the liberation of the people . The united front has become a magic weapon for the victory of the Chinese revolution. After the founding of New China, the people's democratic united front which includes workers, peasants, the urban petty bourgeoisie and the national bourgeoisie has continued to exert great importance in restoring the national economy, consolidating the people's democratic dictatorship and carrying out socialist transformation and building socialism.

Since the 3rd Plenary Session of the 11th CPC Central Committee, our country has entered a new period of reform, opening up and modernization and the united front has entered a new stage of development. In the new historical period, the united front can be said to be more important than ever before. Uniting all forces that can be united, forming the widest possible united front, and maximizing the formation of the broadest alliance of all the socialist laborers, those patriots who support socialism and those patriots who support the reunification of the motherland are the requirement of the cause of building socialism with Chinese characteristics, the requirement of maintaining the overall situation of reform, development and stability, the requirement of meeting the fierce international competition, the requirement of fulfilling the great cause of reunifying the motherland, opposing hegemonism and safeguarding world peace, and the requirement of realizing the great rejuvenation of the Chinese nation. The essence of the united front led by the Communist Party of China is to achieve the broadest unity among all ethnic groups, political parties, all walks of life and people in all fields under one common goal. The united front as an important magic weapon of the Party must never be discarded. As a political superiority of the Party, it must not be weakened. As a long-term policy of the Party, it must not be wavered.

The united front has always been an important part of the proletarian Party's general line and general policy and serves the general line and general tasks of the Party. The work of the united front is to win hearts and gather strength. Building a well-off society in an all-round way and realizing the great rejuvenation of the Chinese nation depend to a large extent on whether the Communist Party of China can mobilize tens of millions of people so that they are of one heart and one mind and can work hard to make concerted efforts. We should always carry forward the great spirit of solidarity of the Chinese nation and conscientiously do well in the work of the united front, including ethnic work, religious work and overseas Chinese affairs. We should mobilize all positive factors to the fullest extent possible and unite all the forces that can be united so that the united front can play an increasingly important role in pushing China to build a well-off society in an all-round way, realizing the complete reunification of the motherland and developing friendly relations and cooperation with foreign countries.

Second, the content and basic tasks of the patriotic united front in the new era

In different historical periods, the united front has different nature and content with the changes of social class relations and the central tasks of the Party and the state. The patriotic united front in the new era of reform, opening up and socialist modernization is led by the working class and is based on the alliance of workers and peasants. It includes the most extensive coalition of all socialist laborers, the builders of the socialist cause, the patriots who support socialism, and the patriots who support unification of the motherland. The united front in the new era includes two areas of alliances: one is the alliance of all laborers, builders and patriots united in the mainland on the political basis of patriotism and socialism, which is the main body and foundation of the united front; The other is an alliance outside mainland China of Taiwan compatriots, compatriots in Hong Kong, Macao and overseas Chinese on the basis of patriotism and advocating the unification of the motherland, which is an important part of the united front. The two alliances are united with each other, promote each other and form a whole, which reflects the unprecedented universality of the united front in the new era.

The basic tasks of the patriotic united front in the new period are as follows: hold high the banner of patriotism and socialism, unite all forces that can be united, mobilize all positive factors to the broadest and most sufficient extent, work in concert with one heart and one mind and make joint efforts to unswervingly implement the Party's basic line and basic program in the primary stage of socialism to serve the promotion of socialist economic, political, cultural and social construction, serve the long-term prosperity and stability of Hong Kong and Macao and the peaceful reunification of motherland, serve the world peace safeguard and common development promotion.

Patriotism is the emotion of loyalty and love to the motherland that people form in the long history, which is manifested in values and codes of conduct that safeguard the motherland's interests and dignity, safeguard the sovereignty and reunification of the motherland, and promote the development and progress of the motherland. The Chinese nation is a great nation with a long tradition of patriotism. Patriotism is the core of the Chinese nation's spirit and an important ideological foundation for the continuous development and expansion of the Chinese nation. For thousands of years, the reason why the Chinese nation has been able to survive the hardships, endured all the bitterness and be steadfast and persevering in face of difficulties is that we have the spirit of patriotism. In the historical process of realizing the great rejuvenation of the Chinese nation, patriotism is a banner that mobilizes and encourages the people to work and fight in unity, which has a strong appeal and cohesion. As pointed out by Hu Jintao, the national spirit with patriotism as the core is an inexhaustible spiritual motive force for us to constantly open up new marches and open up a new future.

Under the banner of patriotism, no matter Taiwan compatriots, Hong Kong or Macao compatriots or overseas Chinese compatriots, as long as they are conducive to our country's modernization, reunifying the motherland and rejuvenating China, as long as they are conducive to national unity and social progress and people's happiness, as long as they are favorable to opposing hegemonism and the maintenance of world peace, they are all important members of the united front.

In contemporary China, patriotism and socialism are in essence highly consistent. The establishment of the socialist basic system has laid a fundamental prerequisite and institutional foundation for all development and progress in contemporary China. the Party and government's administrative idea has intensively embodied the fundamental interests of the broad masses of people and the nation. Most of the members of the united front in the new era are the socialist laborers, builders and patriots who support socialism. The mainstay of the united front is socialism.

In the course of building socialism with Chinese characteristics, we must always hold high the great banner of patriotism and socialism with Chinese characteristics, give full play to the unique advantages of the united front in promoting social harmony, and support the Chinese People's Political Consultative Conference (CPPCC) in carrying out political consultation, democratic supervision and political participation on the two major themes of unity and democracy. We must adhere to the principle of "long-term coexistence, mutual supervision, treating each other with all sincerity and sharing weal and woe", fully mobilize and give play to the enthusiasm and creativity of persons with democratic party and non-party affiliation, continue to strengthen consultation and cooperation with democratic parties and support democratic party and non-party figures in holding leading positions in state organs and further normalize, institutionalize and proceduralize political consultation, democratic supervision and participation in politics, and strengthen solidarity and harmony among political parties, groups, ethnic groups, different social strata and people from all walks of life. We must work hard to build the united front into a united front featuring people-oriented principle and strong cohesion, a united front with an unprecedented universality and inclusiveness, continuously consolidate the most extensive alliance of all socialist laborers and builders of socialism, patriots who support socialist, and patriots who support the reunification of the motherland to create our happy life and a bright future.

The Party's leadership issue is the core issue of the united front. History and reality have shown that only by adhering to the leadership of the Communist Party can an unbreakable united front be formed and can the united front have a correct direction, vigorous vitality and a bright future before it can play its due role. In the new period, upholding the unshakeable leadership of the Communist Party over the united front is determined not only by the nature of the socialist system in our country, but also by the common aspirations and common interests of various personalities inside the united front.

Third, the correct understanding and handling of nationality and religious issues

1. Fully implement the Party's and the nation's ethnic policies and properly handle ethnic issues

To strengthen national unity and promote common development and common prosperity of all ethnic groups is an action program of the nationalities work of the party and state in contemporary China. The ethnic issues have always been very complicated. The handling of ethnic issues is directly related to the unification of the country and social stability. After the founding of New China and the establishment of the socialist system, the history of ethnic oppression and ethnic exploitation ended in China, but this does not mean that ethnic problems have disappeared in China. Especially since our country is in and will be in the primary stage of socialism for a long time, the economic and cultural gaps between the various ethnic groups formed and left over in history can not be eliminated within a short period of time. The hostile forces both at home and abroad are still making use of the ethnic issues for activities of subversion and destruction. To correctly handle ethnic issues is still a long-term, complicated and arduous major task. The ethnic issues under the socialist system are fundamentally different in nature from the ethnic issues under the system of exploitation. Therefore, there are inevitably different ways to solve the ethnic issues. The essence of ethnic issues in the era of socialism is no longer a problem of class contradictions and class struggles. It is a contradiction between the peoples of all ethnic groups on the basis of the unanimity of fundamental interests and should be solved by the correct solution to the contradictions among the people.

The basic principles for handling ethnic issues during the socialist period are: safeguarding the unification of the motherland, opposing national division, insisting on equality among ethnic groups, national unity and common prosperity of all ethnic groups.

Ethnic equality means that regardless of their population size, level of economic and social development, language and culture, customs and religious beliefs, each nation is a part of the Chinese nation and has the same status, they enjoy the same rights and fulfill the same obligations in all aspects of national and social life, we oppose all forms of ethnic oppression, ethnic discrimination and ethnic division. Ethnic equality is the political premise and foundation for ethnic unity and common prosperity of all ethnic groups.

Ethnic unity refers to the harmony, friendship, mutual assistance and alliance among all ethnic groups in social life and communication. Ethnic unity is the fundamental guarantee for safeguarding national unification and achieving common development of all ethnic groups. Without the unity of all ethnic groups, there will be no unification, stability and prosperity of the socialist motherland. The common unity and struggle and common prosperity and development among all ethnic groups are the major themes of ethnic work in the new phase of the new century. Only by helping the ethnic minorities develop their economy and culture and gradually eliminating the gap between the ethnic groups in their economic and cultural development, can we ensure and strengthen ethnic unity.

As the fundamental policy of resolving the ethnic issue, ethnic equality and ethnic unity are stipulated explicitly in the Chinese constitution and relevant laws. The Constitution of the People's Republic of China stipulates: "All ethnic groups in the People's Republic of China are equal. The state guarantees the legitimate rights and interests of ethnic minorities and upholds and develops the relations of equality, solidarity and mutual assistance among all ethnic groups. Discrimination and oppression against any ethnic group are forbidden, and acts that undermine ethnic unity and cause ethnic split are prohibited."

The common prosperity of all ethnic groups is the fundamental starting point and destination for resolving the ethnic issues. To do a good job in ethnic affairs, the most important thing is to actively create the conditions for speeding up economic, scientific and cultural undertakings in ethnic minority areas. To implement ethnic regional autonomy, the most important thing is to improve the economy, otherwise it is of no significance. In ethnic areas, stability and unity can only be achieved after development. We must take economic construction as the center and do everything possible to speed up the economic and social development in ethnic areas and gradually narrow the development gap between ethnic areas and developed areas so as to promote the common prosperity of all ethnic groups.

To adhere to ethnic equality, ethnic unity and common prosperity of all ethnic groups, we must fully implement the Party's ethnic policy and firmly grasp the theme of common unity and progress and common prosperity and development of all ethnic groups. We must firmly establish the principle that "Han people cannot live without ethnic minorities and ethnic minorities cannot be separated from Han nationality and ethnic minorities are inseparable from each other", consolidate and develop the socialist ethnic relations based on equality, solidarity, mutual assistance and harmony. We resolutely oppose big nationalism, local nationalism and ethnic separatism and resolutely expose and crack down all separatist activities by hostile forces inside and outside the country, continuously consolidate and develop the great unity of the Chinese nation, so that the people of all nationalities can live in peace and harmony, work together for a common cause, and develop the society hand in hand.

2. Fully implement the religious policies of the Party and the state and correctly handle religious issues

Religion is a historical phenomenon in the development of human society that has emerged at certain stage. Religious beliefs, religious sentiments and religious rituals and religious organizations related with such beliefs and sentiments are all products of the society and history. China is a socialist country, but religion affects a considerable part of the masses and will persist as a social phenomenon on a long-term basis. The key to correctly understanding the religious issue in our country is to fully understand the long lasting character of religion, the mass character of religious issues and the particular complexity of the religious issues based on the basic national conditions. We must respect the objective law of the emergence, existence and development of religions. We must neither use the power of our administration to destroy religion, nor use the power of our administration to develop religion. The efforts to do a good job in religious work are the need to safeguard the overall situation of reform, development and stability. We should fully implement the Party's policy of freedom of religious belief, administer religious affairs in accordance with the law, and actively guide religions to adapt to the socialist society and uphold the principle of self-administration and running religious affairs independently.

Respecting and protecting the freedom of religious belief is the basic policy for the Party and the state to deal with religious issues. The so-called freedom of religious belief means that each citizen has both the freedom to believe in religion and the freedom not to believe in religion. There is also freedom to believe in one religion and the freedom to believe in other religion. In the same religion, there is freedom to believe in one denomination and also freedom to believe in other denomination; There is freedom for those who not believe in religion in the past now to believe in religion, and also freedom for those who believe religion in the past now not to believe in religion. To fully implement the Party's freedom of religious belief policy and to respect and protect citizens' right to freedom of religious belief is an important manifestation of safeguarding people's interests and respecting and protecting human rights by the Party and the state, and is also the need of unifying the masses to the maximum extent possible.

On the one hand, we must respect each and every one of our citizens for their freedom to believe in religion and their freedom not to believe in religion. On the other hand, we must also demand that religions must act within the limits of their constitutional and legal rights and obligations. In our country, the principle of the separation of religion from politics is practiced. No religion has the privilege of transcending the constitution and laws and cannot interfere in the implementation of state functions such as state administration, judicature and education. At the same time, the government must also administer religious affairs in accordance with the law and regulate its related administrative actions.

To actively guide religions to adapt to socialist society is the fundamental requirement of the religious work of the Party and the state in the primary stage of socialism. Looking at the history of religions in our country and in the world, we can find a common law that any religion should exist and develop in compliance with the society in which it is located. Our country is a socialist country, and our religions must be compatible with socialist society. This is both an objective requirement of the socialist society in our religion and an objective requirement of the own existence of all religions in our country. We should build socialism with Chinese characteristics in conformity with the fundamental interests of the broad masses of people, including those who believe in religion, which is the political basis for doing religious work well. To actively guide the religions to adapt to socialist society does not mean requiring religious people and religious believers to give up their religious beliefs. Instead, we should demand that they love their motherland, support the leadership of the Communist Party of

China, support the socialist system and abide by the country's laws, rules and guidelines and policies. We should require them to obey and serve the highest interests of the country and the nation as a whole in their religious activities; Support them in making religious interpretations that meet the requirements of social progress; Support them in opposing against all illegal activities which make use of religion to endanger the socialist motherland and the people's interests, make contributions to ethnic unity, social development and the unification of the motherland, and make full use of the active role of religion in promoting social harmony. At the same time, in our country, religions must uphold the principle of self-administration and running religious affairs independently, resolutely resist the penetration by use of religions by the overseas forces, resolutely combat the religious extremist force and resolutely oppose and ban the heresy.

Section III

The people's army is an important force in construction of socialism with Chinese characteristics

First, the people's army is a great wall of steel in defense of the motherland and an important force in building socialism with Chinese characteristics

The Chinese People's Liberation Army is a people's army created and led by the CPC and an armed institution carrying out revolutionary political tasks which mainly serves the working class. Under the leadership of the Party, the People's Army has gone through a glorious course that has made an immortal contribution to the victory of the new-democratic revolution and the founding of New China and to safeguarding the socialist revolution and building socialism. In the long-term struggle, the people's army has formed a series of distinctive systems, traditions and styles, including upholding the Party's absolute leadership over the army, wholeheartedly serving the people, treating ideological and political work as the lifeline of the people's army, obeying and serving the revolution and the overall situation of construction.

The sole purpose of the people's army is to serve the people wholeheartedly. Since the people's army came from the people and serve the people, it has always been hailed as "the people's soldiers". In the era of the revolutionary war, Mao Zedong pointed out more than once that the people's army jointed together and battled for the interests of the broad masses of the people and for the interests of the entire nation. "The sole purpose of this army is to stand firmly with the Chinese people and to serve them wholeheartedly."[6] In the new period of reform and opening up and the socialist modernization drive, Deng Xiaoping repeatedly emphasized: The PLA should "steadfastly maintain its own character, that is, that it will continue to belong to the Party, the people and our socialist country… Our army should always be loyal to our Party, to the people, to our country and to socialism."[7]

The people's army is an impregnable great wall to defend the motherland and an important force for building socialism with Chinese characteristics. It is an important guarantee for safeguarding national security and reunification and building an overall well-off society.

First, the people's army is the impregnable great wall that defends the socialist motherland. In today's world, peace and development are the themes of the times. However, the international environment is complicated and changeable. Hegemonism and power politics still exist, and the threat of war has not been basically eliminated. In order to safeguard national sovereignty, security and territorial integrity and promote world peace and development, we must strengthen and consolidate our national defense. As the loyal defender of the motherland, the people's army takes the sacred mission of defending the motherland and safeguarding the unification and security of the motherland.

Second, the people's army is a strong pillar of the people's democratic dictatorship. In the process of building socialism with Chinese characteristics, the fundamental interests of the people are highly consistent. However, acts and hostile elements that endanger and undermine the interests of the country and the people will exist for a long time to a certain extent. To safeguard the unification of the country and social stability and safeguard the people's democratic rights, we must take the people's army as our strong back. The position of the people's army as the mainstay of the state apparatus and the loyal defender of people's interests must not be shaken.

Third, the people's army is an important force for the socialist modernization. On the one hand, effectively building an army and strengthening our national defense are both important elements for comprehensively enhancing the comprehensive national strength of the country and are an important part of the socialist modernization. On the other hand, the people's army obeys and serves the overall national economic construction and actively supports and participate in the building of the country and has made an important contribution to the realization of socialist modernization. In the process of reform and opening up and modernization, the people's army have been highly praised by the Party and the people for their action and spirit

---

6   Selected Works of Mao Zedong, 2nd Edition, Vol.3, p.1039.
7   Selected Works of Deng Xiaoping, 1st edition, Vol.3, p.334.

of courage, endeavor and selfless dedication in the major state-owned construction projects, in major scientific research fields, at the moment when disaster relief is reached, they have been an important force and guarantee for the socialist modernization and building an overall well-off society.

Second, the establishment of the solid national defense capacity is the strategic task of national modernization construction

National defense and army building occupy an important place in the general layout of the cause of socialism with Chinese characteristics. The modernization of the armed forces and national defense is an important part of China's socialist modernization. Consolidated national defense is the basic guarantee for national security and economic development. In the new era of building socialism with Chinese characteristics, in a complex international environment, the people's army must keep up with the tide of military development in the world, win high-tech wars that may happen in the future, and effectively safeguard the country's sovereignty, security and unity. In a society under the condition of market economy and opening to the outside world, the people's army must maintain its own nature, character and style and always become the revolutionary army under the Party's absolute leadership. Being capable of winning battles and never degenerating is the two historic issues that the people's army must solve well in the new situation. The army building and national defense building in the new period must closely focus on these two major issues.

1. Strengthening the building of the people's army in accordance with the requirements of revolutionization, modernization and standardization

After the founding of New China, Mao Zedong proposed that the people's army should be built into a powerful standardized and modernized defense force. In the new historical period, Deng Xiaoping explicitly proposed the general goal of building a revolutionary, modern and regularized people's army. Jiang Zemin pointed out that we must unswervingly follow the path of building a streamlined military with Chinese characteristics in line with the general requirements of being qualified politically and competent militarily and having a fine style of work, strict discipline and adequate logistical support. We must run the armed forces with strict discipline and in accordance with the law, and step up preparations for military struggle. Revolutionization, modernization and standardization are an interconnected whole and none is dispensable. They must be strengthened in all aspects and coordinated and promoted.

First of all, the revolutionization should be given top priority and is the foundation. It determines the nature and direction of the modernization of the armed forces and at the same time provides a powerful spiritual force for the modernization of the people's army. It is an inexhaustible source of long-lasting fighting strength of the people's army. To strengthen the revolutionization building of the army, we must always adhere to the fundamental principle that the Party must absolutely lead the army; We must always adhere to the fundamental principle of serving the people in all aspects and constantly strengthen the army-people unity. At the same time, we should constantly strengthen the unity within the army and consolidate and develop the internal relationship featuring unity, fraternity, harmony and purity of the people's army. We must always place ideological and political work in the first place of all the army's construction and always maintain a firm and correct political orientation.

Second, modernization is the center of army building. All the army's work must be centered on modernization. The modernization of the armed forces includes the basic contents of weapons and equipment, military talent, logistics support, organizational establishment system and modernization of military theories. The modernization of the armed forces in the new period means that we must insist on vitalizing the army through science and technology and according to the strategic goal of building an informationized army and winning an informationized war, speed up the composite development of mechanization and informatization, actively carry out military training under informational conditions, step up cultivation of a large number of highly qualified new military personnel, effectively change the mode of generating combat effectiveness.

Finally, standardization is a necessary requirement of modernization. To strengthen the normalization of the armed forces means that we must implement unified command, unified system, unified establishment, unified disciplinary and uniform training to enhance sense of organization, planning, accuracy and discipline, and take a legal and institutionalized path. Adhere to the principle of administering the army in accordance with the law, strictly control the military, continuously improve the military laws and regulations, improve the scientific management of the armed forces, enhance the quality construction and raise the standardization level so as to systematically constantly ensure the consolidation and enhancement of the combat effectiveness of the armed forces.

Revolutionization, modernization and standardization are interrelated, promote mutually and affect each other, and are dialectically unified in the building of people's army with Chinese characteristics.

2. Carrying out the military strategy of active defense

The military strategy is the basic basis for guiding the construction and use of the armed forces. In order to survive and develop, a country and a nation should gain a foothold in a highly competitive international environment and cannot live without a correct military strategy. The strategic principle of active defense has been the general guideline of the strategy of the Chinese revolutionary war and the important content of Mao Zedong's military thinking. After the founding of New China, it became an important guideline for the national defense construction. After entering a new era of reform, opening up and modernization, Deng Xiaoping continued to emphasize that our strategic guideline is active defense. We are a socialist country that will never seek hegemony or invade others. We strengthen our army and national defense modernization completely for the sake of our defense.

The strategic principle of active defense is fundamentally determined by the nature of China's socialism. The basic goal of China's national defense policy is to consolidate national defense, resist invasion by foreign enemies and safeguard national unity and security. As a socialist country, no matter in the past or in the future, China will neither seek world or regional hegemony nor join any military group, nor will it conduct any kind of arms race, or start a war to invade other countries or control other countries. We strive to avoid and stop the war and strive to solve the international disputes and issues left over by history in a peaceful manner. China's strategic policy of active defense is not an expedient measure but a fundamental national policy. It means that even when China's national defense strength will be greatly enhanced in the future, our policy will still be active defense.

The strategic principle of implementing active defense is the needs to safeguard national security and the socialist modernization. In the complex and ever-changing international environment in which hegemonism, power politics, local wars and terrorism exist, we must provide a strong and secure guarantee for the reform and opening up as well as for the economic construction by constantly strengthening our military and national defense. This determines that our defense is not "passive defense" being in a passive position under attack, but "active defense," that is, we must uphold the self-defense position of "We will not attack unless we are attacked; if we are attacked, we will certainly counterattack" and the strategic principle of attack only after being attacked. Under the guidance of the active defense strategy, we must strengthen national defense and army building to prevent or contain the outbreak of the war and strive for as much peaceful time and enough favorable international environment as possible for the modernization of our country.

In today's world, science and technology, especially information technology, have become increasingly prominent in the war. Local wars under high-tech especially under information technology conditions have been put on the agenda and become the basic form of modern warfare. Under such circumstances, the future war that poses a grave threat to our security will probably be a local war under conditions of informationalization. The basic point for preparing for the military struggle has shifted from the partial warfare under general conditions to the partial warfare under the conditions of winning information technology. This principle has clearly set forth the goals and tasks for preparing the military struggle for the people's army in the new era and solved the direction of the building and reform of the people's army, which is a major development of the active defense strategy.

3. Adhering to the principle of coordinated development of national defense construction and economic construction

Correctly understanding and handling the relationship between economic construction and national defense construction is an important strategic thinking that the Communist Party of China has always adhered to. At the beginning of the founding of New China, Mao Zedong put forward the idea of "grasp with both hands": grasp building national defense with one hand and economic construction with the other hand. In 1956, in his report On the Ten Major Relations, Mao Zedong systematically summarized and elaborated on the issue of correctly handling the relationship between national defense construction and economic construction. He pointed out that "we must strengthen national defense", and strengthening national defense "should first strengthen economic construction" that we should promote national defense construction through economic development. After the 3rd

Plenary Session of the 11th Central Committee of the Party, Deng Xiaoping proposed a strategic change in implementing the guiding ideology of national defense according to the needs of the development of the situation in the new era. He pointed out that the military should take the modernization as its core and follow the path of streamlining the army in the Chinese way and continuously enhance our defense strength; at the same time, obey and serve the overall national economic construction, and actively support and participate in the national economic construction. Jiang Zemin pointed out that it is necessary to comprehensively implement the principle of taking both development and economic construction into consideration and coordinating their development and advance the national defense and the modernization of the armed forces on the basis of economic development. To carry out economic construction and establish a strong national defense are the two strategic tasks of our country's modernization drive. Fundamentally speaking, the two major strategic tasks are unified, but they should be correctly grasped and handled in the light of the national conditions in the initial stage of our socialism. Hu Jintao emphasized that we should conscientiously implement the scientific concept of development in all fields and the entire process of national defense and army building so as to achieve comprehensive, coordinated and sustainable development in national defense and army building. We should make a comprehensive plan for the relationship between national defense construction and economic construction and adhere to the principle of coordinating national defense building and economic development.

First, we must focus on economic construction and concentrate our efforts on boosting the economy. This is the precondition and basis for resolving all the problems in contemporary China, including the building of national defense. Economic construction is the overall situation of the work of the entire Party and the entire country. National defense must and should comply with this overall situation and work closely with this overall situation. Maintaining sustained economic development and greatly enhancing the country's economic strength are necessary for advancing the socialist modernization in our country and also a key point for us to enhance international competitiveness, withstand the pressures of hegemonism and power politics, and safeguard national independence and sovereignty. National defense must rely on economic construction. Only by successful economic construction can the national defense building have a solid material and technological foundation. National defense and army building should closely cooperate with the overall situation of economic construction, and unswervingly adhere to the principle of coordinated development of national defense and economic construction and strive to achieve the unification of a wealthy nation and a strong army.

Second, we must insist on the coordinated development of national defense construction and economic construction, and adapt the strategy of national defense and army development to the strategy of national development. National defense construction and economic construction are two major strategic tasks of state building and development and must be coordinated. On the one hand, with the development of economy, investment in national defense construction should maintain modest growth; on the other hand, the investment in national defense construction must not be too large to overburden the economic development, otherwise it will delay the development of economic construction. In our country, there will be a long-standing conflict between the demand and relative insufficient fund in the national defense and the modernization of the armed forces. Under such circumstances, we must follow the requirements of the scientific concept of development and unswervingly take the path of investing less and more effectively in the national defense and the armed forces to realize their modernization, and further unify the quality and efficiency so that national defense and army building will continue to develop on the basis of increased state financial resources.

Third, we should actively explore the development mechanism of unifying military and civilian industries, embedding military programs in civilian industries and integrating military and civilian development. The development of the modern science and technology revolution, the industrial revolution and the new military revolution have brought the integration of national defense economy, social economy, military technology and civilian technology closer and closer. The army building and combat are unprecedentedly relying on economy, science and technology and society. On the one hand, the modern high-tech war has shown characteristics in its demand for resources such as large in quantity, high in technology and complex in structure. Relying on the national defense economy alone can hardly meet the development needs and we must rely on the entire national economy. On the other hand, modern science and technology especially the rapid development of information technology, has become increasingly blurred the boundary between civil technology and military technology, where many civil high-techs usually serve economic construction at ordinary times, but can be turned into military products with a slight modification in the war. To this end, we must actively explore new ways and means according to the requirements of the times and integrate military with civilian purposes and incorporate military into civilian purposes, to integrate national defense and economic and social development on a wider scale, at a higher level and by a deeper degree, so as to provide rich resources and staying power of the sustained development for the modernization of national defense and the armed forces.

Fourth, enhance the concept of national defense. In peacetime, people's concept of national defense is easy to be indifferent, which may deprive the sustained social momentum of reserve forces. This requires strengthening national defense education and strengthening people's concept of national defense to enable people to establish the thinking of being prepared and having constant alertness and vigilance, so that the reserve forces can gain the care and support from the whole society. Therefore, we must enhance the concept of national defense of the entire people, improve the system of national defense mobilization, stick to the principle of combining a highly capable army with a strong national defense reserve and improve the quality of the reserve army and militia building.

National defense construction and the building of the armed forces are the common cause of the Party and the people of all nationalities in the country. We must uphold the principle of the unification of a wealthy nation and a strong army and uphold the strategic thinking of the people's war. We must rely on the people in running the national defense and continuously increase our national defense strength.

Third, the historical mission of the People's Army in the new century and the military reform with Chinese characteristics

1. The historical mission of the people's army in the new century and the new stage

In the new phase of the new century, Hu Jintao made a scientific proposition of "Three Provides and One Role" to define the historical mission ofthe people's army. "Three Provides" means. "Three Provides" means that the people's army must provide an important force guarantee for the Party's consolidation of its ruling position, provide a strong guarantee for safeguarding the important period of strategic opportunities for national development and provide a strong strategic support for safeguarding the national interest. The "One Role" means that the people's army plays an important role in safeguarding world peace and promoting common development.

In order to accomplish the historic mission of the people's army in the new phase of the new century, we must insist on using the Mao Zedong Military Thought, Deng Xiaoping's thinking on army building in the new era and Jiang Zemin's thinking on national defense and army building as our guidance, using the scientific concept of development to guide army building, and take improving combat effectiveness as the fundamental starting point and foothold of implementing the concept of scientific development, and constantly create new situations of the military construction in the practice of promoting the military reform with Chinese characteristics.

As a guideline for advancing the country's economic, political, cultural and social construction, the scientific concept of development not only reveals and reflects the general laws of economic and social development but also reveals and reflects the basic laws governing national defense and army building. In the military field, the establishment of the scientific concept of development is an inevitable requirement for the sound and rapid development of national defense and army building at a new starting point. In the new phase of the new century, the comprehensiveness, complexity and variability of the national security issue have been further increased. The diversity of military tasks linked to the military's functional mission has further developed. The integration of national defense and economic construction has further deepened. What kind of scientific goal should he national defense and the armed forces have and the question of how to achieve scientific development are historically placed before us. The scientific concept of development has put forward a series of new concepts, new assertions and new ideas for correctly answering and resolving this basic issue in the military field. For example, we must establish a people-centered philosophy as an important concept of army building and administering the military, conscientiously safeguard the fundamental interests of the people and the masses, fully respect the subjective position and creative spirit of the army men and strive to improve the ability to respond to crises, safeguard peace, contain the war and win the war under the conditions of informationization. We must scientifically make overall plan for the army construction in accordance with the principle of revolutionization, modernization and standardization, promote the comprehensive coordinated development of military work, political work, logistics and equipment work. We should intensify the implementation of the strategy of building a strong army based on science and technology and rely on the progress of science and technology to change the mode of generating combat effectiveness. We must strengthen scientific management and optimize the allocation of resources so as to constantly improve the overall efficiency of national defense and army building; we should crack down on various problems in institution and policy system with the spirit of reform and innovation and provide more vigorous institutional and systematic guarantees for the sound and rapid development of army building. We should, from the perspective of realizing the unification of the wealthy country and the strong army, better promote the compatible development of national defense economy and social economy, military technology and civil technology, military personnel and local talents. Taking scientific concept of development as an important guideline for strengthening national defense and army building fully reflects the advancement of the Party's military guidance theory.

2. Actively promote the revolutionization of the military with Chinese characteristics

In today's world, the development of new and high technologies with information technology as the core has effectively promoted the development of new military changes in the world. The widespread application of information technology in the military field has brought a large number of intelligent weaponry and equipment and has also multiplied the combat effectiveness of traditional weaponry and made all kinds of weaponry and combat units become an organic whole, calling for corresponding changes in organizational structure of the army. Informationization is becoming the essence and core of the new military revolution. All developed countries regard informationization as their main goal in the modernization of their armed forces in the new century. China must also regard informationization as the direction for the modernization of its armed forces and base itself on national conditions and military conditions, and actively promote the military changes with Chinese characteristics.

First, actively innovate and develop military theories in accordance with the requirements of iinformationization. Advanced military theory has always been an important condition for the healthy development of army building and an important factor for the victory of war. All countries in the world today attach great importance to the study of military theory. New theories and new ideas on the future military and the future war are continuously being introduced. China's military theory studies have their own characteristics and achievements, but the research on high-tech wars, especially information-based wars, is still far from thorough and systematic. To varying degrees, there are misconception which only emphasize on "hardware" such as weaponry and equipment and neglect "software" such as military theory.

Second, adhere to the basis of mechanization, and oriented by information. To promote the mechanization by information technology, to promote the information technology in the process of mechanization, to achieve the composite development of mechanization and informationization, take the leapfrog development path. Center on the objective of building an information-based army and winning the information-based wars, further implement the strategy of building a strong military through science and technology and rely on scientific and technological progress and innovation to speed up the transformation of the mode of generating combat effectiveness.

Third, create a large number of outstanding new military personnel. The key to promoting military transformation and meeting challenges with information as the center is to train and bring up a large number of new military personnel with excellent ideological and political qualities and excellent military qualifications, such as compound command personnel, think-tank staff officer, and expert-type scientific and technological personnel, etc. Without a large number of highly qualified personnel, there will be no military theory innovation, no creation and use of new combat tactics, no grasp of new weapons and equipment, and therefore no victory in future wars. Therefore, personnel training must be taken as the fundamental plan for the modernization of the armed forces and results should be drawn as soon as possible.

Fourth, we should reform the institutional establishment of the armed forces to gradually form a scientific organizational model, institutional arrangement and mode of operation that combines both the Chinese characteristics and the law governing the building of the modern armed forces. Judging from the trend of the military development in the world today, the issue of unreasonable military establishment in our country is quite prominent. The readjustment and reform of the establishment system should continue to be carried out actively and steadily. In general, we must work toward the direction of moderate scale, reasonable structure and swift and flexible command to be conducive to the needs of future military operations.

Fifth, unswervingly follow the path of elite troops with Chinese characteristics. The elite troops policy display the demand for "quality", and also the demand for "quantity". Therefore, it is imperative to achieve the transformation of the people's army from the quantity and scale model to a quality performance model and from a human-intensive model to a science & technology-intensive model. We must focus on the general goal of building a revolutionary, modern and standardized people's army, embody the principle of "elite troops, sharp weapons, composition and efficiency", further reduce the number of soldiers, optimize the structure, strengthen management and improve the combat effectiveness of the troops by improving the quality so that the People's Liberation Army will carry out its lofty mission of defending the motherland and safeguarding the unification and security of the motherland more effectively.

CHAPTER TWELVE

Socialism with Chinese Characteristics and the Concept of "One Country Two Systems" and Peaceful Reunification of China

Section I

The introduction of the concept of "One Country Two Systems" and peaceful reunification of China and its basic contents

First, national unity and the historical issues of Hong Kong, Macao and Taiwan

Since the founding of New China, especially in the first half of the 1950s, since the liberation of Tibet and the liberation of the Zhoushan Islands and Hainan Island by the PLA Thereafter, the only issues left over by history in the reunification of the country were the Hong Kong and Macao and Taiwan issues. In history, British and Portuguese colonialists had illegally occupied Hong Kong and Macao and the Kuomintang regime had illegally grabbed the Taiwan region. At the beginning of the new period of reform and opening up, "realizing the reunification of the motherland", was proposed, as the "three major issues" and the "three major tasks" of the CPC and the Chinese government, when facing the said historical legacy—the Hong Kong, Macao and Taiwan issues. At the beginning of a new period of reform and opening up, "realizing the reunification of the motherland", which is one of the "three major events" and the "three major tasks" proposed by the CPC and the Chinese government, is facing the same historical legacy—the Hong Kong, Macao and Taiwan issue.

The nature of Hong Kong and Macao issues is one and the same, both of which had seriously undermined China's unification, since the descending period of the Chinese nation in modern times (since 1840s), the western capitalist powers had occupied territories of China by military force and power and unequal treaties which severely damaged China's unification, sovereignty and territorial integrity, and severely damaged the interests of the Chinese nation. They were the marks of humiliation by Western colonialism that the Chinese nation has suffered in the times of enduring impoverishment and long-standing debility.

Therefore, after the founding of New China, the attitude and principled position of the CPC and the Chinese government on the issues of Hong Kong and Macao has been clear and firm: Hong Kong and Macao are part of the sacred and indivisible territory of China, and Hong Kong and Macao residents are sacred inseparable flesh and blood compatriots of the Chinese nation. We do not recognize the changes that the British and Portuguese colonialists have attributed to the sovereignty and the ownership of Hong Kong-Macao in modern times through force and power. We do not recognize Hong Kong and Macao's British and Portuguese "colony" status, all unequal treaties involving Hong Kong and Macao does not bind the Chinese government and the Chinese people, we reserve the highest and the ultimate right to restore sovereignty of Hong Kong and Macao at the right time and under the right conditions.

The nature of the Taiwan issue is different from that of Hong Kong and Macao. The Taiwan issue is a legacy of history of the Chinese civil war. To solve the Taiwan issue and realize national reunification is China's internal affair and interference by any foreign force is rejected seriously.

Taiwan has belonged to China since ancient times. From 1894 to 1895, Japan launched the Sino-Japanese War of 1894-1895 that invaded China and seized Taiwan through the Treaty of Shimonoseki. After the victory of the world anti-fascist war in 1945, the Chinese government regained Taiwan by on the basis of international law–the Cairo Declaration and the Potsdam Proclamation. After World War II, Taiwan was returned to China not only legally but also eventually. The reason for the emergence of the Taiwan issue is that on the one hand, it is the result of the civil war by the Chinese Communist Party and the Kuomintang; on the other hand, it is due to the intervention of foreign forces.

The Taiwan issue has seriously damaged China's unification, sovereignty and territorial integrity, severely undermined the fundamental interests and core interests of the Chinese nation. Therefore, after the founding of New China in 1949, the attitude and the principled position of the CPC and the Chinese government over the Taiwan issue are very clear and firm: Taiwan is a part of the sacred and indivisible territory of China and the residents in Taiwan are the sacred inseparable flesh and blood compatriots of the Chinese nation. There is only one China in the world. China's sovereignty and territorial integrity cannot be divided. Since 1949, although the mainland and Taiwan have not yet reunified, it is not a division of China's territory and sovereignty but a political antagonism left over and extended by the civil war in the mid-to-late 1940s in China. This has not changed the fact that the Mainland and Taiwan belong to one China. The reunification of the two sides of the Strait is not a matter of sovereignty and territorial reintegration, but an end to political antagonism. The core of settling the Taiwan issue is the realization of national reunification with the purpose of safeguarding and ensuring the sovereignty and territorial integrity of the country, pursuing the happiness of all the Chinese people, including the compatriots in Taiwan, and realizing the great rejuvenation of the Chinese nation. The peaceful realization of national reunification best complies with the fundamental interests of the Chinese nation, including compatriots in Taiwan, and is also in line with the trend of the times which seeks peace, development and promote cooperation.

The peaceful settlement of Hong Kong, Macao and Taiwan issues: the "ideological legacy" and "policy heritage" inherited from the first generation of the CPC's central collective leadership".

In the nearly 30 years before the reform and opening up, the guiding principles and the basic policies of the Chinese Communists in dealing with the issue of Hong Kong and Macao are to "maintain the status quo for the time being" in order to "make long-term plans and make full use of it".

During the implementation of the special policy of "maintaining the status quo for the time being" to "make long-term plans and making full use of it", the first generation of the central collective leadership with Mao Zedong as the core proposed many innovative and constructive new ideas and practical concrete measures, and put them into practice one by one. The major ones are as follows: First of all, proceeding from the history and reality of Hong Kong and Macao, "facing" the objective existence of the "de facto right of administration" over Hong Kong and Macao by Britain and Portugal and not interfering in the internal affairs of Hong Kong and Macao and the conflicts with them are strictly controlled in diplomatic field. Second, proceeding from the history and reality of Hong Kong and Macao, fully understanding the "benefits and advantages" political and economic value of "temporal maintenance" of the status quo" of "capitalism in Hong Kong and Macao", which should "not be socialized, nor should they be socialist" for a certain period. Third, to make contact with them, we should comply with their "rules of the game." The depth and height of this ideological understanding are most representative in the speech made by Zhou Enlai on the issue of Hong Kong in 1957 in a forum with the business community in Shanghai. This speech by Zhou Enlai covers all aspects of how to view the sensitive issue of "capitalism in Hong Kong and Macao", which proposes that we should respect the economic laws and characteristics of

Hong Kong and Macao themselves, "Hong Kong should act in full accordance with the capitalist system", and should not be a means "to change the socialist character of the mainland" nor should it "be socialized" and we should cooperate with the bourgeoisie in Hong Kong and Macao, we should "maintain and expand the position of Hong Kong" as "our base for economic ties with other countries", "Hong Kong should become a port economically useful to us", and a series of quite strategic and new ideas with theoretical courage. This speech represents the highest achievement made by the Chinese Communists under the historical conditions of that time on the ideological understanding of this issue.

In the past 30 years before the new period, the guiding principle and the basic principle and policy of the Chinese Communists in handling the Taiwan issue are: "We must liberate Taiwan", nevertheless, we must make efforts to "strive for a peaceful solution to the problem".

In the early days of the People's Republic of China, the fundamental principle and policy of the Chinese Communists in settling the Taiwan issue were "liberation by force", and at the same time efforts to "peaceful liberation" was not ruled out. Starting from the mid 1950s, the first generation of the central collective leadership with Mao Zedong as the core began to formally put forth "peaceful liberation" of Taiwan, that is, by seeking ways of "political negotiation" to peacefully settle the Taiwan issue and realize the principle and policy of peaceful reunification of the motherland. At that time, we mainly considered two "very favorable" background factors: First, the gradual easing of the international situation and the domestic situation–the external "peace force" was growing and the internal work focus has shifted to "large-scale socialist economic construction". Second, all Chinese on both sides of the Taiwan Strait stick to the "one-China" position and oppose the US policy of "Taiwan independence" and "Two Chinas". In May 1955, Zhou Enlai pointed out at the 15th enlarged meeting of the first NPC Standing Committee that there are two possible ways for the Chinese people to liberate Taiwan: the way of war and the way of peace. The Chinese people are willing to work under conditions that are possible to strive to liberate Taiwan peacefully. For the first time to the "new policy" of the Chinese Communists on "peaceful liberation" of Taiwan was "brought into the public". In 1956, the "new policy" of "peaceful liberation" of Taiwan by the CPC and the Chinese government was formally established at the three major conferences held that year–the 8th National Congress of CPC, the 3rd Session of the 1st NPC and the 2nd Session of the 2nd CPPCC National Committee.

From 1956 to 1960, according to changes in the situation across the Taiwan Strait, the first-generation party collective leadership with Mao Zedong as its core conducted a preliminary review and explanation of the specific contents of the "new policy" for the "peaceful liberation" of Taiwan. The basic points were: First, "All patriots belong to one big family", "whether they embrace patriotism earlier or later". Second, "we should promote the third KMT-CPC cooperation." Third, "political negotiations". Fourth, "Three Principles of the People can be as before" and "everything can be as before". For this specific policy, Mao Zedong and Zhou Enlai had "detailed instructions" when they met with Cao Juren, a Hong Kong correspondent in 1956.[1]

In 1960, Zhou Enlai "systematized" the "new policy of" "peaceful liberation" of Taiwan by the first generation of the central collective leadership with Mao Zedong as the core and vividly made the point as "One Head Rope and Four Meshes", namely Taiwan will be re-unified with China. The specific policy is: After Taiwan is returned to the motherland, all military and political powers and personnel arrangements should be consultative with Chiang Kai-shek and Chen Ching and Chiang Ching-kuo. Chiang Kai-shek and Chiang Ching-kuo also note that Chiang Kai-shek and Chiang Ching-kuo also re-use all their military affairs and construction funds. A social reform in Taiwan could be slow and should start once with the conditions are ripe and with the consent of Chiang Kai-shek. The two sides should not send spies and do not undermine solidarity of the other side.[2]

335

Since the Taiwan authorities with Chiang Kai-shek and his son as their core refused to carry out "political negotiations" to "peacefully solve" the Taiwan issue because of their "anti-communist" stance, and the United States, which directly intervened in the Taiwan issue, clung to the the "Cold War" mentality and refused to renounce their "Split China" policy which maintains a situation of "no reunification, no independence, no war and no peace" for the two sides of the Taiwan strait. Meanwhile, because of the internal and external policies of the Communist Party of China and the Chinese government gradually emerged the "Left" deviation mistakes after the mid-1950s, the "new policy" of "peaceful liberation" of Taiwan gradually formed and perfected by the first generation of the central collective leadership with Mao Zedong as the core after the mid-1950s has remained on the level of "policy call" with no conditions to put into practice.

1   See Jin Chongji (editor in chief): Zhou Enlai Biography (3), p.1441, Beijing, Central Literature Publishing House, 1998.
2   See the CPC Central Committee Document Research Series: "Chronicle of Zhou Enlai (1949-1976)" (2), p.321, Beijing, Central Literature Publishing House, 1997.

Second, the scientific conception and basic contents of "peaceful reunification, one country, two systems" in the new era

Since new period, the second generation of the central collective leadership with Deng Xiaoping as the core leader has inherited the unfulfilled will of great reunification and peaceful reunion of the Chinese nation from Mao Zedong and Zhou Enlai and other new China's founders and will continue to take the arduous task of national reunification through solving the issues of Hong Kong, Macao and Taiwan as his own goal and as the "top priority" for the central work of the Party and the country. In the meantime, in accordance with the theme of the times of peace and development, in light of the new changes in the situation at home and abroad, and in light of the history and current situation in Hong Kong, Macao and Taiwan, he has made strategic adjustments for the guiding principles and specific guidelines and policies for solving the issues of Hong Kong, Macao and Taiwan, creatively proposed the scientific concept of "peaceful reunification and one country, two systems" and specifically guided the great practice for the return of Hong Kong and Macao and the development of cross-strait relations.

With the ending of the "Cultural Revolution", Deng Xiaoping, ascended to power for the third time, although he was faced with the devastated situation of the country, put the issue of Taiwan and national reunification as the "top priority". At that time the ongoing negotiations to improve Pacific-wide "great cross-strait relations"—the normalization of the relations between China and the United States—has provided a historic opportunity for a breakthrough in the "small cross-strait relations", i.e. Taiwan Strait. Therefore, during the process of the establishment of diplomatic relations between China and the United States in the second half of 1978, Deng Xiaoping began to concentrate on how to "adopt an appropriate policy to solve the Taiwan issue and realize the reunification of the country according to the actual situation in Taiwan"[3]. From October 1978 to January 1979, in a span of four months, Deng Xiaoping made a "high-density" address on the solution to the Taiwan issue and explained his "new thinking" – "respecting Taiwan's realities." On November 28, 1978, Deng Xiaoping met with American friend Steele and pointed out when talking about the Taiwan issue: "We have said many times that Taiwan will return to China and realize the reunification of the motherland. Under this premise, we will respect Taiwan's reality to solve the Taiwan issue."[4]

---

3   CPCCC Party Literature Research Office: Editorial Office of the CPC Central Committee: "Chronicle of Deng Xiaoping (1975-1997)" (1), p. 189, Beijing, Central Literature Publishing House, 2004.

4   Ibid., p.442.

As of January 29, 1979 to February 5, 1979, Deng Xiaoping paid a visit to the United States and pointed out in Washington to the US Senate and House and Senator's speech on the Taiwan issue: "We will no longer talk about 'liberating Taiwan'. As long as Taiwan returns to the motherland, we will respect the realities and the existing system there."[5]

The basic spirit of Deng Xiaoping's series of conversations is concentratedly reflected in the Message to Taiwan Compatriots published by the Standing Committee of the National People's Congress on January 1, 1979, namely: "We must consider the realities, accomplish the great cause of re-unifying the motherland and when solving the issue of reunification, we should respect the status quo in Taiwan and the opinions of people from all walks of life in Taiwan, adopt fair and reasonable policies and measures to prevent the loss of Taiwanese people." It marks that the Chinese Communists' policy toward the Taiwan issue has begun to walk out from the traditional patterns of "force or peaceful liberation" and "one country, one system", and shifted to the "new thinking", "new policy" of "peaceful reunification" and "one country, two systems" with "unchanged system" as the core.

In September 1981, Ye Jianying, chairman of the Standing Committee of the National People's Congress, formally exposed the concrete content of the "new thinking" and the "new policy" of the CPC and the Chinese government in settling the Taiwan issue by way of a statement to Xinhua News Agency reporters, namely the famous "nine points". In January 1982, when Deng Xiaoping met with Li Yi-zi, chairman of the Chinese American Association, Deng Xiaoping said: "The 'nine-article statement' made in the name of Vice-Chairman Ye, actually means 'one country, two systems'. Two systems are permissible."[6]

This is the first time that Deng Xiaoping formally summed up and summarized the "new thinking" and "new policy" for settling the Taiwan issue as "one country and two systems" or "one country, two systems". In June 1983, Deng Xiaoping met with Yang Liyu, a professor at Northwestern University in New Jersey, and when talking about the Taiwan issue, he further systematized the concrete contents of the "new thinking" and the "new policy" of the CPC and the Chinese government for settling the Taiwan issue, put forward the famous "Deng's Six Conceptions". By now, the "new thinking" and "new policy" which is called the "Taiwan Plan" overseas, namely the "one country, two systems" of the Communist Party of China and the Chinese government in settling the Taiwan issue have basically taken shape.

---

5   Ibid., p.478.
6   Ibid., p.189.

Regrettably, the new conception, good faith and goodwill of the "new thinking" and "new policy" of the Communist Party of China and the Chinese government in settling the Taiwan issue were not recognized by the Taiwan Kuomintang authorities across the Taiwan Strait. Chiang Ching-kuo rejected the constructive proposal made by the Communist Party of China to jointly promote the negotiations between the two Parties on an equal footing, carrying out the third cooperation and realizing the peaceful unification of the motherland, he claimed "no contact, no negotiation and no compromise" and even proposed the slogan of unifying China with the "Three People's Principles" to oppose "one country, two systems ". The political calls made by the Communist Party of China and the Chinese government from the Message to Taiwan Compatriots to the "Ye's Nine Principles" and the "Deng's Six Conceptions" were both rejected by the Kuomintang authorities in Taiwan as a "united front conspiracy". The stalemate in cross-strait relations was still frozen. Under such circumstances, the CPC and the Chinese government cannot but consider the re-selection of the "breakthrough" in the "peaceful reunification and one country, two systems" project of contemporary China, and cannot but bring the of the "time-table" for solving the Hong Kong and Macao issue" in advance, whose condition and opportunity are "relatively mature". we cannot but try to implement the "Taiwan Plan" under " one country, two systems" in the "Hong Kong-Macao Way" and take the "Hong Kong-Macao Model" under "one country, two systems" as the "First Example" to finally solve the Taiwan issue.

For the first time, Deng Xiaoping formally declared his position on the future of Hong Kong when he met with Governor MacLehose, who visited Beijing in March 1979. Deng Xiaoping explicitly said that, we have always believed that the sovereignty of Hong Kong belongs to the People's Republic of China, but Hong Kong has its special status. Hong Kong is a part of China and the issue itself is not negotiable. But what is certain is that even when this problem is solved in 1997, we will still respect the special status of Hong Kong. What worries people now is that their investments in Hong Kong may not be sustained. At this point, the Chinese government can tell you explicitly and tell the British government that even if a certain political settlement is made then, it will not hurt the interests of the investors who continue to invest. Please rest assured investors, this is a long-term policy. That is: Hong Kong can engage in its capitalism for quite some time in the 20th and early 21st century. We shall pursue our socialism.[7]

From the first half of 1979 to the first half of 1982, Deng Xiaoping conducted a three-year investigation and study on the Hong Kong issue. Based on the "Taiwan Plan" of the scientific concept of "one country, two systems", Deng Xiaoping initially formed the decision-making and policy to

7   Ibid., p.500f.

solve the Hong Kong issue–the "Twelve Special Policies", and the later Sino-British negotiations were based on these "Twelve Special Policies".

During the formation and development of the "Taiwan Plan" under "one country, two systems" and the "Hong Kong Plan" under "one country, two systems", the "new thinking" and "new policy" of the CPC and the Chinese government on solving the Hong Kong, Macao and Taiwan issue–"the peaceful reunification and one country, two systems" were also uplifted to the level of the basic principles, policies and basic national policies of the Party and the country and were standardized, institutionalized and legalized. In December 1982, the Constitution of the People's Republic of China adopted by the Fifth Session of the Fifth National People's Congress stipulated in Article 31 that the state may set up a special administrative region when necessary. The system implemented in the special administrative region shall be prescribed by law by the National People's Congress in accordance with the specific conditions. In mid-May 1984, Zhao Ziyang, premier of the State Council, made the Report on the Work of the Government at the 2nd Session of the 6th National People's Congress, which comprehensively explained the decisions and policies of the Communist Party of China and the Chinese government in settling the issue of Hong Kong, that is, the "Hong Kong Plan" of "one country, two systems". By the end of May, the 2nd Session of the 6th National People's Congress passed the Report on the Work of the Government by Premier Zhao Ziyang. In October 1984, the Outlook Weekly published an article entitled "One Country and Two Systems" by Deng Xiaoping, further systematizing and theorizing the scientific concept and basic national policy of "peaceful reunification and one country, two systems".

The core contents of the scientific concept and basic national policy of "peaceful reunification and one country, two systems" are as follows:

First, one China. There is only one China in the world. The Mainland (interior areas) region and Hong Kong, Macao and Taiwan regions are all inseparable parts of China. China's sovereignty and territorial integrity are inseparable. The only legitimate government that represents China in the international community is the government of the People's Republic of China. This is the precondition and foundation for the peaceful reunification of our country.

Second, two systems. Under the premise of one China, the main body of China, i.e. the mainland (interior areas) has implemented the socialist system. Hong Kong, Macao and Taiwan maintain their original capitalist system, their social and economic systems remain unchanged, their lifestyles remain unchanged, their laws remain basically unchanged, and they keep the same economic and cultural ties with foreign countries, we will coexist for long-term and seek common development.

Third, a high degree of autonomy, self-administration. After the peaceful reunification of the country, Hong Kong and Macao established special administrative regions directly under the jurisdiction of Central Government and enjoyed a high degree of autonomy, including administrative powers, legislative powers, independent judicial power and power of final adjudications, and certain foreign affairs powers. Taiwan can also preserve its army.

Fourth, diplomatic negotiations, political negotiations and peaceful reunification. Through diplomatic and political negotiations, we can achieve the peaceful unification of our country, but at the same time, we will not make any commitment to renounce the use of force. This is not aimed at our own countrymen, but for the separatist conspiracy of various separatist forces at home and abroad.

Before and after the introduction of the scientific concept and basic national policy of "new thinking" and "new policy"–"peaceful reunification and one country, two systems" of the Communist Party of China and Chinese government for solving the Hong Kong, Macao and Taiwan issue, there have been a great variety of state unification patterns in the international community, such as the "model of the Civil War" in the United States, the "Vietnam Model", the "Yemen model" and the "German model", there are two important common grounds: the first is "solution by the armed forces" and the second is "one country one system". The realization of national reunification in the manner of "peaceful reunification" and "one country, two systems" conforms to the current theme of peace and development and the trend of democratization, multi-polarity and diversification in the contemporary world, is in the fundamental interest and the long-term interest of the Chinese people and the people of the world, which is a great pioneering undertaking of the CPC and the Chinese government on political civilization and a great contribution made by the Communist Party of China and the Chinese government to the cause of human peace and justice.

Section II

The return of Hong Kong and Macao to the motherland under the guidance of scientific concept of "One Country, Two Systems"

First, "One Country, Two Systems" and the "Hong Kong and Macao model"

As the prelude to the return of Hong Kong and Macao, the Sino-British negotiations and the Sino-Portuguese negotiations were basically conducted under the guidance of Deng Xiaoping's scientific concept of "peaceful unification and one country, two systems", which was based on the general principles, namely, a unification which will "resume the exercise of sovereignty, maintain stability and prosperity" and a unification that "sees off colonialism and preserves capitalism". China's precondition for the negotiation was that "the sovereignty issue cannot be compromised." The Chinese government should resume the exercise of sovereignty in Hong Kong and Macao in 1997 and 1999 and only after reaching a consensus on this key issue would it possible to discuss how to implement the "one country, two systems" after Hong Kong and Macao will be returned to China, in "1997" and "1999".

The Sino-British talks were "unveiled" by the visit of British Prime Minister Margaret Thatcher in 1982. Deng Xiaoping made a clear-cut stand during the talks: "We have a clear-cut position regarding the Hong Kong issue, which involves three things. First, it involves the issue of sovereignty. Second question is about what method China will adopt to govern Hong Kong after 1997. The third question is that both the Chinese and British governments should carefully discuss how to ensure that no major fluctuations will occur in Hong Kong from 1982 to 1997."[8]

On the first question, Deng Xiaoping clearly explained the three basic positions that the Communist Party of China and the Chinese government adhere to: First, "the question of sovereignty is not a question that can be discussed". Second, "China will regain sovereignty over Hong Kong in 1997". Third, China wants to recover "not only the New Territories, but also Hong Kong Island and Kowloon". Deng Xiaoping pointed out: "China has no room for maneuver on this issue! On the second question, Deng expressed full confidence: "I am not worried about this." "I believe we will formulate a policy that should be implemented and is acceptable to all sectors after the return of Hong Kong". On the third question, Deng Xiaoping did not dissemble his concern: "What I'm worried about is how to make a perfect transition during the transitional period in the next 15 years. I am worried that there will be a lot of chaos during this period, which is generated by human factors". Mrs Thatcher had to accept these points.

The Sino-British negotiations lasted a full two years. According to the content, it can be divided into two stages: secret consultation (September 1982 to June 1983) and formal talks (July 1983 to September 1984). The diplomatic negotiations between China and the United Kingdom, which were held in the first phase through secret negotiations, mainly addressed the basic issues of "topics" and "procedures". The diplomatic negotiations between China and the United Kingdom in the second phase, which were formal talks, took 22 rounds. The 22 rounds of formal talks can be divided into three smaller stages, depending on the content involved. The first to

8   Anthology of Deng Xiaoping, 1st edition, Vol.3, p.12.

sixth rounds of formal talks from July 1983 to November 1983 was the first stage. The main agenda was the overall arrangement after Hong Kong was taken back in 1997. The seventh to twelfth rounds of formal talks from December 1983 to April 1984 was the second stage. The main agenda is on the basis of the "Twelve Special Policies" proposed by China on solving the Hong Kong issue to discuss the substantive arrangements after the resumption of Hong Kong in 1997. The thirteenth to the twenty-second rounds of formal talks from April 1984 to September 1984 was the third stage. The main agenda is to resolve the remaining issues of the formal talks in the previous stage and discuss the arrangements, transfer of power issues and the preparation of the agreement during the transitional period of Hong Kong. In the process of diplomatic negotiations, China has taken full advantage of the political intelligence and the art of struggle, which are highly integrated with the firmness of principle and the flexibility of tactics, and all the problems encountered in formal talks were solved one by one.

On December 19, 1984, the formal signing ceremony of the Sino-British Joint Declaration was held in Beijing's Great Hall of the People. On the same day, People's Daily published an editorial titled "Important Events in the History of the World Today–Congratulating the Official Signature of the Declaration on the Issue of Hong Kong by China and the United Kingdom, stating: Both the Chinese and British governments take the overall interests as their priority, base on friendly cooperation, mutual understanding and mutual accommodation, and solve the issues of Hong Kong left over by history through negotiation. This will not only help maintain the long-term stability and prosperity of Hong Kong, but also further promote the friendly and cooperative relations between China and Britain as well as safeguard the peace in Asia and the world. It will not only serve the interests and demands of the British people but also the interests and demands of the entire Chinese people including Hong Kong and Taiwan compatriots. The formal signing of the joint declaration on the issue of Hong Kong between the two countries is not only a major event in the relations between China and Britain, but also a major event in international politics. It provides an example for the international community to solve issues left over by history through peaceful and friendly consultations.

After the Sino-British Joint Declaration was put into effect and entered the "12 years of transitional period" (1985-1997) from "old Hong Kong" to "new Hong Kong", in order to fully implement the basic spirit and specific contents of the Sino-British Joint Declaration, and to achieve the smooth transition and smooth handover before "1997" and the strategic goal of "maintaining stability and prosperity" after "1997", China mainly carried out the two major tasks of making the "Hong Kong Basic Law" and the preparation of "New Hong Kong".

From 1985 to 1990, the Drafting Committee of the Basic Law of Hong Kong passed nine plenary meetings, 25 general board meetings, 73 panel meetings and three general working group meetings. After two times of more than one year of seeking for opinions on the Basic Law of Hong Kong (Draft) for Comments and the Basic Law of Hong Kong (Draft) in Hong Kong, across the country and all departments, and after several discussions and repeated revisions, the extremely precious Grand Code of "one country, two systems" was launched . On April 4, 1990, the Third Session of the Seventh National People's Congress passed the Basic Law of the Hong Kong Special Administrative Region of the People's Republic of China.

The formulation of the "Basic Law" which guarantees the "small constitution" of "one country, two systems" that has remained unchanged in Hong Kong for 50 years has aroused strong repercussions at home and abroad. It is considered as another milestone of Hong Kong's return journey after the signing of the "Sino-British Joint Declaration". Deng Xiaoping highly praised it: "By historic I mean it is significant not only for the past and the present but also for the future. By international and far-reaching I mean it is significant not only for the Third World but for all mankind. This document is a creative masterpiece."[9]

The preparation of "New Hong Kong" follows the steps of the generation of "Preparatory Commission", "Organizing Commission", and "Selection Commission", the generation of the Chief Executive, the generation of 3 groups of administrative, legislative and judicial teams headed by the Chief Executive, and the preparatory process "Handover Ceremony". Its "parent machine" of work is the "Organizing Commission" and the "Selection Commission, and its "head" is the first chief executive. On December 11, 1996, the 3rd Plenary Session of the "Selection Commission" elected Tung Chee Hwa as the first Chief Executive by an absolute majority of 320 votes.

From June 30 to July 1, 1997, the "new" and "old" Hong Kong was "docked". The "handover ceremony" of Hong Kong mainly meant "farewell" to the "old master", handover of Hong Kong from Britain to PRC, and the establishment ceremony of the SAR and SAR (Special Administrative Region) government of the Hong Kong as the "new master". On July 1, Chinese President Jiang Zemin solemnly declared to the world in Hong Kong: "Chinese and British Governments have held the handover ceremony of Hong Kong, solemnly announcing the resumption by the Chinese Government of the exercise of sovereignty over Hong Kong. Now, the Hong Kong Special Administrative Region of the People's Republic of China is formally established, which is an event of great importance and far-reaching influence for Hong Kong, for China and even for the whole world. I

---

9   Selected Works of Deng Xiaoping, 1st edition, Vol.3, p.352.

take this as a red letter day not only for the Hong Kong compatriots, but also for the Chinese people and the entire Chines nation… Hong Kong's return to the motherland is a shining page in the annals of the Chinese nation. From now on, the Hong Kong compatriots will truly become masters, and in this region new page of history is opened in the annals of Hong Kong."[10]

The return of Macao basically follows the successful return model and successful experience of Hong Kong's "First Example".

From June 1986 to March 1987, the Sino-Portuguese negotiations were held in Beijing and four rounds of formal talks were held. On April 13, 1987, Sino-Portuguese Joint Declaration was officially signed in Beijing. The Joint Declaration announced: The government of the People's Republic of China resumed its exercise of sovereignty over Macao on December 20, 1999. After the "historical issues" of Hong Kong between China and Britain, which lasted for a century and a half, has been solved, the "historical issues" of Macao between China and Portugal, which has lasted for four and a half centuries, has finally been successfully solved in the era in which the Chinese Communists came to power, in the era of the People's Republic of China where people are the masters of their country, and in the era of rejuvenation and peaceful development of the Chinese nation. The disgrace of several generations was wiped out and the dream of reunification of several generations came true.

From December 19, 1999 to December 20, 1999, the "new" and "old" Macao "docked." The "handover ceremony" of Macao consists mainly of "farewell" to the "old master", the handover ceremony of the Macao regime between China and Portugal, and the establishment ceremony of the SAR and SAR government as the "new master". On December 20, Chinese President Jiang Zemin solemnly announced to the world in Macao: "The government of China and the government of Portugal are holding a solemn ceremony here to mark the transfer of government of Macau and to announce the Chinese Government's resumption of the exercise of sovereignty over Macau."[11] "This signifies that henceforth our compatriots in Macao have become the masters of this land and that Macao has entered upon a brand new era in its development. This great event of the Chinese nation will shine forever in the annals of history."[12]

Peaceful settlement of the territorial and sovereignty disputes left over from history by means of diplomatic negotiations and peaceful resolving of the issue of national unification of Chinese regions implementing different social systems with the "one country, two systems" policy, and "seeking a

10   Selected Works of Jiang Zemin, Vol.1, p.651.
11   Selected Works of Jiang Zemin, Vol.2, p.484.
12   Ibid., p.486.

344

global cooperation between the two systems" has been a great innovative contribution made by the Communist Party of China and the Chinese government to the development and practice of the Marxist nation-state theory and to the history of human political civilization and to the contemporary world with the theme of peace and development. The "Hong Kong-Macau model" of "peaceful reunification and one country, two systems" with the "Twelve Special Policies", Joint Declaration and the Basic Law as the main contents and the successful practice of the return of Hong Kong and Macao opened up a new path for the development history of Marxism, the development history of human political civilizations, and the unification of nation-states and the integration of nation-states in the contemporary world, which not only provides a First Example of reference and enlightenment for contemporary China to continue resolving similar issues of national unification such as the Taiwan issue and resolving similar border territorial disputes such as the Sino-India Boundary Issue, it is also beneficial to the contemporary world to continue to solve the similar problems of national unification such as the issue of the Korean Peninsula and to solve similar territorial disputes such as the Malvinas Islands Issue between Britain and Argentina, which also can be used as the First Example of reference and enlightenment. British Prime Minister Thatcher once spoke highly of Deng Xiaoping's scientific concept of "one country, two systems" as "the most talented creation." She said: "There is no precedent for the idea of 'one country, two systems', that is, to retain two different political, social and economic systems in one country. It provides an imaginative answer to the special historical environment of Hong Kong. This concept sets an example of how the seemingly insoluble problem can be solved and how it should be solved." Javier Perez de Cuellar, the then UN Secretary-General, said: "The way in which the two countries solved the Hong Kong issue should be vigorously promoted. This is undoubtedly a very prominent example when tension and confrontation are unfortunately covering many parts of the world. "

345

Second, "One country, two systems" and a new type of governance suited for Hong Kong and Macao

As early as 1985 when the Sino-British Joint Declaration was signed and took effect by exchange of the instruments. Hong Kong just stepped into the "12-year transitional period", Deng Xiaoping has proposed and repeatedly emphasized the two "simple" standards to judge whether the practice of "one country, two systems" is really successful in Hong Kong and Macao: the first is whether we can achieve a smooth transition and a smooth handover before "1997" and "1999"; the other is whether we can maintain long-term stability and prosperity after "1997" and "1999". As for the first test, after overcoming the "expected difficulties" both inside and outside Hong Kong-Macao society and after concerted efforts by the Chinese Central Government, the governments of Hong Kong and Macao SAR, Hong Kong and Macao compatriots, we have finally submitted a "world-wide appreciated" excellent answer–the "handover ceremonies" of Hong Kong and Macao "without occurrence of any unpleasant major accident". For the latter test of criterion, Deng Xiaoping has proposed: if, under the general background of economic globalization and the peaceful rise of mainland China, after the "new" Hong Kong and Macao can overcome various kinds of "unexpected difficulties" inside and outside Hong Kong and Macao societies, by the joint efforts of Central Government, and the governments of Hong Kong and Macao Special Administrative Regions, as well as compatriots in Hong Kong and Macao, we will also submit a second answer which will be "fairly appreciated by the whole world".

Just at the beginning of the construction of "one country, two systems" of "new" Hong Kong and Macao, on the question of how to "observe and assess the situation in Hong Kong and Macao", Chinese President Jiang Zemin also proactively put forward four basic preconditions: the great concept of "one country, two systems" proposed by Deng Xiaoping and the concept of "Hong Kong people ruling Hong Kong", "Macao people administering Macao", a high degree of autonomy is completely correct; compatriots in Hong Kong and Macao are fully capable of managing Hong Kong and Macao well; the wisdom and experience of the SAR government can handle complex situations; the great socialist motherland is the strong backing for Hong Kong and Macao in maintaining prosperity, stability and the difficulties and risks ahead of victory.[13]

He expressed the sincere hope and firm confidence in the "new era of Hong Kong and Macao history" and "better tomorrow in Hong Kong and Macao" of the Central Government and people of all nationalities in the country. For more than a decade since the return of Hong Kong and Macao, the construction and practice of "one country, two systems" in the "new" Hong Kong and Macao has fully proved the correctness of this scientific judgment.

The return of Hong Kong and Macao and the "one country, two systems" construction of "new" Hong Kong and Maucao are the two experimental fields that set the example for "peaceful unification" project under "one country, two systems" in contemporary China. Since the return of Hong Kong and Macao and the start of "Hong Kong people administering Hong

13   See "Conversations of Jiang Zemin Attending the Discussions of the Hong Kong Delegation to the Second Session of the Ninth National People's Congress", People's Daily, 19990308; "Conversations of Jiang Zemin at the Discussion on the Macao Delegation to the Third Session of the Ninth National People's Congress" People's Daily, 2000/03/09.

Kong" and "Macao people administering Macao", the "new" Hong Kong and Macao, faced with the "dilemmas" of "change" and "unchange", under the impacts of the negative Asian financial storm, SARS and the global financial crisis on one hand, and the positive double challenges of the Mainland's entry into WTO, the signing of "Closer Economic Partnership Arrangement" with Hong Kong and Macao and the opportunity of Hong Kong and Macao opening up the "Individual Visit Scheme" and "Individual Traveler Policy" to some provinces and cities on the other hand. We made the best use of the opportunity of the worldwide trend of political multi-polarization, economic diversification and cultural diversification, and for the building of an all-round capitalist material civilization, spiritual civilization, political civilization and "harmonious society" with Hong Kong and Macao characteristics, we found a new path to keep maintaining the traditional and regional advantages of the status of "free port", "independent customs territory" and "international economic center" and "the center of East-West cultural exchanges", and continued to maintain the tradition and core values of "freedom, democracy, human rights and the rule of law", that is, the construction of the "Hong Kong-Macau model" under "one country, two systems" of "continuing to maintain long-term stability and prosperity".

For the general political and economic development trend since the re-unification of Hong Kong and Macao, the Central Government, the SAR government, compatriots in Hong Kong and Macao and the international community have a basic assessment: in the "new" Hong Kong and Macao, "the concept of "one country, two systems" has been transformed from a scientific concept to a vivid reality"; "'One country, two systems' has been integrated into the life of 'new' Hong Kong and Macao". On July 1, 2007, at the celebration of the 10th anniversary of Hong Kong's return to the motherland, Chinese President Hu Jintao delivered a speech comprehensively summarizing the great achievements made in the construction of "one country, two systems" in the "new Hong Kong". He pointed out: Over the past 10 years, the Central Government has earnestly implemented the principle of "one country, two systems", Hong Kong people administering Hong Kong" and a high degree of autonomy. We must strictly abide by the Basic Law of the Hong Kong Special Administrative Region and unswervingly safeguard Hong Kong's prosperity and stability. Hong Kong continues to maintain its existing capitalist system and way of life, fully exercising its administrative power, legislative power, independent judicial power and final adjudication power under the Basic Law of the Hong Kong Special Administrative Region. Hong Kong residents enjoy extensive democratic rights and freedoms, "Hong Kong people administering Hong Kong" and a high degree of autonomy has become a vivid reality. Over the past 10 years, under the strong support of the Central Government and the motherland, the Chief Executive Tung Chee Hwa and Donald Tsang successively led the SAR government together with the broad masses of Hong Kong compatriots to overcome serious difficulties and challenges caused by the Asian financial crisis and the SARS epidemic, which have safeguarded Hong Kong's overall social stability and achieved economic recovery, and made great strides in various undertakings in Hong Kong. In the past 10 years, the community of Hong Kong has maintained its stability, the economy is more prosperous, the democratic and orderly development is achieved, and the people live and work in peace and contentment, showing a thriving scene. Facts have indisputably proved that the principle of "one country, two systems" is completely correct. Hong Kong compatriots are completely wise and capable of managing well. Building a good Hong Kong and a great motherland have always been the strong backing of Hong Kong's prosperity and stability! On December 20, 2009, On the occasion of the 10th anniversary celebration of Macao's return to the motherland, Hu Jintao delivered a speech comprehensively summarizing the great achievements made in the construction of "one country, two systems" in "New Macao". He pointed out: In the 10 years since Macao's return to the motherland, with the vigorous support from the Central Government and the motherland, the Macao Special Administrative Region and its Chief Executive, H.E. Edmund Ho, and the SAR government lead the people of all walks of life in Macao to work hard in unity and pragmatism to actively deal with the severe challenges posed by the Asian financial crisis, the SARS outbreak and the international financial crisis, and work hard to overcome the difficulties encountered in the process of Macao's development, maintain the prosperity and stability of Macao and make great strides in various undertakings, thus Macao, the famous historic city of commerce, emerged an unprecedented vitality. The successful practice of "one country, two systems" in Macao has created a brilliant chapter for the development of Macao and added dazzling luster to the development of the country. The successful practice of "one country, two systems" in Macao has opened a brilliant chapter for the development of Macao and added dazzling luster to the development of the country. The 10 years since Macao's return to the motherland have been the successful practice of "one country, two systems". It is a 10-year period of the successful implementation of the Basic Law in Macao. It is also a period of 10 years in which Macao people from all walks of life actively have explored ways of development that are in line with Macao's realities and have made constant progress!

Recalling the 10plus years after the return of Hong Kong and Macao, we can draw a historic conclusion: the practice of "one country, two systems" in Hong Kong and Macao is a success. The "Hong Kong-Macao model" under "one country, two systems" is viable. Moreover, "one country, two systems" provides a system guarantee for "better tomorrow of Hong Kong and Macao". Practice has proved that the principle of "one country, two systems" is completely correct and has strong vitality.

On October 15, 2007, Hu Jintao once again raised the issue of "maintaining long-term prosperity and stability in Hong Kong and Macao" to the strategic height of "a major issue confronting the Party's state administration under the new situation", he emphatically pointed out: Since the return of Hong Kong and Macao, the practice of "one country, two systems" has been increasingly enriched. "One country, two systems" is completely correct and has strong vitality. A major task the Party faces in running the country in the new circumstances is to ensure long-term prosperity and stability in Hong Kong and Macao. We will unswervingly implement the system under which Hong Kong people administer Hong Kong and Macao people administer Macao with a high degree of autonomy, and act in strict accordance with the basic laws of the two special administrative regions. We support to the governments of the two regions in their administration in accordance with the law and in their efforts to promote economic growth, improve people's lives and advance democracy. We encourage people from all walks of life in Hong Kong and Macao to work with one accord to promote social amity under the banner of love for the motherland and devotion to their respective regions. We will increase exchanges and cooperation between the mainland and the two regions so that they can draw on each other's strengths and develop side by side. We will actively support the two regions in their external exchanges and firmly oppose attempts by any external force to interfere in their affairs. Our compatriots in Hong Kong and Macao, without doubt, have the wisdom and ability to successfully administer and develop their regions. Both regions have played and will continue to play an important role in China's modernization drive, and the great motherland will always provide them with strong backing for their prosperity and stability.

Section III

The breakthrough in cross-strait relations and the new situation of peaceful development in cross-strait relations

First, the basic state policy of "peaceful reunification and one country, two systems" and breakthrough in Cross-Strait relations

In current China, to solve the Taiwan issue—"peaceful reunification of the motherland and one country two systems"—is a "top priority" strategy among its great undertakings. In the late 1970s and early 1980s, Deng

Xiaoping's scientific concept of "one country, two systems" was originally designed to solve the Taiwan issue. Only when the stalemate in the Taiwan issue was not easy to be solved in a short period of time, he chose to solve the problem of Hong Kong and Macao whose timing and conditions are relatively ripe as a sally port, make use of the First Example by reunifying Hong Kong and Macao with the "Hong Kong-Macao model" under "one country, two systems" to accumulate experience and create conditions for a final solution to the Taiwan issue. Since the 1990s and the 21st century, the third generation of the central collective leadership with Jiang Zemin at the core and the Party Central Committee with Hu Jintao as the general secretary have carried out new theoretical and practical innovations on the basis of inheriting and developing this scientific concept, On the one hand, made efforts to bring about the return of Hong Kong and Macao and constructed the "Hong Kong and Macao model" under "one country, two systems", on the other hand, shifted the strategic focus of the great project of "peaceful reunification and one country under two systems" in contemporary China to the settlement of Taiwan issue. According to the new changes in China's domestic situation and the international situation, according to the evolution of political ecology in Taiwan and the new changes in the cross-Strait relations in the "post-Cold War era", it is necessary to fully readjust our strategic thinking and specific policies on the work related to Taiwan affairs

which should focus on anti-independence rather than equally focus on anti-independence and promoting reunification, we should shift from placing the hope on the "passive reaction" of Taiwan authorities to our initiating action, shift from placing the hope on "the Taiwan people's" "hard and soft tactics" to the "harder" and "softer" "active control". We have formed a set of comprehensive and systematic theoretical and policy guidelines such as The Issue of Taiwan and China's Reunification and the white book of The One-China Principle and the Taiwan Issue, the "5.17 Statement", The Anti-Secession Law of the Republic of China, "Jiang's 8-points", "Hu's 4-points" and "Hu's 6-points", for the work related to Taiwan affairs and further opened up a new situation for the peaceful development of cross-Strait relations and laying a solid foundation for settling the Taiwan issue and for realizing the ultimate goal of "peaceful reunification and one country under two systems" in contemporary China.

Since the entry into the new period, the Communist Party of China and the Chinese government have always tried their utmost to carry out their utmost sincerity and strive for the realization of peaceful reunification through the principle of "one country, two systems", and adopted a series of pro-active policies and measures to comprehensively promote the peaceful development in cross-Strait relations, our sincerity, goodwill and new ideas are gradually gaining the understanding and support of more and more Taiwan compatriots, compatriots in Hong Kong, Macao and overseas

Chinese. The vast majority of Taiwan compatriots have also made great efforts to promote the development of cross-Strait relations. From the late 1980s on, there have been signs of loosening over the stalled impasse in the Taiwan issue.

At the end of 1987, Chiang Ching-kuo, the leader of the Kuomintang authorities in Taiwan, made the decisions of his most important and direct influence on the evolution of political ecology on the island of Taiwan and the development of cross-Strait relations–"lifting the ban on political parties" and "opening up family visits from the mainland". The cross-strait relations have begun to enter a new stage of historical development. Since the late 1980s and early 1990s, in just a few short years, the isolation between the two sides of the Taiwan Strait has been broken, and the cross-Strait economic and cultural exchanges and personnel exchanges have made great strides. In order to properly settle the specific problems arising from the exchanges of compatriots on both sides of the Strait through negotiation, in November 1992, the mainland's Association for Relations Across the Taiwan Straits (ARATS) and the Taiwan's Straits Exchange Foundation (SEF) reached an agreement that each of them verbally states "both sides of the Strait uphold the one China principle" in conducting transactional talks, namely the so-called "1992 Consensus" (mainland China's understanding and interpretation are "there is only one China and both sides agree to accept it", and Taiwan's understanding and explanation are "both sides agree to accept there is one China"). On the basis of this, the leaders of the ARATS and SEF successfully held the first "Wang (Wang Daohan) -Koo (Koo Chen-fu) Talks" in April 1993 and signed four agreements on protecting the legitimate rights and interests of compatriots on both sides of the Taiwan Strait. In October 1998, the leaders of the ARATS and SEF held a meeting in Shanghai and successfully held the second "Wang-Ku Talks", which opened the process for cross-Strait political dialogue.

Since the mid-1990s, because that the leader of Taiwan's authorities Lee Teng-hui and Chen Shui-bian gradually abandoned the one-China principle and vigorously pushed forward the separatist policy of "Taiwan Independence" with "two Chinas" or "one China, one Taiwan" at the core, the newly opened process of political dialogue across the Taiwan Strait has been interrupted. The Communist Party of China and the Chinese government considered the current situation, conformed to the new situation of the evolution of political ecology on the island of Taiwan and the development of cross-Strait relations, and open up a new situation in the exchange of political parties across the Taiwan Strait. In 2005, the CPC successively invited the leaders of the three parties on the island of Taiwan, the Kuomintang, the People First Party and the New Party, who have always been adhering to the one-China principle, to visit the mainland and successfully realized the direct dialogue among political party leaders–"Hu (Hu Jintao) Lien (Lien Chan) Meeting", "Hu (Hu Jintao) Song (James Soong) Meeting", and Hu (Hu Jintao) Yu (Yok Mu-ming) meeting". In particular, the so-called "third handshake" of the Kuomintang and Communist Party on the "Hu Lien Meeting" held on April 29, 2005 is of extraordinary significance. At the meeting, both sides jointly published the "Common Prospect of Peace and Development on Both Sides of the Taiwan Strait", jointly establishing the "Three Recognitions" and the "Five Promotions", which set a foreshadow for resuming the political dialogue between Taiwan and mainland on the basis of "1992 Consensus" after the Kuomintang party again won the Taiwan government in 2008.

Compared with the stalemate in the political exchanges between the two sides of the Strait, which have been intermittent and slow in political dialogue since the isolation between the two sides of the Strait was broken in the late 1980s, the momentum of cross-Strait economic exchanges and personnel exchanges has always been unstoppable. By the end of 2007, more than 47.03 million Taiwanese residents came to the mainland and mainland residents totaled more than 1.63 million to Taiwan. The mainland has totally approved 75,146 Taiwanese investment projects and Taiwan businessmen actually invested 45.76 billion U.S. dollars. According to statistics on actual use of foreign investment, Taiwan's investment in mainland China accumulatively absorbs 6.0% of the overseas investment in the mainland. The trade volume between the two sides of the Taiwan Strait amounted to 728.1 billion U.S. dollars, of which 125.9 billion US dollars were exported to Taiwan, 602.2 billion U.S. dollars were imported from Taiwan and the deficit of the Mainland added up 476.3 billion US dollars. In 2010, the trade volume between the mainland and Taiwan was 145.37 billion US dollars, and 3,072 Taiwanese investment projects were approved. By the end of December 2010, 83,133 Taiwan-funded projects had been approved by the mainland, actually utilizing 52.02 billion US dollars. At present, Taiwan is the mainland's seventh largest trading partner, the ninth largest export market and the fifth largest source of imports. The mainland is Taiwan's largest trading partner, the largest export market and the largest source of trade surplus. The general trend of the peaceful development of cross-Strait relations has become irreversible.

Second, the basic national policy of "peaceful reunification, one country, two systems" and the new situation of peaceful development in cross-strait relations

At the turn of the century, the third generation of the central collective leadership with Jiang Zemin at the core and the Party Central Committee with Hu Jintao as general secretary have always held high the banner of adhering to the One-China principle in settling the Taiwan issue and developing cross-Strait relations." Jiang Zemin emphasized: "Adherence to one China principle is the basis for resolution of the Peaceful Reunification of the Motherland."[14]

Hu Jintao emphasized: "Adhering to the one-China principle is the cornerstone of developing cross-Strait relations and realizing the motherland's peaceful reunification."[15]

On January 30, 1995, Jiang Zemin delivered a speech entitled "Keep Striving to Promote the Great Cause of the Reunification of the Motherland". He put forward eight propositions of "developing cross-Strait relations at this stage and advancing the process of peaceful reunification of the motherland", namely, the famous "Jiang's 8-points", for the first time he clearly put forward the issue of "adhering to the one-China principle" and pointed out:" Adhering to the 'one-China' principle is the basis and premise for realizing peaceful reunification." Since the beginning of the 21st century, on February 21, 2000, the Chinese government issued a white paper entitled "The One-China Principle and the Taiwan Issue". It has conducted a comprehensive and systematic study of Jiang Zemin's "Adherence to the One-China Principle" from different angles and aspects and concretely explained: "The One-China Principle is the foundation stone for the Chinese government's policy on Taiwan."[16]

Since the 16th CPC National Congress, the party Central Committee with Hu Jintao as General Secretary has repeatedly emphasized that upholding the one-China principle is the basis for developing cross-Strait relations and realizing peaceful unification. On this issue of non-trivial matter relating to the fundamental interests of the Chinese nation, our stance is firm and consistent.[17]

On March 14, 2005, the "Anti-Secession Law of the People's Republic of China" passed at the Third Session of the Tenth National People's Congress made it clear for the first time in the legal language that reflects the will of the state: "Adherence to the One-China Principle is the Realization of Peaceful Reunification of the Motherland The foundation."

Since the beginning of the new century, in order to demonstrate the sincerity, goodwill and new ideas of the CPC and the Chinese government in upholding the "One-China Principle," our party has also adjusted the concrete connotation of "One-China principle" with keeping pace with

14   Selected Works of Jiang Zemin, Vol. 1, p.421.
15   Hu Jintao: "We will never waver in upholding the One China principle", see Xinhuanet.com, 2005/03/04.
16   See "The One-China Principle–the Basis and Prerequisite of Peaceful Reunification", People's Daily, 2000/02/22.
17   See Hu Jintao: "We will never waver in upholding the One China principle", see Xinhuanet.com, 2005/03/04.

the times: since the traditional "world there is one China, Taiwan is part of China, the sole legal government that represents China in the international community" is the "old" "syllogism" "government of the People's Republic of China". At this stage there is "only one China in the world; both the mainland and Taiwan belong to one China, China's sovereignty and territorial integrity cannot be divided"[18].

From the only one China in the world in the "new" "syllogism" to that in "Hu's 6-points", China's sovereignty and territorial integrity cannot be divided. Since 1949, although the mainland and Taiwan have not yet reunified, it is not a division of China's territory and sovereignty but a political antagonism left over and extended by the civil war in the mid-to-late 1940s in China. This has not changed the fact that the mainland and Taiwan belong to one China. For the two sides of the Straits, to return to unity is not the recreation of sovereignty or territory, but an end to political antagonism.[19]

It is a basic political view on settling the Taiwan issue of the first generation of the central collective leadership of the Party with Mao Zedong as the core and the second with Deng Xiaoping as its core before the 1990s that through the negotiation of the two ruling Parties, the Communist Party of China and the Kuomintang, to settle the Taiwan issue with equal terms to realize the peaceful reunification of contemporary China. In the first half of the 1990s, when the Kuomintang still took power in Taiwan and still did not give up its "one-China" stance, the third-generation central leadership collective with Jiang Zemin as its core also continued to adhere to the "third KMT-CPC cooperation" for the settlement the Taiwan issue in order to achieve the peaceful unification of contemporary China.

Starting from the mid-1990s, in response to the evolution of Taiwan's domestic political ecology, including the increasingly serious and even rampant "Taiwan Independence" split trend and the "Taiwan Independence" division situation within the Kuomintang, the leading collectives of the third generation of the Party with Jiang Zemin as its core, while continuing to "hold high the banner of political negotiations across the Strait", made strategic and even structural adjustments to the targets, procedures and specific contents of the cross-Strait political negotiations and put forward a series of new political propositions. Among them, the most important thing is to explicitly put forward the principle of "upholding the one-China principle is the basic premise and the political foundation for political negotiations across the Taiwan Strait", "diluting the object of political negotiations–the

---

18   Selected Works of Jiang Zemin, Vol. 3, p. 564.
19   See Hu Jintao, "Let Us Join Hands to Promote the Peaceful Development of Cross-Straits Relations and Strive with a United Resolve for the Great Rejuvenation of the Chinese Nation–Speech at the Forum Marking the 30th Anniversary of the Issuance of the Message to Compatriots in Taiwan," People's Daily, 2009/01/01.

sole subjectivity of the Chinese Kuomintang" and "phased political negotiations ", and so on.

This "new thinking" is mainly reflected in Jiang Zemin's speech at
the Spring Tea Party held by the Taiwan Work Office of the CPC Central
Committee and the Taiwan Affairs Office of the State Council (Jiang's
8-points). Jiang zemin pointed out: "It has been our consistent stand to hold
negotiations with the Taiwan authorities on the peaceful reunification of the
motherland.... We have proposed time and again that negotiations should
be held on officially ending the state of hostility between the two sides and
accomplishing peaceful reunification step by step. Here again I solemnly
propose that such negotiations be held. I suggest that, as the first step, negotiations should be held and an agreement reached on officially ending
the state of hostility between the two sides in accordance with the principle
that there is only one China. On this basis, the two sides should undertake
jointly to safeguard China sovereignty and territorial integrity and map out
plans for the future development of their relations. As regards the name,
place and form of these political talks, a solution acceptable to both sides
can certainly be found so long as consultations on an equal footing can be
held at an early date... Leaders of the Taiwan authorities are welcome to
pay visits in appropriate capacities. We are also ready to accept invitations
from the Taiwan side to visit Taiwan. We can discuss state affairs, or exchange ideas on certain questions first. Even a simple visit to the other side
will be useful."[20]

Since then, Jiang Zemin reiterated this basic political stance on different
political occasions.

As for the specific content of "political negotiations across the Taiwan
Strait", the basic open stance of the third-generation central leadership collective with Jiang Zemin at its core and the CPC Central Committee with
Hu Jintao as general secretary since the 1990s and the 21st century has always remained the same–"Under the premise of one-China, any problem
can be discussed", "our status is equal and the topic for discussion is open".
In 1992, at the 14th Congress of the Party, Jiang Zemin pointed out: "On
the premise that there is only one China, we are prepared to talk with the
Taiwan authorities about any matter, including the form that official negotiations should take, a form that would be acceptable to both sides."[21]

In 2002, Jiang Zemin pointed out in the report of the party's 16th National
Congress that "On the premise of the one-China principle, all issues can be
discussed. We may discuss how to end the cross-straits hostility formally.
We may also discuss the international space in which the Taiwan region may

20   Selected Works of Jiang Zemin, Vol.1, pp.421-423.
21   Ibid., p.252.

conduct economic, cultural and social activities compatible with its status, or discuss the political status of the Taiwan authorities or other issues."[22]

And Jiang Zemin for the first time, proposed focusing and opening "three links" across the Taiwan Strait, namely direct trade, transportation, and postal links.

After the 16th National Congress of the CPC, the Party Central Committee with Hu Jintao as general secretary continued to "hold high the banner of cross-Strait political negotiations" and at the same time the targets and topics for cross-Strait political negotiations were further opened and the "flexible" space was further increased, which fully demonstrated the sincerity, goodwill and new idea of the CPC and the Chinese government in settling the Taiwan issue through cross-Strait political negotiations and realizing the peaceful unification of contemporary China.

On March 4, 2005, Hu Jintao, when visiting some members of the 3rd Plenary Meeting of the 10th CPPCC National Committee, proposed four points of views on cross-Strait development under the new situation ("Hu's 4-points"): "As long as the Taiwan authorities recognize the "1992 Consensus', the cross-Strait dialogue and negotiation can be resumed, and any questions can be discussed. We can not only talk about the issues we have already proposed that formally put an end to the state of hostility on the two sides of the Strait and establish mutual trust in the military, the space for the activities of the Taiwan region fitting in with its status internationally, the political status of the Taiwan authorities and the framework for the peaceful and stable development of cross-Strait relations. All the problems that need to be solved in the process of peaceful reunification can also be discussed. We welcome all the efforts made by any person and political party in Taiwan to recognize the one-China principle. As long the One-China Principle and the '1992 Consensus' is recognized, no matter who they are or what political parties they are or what they have said in the past, we are willing to talk with them about the issue of developing cross-Strait relations and promoting peaceful unification."[23]

On March 14, 2005, the 3rd Plenary Session of the 10th National People's Congress passed the Anti-Secession Law of the People's Republic of China which is the first time that the three "can be talked" at the policy level of the ruling party on "cross-Strait political negotiations" are further substantiated and upgraded to the six "can be talked" on the national legal level.

---

22   Selected Works of Jiang Zemin, Vol.3, pp.564.
23   "All Chinese Sons and Daughters including Taiwan Compatriots Are United In Their Work Together To Promote the Great Cause of Peaceful Reunification of The Motherland", People's Daily, 2005/03/05.

On March 4, 2008, Hu Jintao pointed out during his visit to some members of the 1st Session of the 11th CPPCC National Committee the important suggestions on developing cross-Strait relations that if any political party in Taiwan who recognizes that both sides belong to the same China, we are willing to exchange and negotiate with them. The status of each party in the negotiations is equal. The topics are open and any questions can be discussed. Through negotiations, the two sides should seek solutions to important issues such as politics, economy, military affairs, culture and foreign exchange between the two sides of the Taiwan Strait and plan the future development of cross-Strait relations. We expect that both sides of the Strait will work together to create the conditions for the two sides to negotiate and formally conclude the state of hostility on the basis of the one-China principle, reach a peace agreement, establish a framework for the peaceful development of cross-Strait relations and create a new phase for the peaceful development of cross-Strait relations. We must also strive to unify with people who have previously nursed illusions of Taiwan's independence, advocated independence or even engaged in independence activities. As long as they return to the correct path of promoting the peaceful development of cross-Strait relations, they will all be warmly welcome.[24]

On December 31, 2008, in his important speech at the symposium commemorating the 30th anniversary of the publication of the Message to Taiwan Compatriots, Hu Jintao further released his sincerity, goodwill and new ideas in pushing for political negotiations across the Taiwan Strait, and released his self-confidence, grace and mind-set for the promotion of cross-Strait political negotiation. He said: "In order to facilitate consultations and negotiations between the two sides of the Strait and make arrangements for reciprocal transactions, the two sides of the strait should pragmatically discuss the political relations under special circumstances in which the state has not yet been unified. In order to be in a position to stabilize the situation in the Taiwan Strait and ease military security concerns, both sides of the Strait can conduct timely contact and exchange on military issues and discuss the issue of establishing a mechanism for mutual trust in military security. On the basis of the one-China principle, we once again called for consultations to formally end the hostile state across the Strait, to reach a peace agreement and establish a framework for the peaceful development of cross-Strait relations". "With regard to Taiwan's activities in participating in international organizations, it is possible to make fair and reasonable arrangements through pragmatic consultations between the two sides on the premise of not creating 'two Chinas' and

24   See "Firmly Grasping the Peaceful Development Theme of the Cross-Strait Relationship, Sincerely Seeking Welfare for the Compatriots on Both Sides and Seeking Peace Across the Taiwan Strait", People's Daily, 2008/03/05.

'one China, one Taiwan'." Hu Jintao also stressed once again: "We also warmly welcome those who, in the past, stood for, engaged in and pursued "Taiwan independence" to change course and join us in promoting the peaceful development of cross-Straits relations. We hope the DPP will come to a clear judgment of the current situation and stop the separatist activities aimed at "Taiwan independence" rather than going against the common aspiration of the nation. As long as the DPP changes its separatist stance and stop pursuing "Taiwan independence", we are ready to respond positively."[25]

To solve the Taiwan issue (including the "cross-Strait political negotiations" with the Taiwan authorities), a precondition and a basic condition for the peaceful unification of contemporary China is that we must solve the problem of "return of people's hearts" of the people in Taiwan, that is the "Placing Hope on Taiwan People" that the Communist Party of China and the Chinese government have always stressed. Since the 1990s and the 21st century, the third generation of the central collective leadership with Jiang Zemin at the core and the Party Central Committee with Hu Jintao as the general secretary have attached great importance to resolving the issue of "return of people's hearts" of the people in Taiwan. They have always regarded "doing well the work of Taiwan people" as one of the most important goals of the CPC and the Chinese government in their work on Taiwan.

The CPC and the Chinese government made it clear that the 23 million compatriots in Taiwan are our brothers and sisters and have a glorious tradition of patriotism. They are the basis for the peaceful development of cross-Strait relations and the anchor for the realization of the motherland's peaceful reunification. They are also the current foundation and subjectivity forces for the opposition and containment of "Taiwan Independence" separatist forces and splitting activities. To solve the Taiwan issue and realize the peaceful unification of the motherland requires not only "Chinese do not fight Chinese" but also "Chinese people solve their own affairs". To solve the Taiwan issue "mainly with our power", we must work together through the efforts of 1.3 billion mainland China compatriots and 23 million Taiwan compatriots.

Over the past 30 years or so, the specific content of the scientific concept and basic national policy of "peaceful reunification and one country, two systems" has been constantly adjusted due to the evolution of political ecology in Taiwan and changes in the cross-Strait relations, which undergone transmutation and transformation from two different "placing hopes"

25   Hu Jintao: "Promoting The Peaceful Development of Cross-Strait Relations and and Achieve the Great Revival of the Chinese Nation–Speech at the Ceremony on Commemorating the 30th Anniversary of Message to Compatriots in Taiwan", People's Daily, 2009/01/01.

principles, namely "place hope on Taiwan people and also place hope on Taiwan authorities" and "place hope on Taiwan authorities and place more hope on the people of Taiwan", to the sole "placing hope" principle, namely "place hope on Taiwan people", which was more pragmatic and targeted.

Since the 1990s and the 21st century, all previous meetings of the CPC and the Chinese government on the work of Taiwan, the policy documents and relevant laws and regulations issued to Taiwan in the past and the talks made by previous leaders and Taiwan-related officials both at home and abroad have, without exception, taken "doing good things regarding the Taiwan Strait work", and "winning the hearts and minds of the Taiwan people" was raised to the strategic height to resolve the Taiwan issue and realize the peaceful reunification of China.

Since the 16th National Party Congress in 2002, the Party Central Committee with Hu Jintao as general secretary has continued to hold high the banner of "placing hope on the Taiwan people" and doing a good job in "winning the hearts and minds of the Taiwan people". Hu Jintao made it clear that "the principle of implementing 'placing hope on Taiwan people' will never change". On March 4, 2005, Hu Jintao, while visiting some members of the 3rd Plenary Session of the 10th CPPCC National Committee, pointed out when he put forward the four points guideline on developing cross-Strait relations under the new situation "The Taiwan compatriots are our flesh-and-blood brothers, as well as an importance force in developing cross-Straits relations and checking the "Taiwan independence" secessionist activities. The more the "Taiwan independence" secessionist forces want to isolate the Taiwan compatriots from us, the more closely we have to unite with them. Under whatever circumstances, we shall always respect, trust and rely on the Taiwan compatriots, land ourselves in their position to think of their difficulties, and do everything we can to look after and safeguard their legitimate rights and interests... And here in the following Hu Jintao defined his idea of "4 conductives" as the following Anything beneficial to the Taiwan compatriots and conducive to the promotion of cross-Straits exchanges, to the maintenance of peace in the Taiwan Straits region and to the motherland's peaceful reunification, we will do it with our utmost efforts and will do it well. This is our solemn commitment to the broad masses of the Taiwan compatriots."[26]

For the first time, the idea of "4 conductives" was formally proposed in the context of "doing a good job in winning the hearts and minds of the Taiwan people".

359

26 "All Chinese Sons and Daughters including Taiwan Compatriots Are United In Their Work Together To Promote the Great Cause of Peaceful Reunification of The Motherland", People's Daily, 2005/03/05.

Since the 16th National Congress of the CPC, the Party Central Committee with Hu Jintao as the general secretary has further advocated the new thinking, new idea that the people on both sides of the Strait should be a "community of common destiny" based on the guiding thought and basic principle of keeping "unswervingly implementing the principle of placing hope on the people of Taiwan".

Hu Jintao pointed out explicitly: "No matter the past, the present or future, 1.3 billion mainland compatriots and 23 million Taiwan compatriots are all connected by a common destiny."[27] The long history of 5,000 years of compatriots on both sides of the Taiwan Straits, and splendid culture, we are all closely linked. We are all descendants of the Chinese nation. We all should take our great nation as our pride. We should all also take our responsibility to rejuvenate this great nation."[28]

"China belongs to the 1.3 billion Chinese people including 23 million Taiwan compatriots. The Mainland belongs to the 1.3 billion Chinese people including 23 million Taiwan compatriots. Taiwan belongs to the 1.3 billion Chinese people including 23 million Taiwan compatriots. Any issue involving China's sovereignty and territorial integrity must be decided collectively by the entire 1.3 billion Chinese people."[29]

In October 2007, for the first time, Hu Jintao put forward the important idea of "firm grasping the theme of peaceful development of cross-Straits relations" in the Report to the 17th National Congress of the Communist Party of China and emphasized that "China is the common homeland for the compatriots on both sides of the Straits, who have every reason to join hands to safeguard and develop this homeland".[30]

This set the main tune for the work on Taiwan and the Taiwan policy of the Communist Party of China and the Chinese government at a later time.

On December 31, 2008, in his important address on the symposium to commemorate the 30th anniversary of the publication of the Message to Taiwan Compatriots, Hu Jintao put forward six suggestions on "firmly grasp the theme of peaceful development of cross-Strait relations and actively promote the peaceful development of cross-Strait relations". First, abide by one China and enhance mutual political trust. Second, promote

27   See "Firmly Grasping the Peaceful Development Theme of the Cross-Strait Relationship, Sincerely Seeking Welfare for the Compatriots on Both Sides and Seeking Peace for the Taiwan Strait Area", People's Daily, 2008/03/05.
28   See "Hu Jintao Meets with PFP Mainland Delegation", People's Daily, 2005/05/13.
29   "All Chinese Sons and Daughters including Taiwan Compatriots Are United In Their Work Together To Promote the Great Cause of Peaceful Reunification of The Motherland", People's Daily, 2005/03/05.
30   CPCCC Party Literature Research Office: "Selection of Important Literature since the 17th National Congress" (Vol.II), p.34.

economic cooperation and promote common development. Third, promote Chinese culture and strengthen spiritual ties. Fourth, strengthen personnel exchanges and expand exchanges between people from all walks of life. Fifth, safeguard national sovereignty and negotiate foreign affairs. Sixth, put an end to hostilities and reach a peace agreement. This is the famous "Hu's 6-points" "Hu's 6-points" which once again demonstrated the goodwill, sincerity and new ideas of the CPC and the Chinese government in settling the Taiwan issue and is a new programmatic document for the CPC and the Chinese government in settling the Taiwan issue.

Since March 2008, under the correct guidance and active promotion of the CPC and the Chinese government, with the joint efforts of compatriots on both sides of the Taiwan Strait, there has been a significant positive change in the political ecology in Taiwan and in cross-Strait relations. The cross-Strait relations ushered in a rare historic opportunity. Before and after Kuomintang, who opposed "Taiwan Independence" and acknowledged the "1992 Consensus", "holding power" in Taiwan, it showed great enthusiasm for the development of "normalized" cross-Strait relations and put forward the new idea of "facing reality, opening up the future, shelving controversy, and pursuing win-win cooperation" for the development of cross-Strait relations. For that, we gave a positive response. On April 29, 2008, Hu Jintao met with Lien Chan, Honorary Chairman of the KMT, and exchanged views on the issue of developing cross-Strait relations. Hu pointed out explicitly that the situation in Taiwan has undergone positive changes and the cross-Strait relations have shown a good momentum of development. Both sides of the Strait should make joint efforts to "build mutual trust, lay aside disputes, seek consensus and shelve differences, and jointly create a win-win situation."[31]

On May 28, Hu Jintao met with Wu Po-hsiung, chairman of the Kuomintang, and exchanged in-depth views on promoting the improvement and development of cross-Strait relations under the new situation. Hu Jintao told Wu Po-hsiung earnestly that with the joint efforts of the Kuomintang and the Communist Party and compatriots on both sides of the Taiwan Strait, the situation in Taiwan has undergone a positive change and the development of cross-Strait relations is facing a rare historical opportunity. This situation is not easy, it is worth cherishing.[32]

Since June 2008, thanks to the concerted efforts of the two sides of the Taiwan Strait, the channels and mechanisms for communication between ARATS and SEF, which were forced to be shelved for a relatively long period of time, have been restored. Consultations on developing the direct

---

31   "Hu Jintao meets with Lien Chan and his entourage", in: "People's Daily", 2008/04/30.
32   See "CPC Central Committee General Secretary Hu Jintao Hold Talks with *Wu* Po-hsiung, Chairman of the Kuomintang," People's Daily, 2008/05/29.

"Three Links" and comprehensive economic exchange and cooperation and other issues between the two sides of the Taiwan Strait were held, and a series of important progress and breakthrough results were made. From June 12 to June 13 to December 20 to December 20, Chen Yunlin, the new ARATS president, and Chiang Pin-kung, the new chairman of SEF, conducted six consecutive "Chen Chiang Meeting" and co-signed the "Cross-Strait Meeting Minutes on Chartered Airplane", "Cross-Strait Agreement on Mainland Residents Travelling to Taiwan", "Cross-Strait Air Transport Agreements", "Cross-Strait Maritime Transport Agreements", "Cross-Strait Postal Services Agreements", "Cross-Strait Food Safety Agreements", "Cross-Strait Financial Cooperation Agreement", "Cross-Strait Supplementary Agreement on Air Transport", "Cross-Strait Joint Anti-Crime and Judicial Mutual Assistance Agreement", "Cross-Strait Labor Cooperation Agreement on Fishing Vessel Crew Members", "Cross-Strait Cooperation Agreement on Quarantine and Inspection of Agricultural Products", "Cross-Strait Cooperation Agreement on Standard Metrological Verification Certification", "Cross-Strait Economic Cooperation Framework Agreement" (ECFA), "Cross-Strait Intellectual Property Protection Cooperation Agreement", "Cross-Strait Agreement on Pharmaceutical and Health Cooperation", and so on. The signing of these cooperation agreements not only satisfactorily resolved the issue of the "Full Three Links" that the two sides of the strait have suspended for a long time, but also gradually brought the cross-Strait economic exchanges and cooperation into an institutionalized track, becoming more and more comprehensive and in-depth.

At present, the cross-Strait relations have seen gratifying new developments. Both sides properly handle a series of issues, maintain the momentum of improvement and development of cross-Strait relations and promote the prospects for the peaceful development of cross-Strait relations. There have emerged unprecedented frequent contacts, close economic ties, thriving cultural exchanges, and vast common interests between the compatriots on both sides of the Strait. The Chinese people have increasingly won the understanding and support of the international community in safeguarding the peace across the Taiwan Strait, promoting the development of cross-Strait relations and realizing the peaceful reunification of the motherland. The majority countries in the world have generally recognized the continuous consolidation and development of the "one China" pattern. After experiencing a certain "freezing period", the relations between the two sides of the strait have ushered in a "new spring" after the snow melt.

At present, the peaceful development of cross-Strait relations has become the common will and the common goal of the compatriots on both sides of the Taiwan Strait. The peaceful development of cross-Strait relations is the prerequisite and foundation for the peaceful unification of the two sides of the Taiwan Strait and the preparation and accumulation for the cross-Strait peaceful reunification. Although the peaceful development of cross-Strait relations still faces numerous hindrance and obstacles, it will inevitably undergo twists and turns in the future. However, we firmly believe in the peaceful development of cross-Strait relations, and we will never falter. The future of the peaceful development of cross-Strait relations lies in the hands of compatriots on both sides of the Taiwan Strait. The bright future of the great rejuvenation of the Chinese nation belongs to all the Chinese people, including the compatriots in Taiwan. We believe that compatriots on both sides of the Taiwan Straits have enough wisdom and ability to jointly create a new situation of peaceful development of cross-Strait relations and jointly welcome the prosperous future of the Chinese nation.

CHAPTER THIRTEEN

Peaceful Foreign Diplomacy with Chinese Characteristics

Section I

The Development and changes in the international situation in the new period of Reform and Opening-up and basic characteristics of the international situation

First, peace and development remain to be the two main themes of the times

The so-called era refers to a historical development process and a historical development stage of a social form gradually forming, maturing and starting to decline and change to a new social form. The theme of the times refers to the major issues that need to be resolved in the process of world history under certain historical conditions and is determined by the major contradictions in the world and reflects the basic characteristics of the world situation. It is also a big issue which has a global impact and strategic significance for the development of the world situation. The themes of the times are generally transformed along with the development and changes in the world's major contradictions and the international situation. In the 20th century, two major changes took place in the theme of the times: in the first half of the 20th century, the theme of the times in the development of world history was "War and Revolution"; In the second half of the 20th century, especially since the 1970s, the theme of the times in the development of the world's history was gradually replaced by "Peace and Development".

After the late 1970s, Deng Xiaoping gained a profound insight into the new changes in the current world situation. He seized the major contradictions in the contemporary world from the numerous and complicated contradictions existing in the contemporary international community and made the remark that "peace and development are the two outstanding issues in the world today" and great issues confronting the world today, issues of global strategic significance"[1].

Which was a scientific thesis. The 13th CPC National Congress in 1987 confirmed the new thesis that peace and development are two major themes in the world today. This new judgment on the theme of the times of the contemporary world reflects not only the objective laws governing the development of the world history but also the common aspirations of the people in the world and fundamentally reversed the traditional mindset of "War and Revolution".

In the new period of reform and opening up, China's diplomacy has achieved two important adjustments and changes in its diplomatic ideology, diplomatic strategy and foreign policy. First, it has changed the estimate of inevitable world war and believed that it is possible to strive for a long-term general peace. To this end, it takes the maintenance of world peace and promoting common development as the fundamental purposes and basic guiding ideology of New China's diplomacy and has formulated a policy of opening to the outside world in all respects. The second step was to adjust and change the strategy of "One Line and A Vast Area"[2] and the decision not to ally with any big powers and not to support either party to oppose the other party thus China gave a new meaning and contents to its former "independence" policy. And China decided not to delineate and determine its relationships with other countries based on social systems and ideologies. Since then, the diplomacy of New China has been constantly maturing, and developed from "Friend-Enemy Diplomacy" to "All-round Diplomacy". Since the mid-1990s, China's diplomacy has not only broadened the scope and scale of its diplomacy, but also deepened the content and level of exchanges, creating a new situation in its foreign relations.

Peace and development have become the theme of the times in the contemporary world. They are the result of the concerted efforts of the development and changes of various contradictions in the world and the world's

1   Selected Works of Deng Xiaoping, 1st Edition, Vol.3, p.105.
2   In order to find a solution to the situation that China was caught in the power struggle between the two superpowers, Mao Zedong took a farsighted decision: to establish an anti-hegemony "united front" extending from China through the Middle East, Turkey, Iran, to Western Europe, which also included the Atlantic to Canada and the United States, and then through the Pacific to Japan, including Australia and New Zealand, and also included vast areas of Asian, African and Latin American countries along the line. This is known as the strategic diplomatic thought of "One Line and a Vast Area."

growing inhibition of the war. First, since the end of the Second World War, the new world wars have not taken place. The current world is in a long period of relative peace. Although local wars and regional conflicts continue, the local wars cannot change the general trend of the world which remains in a relatively peaceful situation. Second, although the danger of war exists, the growth of the peace force exceeds the growth of the war factors.

The world-wide Anti-Fascist War completely defeated the German, Italian and Japanese fascism, cleared the biggest obstacle in the democratization process of the world and greatly changed the contrast of international forces. The large number of socialist countries emerging after the war and the emerging independent nationalities in the country have created extremely favorable conditions for world peace and development. In the 20th century, humankind experienced the catastrophes of the two world wars and also experienced the hardships of confrontation between the two poles and the Cold War, paying a huge price. The anti-war sentiments of all peoples are on the rise, and they are longing for peace. Third, the rise of the new scientific and technological revolution has made the decisive role of the productive forces in the economic and social development of the world economy increasingly prominent. It has also promoted the world economy to develop in the direction of globalization. Economic globalization has made the issue of development a global issue. Fourth, evaluating from a worldwide perspective, the epoch of proletarian socialist revolution has not yet arrived. The proletarian revolutionary movement in the developed capitalist countries is at a low ebb. The world socialist movement is at a low ebb. The emphasis, themes and forms of relations between the capitalist and the socialist countries has taken a significant turn.

The contemporary world is undergoing major changes and adjustments, peace and development are still the two main themes of the times. the world needs peace, peoples of whole countries demand cooperation, countries demand development, societies demand reform and improvement, these have become an irresistible trend of the current times.

However, we must also point out that we should read even more profound implication from Deng Xiaoping's interpretation of the theme of the contemporary world era. Although he pointed out that "there is hope for peace", "world war can be put off and peace maintained for a longer time if the struggle against hegemonism is carried on effectively".[3]

However, Deng Xiaoping never talked about global peace and that war will not happen again. Instead, he is affirming that peace is the major trend of the world. While the new world war is likely to be avoided, there is also a clear understanding of the dangers of war. On different occasions, Deng

---

3 Selected Works of Deng Xiaoping, 2nd Edition, Vol.2, p.241.

Xiaoping repeatedly stressed: "Peace and development are the two major issues in the world, and neither one has been resolved"[4], at present, "generally speaking, the forces for world peace are growing, but the danger of war still exists"[5], "small wars will be unavoidable. The current wars between underdeveloped countries are actually what the developed countries need. Their policy of bullying backward countries has not changed"[6].

The western world and the United States in particular, "In by inciting unrest in many countries, they are actually playing power politics and seeking hegemony. They are trying to bring into their sphere of influence those countries that—up to today—heretofore they have not been able to control."[7] In his report to the 17th National Party Congress, Hu Jintao insisted on Deng Xiaoping's dialectical thinking on the theme of the times of the contemporary world. After affirming the overall stability in the international situation, he immediately and profoundly pointed out: "The world remains far from tranquil. Hegemonism and power politics still exist, local conflicts and hotspot issues keep emerging... All this poses difficulties and challenges to world peace and development."[8]

Since the end of the Cold War, the international situation has witnessed the most profound change since the Second World War ended. Hegemonism and power politics have also emerged in new forms in the world political arena. Utilizing so-called "human rights" and "universal values" and other issues to rampantly interfere in the internal affairs of other countries, expand military blocs, strengthen military alliances, push for power over socialist countries and developing countries in the Third World, make peaceful evolution and implement economic sanctions have become the dominant tactics of hegemony and power politics nowadays. As the only major socialist country in the contemporary world, China has become the main target of the peaceful evolution of the West. The task of opposing hegemonism and power politics is still arduous. We must also remain high vigilant and never allow it to be taken lightly.

---

4   Selected Works of Deng Xiaoping, 1st Edition, Vol.3, p.383.
5   Ibid., p.105.
6   Selected Works of Deng Xiaoping, 1st Edition, Vol.3, p.319.
7   Ibid., p.348.
8   CPCCC Party Literature Research Office: "Selection of Important Literature since the 17th National Congress" (Vol.I), p.36-37.

Second, the development trend of contemporary world politics and economics

1. The irreversible trend of multi-polarization

The multi-polarization of the world politics refers to a historical trend of development that develops towards a multi-polar pattern through the interaction of basic political forces such as countries and groups of countries that have an important influence on international relations in a certain period of time.

In the 1960s and 1970s, political multi-polarization broke through the two major systems controlled by the two superpowers—the United States and the Soviet Union at that time and first revealed the momentum of development, and the two superpowers of the United States and the Soviet Union tried their best to stop it but failed. The "Gaulleism" in Europe broke the domination of the United States in the capitalist world. The ideological trend of opposition to Soviet control in Eastern Europe, as well as the breakdown of Sino-Soviet relations and the breakdown of the relations between the Soviet Union and Afghanistan, ended the epoch of the unified socialist camp. Since then, the trend of political multi-polarization has become increasingly evident. Now that the bipolarity cold war situation has collapsed, it is even harder for the remaining superpower to stop the development of political multi-polarization.

The fundamental reason why the development trend of political multi-polarization is irreversible lies in the interaction and mutual influence of various forces in the world and in the mutual growth and decline of various forces. Specifically, the reason why the trend of political multi-polarization is irreversibly strengthened and accelerated is that the United States wants to establish a uni-polar world, but is powerless and that the big powers such as China and Russia resolutely oppose it, and the EU does not agree with it. The United States hegemonism has been opposed by the people of all countries in the world. The diversified combination of various forces in the world and the profound readjustments in the relations among major powers is conducive to the development of political multi-polarization. Science and technology and economic strength have become increasingly important factors that affect the development of international relations. In the rapid development of science and technology and economy, no force is ever able to occupy an absolute superiority in all aspects and control the world at its will. The process of economic globalization has greatly reduced the possibility of building a uni-polar world. The imbalance of economic development has led to changes in the political status and role of all countries. As China's overall national strength increases, and Russia is committed to revitalizing its economy and restoring its position as a big power, developing countries are developing themselves in adjustment, the EU as a whole has a growing influence in global affairs, Japan's economy is strong and Japan has the ambition of being both a major political power and a military power, these major world countries and major regional powers (countries) invariably advocate that the world should develop toward multi-polarization.

In this epoch the development of a multi-polar world pattern demonstrates a progressive demand and serves the common interest of all peoples. Multi-polarization will enable all forces in the world to gradually form a relationship of mutual support and mutual restraint and counterbalance so as to avoid the outbreak of a new world war and to contain hegemonism and power politics and promote the establishment of a just and reasonable international new political and economic order, which will be conducive to the good pursuit of peace, stability and prosperity of the peoples of all countries in the new world.

However, the formation of a multi-polar world pattern will be a long-term process. This is because: First, the US hegemonism and its attempt to construct a uni-polar world are the biggest obstacles to multi-polarization. Second, the continuation of the Cold War mentality in the world and the widening gap between the rich and the poor in the North and the South have all produced various disruptions and impacts on the multi-polarization trend. Third, the formation of a multi-polar pattern is a process of reorganization and redistribution of various forces in the world. As a result, there will be many uncertainties and the process of world multi-polarization will be full of contradictions and struggles.

In this long process of political multi-polarization in the contemporary world, the cooperation in competition and the competition in cooperation have become the main features. In the increasingly fierce competition for comprehensive national strength, scientific and technological forces and economic forces are at the center. The scientific and technological strength and economic strength of a country can become the fundamental condition for it to be one of the world's poles. Therefore, all countries give top priority to the development of science and technology and the development of economy. Whether the multi-polarization of the world pattern can become a reality depends on the rapid development of science and technology and economy at the major centers of powers in the world and on whether the technological and economic development in developing countries will take off so as to enhance their political and economic development driving force in the world.

2. Economic globalization that is developing in depth

Economic globalization refers to the breakthrough in national economic borders between countries. The economies of all countries are interdependent and interpenetrated. They are closely linked with each other in their economic sectors and various economic links, exercise different levels of cooperation and coordination and develop toward integration.

Since the end of the Second World War, the new scientific and technological revolution and its achievements have been rapidly transformed into direct productivity, which has greatly enhanced labor productivity, promoted the internationalization of all countries, boosted the development of world trade and increased the degree of economic interdependence among all countries, brought the world economy to the direction of globalization. These are mainly manifested in: the growth of international direct investment has brought about the internationalization of capital; brought about the internationalization of trade and made trade become the most active link in international exchanges and an indispensable part of the economic development of all countries; and the growth of the world's total import and export trade volume is at a much higher rate than that of production, which has become a basic feature of international economic relations; it has brought about internationalization of finance, with international financial transactions far exceeding world production and trade in commodities; and transnational corporations have increasingly become the dominant force in the world economy.

The development of economic globalization is conducive to the rational flow of factors of production both at global and regional levels, forming complementary advantages with each other, promoting the growth of global productivity, boosting the new round of global industrial restructuring and promoting the development of world economy. However, the negative impact of economic globalization cannot be ignored. The prominent weaknesses of the market economy and the acceleration of the globalization process have exposed all countries to different opportunities and challenges. For developing countries, economic globalization is both an opportunity and a challenge. Economic globalization will help them to obtain more funds, especially direct investment by multinational corporations, and speed up economic development and structural readjustment. It will help them make better use of their own advantages, open up international markets and develop foreign economy and trade. it will help them quick access to advanced technology and management experience, play the late-starting advantage, and achieve technological leaps. However, economic globalization has also had a negative impact. It has exacerbated the imbalances in the development of various countries and regions. In particular, it has widened the development gap between North and South and widened the gap between the rich and the poor. It has also made developing countries more vulnerable to external economic fluctuations and financial crises, and the problem is even worse when the developed countries intend to use globalization to intervene in developing countries.

Faced with the opportunities and challenges brought about by the economic globalization, the vast number of developing countries should, in accordance with its specific conditions, increase its ability to guard against and resist risks step by step while expanding its opening to the outside world. As the deepening economic globalization has deepened the interdependence and mutual influence of all countries in the world and spread the crisis around the world, the challenge of globalization requires global cooperation. All countries should strengthen their international cooperation whit a responsibility and risk-sharing spirit and jointly safeguard the steady development of the international economy so as to jointly promote the globalization toward a balanced, inclusive and win-win situation.

The current economic globalization has far exceeded the economic sphere and is now having an increasingly widespread impact on the international political, security, social and cultural fields. For example, economic globalization has led to the expansion of security connotations. Security has expanded from traditional security domains to non-traditional security domains. Terrorism, economic security, deteriorating environment, climate warming, epidemic spread, waves of immigration and cross-border crimes and other non-traditional security threats are increasing, and these threats are not solvable by any single country. Strengthening international security cooperation is extremely urgent. One typical example is that after the Sept.11 terrorist attacks in 2001, the U.S. President George W. Bush, who was seeking "unilateralism" immediately called for international cooperation in the fight against terrorism. As another example, the trend of economic globalization resulting in the deeper interdependence of international political and economic relations has been. The rules governing the world's political and economic development are no longer represented by the traditional "zero sum" but replaced by the "win-win" principle. This made compromises and cooperation, coexistence become the general trend of international relations. The ways of settling political conflicts and economic disputes have increasingly relied on diplomatic negotiations and the arbitration and involvement of international organizations.

Section II

The independent and peaceful foreign diplomatic policy

First, safeguarding world peace and promoting common development as the basic goals of China's diplomatic strategy and policy

In the new period of reform and opening up, the Communist Party of China and the Chinese government continue to adhere to the independent and peaceful diplomacy strategy and policy, unite with all peace-loving people in the world, strive to maintain lasting peace in the world, actively promote the common prosperity of all countries and make best efforts to seek justice in the international community and international affairs, strive for and create a peaceful international environment and favorable external conditions for the construction and development of socialism with Chinese characteristics, so that China's comprehensive strength has be continuously enhanced and its international status, image and influence continuously improved . The socialist nature, international status and vital interests of China all determine that the purpose of China's foreign policy is to safeguard world peace and promote common development, which is reflected in the basic objective of foreign policy but also in promoting peace and development, since the founding of new China, its foreign policy has undergone major adjustments in different historical periods, but the basic objective of this purpose and its embodiment, namely the foreign policy has remained unchanged.

The world needs peace, the country needs development, the society needs progress, the economy needs prosperity, and life needs to be enhanced. It is the common aspiration and fundamental interest of the people of all countries in the world. The first constitution after New China–The Constitution of the People's Republic of China in 1954 clearly stipulated: In international affairs, our unswerving policy is to fight for the lofty goal of world peace and human progress. Since the founding of New China, we have always adhered to this principle and made our own contribution to safeguarding world peace and the cause of progress in mankind.

In order to safeguard world peace, China has always opposed the arms race. China attaches importance to and supports international arms control, disarmament and non-proliferation and takes practical measures to strictly comply with relevant international obligations and works with the international community to abide by the purposes and principles of the "UN Charter", as well as other universally recognized norms governing international relations, and to safeguard the international strategic stability and promote the common security of all nations, on which basis to consolidate and strengthen the existing international arms control, disarmament and non-proliferation systems. China supports the early entry into force of the Comprehensive Nuclear Test Ban Treaty and will continue to abide by the "moratorium on tests" promise. China supports the preparatory work done by the Preparatory Committee of the Treaty Organization for the entry into force of the Treaty and actively participates in the construction of the international monitoring system. China strictly abides by its commitment of not to be the first to use nuclear weapons at any time and to its commitment of not to use or threat to use nuclear weapons on non-nuclear weapon states or regions under any circumstances, and calls on other nuclear-weapon states to make the same commitments and conclude relevant international legal instruments. China has signed all relevant protocols to the Treaty on Nuclear-Weapon-Free Zone that are open for signature and has already agreed with ASEAN on relevant issues of the Protocol to the Treaty on South-East Asia Nuclear-Weapon-Free Zone, China also welcomes the signing by the five Central Asian countries of the Treaty on the Nuclear-Weapon-Free Zone in Central Asia. China has conscientiously fulfilled all obligations under the Chemical Weapons Convention and established implementation agencies at all levels from the central government to the local authorities. China has joined all international treaties and international organizations in the field of non-proliferation. It attaches great importance to the role of the Treaty on the Non-proliferation of Nuclear Weapons (NPT), the Biological Weapons Convention (BWC) and the Chemical Weapons Convention (CWC) in preventing the proliferation of WMD. China supports the role played by the UN in the field of non-proliferation, and has conscientiously implemented the relevant resolutions of the UN Security Council. China attaches great importance to military transparency, and makes unremitting efforts to enhance military transparency and promote mutual trust with other countries in the military sphere. In 2007 China joined the UN Standardized Instrument for Reporting Military Expenditures, and reports annually to the UN the basic data of its military expenditures for the latest fiscal year.[9]

In order to safeguard world peace, China has always advocated the peaceful settlement of disputes between two sides through peaceful negotiations. They should not resort to or threaten to use force. They should not interfere in the internal affairs of any country on any pretext, let alone bullying, invading or subverting other countries. In response to the fact that some developed countries in the world do not respect the diversity of the world and attempt to transform the hegemonist acts of other countries from the political systems, economic development models and values of the developed western countries, Jiang Zemin pointed out: "Any country that bases

9   See Information Office of the State Council of the People's Republic of China: "China's National Defense in 2008", People's Daily, 2009/01/20.

itself on its mightiness and superstition to seek hegemony and promotes its expansion policy is doomed to failure. Making an excuse to infringe on the sovereignty of other countries and interfere in the internal affairs of other countries will eventually bring its own fruits. In spite of the objective reality of the colorful world in the contemporary world, attempts to impose one's own social system, development model and values on one's own are often threatened with isolation and sanctions. Such overbearing behavior can only be judged as a harmful way, and will also end in harming oneself. With unfair and irrational international economic order, it is unpopular for us to build our own development on the basis of poverty and backwardness in other countries. The attempt to swell the world affairs and dominate the fate of other peoples has become increasingly unreasonable."[10]

"Historical experience, especially nearly a century of historical experience, has repeatedly warned people that the consequences of imposing one's development mode to other countries will be grave and will always give rise to confrontation, turmoil and even wars. We should learn from this. The diversity of the world is an objective reality. We should face it and adapt to it. This requires that all countries respect each other, do not interfere in each other's internal affairs, treat each other as equals, seek common ground while shelving differences, coexist peacefully and develop cooperation. Only in this way will it be possible to maintain lasting peace and stability and create the necessary international environment for the common development of all nations."[11]

In order to safeguard world peace, China has actively advocated a new concept of security. Hu Jintao pointed out at the summit of the 60th anniversary of the United Nations: "We must abandon the Cold War mentality, cultivate a new security concept featuring trust, mutual benefit, equality and cooperation, and build a fair and effective collective security mechanism aimed at preventing war and conflict and safeguarding world peace and security."[12]

The new concept of security is based on mutual trust and opposes the expansion of military alliances and the intensification of the arms race to achieve their own safety. It advocates that all countries resolve disputes through consultation and dialogue. It emphasizes the principle of equality and mutual benefit and advocates that we should surmount the traditional thinking of "zero sum game" and achieve the win-win situation on the basis of mutual benefits; it advocates to promote cooperation for security. History

---

10   Selected Works of Jiang Zemin, Vol.1, p.478.
11   Ibid., p.331.
12   Hu Jintao: "Striving to Building a Harmonious World of Lasting Peace and Common Prosperity–Addressing the Summit Meeting Celebrating the 60th Anniversary of the United Nations", People's Daily, 2005/09/16.

has proved that force cannot conclude peace, power cannot ensure security, only through sincere and effective cooperation can we prevent conflicts and wars and safeguard common security.

In order to promote common development, China has actively promoted the reform of the unreasonable old international economic order and established a just and reasonable new international economic order. In the meantime, China is committed to its own reform, opening up and modernization drive. It also vigorously promotes "South-South cooperation", promotes "North-South dialogue", and creates a favorable environment for the world's prosperity. The third world countries are populous, rich in resources and vast in market. The development of "South-South cooperation" not only has great potential but also helps to enhance the overall strength of developing countries. As the largest developing country, China has been actively promoting "South-South cooperation". In the process of promoting "South-South cooperation", China respects the independence and sovereignty of developing countries, supports and promotes the solidarity and cooperation among developing countries. It emphasizes on unity and common interests and taking a restrained attitude and solving the problems and divergences among developing countries through peace talks. In the February 1982 consultation on "South-South cooperation" in New Delhi, China proposed the following five principles for "South-South cooperation": "South-South cooperation" should unswervingly move towards developing an independent national economy and strengthening collective self-reliance, and follow the principle of equality and mutual benefit and mutual care; the general plan of "South-South cooperation" should take into account the different interests and demands of developing countries so as to benefit all parties participating in the cooperation; and the cooperation projects should be based on the actual situation and should be realistic, pragmatic, give full play to their respective economic advantages and jointly improve their capability for self-reliance. Interregional and global economic cooperation should mutually reinforce and complement each other; "South-South cooperation" should help promote and develop the unity of the developing countries so as to enhance the negotiation status with the developed countries and promote the establishment of a new international economic order. The deepening of "South-South cooperation" has increased the overall strength of developing countries and brought them increasing influence and role in international affairs. Since the 21st century, China has used all kinds of opportunities and platforms to advance "South-South cooperation" and promote "North-South dialogue". In July 2008, Hu Jintao took the opportunity of the dialogue meeting between leaders of the Group of Eight and developing countries to further elaborate the Chinese government's proposal of strengthening "South-South cooperation" and promoting "North-South dialogue": The "South-South cooperation" is a way for developing countries to complement each other's strengths, and an important way to achieve common development. We should play an exemplary role in making a positive contribution to the promotion of "South-South cooperation". On the one hand, we should jointly promote the democratization of multilateralism and international relations, enhance the participation and decision-making power of developing countries in international affairs and strive for a favorable external environment for the development of developing countries. On the other hand, we should actively promote the reform of the international economic, financial, trade and development systems, safeguard the legitimate rights and interests of developing countries, enhance the ability of developing countries to deal with various risks and challenges, and promote a balanced, coordinated and sustainable development of the world economy. Take a long-term perspective, promote "North-South dialogue". Under the conditions of deepening economic globalization, all countries in the world have the connected interests and common destiny. If the developing countries lag behind, the world economy will not achieve lasting development. Only by working together can the developed countries and developing countries effectively solve global problems. We should continue to adhere to the principle of seeking truth from facts and seeking common grounds while reserving differences, and promote the establishment of a new type of partnership based on equality, mutual benefit, cooperation and win-win by both countries. We should strengthen consultation with the developed countries, push them to listen more to the voices of developing countries, make full use of the resources of the international community and increase their investment in promoting global development.[13]

Second, independence as the fundamental principle of China's foreign strategy and policy

Independence is the safeguarding of the sovereignty of the country and not giving in to any external pressure or interference in our domestic and foreign affairs and handling all our internal and external affairs independently and autonomously according to our own actual conditions and the development of the international situation.

The principle of independence and self-government are the basic principles of safeguarding national sovereignty, national security, national interests and national dignity. It is the crystallization of the Chinese people's historical experience of striving for national independence and the liberation of the people over the past century. It is also the summary of the historical experience in the international struggle since the founding of People's Republic of China, although many important strategic adjustments have

---

13　See Hu Jintao: "Addressing the Collective Meeting of Leaders of Five Developing Countries," People's Daily, 2008/07/09.

taken place in the diplomacy of New China during different historical periods, the principle of independence and autonomy is always unswerving. No matter how the international situation changes, China has never sacrificed its principle of independence. Deng Xiaoping emphasized in the opening speech of the 12th National Congress of the CPC: "Independence and self-reliance have always been and will always be their basic stand. While the Chinese people value their friendship and cooperation with other countries and other peoples, they value even more their hard-won independence and sovereign rights. No foreign country should expect China to be its vassal or to allow any act that will harm China's interests."[14]

Hu Jintao pointed out more clearly: In a populous developing socialist country like us, we must regard independence, soverignity, self-reliance as the fundamental starting point for our own development at any time. We must uphold the social system and development path chosen by the Chinese people at any time, always give top priority to the sovereignty and security of our country, resolutely safeguard interests of national sovereignty, security and development, insist on handling the affairs of China in accordance with the situation in China and rely on the Chinese people's own strength to manage these affairs, and resolutely oppose the interference of external forces in our domestic affairs. In all international affairs, we must proceed from the fundamental interests of the Chinese people and the common interests of all world peoples, determine our policies based on the merits of each other, and follow the principle of calm observation, sober response and mutual respect, and seek common grounds while reserving differences. Deal with any external pressure, and not succumb to any external interference.[15]

Since the 1980s, China has given new connotations and characteristics to the principle of independence and sovereignty, namely "genuine non-alignment", alliance with no major power, and no support for any opposition of one party to the other, which better safeguarded China's independence and sovereignty. After the end of the Cold War, China has established a strategic partnership with some major powers but it does not mean alliance but rather friendly cooperation. It does not aim at any third party, nor does it pose a threat to any country. Its purpose is to strengthen cooperation and exchanges among big powers, and promote our own development. This not only helps safeguard the independence and sovereignty of China, but also helps promote the just cause of world peace and development.

China's unswerving pursuit of an independent and sovereign foreign policy is determined by China's socialist nature and its position on the

14 Anthology of Deng Xiaoping, 1st edition, Vol.3, p.3.
15 CPCCC Party Literature Research Office: "Selection of Important Literature since the 17th National Congress" (Vol.I), p.805.

international stage. To adhere to an independent and autonomous foreign policy is to give top priority to state sovereignty and security, resolutely safeguard China's national interest, and oppose any country's detriment to China's independence, sovereignty, security, interests and dignity; that is, starting from the fundamental interests of the Chinese people and the people of the world, we must make decisions on our own positions and policies based on the merits of all international affairs and not give in to any external pressure; we should insist that the affairs of all countries be decided by the governments and peoples of various countries and that affairs in the world should be equally consulted between the government and people of all countries and oppose all forms of hegemonism and power politics. Instead of deciding on the similarities and differences between social systems and ideologies, we should adhere to the Five Principles of Peaceful Coexistence with all other countries to build and develop friendly relations; We should adhere not to ally with any major power or groups of major powers, not to engage in an arms race, not to participate in an arms race, not to carry out military expansion, and never seek hegemony.

In the ever-changing international situation, China upholds its independent and autonomous foreign policy, resolutely defends its independence, sovereignty, security, interests and dignity, strengthens the good-neighborly and friendly relations with neighboring countries, consolidates and develops solidarity and cooperation with the vast number of developing countries, improve and develop relations with the developed countries, take an active part in multilateral diplomatic activities, work hard to promote the establishment of a fair and rational new international political and economic order, and fight resolutely with various acts and schemes aimed at splitting and overthrowing the country, safeguard the integrity of the territory and sovereignty, promote the great cause of peaceful reunification of the country and thus further enhance the international status, image and influence of China.

Third, Five Principles of Peaceful Coexistence as the basic criteria in dealing with the relationships between countries

The Five Principles of Peaceful Coexistence are the basic principles for New China in handling all the national relations. China put forward the Five Principles of Peaceful Coexistence originally used to deal with the relations with the nationalist countries and then gradually recognized by the international community and become recognized as a universal principle of international relations.

The Five Principles of Peaceful Coexistence are the mutual respect for sovereignty and territorial integrity, mutual non-aggression, non-interference in each other's internal affairs, equality and mutual benefit and peaceful coexistence. The five principles are interrelated and are essentially against aggression and expansion and safeguarding the independence, sovereignty, safety, interests and dignity of the country. China is not only an advocate of the Five Principles of Peaceful Coexistence, but also a loyal defender and executor.

Based on the Five Principles of Peaceful Coexistence, China has developed friendly relations and cooperation with all other countries in the world and promoted peaceful coexistence and equal treatment among nations. China adheres to the principle of "Friendship and Partnership" with its neighbors and its friendly relations and cooperation with its neighboring countries and other Asian countries have continued to develop and their common interests have been constantly expanded. China has established various forms of cooperative relations with major powers, between whom the dialogue, exchanges and cooperation have been continuously strengthened. China constantly strengthens its cooperation with the vast number of developing countries and, under the framework of "South-South cooperation", tries its best to achieve complementary and common development.

In the late 1980s, when the old world pattern was transforming to the new one, Deng Xiaoping continued to emphasize the establishment of a new international economic and political order guided by the Five Principles of Peaceful Coexistence. In December 1988, when Deng Xiaoping met with the Indian Prime Minister, he said: "The general world situation is changing, and every country is thinking about appropriate new policies to establish a new international order. Hegemonism, bloc politics and treaty organizations no longer work. Then what principle should we apply to guide the new international relations? I have talked about this matter recently with some foreign leaders and friends. Two things have to be done at the same time. One is to establish a new international political order; the other is to establish a new international economic order. With regard to the latter, I spent a long time on the subject when I spoke at the United Nations General Assembly in 1974. We have been talking about it all along, and we shall go on talking about it. As for a new international political order, I think the Five Principles of Peaceful Coexistence, initiated by China and India, can withstand all tests."[16]

In October 1989, Deng Xiaoping said in talks with Prime Minister Chatichai Choonhavan of Thailand: "A new international economic order should be established, so as to settle the North-South question. A new international political order should also be established that would be in conformity with the new international economic order. I have especially recommended that the Five Principles of Peaceful Coexistence, which we Asians put forward in the 1950s, be made norms governing the future international political order."[17]

16   Selected Works of Deng Xiaoping, 1st edition, Vol.3, p.282-283.
17   Selected Works of Deng Xiaoping, 1st edition, Vol.3, p.328.

380

The Five Principles of Peaceful Coexistence are based on the principle of national sovereignty and go beyond the similarities and differences in ideology, social system and development path in handling the paradigm of international relations. To establish a new international political and economic order guided by the Five Principles of Peaceful Coexistence, we must respect each country's right to independently choose its own social system and development path according to its own national conditions. No country should impose its own social system, ideology and development model on other countries and can interfere in the internal affairs of other countries on any pretext. Although the in-depth development of economic globalization has brought the relations between countries in close contact with each other and the exchange and integration of various cultures reached unprecedented heights, at the same time, all countries were forced to pay more attention to the national characteristics of their culture. It is impossible for the world to be governed by a single culture. It is unrealistic, harmful and even dangerous for some countries to try to enclose the rich and colorful world in a single mode. As Jiang Zemin pointed out: "We have thousands of nations, more than 200 countries and regions on this earth. We live in different natural environments and have different social development experiences. We have formed a great variety of lifestyles, values, religious beliefs and cultural traditions. It is reasonable and deserves respect for peoples of all countries to choose effective social systems and modes of development that are in keeping with their actual conditions and to formulate effective laws and policies according to their national conditions... People of all countries know best the specific conditions of their own country and are most qualified to find a suitable development path for their own country. Therefore, the affairs of all countries should, in the final analysis, be governed by their own governments and people themselves and should not interfere with others."[18] Hu Jintao further stressed at the summit on the 60th anniversary of the United Nations: "We should respect the right of all countries to independently choose their own social systems and develop their paths of development. We should learn from each other instead of deliberately excluding each other rather than being one. We should encourage all countries to rejuvenate and develop according to their national conditions. Dialogue and exchanges among civilizations should be strengthened. Make concerted efforts to seek common development while reserving differences, work hard to eliminate mutual doubts and estrangements, make mankind more harmonious and make the world more colorful and rich. We should safeguard the diversity of civilizations in an equal and open spirit, promote the democratization of international relations and work together to build a civilized and inclusive world of harmony."[19]

---

18   Selected Works of Jiang Zemin, Vol.1, p.331.
19   CPCCC Party Literature Research Office: "Selection of Important Literature since the 16th National Congress" (Vol.II), p.997.

Fourth, following an opening-up strategy of mutual benefit and pursuing a win-win situation

Since the 3rd Plenary Session of the 11th CPC Central Committee, the opening up to the outside world has been a major strategy formulated by the CPC and the Chinese government in light of the development and changes in the international situation as well as the requirements of the Party and the country's central work. It is one of the basic national policy on building and developing socialism with Chinese characteristics. The future and destiny of contemporary China are increasingly closely linked with the future and destiny of the world. The development of China cannot be separated from the world and the development of the world needs China. "In today's world, no country can succeed in shutting its doors and doing construction. We have comprehensively analyzed and judged the external environment in which the trend toward multi-polarization in the world is strengthening and the development of economic globalization is deepening. We comprehensively grasp the opportunities and challenges brought about by the development and changes in the world today. We not only uphold independence and autonomy but also bravely participate in economic globalization." "We will continue to expand our opening to the outside world and closely integrate 'bringing in' and 'going out'. We will consciously study and draw lessons from all civilized achievements created by human society and adhere to the principle of seeking benefits and avoiding disadvantages so as to take part in international economic cooperation and competition under the conditions of economic globalization. Advantage and promote the development of economic globalization in a balanced, inclusive and win-win manner. Together, we should care for the earthly homeland on which mankind depends and promote the prosperity and progress of human civilization." "We should not only use the peaceful international environment to develop itself, but also maintain world peace through own development."[20]

Under the planned economy system of the traditional socialism that began before the new period of reform and opening up, China's foreign economic relations and cooperation were basically closed and stagnant. Although the 3rd Plenary Session of the 11th Central Committee of the Communist Party of China historically proposed the basic requirements of opening up to the outside world in 1978, the development of China's foreign economic exchange and cooperation in the first ten years of the new period of reform and opening up was actually rather slow. After Deng Xiaoping's South Talks in 1992, especially after the Party's 14th National Congress, China's foreign economic exchange and cooperation began to rapidly develop and was fully improved. The more than 30 years of practice of opening up to the

---

20   CPCCC Party Literature Research Office: "Selection of Important Literature since the 17th National Congress" (Vol.II), p.805.

outside world in the new period of reform and opening up has transformed China from a relatively closed economy into one of the most open developing economies. Its opening up to the outside world has gone through an early phase of pilot exploration, the phase of expansion of the opening in the 1990s, and the institutional opening phase after accession to WTO. Opening to the outside world has strongly promoted the process of industrialization in China, greatly enhanced the international competitiveness of the Chinese economy and its influence in the world economy. China has fused with the world economy in a wider area and at a deeper level. Practice has fully proved that opening to the outside world and making full use of both the international and domestic markets and resources are conducive to promoting China's economic and social development, promoting scientific and technological progress and innovation in China, improving China's international competitiveness and influence, and contributing to create a favorable international environment for the development of China, this is the only way to push forward China's socialist modernization.

With the deepening of economic globalization and the continuous improvement of the socialist market economic system in China, profound changes are taking place in the internal and external conditions China faces for its opening up. This not only provides a good opportunity for us to expand opening up to the outside world and promote a sound and rapid economic development, but also poses a severe challenge to our firm grasp of the initiative of China's economic development in the increasingly fierce international competition and the effective safeguarding of the country's economic security. Facing such a new situation, the report of the 17th National Congress of the CPC made a concrete plan for China to continue expanding the breadth and depth of its opening up to the outside world: adhere to the basic national policy of opening up, better combine "bringing in" with "going out" , expand the field of opening, optimize the opening structure, improve the quality of opening, and improve the open economic system featuring internal and external linkage, mutual benefits and win-win results, safety and efficiency, thus forming a new advantage of participating in international economic cooperation and competition under the condition of economic globalization. Deepen the opening up of the coastal areas, speed up the opening up of the interior areas, enhance the opening up along the borders, and mutually promote the opening up to the domestic and outside market. We will speed up the transformation of the pattern of growth of foreign trade, base ourselves on winning by quality, adjusting the structure of imports and exports, promoting the transformation and upgrading of the processing trade and vigorously developing the service trade. Make innovations in the use of foreign capital, optimize the structure of foreign capital utilization, and play the positive role of utilizing foreign capital to promote independent innovation, industrial upgrading and coordinated regional development. Innovate the ways of overseas investment and cooperation, support enterprises to carry out international operations in R & D, production and sales, and speed up the cultivation of multinationals and international famous brands in China. We will vigorously carry out mutually beneficial international cooperation in energy and resources. Implement the strategy of a free trade zone and strengthen bilateral and multilateral trade and economic cooperation. Adopt comprehensive measures to promote the basic international balance of payments and pay attention to preventing international economic risks.

The new strategy of opening up to the outside world formulated in the report of the 17th National Congress of the CPC has profound meaning and reflects the new characteristics and new trends of China's opening to the outside world: improving the quality of opening, strengthening internal and external linkage and paying attention to mutual benefit and win-win results. Internally, this new strategy of opening to the outside world is to make full use of international resources to support the transformation of the mode of development, achieve scientific development and guarantee the grand goal of building a well-off society in an all-round way. Internationally, it is to create a favorable international environment for peaceful development and safeguard China's peaceful rise.

384 Section III

Unswervingly follow the path of peaceful development and promote building a harmonious world

First, unswervingly follow the path of peaceful development

As a specific political concept, the path of peaceful development of China was proposed in recent years. Initially, the term "peaceful rise" was used. In December 2003, in his speech at the General Meeting commemorating the 110th anniversary of Mao Zedong, Hu Jintao pointed out that China must stick to the path of development with peaceful rise. Starting from April 2004, the official document of the Communist Party of China and the Chinese government began to use the expression "peaceful development". On August 22, 2004, Hu Jintao formally proposed to the General Meeting in commemoration of the 100th anniversary of Deng Xiaoping the important proposition of "adhering to the path of peaceful development". In March 2005, Premier Wen Jiabao for the first time comprehensively elaborated on the idea of "peaceful development" in his Report on the Work of the Government. On December 22, 2005, the State Council Information Office published a white paper entitled "China's Path of Peaceful Development". For the first time, it systematically addressed the issue of China's peaceful development in the form of government's announcement. In August 2006, at a conference on foreign affairs held by the Central Government, Hu Jintao listed "adhering to the path of peaceful development" in his speech as one of the six key tasks to be done in the future. In October the same year, the Decision of the CPC Central Committee on Several Major Issues concerning Building a Harmonious Socialist Society adopted by the 6th Plenary Session of the 16th CPC Central Committee for the first time made a explicit and clear statement of the path of peaceful development in the resolution document of the Party Central Committee. In October 2007, Hu Jintao set forth a separate section on the path of peaceful development in the report to the 17th National Congress of the Communist Party of China, which is of great practical and far-reaching historical significance for the development and layout of China's diplomacy. In September 2011, the State Council Information Office again promulgated the white paper entitled "China's Peaceful Development," responding to world concerns and elaborating on the chosen path of development for China. Answered in detail the issue of "what kind of development path has China chosen and what does China's development mean to the world", a world focused question. This is the second time after six years that the Chinese government once again published a white paper on the issue of "peaceful development".

To realize peaceful development is the sincere desire and unswerving pursuit of the Chinese people. Since the implementation of the basic national policy of reform and opening up in the late 1970s, China has successfully embarked on a path of peaceful development suited to its own national conditions and characteristics of the times. China's path of peaceful development is a brand-new way for mankind to pursue progress in civilization. It is the only way for China's modernization and a serious choice and solemn commitment of the Chinese government and the Chinese people. China unswervingly follows the path of peaceful development as an inevitable choice based on China's national conditions; it is an inevitable choice based on the tradition of Chinese history and culture; and an inevitable choice based on the development trend of the present world. Looking back on history, based on reality and looking forward to the future, China will unswervingly follow the path of peaceful development and strive to achieve scientific development, independent development, open development, peaceful development, cooperative development and common development.

At present, the international situation is undergoing complicated and profound changes. Peace and development remain the main themes of present era. The path of China's socialist modernization is a path of peaceful development. This path is to use the favorable opportunity of world peace to realize our own development and to better safeguard and promote world peace by our own development. It is, while actively participating in economic globalization and regional cooperation, to achieve development relying mainly on our own strength and on reform and innovation. It is to adhere to the principle of opening up to the outside world and actively develop cooperation with all countries in the world on the basis of equality and mutual benefit; It is to concentrate on the construction and wholeheartedly seek for development, and maintain the peaceful international environment and a good surrounding environment for long-term; It means, never to seek hegemony, always be a staunch force in safeguarding world peace and promoting common development.

As we adhere to the path of peaceful development, we must unswervingly hold high the banner of peace, development and cooperation, always follow the independent and autonomous foreign policy of peace, implement the opening-up strategy of mutual benefit and win-win results, safeguard national sovereignty, security and development interests and actively strive for a peaceful and stable international environment, a neighborhood with neighbourly and friendly relations, a cooperative environment of equality and mutual benefit, a safe environment of mutual trust and cooperation, and an objective and friendly public opinion environment. Adhere to the basic national policy of opening up to the outside world, improve the level of opening up to the outside world, actively develop economic and technological cooperation with foreign countries, vigorously carry out cultural exchanges with other countries, make better use of both domestic and international markets and resources, and pay more attention to strengthening mutually beneficial cooperation and common development. In accordance with the Five Principles of Peaceful Coexistence and other universally recognized norms governing international relations, we should develop friendly relations with all countries in the world and create a favorable external environment.

Peace, openness, cooperation, harmony and win-win are our ideas, our philosophy, our principles and our pursuit. To take the path of peaceful development is to unite China's domestic development with opening to the outside world, link China's development with the development of the world, combine the fundamental interests of the Chinese people with the common interests of the peoples of the world, and promote the peace and development of the world by our own development.

Peace is the foundation of development and development is the basis of peace. For a long time, the Chinese government and Chinese people have worked tirelessly for the peaceful international environment and have cherished the peaceful international environment which was won through struggle of the peace-loving and progress-seeking countries and people all over the world. "The Chinese nation is a peace-loving nation. China has always been a staunch force in safeguarding world peace. We insist on combining the interests of the Chinese people with the common interests of all peoples, upholding justice and doing justice. We insist that all countries, big or small, strong or weak, rich or poor are equal and respect the right of peoples to choose their own path of development. We will neither interfere in other countries' internal affairs nor impose our own will on others. China is committed to resolving international disputes and hot issues peacefully, promoting international and regional security cooperation and opposing all forms of terrorism. China pursues a defensive national defense policy, does not engage in an arms race and does not pose a militarythreat to any country. China opposes all forms of hegemonism and power politics. It will never engage in expansion.[21]

China's development is an important part of the development of the world. We persist in concentrating ourselves on construction and whole-heartedly seeking development. Through our own development, we continuously add positive factors to the development of human society and promote the development of the cause of human civilization and progress. Hu Jintao solemnly pointed out in the report to the 17th National Congress of the CPC: "We will continue to contribute to regional and global development through our own development, and expand the areas where our interests meet with those of various sides. While securing our own development, we will accommodate the legitimate concerns of other countries, especially other developing countries. We will increase market access in accordance with internationally recognized economic and trade rules, and protect the rights and interests of our partners in accordance with the law. We support international efforts to help developing countries enhance their capacity for independent development and improve the lives of their people, so as to narrow the North-South gap. We support efforts to improve international trade and financial systems, advance the liberalization and facilitation of trade and investment, and properly resolve economic and trade frictions through consultation and collaboration. China will never seek benefits for itself at the expense of other countries or shift its troubles onto others."[22]

Under the guidance of mutually beneficial win-win and open strategy, a more open and rapidly developing China is conducive to the common prosperity and stability of all countries in the world. First of all, China's opening up and development will make the world situation more stable and world peace more secure. Because today's China is a responsible world power in the international community, it is an active participant in the building of the international order and economic cooperation, it is a staunch force in safeguarding world peace and stability. Second, the sustained, rapid,

---

21   CPCCC Party Literature Research Office: "Selection of Important Literature since the 17th National Congress" (Vol.II), p.36-37.
22   Ibid., p.37.

coordinated and healthy development of China's economy will surely continue to bring more opportunities and greater space for cooperation to the international community. It will create more community of interests and communities of stakeholders so as to benefit the world economy and help to promote the common development of all countries. Finally, China's peaceful development will provide the international community with a brand-new development model. Instead of going through the traditional military expansion, struggle for hegemony or hegemony, China will, through peaceful means and gradual advance, make the best use of the situation, seek advantages and avoid disadvantages in its progress path closely linked with economic globalization. It not only applies the entire international community with all-round opening up, but also insists on independence and autonomy. It relies mainly on its own strength to expand domestic demand, tap potential and take the path of modernization to enrich the people and strengthen the state with Chinese characteristics. This will have great reference and inspiration significance to the international community.

In the meantime, the Chinese government and Chinese people are also soberly aware that China is still a developing country and still faces many difficulties and problems in its development. There is still a long way from China's modernization drive. It is in the fundamental interests of the Chinese people to take the path of peaceful development, which also meets the objective requirements of the development and progress of human society. China must take the path of peaceful development today and must stick to the path of peaceful development even it is strong in the future. The determination of the Chinese government and the Chinese people to follow the path of peaceful development is firm and unwavering. China has made it clear that its goal for the first two decades of the 21st century is to build a well-off society at a higher level in an all-round way that benefits the population of billions, which will make the economy more developed, the democracy more complete, the science and education more advanced, the culture more prosperous, the society more harmonious, and the people's life more affluent. By that time, China will definitely make greater contributions to the lofty cause of peace and development.

Second, the construction of a harmonious world of lasting peace and common prosperity

"Promoting the construction of a harmonious world of lasting peace and common prosperity" is a major diplomatic ideology and diplomatic strategy put forward by the Party Central Committee with Hu Jintao as its general secretary. In April 2005, at the Asian-African Summit in Jakarta, Hu Jintao put forward the proposal that Asian and African countries should promote friendly coexistence, equal dialogue, and development and prosperity among different civilizations and jointly build a harmonious world.

This is the first time that the concept of "harmonious world" appeared on the international stage. On July 1, more than two months later, when Hu Jintao visited Moscow. "Harmonious World" was written into the Sino-Russian Joint Statement on the International Order of the 21st Century. It was first time recognized as a consensus on the relations among nations, marking this new concept gradually entered the horizons of the international community. Chinese leaders are also gradually deepening their thinking on building a "Harmonious World". In September 2005, at the summit of the 60th anniversary of the United Nations, Hu Jintao delivered a speech entitled "Striving to Build a Harmonious World of Lasting Peace, Common Prosperity", in which he comprehensively expounded the profound connotation of "Harmonious World". The speech aroused a warm response from participants. The foreign media also paid high attention and make positive comments on the speech, they thought it was a message to the contemporary world that China is eager for peace, is willing to be a responsible great power and hopes to build a peaceful, prosperous and harmonious world with other countries. There is only one earth for human being and it is the common aspiration of all the peoples in the world and the lofty goal of China to follow the path of peace and development to build a harmonious world of lasting peace and common prosperity.

After the catastrophes of the two world wars, the people of all countries in the world doubly cherished peace and hoped to establish a harmonious and beautiful world, regardless of their nationality, race or color, equally and peacefully achieve international cooperation. However, the current international environment has both advantages and disadvantages for building a harmonious world. On the one hand, peace and development are still the theme of the times in the contemporary world. The overall situation in the world is moving towards relaxation. The world's forces for maintaining peace continue to grow. The factors that restrict the war not only still exist but will continue to grow. At the same time, with the rapid development of economic globalization and the world's scientific and technological progress, the interdependence and mutual needs of all countries have been deepened, the interests of China and other countries in the world have been closely linked and their common interest has been steadily growing. As a result, achieve common development through win-win and multi-win approaches become possible. The global economy needs global cooperation. On the other hand, hegemony impedes the democratization of international relations. Terrorism, the Cold War mentality and extreme thinking pose a grave threat to world peace and security. The widening gap between the rich and the poor has led to the imbalance of global development. The legacy of colonialism has sparked hot spots in the region and globalization has brought the world into a period of high incidence of contradictions. In the face of great revolution and adjustment of the world, what kind of view on world order is advocated by the Communist Party of China and the Chinese government? This is an important issue that has attracted worldwide attention. The report of the 17th National Congress of the Party made a distinct and profound answer to this question: "We maintain that the people of all countries should join hands and strive to build a harmonious world of lasting peace and common prosperity. To this end, all countries should uphold the purposes and principles of the United Nations Charter, observe international law and universally recognized norms of international relations, and promote democracy, harmony, collaboration and win-win solutions in international relations. Politically, all countries should respect each other and conduct consultations on an equal footing in a common endeavor to promote democracy in international relations. Economically, they should cooperate with each other, draw on each other's strengths and work together to advance economic globalization in the direction of balanced development, shared benefits and win-win progress. Culturally, they should learn from each other in the spirit of seeking common ground while shelving differences, respect the diversity of the world, and make joint efforts to advance human civilization. In the area of security, they should trust each other, strengthen cooperation, settle international disputes by peaceful means rather than by war, and work together to safeguard peace and stability in the world. On environmental issues, they should assist and cooperate with each other in conservation efforts to take good care of the Earth, the only home of human beings."[23]

This thesis accurately expresses the basic proposition of the CPC and the Chinese government on the reasonable trend of the contemporary world, profoundly expounds the concept of world order advocated by the CPC and the Chinese government, and shows the broad mind that the Chinese Communists and the Chinese government base on and fight for the fundamental interests of the Chinese people and the people around the world.

The new concept and new strategy of a harmonious world have seized the main theme of the development of the times and is the inheritance, development and innovation of the independent and peaceful foreign policy that China has long pursued. It has inherited and deepened the Five Principles of Peaceful Coexistence, developed the just and rational view of a new international order China has always advocated, and integrated the new concept of security based on mutual trust, mutual benefit, equality and cooperation advocated by China. It summed up the new development concept of mutual benefit, win-win and sustainable development proposed by China in recent years, and the new concept of civilization that respects diversity and mutual tolerance.

---

23   Ibid., p.36.

The harmonious world we advocate is a peaceful and stable world in which all nations trust and live in harmony with each other and jointly safeguard the peace and security of the world through fair and effective security mechanisms. The harmonious world we advocate is a democratic and just world in which sovereignty and sovereignty of all countries are equal and international relations are based on the rule of law and multilateralism and the affairs of the world are settled through consultations among all nations. The harmonious world we advocate is a mutually beneficial and cooperative world, in which the economic globalization and progress in science and technology are conducive to the common development of the international community, especially to the developing countries. The harmonious world we advocate is an open and inclusive world, in which different civilizations conduct dialogues with each other, learn from each other, different social systems and development models learn from each other and seek common development.

The way to achieve a harmonious world means that all countries in the world are on the path of peaceful development. Without peace, a harmonious world cannot be established. To keep peace requires that all countries in the world take the path of peaceful development. There will be no world peace when only a part of the countries follow the path of peaceful development. As a practitioner of building a harmonious world and following the path of peaceful development, China upholds the banner of "peace, development and cooperation". It emphasizes developing friendly cooperation with all countries on the basis of the Five Principles of Peaceful Coexistence, which means that China will pursue a policy of no hostile country. In other words, China does not set any country as its enemy. All countries in the world can become friends of China. China is also willing to make friends with all the countries in the world. In developing relations with big powers, China places greater emphasis on the development of various "partnership" and "cooperative relations"; China has formulated the policy of "bringing harmony, security, prosperity and strength to neighbors" in advancing the relations with neighboring countries, adhere to the principle of "Friendship and Partnership". In addition, China's diplomacy has further diluted the ideological colors and emphasized the friendly cooperation between countries with different ideologies. This proves that in the diplomatic concept of China, the common interest in peace and development of all countries in the world goes beyond ideological interests. China attaches importance to common development and common prosperity and pursues an open strategy of mutual benefit and win-win. It emphasizes the democratization of international relations and promote democracy, harmony, cooperation and win-win spirit. It upholds the new concept of security based on mutual trust, mutual benefit, equality and coordination. It consolidates the cultural exchanges among various countries, draws on each other's cultural accomplishments and seeks common ground while shelving differences with other countries in the world. It strengthens cooperation with other countries in the world on environmental issues and attaches importance to assuming corresponding responsibilities in international affairs.

Building a harmonious world of lasting peace and common prosperity cannot be achieved without the joint efforts of all mankind and long-term struggle, which is by no means an overnight event. In the important historic period in which both opportunities and challenges coexist, what kind of appearance the world will ultimately assume is both objective and necessary and also inseparable from our expectations and efforts toward the expected direction. In September 2009, Hu Jintao emphasized at the 64th UN General Assembly that in the face of unprecedented opportunities and challenges, the international community should continue to work hand in hand to maintain the concept of peace, development, cooperation, win-win results and tolerance and promote the building of a harmonious world with lasting peace and common prosperity and make unremitting efforts for the lofty cause of mankind's peace and development. Hu Jintao put forward four propositions in this regard: First, examine security with a broader perspective and safeguard world peace and stability. Second, take a more holistic view of development and promote common prosperity. Without the universal development and equal participation of developing countries, there can be no common prosperity of the world and a more just and reasonable international economic order cannot be established. Third, carry out cooperation with a more open mind and promote mutual benefit and win-win results. Fourth, contain each other with a broader mind and achieve harmonious coexistence.

The harmonious world of lasting peace and common prosperity is the common aspiration of all peoples around the world, and promoting the construction of such a world is in the fundamental interest of all mankind. To establish such a goal and work towards it is to demonstrate the expectations and pursuit of the Chinese Communists and Chinese people towards the development of the world and to show the value orientation we take in various actions. The proposal of the CPC and the Chinese government on building a harmonious world seeks to arouse countries and peoples with similar ideals to form a just force for the pursuit of peace, development and cooperation so as to guide the correct course of the world. No matter how far and how hard the ultimate realization of a harmonious world is, some people have to advocate and attract everyone to make unremitting efforts. We believe that as long as all the countries in the world closely unite to seize the opportunities and meet the challenges, we will be able to create a bright future for the development of human society and can truly build a harmonious world of lasting peace and common prosperity.

CHAPTER FOURTEEN

The Concept and Practice of the Core of Leadership of Socialism with Chinese Characteristics

Section I

The strengthening and improvement of the Party's leadership

First, the leadership of the CPC is the choice of history and people

The core position of the leadership of the CPC has been formed in the long-term revolutionary struggle and is the inevitable result of the development of the Chinese modern history and the long-term choice of the Chinese people.

After 1840, due to the invasion by the Western powers, China gradually became a semi-colonial and semi-feudal society and the national crisis and the social crisis deepened all the way. In order to get rid of the double oppression of imperialism and feudalism, the Chinese people conducted an indomitable struggle, but all failed. China is looking forward to new social forces and new ideological theories so as to open up a new path to save the country and people. In 1921, in the process of integrating Marxism-Leninism with the Chinese workers' movement, the Communist Party of China came into being. Since then, the great mission of leading the revolutionary struggle against imperialism and feudalism, winning national independence and liberating the people, and rejuvenating China has historically fallen upon the shoulders of the Communist Party of China. The Chinese revolution entered a completely new stage of development.

After the founding of the Communist Party of China, it persisted in combining the basic principles of Marxism with the concrete reality of the Chinese revolution and led the Chinese people in winning the democratic revolution and establishing the People's Republic of China. After the founding of New China, the Communist Party of China became the leading core of China and the cause of socialism. Deng Xiaoping pointed out: "China always used to be described as 'a heap of loose sand'. But when our Party came to power and rallied the whole country around it, the disunity resulting from the partitioning of the country by various forces was brought to an end. So long as the Party exercises correct leadership, it can rally not only its whole membership but also the whole nation to accomplish any mighty undertaking."[1]

In fact, the Communist Party of China has led the Chinese people to establish a socialist system and to realize the most extensive and profound social change in Chinese history. It has also initiated the cause of building socialism with Chinese characteristics and opened the correct path for the great rejuvenation of the Chinese nation. It established the people's democratic dictatorship in the state power and the Chinese people take charge of their own destiny; It established an independent and relatively complete system of national economy, which markedly enhanced the economic strength and overall national strength; It developed the socialist culture and enriched the spiritual life of the people throughout the country; it completely ended the situation of a heap of loose sand in old China, achieved a high degree of unification of the country and unprecedented unification of all ethnic groups; It forged a people's army under the absolute leadership of the Party and established a fortified national defense; It insisted on an independent and autonomous foreign policy of peace and made an important contribution to the peace and development of the world. The socialist country of China enjoys increasing international status and international influence. Without the communist party, there will be no new China; with the communist party, the situation of China is completely renewed. This is the most basic and important conclusion drawn by the Chinese people in the course of long-term struggle.

In the new phase of the new century, if China is to realize the prosperity and strength of the country and the common prosperity of the people, it also must rely on the leadership of the Communist Party of China. Because in China only the Communist Party of China is the political forces who can unite and lead the people of all ethnic groups across the country to achieve the great rejuvenation the Chinese nation.

First of all, to ensure the correct direction of China's modernization drive requires the leadership of the Communist Party of China. To achieve modernization and national rejuvenation is a century-long pursuit and dream of the Chinese people. History proves that only by taking the path of socialism can China realize its modernization. Therefore, to ensure the correct

---

1   Selected Works of Deng Xiaoping, 2nd Edition, Vol.2, p.267.

direction of China's modernization, we must adhere to the leadership of the Communist Party. Only by adhering to the leadership of the Communist Party of China and following the path of socialism with Chinese characteristics can we formulate and implement the correct guidelines and policies and ensure that the cause of modernization will continue to make progress and eventually realize the great rejuvenation of the Chinese nation.

Second, safeguarding national reunification and social harmony and stability requires the leadership of the Communist Party of China. The unification of the country and the social harmony and stability are the necessary prerequisites for the prosperity and strength of the country and for the people to live and work in peace and contentment. The warlordism, disintegration and political turmoil brought disaster after disaster to contemporary China. It is engraved in the bones and printed on the heart of the Chinese people. Under the leadership of the Communist Party of China, the New China has completely ended the history of national disunity and the political turmoil, and has formed a brand-new situation in which the reunification of the country and the unity of the people of all ethnic groups across the country have been achieved. In the new phase of the new century, by virtue of its rich ruling experience and ability to control the overall situation, only the Communist Party of China can make overall plans for the economic and social development and maintain the unity of the country and the social harmony and stability.

Once again, taking overall control of the entire situation, coordinating all parties, pooling the wisdom of people and bringing together forces all call for the leadership of the Communist Party of China. With its vast territory and large population, China has unbalanced development and great differences between urban and rural areas and between regions, and faces various complicated social conflicts. Only by properly adjusting and coordinating the relations of interest in all aspects can we mobilize all positive factors to the maximum extent, concentrate all resources, strength and wisdom on major issues concerning the national economy and the people's livelihood so as to ensure the sustainable economic and social development. In China, to smoothly resolve all kinds of difficulties and problems in its progress, to effectively handle various complicated social conflicts, to unify and unite the thoughts and forces of over a billion people, and to build a beautiful future are inconceivable without the leadership of the Communist Party of China.

Finally, coping with the complicated international environment requires the leadership of the Communist Party of China. In today's world, economic globalization and world multi-polarization are developing with twists and turns. Science and technology are changing with each passing day. Competition in overall national strength is becoming increasingly fierce.

Confrontation and cooperation, hegemony, nationalism and terrorism are all intertwined. In a complicated international environment, if China is to take an independent and peaceful path of development, it must have a strong political core to unite the people of all ethnic groups across the country. In China, only the Communist Party of China is qualified and capable of serving as the political core.

The key of Chinese issue is the Party, the leadership of the Communist Party of China is the fundamental guarantee for the success of modernization and the reform and opening up. It is the fundamental guarantee for uniting the people of all nationalities across the country and rejuvenating the Chinese nation. By their individual experiences, the Chinese people have deeply recognized this point and resolutely support the leadership of the Communist Party of China.

Second, the nature and the goal of the CPC

The Communist Party of China is the vanguard of the Chinese working class. At the same time it is the vanguard of the Chinese people and the Chinese nation. It is the leading core of the cause of socialism with Chinese characteristics. It represents the development requirements of China's advanced productive forces, represents the way forward for China's advanced culture and represents the most fundamental interests of the broad masses of people.

The leadership of the Communist Party of China in contemporary China is closely linked with its nature and purpose.

1. The Communist Party of China is the vanguard of the Chinese working class

Political parties have nature of class. Any political party represents the interests of a certain class and has the class basis on which they exist and develop. Since its founding, the Communist Party of China has been political party of the Chinese working class and has always adhered to the nature of the vanguard of the working class.

First of all, the Communist Party of China is the product of the combination of Marxism-Leninism and the Chinese workers' movement, and the working class is the class basis of the Communist Party of China. The Chinese working class is the product of the mechanized big industry in modern times, the undertaker of mass production, the representative of advanced productive forces and relations of production, and has the outstanding characters of selflessness, strict organizational discipline, and being resolute and thorough in revolution. The Communist Party of China is a concentrated crystallization of the characteristics and excellent qualities of the working class in China.

Second, the Communist Party of China is made up of the advanced elements of the working class. the Party has gathered the advanced elements in the working class with communist consciousness. They are infinitely loyal to the cause of communism and have the spirit of devoting their lives to the fundamental interests of the working class and the people of all nationalities. In the meantime, the Party also recruited people with other class backgrounds who meet the conditions for joining the Party to join the Party organization. In the process of building socialism with Chinese characteristics, we admit outstanding individuals from other strata (including from new emerging strata) who believe in communism, and accept and practice the Party's program and constitution, consciously strive for the Party's line and program, go through long tests, and conform to the conditions of Party members into the Party so as to continuously enhance the Party's class basis, expand the mass base of the Party and continuously raise the Party's influence and cohesion in the whole society, these are the requirement of the times. This will not change the nature of the vanguard of the working class of the Party. Judging the nature of a political party depends mainly on the interests of which class its theory and program represent. The theory and program of the Communist Party of China represent the interests of the working class and represent the fundamental interests of the overwhelming majority of the people.

Finally, taking the Marxism as our theoretical basis and guiding action, the Communist Party of China holds a scientific world outlook and methodology and can grasp the law of historical development on the whole and represents the correct direction for the development of Chinese society. The Party attaches great importance to ideologically building the Party and insist on educating and arming all party members with Marxist theories. It not only requires that party members organizationally join the Party, but also requires party members to ideologically join the Party at first and guide them to fight for the Party's program and tasks.

2. The Communist Party of China is also the vanguard of the Chinese people and the Chinese nation

The CPC has always represented the long-term interests and fundamental interests of the Chinese people and the Chinese nation. In keeping with China's reality and the wishes of the Chinese people, as the core of the Chinese people and the Chinese nation, the CPC has brought together the forces of the entire nation and society to a high degree to strive for the common ideals and goals of our country and benefit our motherland and our people.

As a political party of the Chinese working class, the reason why the Communist Party of China is both the vanguard of the Chinese people and the Chinese nation lies in the fact that:

First, the fundamental interests of the Chinese working class are in line with the fundamental interests of the Chinese people and the Chinese nation. Marxism believes that only by liberating all mankind can the working class ultimately liberate itself. The interests of the Chinese working class have always been closely linked with the fundamental interests of the Chinese people and the Chinese nation. Its historical destiny is also closely linked with the historical fate of the whole Chinese people and the entire Chinese nation. In order to accomplish the historic mission of the working class means that the Communist Party have to struggle for the benefit of the working class and at the same time strive for the benefit of all the people and the entire nation. Since its entry into the historical arena, the Communist Party of China has both the dual mission of eliminating class oppression and realizing national independence. The Wayaobao meeting held in 1935 pointed out that the Communist Party of China is the vanguard of the Chinese proletariat and the vanguard of the entire nation. Over the past 90 years since the founding of the Party, no matter in leading the revolutionary cause of anti-imperialism and anti-feudalism, striving for national independence and the liberation of the people, or in leading the cause of socialist modernization after assuming power, the Party was all aimed at realizing the prosperity of the country and the common prosperity of the people. Undoubtedly, this will accord with and represent the interests of the Chinese working class as well as the long-term interests and fundamental interests of the Chinese people and the Chinese nation.

Second, achieving to become the vanguard of the Chinese people and the Chinese nation, is an inherent requirement of the Communist Party of China to perform its ruling mission. It is also the political requirement for leading the people and the nation as the ruling party. The essence of the communist party's ruling is to use the power entrusted by the people to serve the people and to effectively safeguard, achieve and develop the fundamental interests of the overwhelming majority of the people. History and reality show that the interests of the overwhelming majority are the most crucial and the most decisive factor. As a ruling party, it will risk losing its qualification of ruling if it does not stand in the position of the vanguard of the Chinese nation to consciously care for the interests of the overwhelming majority and take care of the overall interest of the country and nation according to the will of the overwhelming majority. The Communist Party of China in the ruling position has always had a problem of strengthening the mass base. One of the important reasons why some veteran ruling parties in the world have lost their ruling position is that this problem has not been solved. The Communist Party of China fulfills its ruling mission in the capacity of the faithful representative of the entire people and the entire nation. With the deepening of reform and opening up, new changes have taken place in the structure of social strata in our country and new social strata have emerged.

the Party must take the initiative to stand on the position of the vanguard of the Chinese people and the Chinese nation. While continuing to rely on the working class and strengthening the alliance between workers and peasants, the Party should conscientiously treat the new social classes as an important part of the social mass base of its ruling and attaches importance to them. Only in this way can the Party's social mass base of ruling expand and consolidate day by day.

Third, becoming the vanguard of the Chinese people and the Chinese nation is also an inevitable choice for the Party while it takes the national rejuvenation as its own responsibility. As conscientious and resolute patriots, the Chinese Communists have always taken the realization of the great rejuvenation of the Chinese nation as their noble historic responsibility. To realize the great rejuvenation of the Chinese nation in accordance with the Party's struggle program is to gradually build China into a prosperous, democratic and civilized socialist modern country. To shoulder the lofty responsibility of accomplishing this great cause of history, the Chinese Communists must take the stance of the vanguard of the Chinese people and the Chinese nation and always adhere to the principle of combining Marxism with China's concrete reality and in the process of working hard to realize the localization of Marxism in China, we must constantly open up new ideas and new realms for rejuvenating the nation. We must carry forward the outstanding cultural traditions of the Chinese nation with great ambition and bread vision, and at the same time, make active use of and draw on the achievements of all advanced civilizations in the world today. We must unite the forces of the entire nation to maximize the mobilization and development of all positive factors and unite all the positive social forces that are interested in strengthening China and mobilize all the positive social factors conducive to promote the great cause of rejuvenating the Chinese nation; we must actively admit outstanding individuals from all walks of life of the entire nation, into the Party so that we can truly become the "backbone" of the rejuvenation cause of the Chinese nation. The more consciously the Communist Party of China becomes the vanguard of the Chinese people and the Chinese nation, the greater contribution it can make for national rejuvenation.

The "Two Vanguards" is an organic unity. On the one hand, always becoming the vanguard of the working class in China is the political premise that the Party truly becomes the vanguard of the Chinese people and the Chinese nation. Only by becoming the vanguard of the Chinese working class and by consciously fulfilling the fundamental guiding ideology of Marxism and taking communism as the ultimate goal can the Party truly have the scientific guidance, political foresight and board vision necessary to be the vanguard of the Chinese people and the Chinese nation. On the other hand, consciously becoming the vanguard of the Chinese people and the Chinese nation is the inevitable requirement of the Party, who is the vanguard of the working class in China. Only by consistently representing the interest of the entire people and the entire nation can the Party fully reflect its nature of the vanguard of the working class. Since the reform and opening up, while admitting the Party members among workers and peasants, the Party also paid attention to absorb the outstanding elements from all walks of life. To uphold that the Party is the vanguard of the Chinese working class and the vanguard of the Chinese people and the Chinese nation will continuously enhance the Party's class foundation, expand the Party's mass base, improve the Party's influence and cohesion in the whole society, and fulfill the solemn mission the times bestows the Party.

3. The purpose of the Communist Party of China is to serve the people wholeheartedly

Serving the people wholeheartedly is the purpose of the Communist Party of China and one of the distinctive hallmarks of the CPC from the other political parties. Mao Zedong pointed out: "Our point of departure is to serve the people wholeheartedly and never for a moment divorce ourselves from the masses, to proceed in all cases from the interests of the people and not from one's self-interest or from the interests of a small group, and to identify our responsibility to the people with our responsibility to the leading organs of the Party."[2]

Deng Xiaoping has repeatedly stressed that the Communist Party must take wholeheartedly serving the people as its criterion. He proposed that all our work should be based on the criteria of the support, approval, liking and consent of the people. This is both the guiding ideology for the Party in formulating guidelines and policies and the best explanation for the purpose of serving the people wholeheartedly.

First of all, the nature of the Communist Party of China determines that its purpose is to serve the people wholeheartedly. The Communist Party is the vanguard of the working class. Only by completely liberating all mankind can the working class ultimately liberate itself. Therefore, the working class party is a party that completely takes up the standpoint of the vast majority of working people and serves the interests of the masses. The Communist Party of China represents the interests of the Chinese working class and at the same time represents the interests of the Chinese people and the Chinese nation. Aside from the interests of the working class and the broad masses of the people, the CPC has no special interests of its own.

---

2   Selected Works of Mao Zedong, 2nd Edition, Vol.3, pp.1094-1095.

Second, upholding the purpose of serving the people wholeheartedly is the fundamental requirement of upholding the historical materialism of Marxism. The historical materialism holds that the masses of people are the creators of history, the creators of the material and spiritual wealth of the society, the driving force and the ultimate deciding force for the development of history. It shows that whoever can conform to the requirements of the masses in creating social history, they can lead the people to victory, otherwise they can only be discarded by history. Only by relying on the broad masses of the people can the Party realize its historic mission. Only by relying on the masses of the people can the Party have strength. Only by serving the people can the Party have its internal reason of existence.

Thirdly, serving the people wholeheartedly is the fundamental guarantee for the Party to succeed in socialist revolution and construction. On the one hand, since the founding of the Communist Party of China, it has regarded serving the people as its highest principle. The history of the struggle of the Communist Party of China is the history of serving the people wholeheartedly. Leading the new-democratic revolution, winning national independence and liberating the people, or leading the construction of socialism with Chinese characteristics, and realizing the prosperity of the country and the affluence of the people all are aimed at realizing the common interests of the people of all ethnic groups across the country. Serving the people wholeheartedly is the essential feature of the Communist Party of China. On the other hand, just because the Party starts from the interests of the people and serves the people wholeheartedly, it wins the support of the broad masses of the people, defeats the hardships and dangers on the road of advance, and wins one victory after another in revolution and construction. The fundamental reason why the Party has strength is that the Party can faithfully represent the interests of the people and the masses. This is the decisive factor that the Party will always be invincible.

4. Adhering to and improvement of party leadership

Jiang Zemin pointed out: The key to handle China's affairs well is our Party. This on the one hand means that building socialism with Chinese characteristics cannot succeed without Party leadership and must uphold the leadership of the Party. Furthermore, we must insist on the Party's core leadership position in the cause of building socialism with Chinese characteristics, adhere to the Party's political leadership over the policies and overall work of the state, uphold the Party's absolute leadership over the army, stick to the principle of Party supervising its cadres and uphold the Party's leading role in ideology, etc. On the other hand, what is even more important is that we must strengthen party building and improve leadership of the Party, to which the key is to constantly strive to solve the new situations and new problems encountered in Party building in light of the development of the situation and tasks. What kind of Party should be built and how to build the Party are the basic issues for strengthening and promoting Party building under the new historical conditions.

It is a dialectical unity to uphold the Party's leadership and improve the Party's leadership. If insisting the Party's leadership should solve the issue of whether or not the socialist cause needs the leadership of the Party and the Party's position and role in the cause of socialism, then improving the Party's leadership needs to solve the problems of further reforming and improving the Party's leading methods and ways of governing and better realizing the Party's leadership over the cause of socialist construction. If we do not adhere to the leadership of the Party, we will not be able to improve the Party's leadership. To improve the Party's leadership is to better adhere to the Party's leadership. Under the new historical conditions, only by improving the leadership of the Party can we uphold and strengthen the Party's leadership. This is because:

Judging from the international environment, the world today is undergoing major realignments and adjustments. Judging from the domestic perspective, our country has entered a new stage of development in building an overall well-off society and accelerating the socialist modernization drive. In the face of the new situation and new tasks, if the Party's ideology, leadership style, working methods and specific systems are not improved or perfected, they will be out of touch with the reality and the masses and the Party's leadership and combat effectiveness will be weakened, and insisting on the Party's leadership will become an empty and a dull slogan.

Judging from the status of the Party itself, after more than 90 years of development, great changes have taken place in the Party's status, tasks, personnel conditions and environment. The Party has turned from a Party that has led the people in their struggle to seize the power of the entire country, to a Party that leads the people in running the entire country and to a party which is in power for a long time. The Party's governing environment has changed from being externally and internationally blocked and implementing planned economy to opening up to the outside world and developing the socialist market economy; The number of new Party members is increasing substantially and the succession of new cadres is continuously proceeding. The actual situation of the Party is still far out of accord with the glorious mission that the Party shoulders to lead the socialist modernization. For example, the Party's ability to govern is not fully adapted to the new situation and new tasks, some party members and cadres do not have the correct style of work, whose formalism and bureaucratism are rather prominent and negative conducts such as extravagance, waste and corruption are still serious. Quite a number of grassroots Party organizations are weak, lax and loose, etc. All these need to be solved by improving the Party's leadership.

In the new phase of the new century, strengthening the building of the Party and improving the leadership of the Party in particular need to solve the following problems:

First, we must fully understand and grasp the connotation of the Party's leadership. After the Party came into power, the Party's leadership was once understood that Party organizations at all levels made direct decisions and handled various issues. This understanding and practice have seriously affected the correct functioning of the Party's leadership. In the new period of reform, opening up and modernization, on the basis of earnestly summing up the ruling experience, the Party made a scientific summary of the Party's leadership, that is, the Party's leadership is mainly political, ideological and organizational leadership. Among them, the political leadership is the core and the foundation; ideological leadership is the basis and premise of political leadership; organizational leadership is the guarantee of political leadership. This requires that in the practice of improving leadership, on the one hand the Party should overcome the tendency of substituting the Party for the regime in the past; on the other hand, it must overcome the tendency of simply emphasizing one aspect of the Party's leadership and neglecting others.

Second, we should strengthen Party building in accordance with the two historic issues of raising the level of the Party's leadership and governance and raising the capacity to resist corruption and prevent degeneration and withstand risks. With the power of mobilizing resources from all over the country, such as the people, property and other resources, the Communist Party of China is ruling a big country with more than 1.3 billion people. Along with the progress of its modernization, the social and economic components, the organization forms and the relations of interests in our country are increasingly diversified. The selectivity and difference of people's thoughts and behaviors have obviously increased; In addition, we are in an open era, the impact of the international situation, especially the economic globalization, on national security, especially economic security, has become more and more direct. This requires that in the environment of developing the socialist market economy, the Party must continuously enhance its ability to coordinate all parties, resolve conflicts, gather strength and resist risks and must continuously enhance its ability to resist corruption and prevent degeneration. the Party must keep pace with the times, keep pushing forward inner-party democracy, promote the entire social democracy through inner-party democracy, promote the democratization and scientification of decision-making, and continuously raise the Party's leadership and governance level; We must harshly punish the corruptive phenomenon within the Party, combine strict discipline, strict law enforcement with strengthening ideological education to establish and perfect the two lines of defense, namely ideological and moral construction and Party discipline and state law binding, so as to form a governance and supervision system that strictly controls the Party and advanced nature and purity should be completely cured and all tumors grown on the healthy organism of the Party be removed.

Third, we must reform and improve the leadership system of the Party and the state. In the era of revolutionary war, the Communist Party of China practiced a highly centralized leadership system, which was compatible with the tasks and environment the Party faced at that time. After the founding of new China, the Party still followed this system and leadership style for a long period of time. Practice has proved that leadership form of substituting the Party for the regime and party organizations directly monopolizing everything is not conducive to establishing the authority of the organs of state power where the people are the masters of the country, to the construction of a socialist democratic legal system and to the enhancement of the scientific and efficient decision-making, it is also easy to occur excessively centralized power, patriarchal system and individual arbitrariness and other malpractices. Therefore, we must reform the leadership system of the Party and the state in accordance with the principle of overall consideration of the entire situation and coordination of all parties to both ensure the central role of the Party and give full play to the functions of the NPC, the government, the CPPCC, the people's organizations and economic organizations. The key to reform is to correctly handle the relationship between the Party and the government and solve the problem of how the Party can exercise leadership. The ruling party's leadership over the state power system is achieved through the exertion of political influence, the recommendation of important cadres, the management of Party organizations and Party members in the power agencies, the proposition of major affairs concerning the state and the passing it through legal procedures to become the will of the state. During the process of governing, Party and government have their own functions and should not be confused or united at will.

Finally, we must conscientiously implement the basic strategy of governing the country according to law and building a socialist country ruled by law. To lead the people in formulating Constitutions and laws, the Party must inevitably lead the people in observing and implementing the Constitution and the law. The Party's own activities must also be carried out within the framework of the Constitution and laws, and become a model for observing and implementing the Constitution and laws. On such basis can the Party's leadership over state affairs be united with the rule of law, can we truly improve the Party's leadership.

Section II

The power of the Party rooted in people and a party for the people

First, all rely on the people, everything for the people

In everything we do, having people in our minds, relying on them, doing everything for the people's interests, serving the people wholeheartedly, is the purpose and the fundamental position of the CPC, represented by Mao Zedong, has gradually formed the mass line of "integrating ourselves with the masses in all things, rely on them, and aim everything for the people". This mass line is the fundamental political line and organizational line of the CPC.

Deng Xiaoping pointed out: "The masses are the source of our strength and the mass viewpoint and the mass line are our cherished traditions."[3] "Only by consistently relying on the masses, maintaining close ties with them, listening to what they have to say, understanding their feelings and always representing their interests can the Party become a powerful force capable of smoothly accomplishing its tasks."[4] Jiang Zemin repeatedly stressed: "The cause of building socialism with Chinese characteristics is a creative undertaking with broad participation of hundreds of millions of people. We must always uphold the party's mass line of believing in the masses, relying on the masses in everything, coming from the masses going to the masses, respect the creation of masses of people and listen to their voices, reflect their wishes and concentrate their wisdom and strength on the development of our various undertakings."[5] In the new phase of the new century, Hu Jintao pointed out: "Only by profoundly understanding the people's great force of making history and sincerely representing the fundamental interests of the overwhelming majority of the Chinese people, all is done for the people, all depends on the people can our party win the full the trust and support of the people and be victorious."[6]

Firstly, the conduct of "in everything we do, having people in our minds, relying on them, doing everything for the people's interests, is a necessary conclusion derived from Marxist historical materialism and an essential requirement of a Marxist political party. The people are the creators of history, which is a basic Marxist view. The Communist Party of China upholds

---

3   Selected Works of Deng Xiaoping, 2nd Edition, Vol. 2, p.368.
4   Ibid., p.342.
5   CPCCC Party Literature Research Office: "Selection of Important Literature since the 15th National Congress" (Vol. I), p.692.
6   CPCCC Party Literature Research Office: "Selection of Important Literature since the 16th National Congress" (Vol. II), p.522.

the interests of the people above all else and does not pursue any interests of its own apart from the interests of the overwhelming majority of the people. At all times, the Communist Party of China must uphold the principle of respecting the law of social development and respect the main status of the people in making history, adhere to combine striving for lofty ideals with working for the interests of the overwhelming majority of the people, adhere to the consistency of striving for lofty ideals and working for the benefits of the overwhelming majority of the people, adhere to the consistency of accomplishing all aspects of Party work and realizing the interests of the people. Only in this way can we fully display the essential characteristics of establishing the Party for the public and do governing work for the people, i.e. the fundamental nature of a Marxist political party.

Second, doing everything for the people and relying on the people for everything is the fundamental guarantee for the Communist Party of China to overcome various difficulties and risks and continuously achieve the success of its cause. The historical experience of China's revolution and construction has repeatedly proved that insisting on the Party's mass line and always keeping the flesh-and-blood relationship with the people and the revolution and the cause of construction will proceed and succeed; violating the Party's mass line and seriously detaching itself from the masses, the cause of revolution and construction will suffer setbacks or even failure. The masses of the people are the decisive force in promoting historical development and social change. They are the source of strength and the foundation of victory of the Communist Party of China. Under no circumstances, the Party cannot change its conduct of sharing the same fate with the people, its purpose of serving the people wholeheartedly, the Party cannot discard the historical materialistic point of view that the masses are the true heroes who make history. The Party cannot be separated from the people and the people cannot be separated from the Party.

Finally, doing everything for the people and relying on the people for everything, and always maintaining the flesh-and-blood ties with the people are the keys to the Party's long-term governance. Winning The hearts and support of people is the fundamental factor that determines the rise and fall of a political party and a political power. The Party's theoretical line, principles and policies as well as all its work can only remain invincible if it is carried out in accordance with the wishes of the people, the interests of the people and the hearts of the people. We must always regard the will and interests of the masses as the starting point and end aim for all our work and always regard relying on the wisdom and strength of the people as the fundamental line of work in promoting the cause of socialism with Chinese characteristics.

Being in close contact with the masses is the greatest political advantage of the Communist Party of China and being divorced from the masses is the greatest danger after the Party is in power. In the era of revolutionary war, the Party survived and developed only under the cover and direct support of the masses, thus forming the flesh-and-blood ties between the Party and the masses. After the Party came to power, on the one hand, it has obtained the conditions for better serving the people and on the other hand it has also increased the danger of being divorced from the masses. At the 8th National Congress of CPC, Deng Xiaoping once pointed out: For Party organizations and Party members, there is not less but more danger than in the past of becoming divorced from the masses after their coming to power. The reason why the ruling party is easy to be divorced from the masses is that the ruling party has the power and the various resources in hand and easy to set themselves up over the masses and give orders, and issue orders to get things done. The long-term ruling status of the CPC makes it easy for Party organizations and Party members and cadres to ignore or even disregard the aspirations and demands of the people, neglect or even disregard criticism and supervision, and develop a tendency to be arrogant and only account-able to the superior; Some Party members and cadres treat themselves as advanced elements and leaders and are far more knowledgeable than the masses, they don't learn from and discuss with masses, and thus seriously violate the actual situation and abuse the Party's prestige. Some cadres use the power in their hands to seek the personal interests or interests of small groups, resulting in corruption and degeneration, which undermines the Party-masses relations."

The Communist Party of China has always maintained a high degree of vigilance toward the tendency to be easily separated from the masses after it came to power. The Second Plenary Session of the Seventh Central Committee of the Party held on the eve of the founding of new China re-minds the entire Party of the need to be vigilant against the growth of the airs of arrogance and self-satisfaction and self-styled hero. After the found-ing of New China, the Party Central Committee has always carried out the principle of closing the Party-masses relations in the form of cyclically con-solidating the Party and rectifying its style of work. It has always conducted an uncompromising struggle against the phenomena of bureaucratism, or-derism, formalism and specialization that separate the Party from the mass-es, which exists in government organs and Party members and cadres. In the new phase of the new century, the Party Central Committee repeatedly stressed that whether it can always maintain its flesh-and-blood ties with the people and the masses is directly related to the Party's life and death. Understanding the relationship between the Party and the masses from the perspective of life and death is of great significance to close the relationship between the Party and the masses under the conditions of reform and opening up and the market economy.

To enhance the Party-masses relations must be implemented in all the work of the Party and the state. Among them, strengthening the construction of the Party's style of work has a special importance. The work style construction is related to the image of the Party and the life of the Party. The core of building the Party's work style is to maintain the flesh-and-blood ties with the masses of the people. Under the conditions of a market economy, the most important issue that affects the Party style and the relations between the Party and the masses is corruption. Therefore, constantly improving the ability to resist corruption and prevent degeneration and severely punish corruption have become the top priorities in the Party's work style construction. Corruption is a social phenomenon which has complex and profound social roots and ideological roots. China is in the primary stage of socialism, carrying out the policy of reform and opening up and developing the socialist market economy.China's new system in many aspects is still imperfect and provides a breeding ground for corruption, on the other hand, since the Party has long been in ruling status, some Party members and cadres can be easily divorced from the masses, due to false pride, ignorance or due to lack of internal and external supervision. Besides, some branches and departments are not strict in governing the Party, and their political and ideological and organizational construction work are not properly handled. There are situations wherein the bourgeoisie decadent ideas and remnant of feudal ideas and conducts which has gifted the Party ranks. Some Party members and cadres have ignored remolding of their world view, thus their ideals, beliefs and, their revolutionary aspirations have weakened, they cannot resist the tests of power, money and sex. The existence of these phenomena determines that the task of fighting corruption must be long-term and arduous. The more the time Party holds the ruling status, the more arduous must be its task is to resist corruption and prevent degeneration.

The nature and purpose of the Communist Party of China determines that the Party is incompatible with all kinds of negative corrupt practices. In the process of building socialism with Chinese characteristics, the stance and attitude of the CPC Central Committee toward fighting corruption have always been clear, the Party thinks that without resolutely quelling corruption, the flesh-blood ties between the Party and the people will be seriously damaged and the Party will face the risk of losing its ruling status and is likely to move toward self-destruction. Fighting corruption and advocacy of clean government are not only a major task for the Party's work style building, but also a major task of strengthening the building of the Party's governing ability and advanced nature, as well as an urgent task of safeguarding social fairness and justice and promoting social harmony. In the new phase of the new century, the CPC has fully realized the long-term, complex and arduous nature of the fight against corruption, placed the anti-corruption building on a more prominent position and clearly opposed corruption. The report of the 17th National Congress of the Communist Party of China emphasized that we should adhere to the policy of tackling both the root cause and the symptoms of corruption, comprehensively treating, punishing and guarding at the same time and paying attention to prevention. We must earnestly prevent and punish corruption and at the same time of resolutely punishing corruption, pay more attention to the root causes, focus on system construction which will prevent it, broaden work areas to prevent corruption at the source and gradually build a long-term mechanism of education for corruption prevention, a system of combating corruption and building a clean government, and a monitoring mechanism over the exercise of power. We must strictly investigate and punish all violations of the law and discipline, earnestly handle problems concerning leading cadres' honesty and self-discipline, resolutely rectify malpractices that bring damage to the people's interests, enact and improve laws and systems on combating corruption and building a clean government. We should raise the ability of Party members and cadres to resist corruption and implement the responsibility system for improving Party style and building a clean government and resolutely correct unhealthy trends that harm the interests of the people and earnestly solve the problems that masses have shown strong reactions. Only by constantly strengthening anti-corruption efforts and building a clean government can the Communist Party of China be able to prevent and curb corruption more effectively, continuously improve its ability to resist corruption and prevent degeneration, and strengthen its flesh-and-blood ties with the people.

Second, caring about the people, working so as to benefit the people and developing the fundamental interests of the majority of the people

Realizing, maintaining and developing the fundamental interests of the overwhelming majority of the people is the fundamental objective of building socialism with Chinese characteristics and the starting point and the foothold of all the work of the Communist Party of China. The so-called "maintaining" policy is to safeguard and maintain the interests of the masses, through various systems, policies and measures and to ensure that the people exercise extensive rights conferred to them by the Constitution and laws and see that their rights are never unjustly infringed. Thirdly, the so-called "developing" policy aims to treat the interests of the masses with a development perspective, by starting from the characteristics of the times and proceed from the short-term and long-term prospects of development, and profoundly recognize the changes and trends regarding the interest of the people. On the other hand, with the deepening of reform and opening up and the modernization drive, we will continue to enhance and enrich the interests of the people, expand and increase the rights and interests of the people. Realizing, maintaining and developing the fundamental interests of the overwhelming majority of the people is a closely integrated whole. Realizing is the foundation, maintaining is the guarantee, and developing is the prospect. If they cannot be well realized, they cannot be truly maintained; without realizing and maintaining, the development become empty talk. At the same time, realization and maintenance are dynamic and we must continuously realize and maintain in the light of development. Only in this way, development and maintenance can be fully effective.

With the deepening of reform and opening up and the development of market economy, interests of people have diversified and new interests demands have requirements inevitably arisen. Only when the Communist Party of China realizes, maintains and develops the interests of the overwhelming majority of the people can it be true to its purpose and ideals as the Party that has always represented the fundamental interests of the overwhelming majority and that has served the people wholeheartedly.

First, for the Party, it is the fundamental starting point to consider and satisfy the interests of the overwhelming majority. The interests of the majority are the most crucial and the most decisive factors, which is always related to the overall situation in which the Party is in power and the overall economic and social development of the country, and the overall situation of the unity of the people of all nationalities in the country and the stability of the community. The overall interests of the people are always made up of the specific interests of all parties. In order to truly represent the fundamental interests of the overwhelming majority of the people, the CPC must make efforts to handle the relations among the three parties: First, to correctly handle the relationship between current interests and long-term interests, correctly unite current interests with long-term interests, and unify reform, stability and development. The second is to properly handle the relationship between local interests and overall interests, and consciously take the overall interests as the priority and the local ones as subordinate to the overall situation. The third is to correctly handle the relationship between the diversified specific interest and the fundamental interest. Correctly reflect and give consideration to the interests of the masses at different levels and in different aspects so that all the people will make steady progress towards common prosperity.

Secondly, we should properly handle and give consideration to the interests of the masses at different levels and in different aspects. As a ruling party, the Communist Party of China must deeply recognize the interest demands of people from all aspects, so that workers, peasants, intellectuals and other strata can enjoy the fruits of economic and social development and the Party can win the support of the masses from all walks of life all levels to the maximum extent possible. In this way, can we better lay a solid social foundation for its governance and consolidate its ruling position.

Finally, we must earnestly solve the practical problems that concern the people's interests. To realize, maintain and develop the interests of the overwhelming majority of the people, we must concretely solve the most immediate, practical and concern interests of the people, and concretely solve the actual problems of the production and livelihood of the masses.

Building the Party for the public and governing for the people are the fundamental embodiment of the purpose of the Communist Party of China. The highest criteria, in judging the quality of all work and policies of the Party and the state, should be whether, they serve the fundamental interest of the overwhelming majority. Only by upholding the principle of building the Party for the public and assume governing for the people, can the Party adhere to the principle of putting the interests of people to the supreme status, and formulate correct lines, guidelines and policies in this direction, only in this way can we uphold the principle of exercising power for the people, showing concern for them and working for their interests, can we fully respect the people's dominant position, give play to the pioneering spirit of the people, safeguard the rights and interests of the people and take the path of common prosperity, can we promote the all-round development of the people, and achieve the ideal of"development for people", "development relying on the people", and achieve the ideal that the fruits of development are shared by the people.

Section III

Promote the party's task to build itself in an all-round way with a spirit of reform and innovation

First, the Party building as a great undertaking project

In the course of leading the new democratic revolution, Mao Zedong defined the building of a nationwide, mass based, an ideologically, politically and organizationally advanced, true Marxist political party as a great project or great undertaking. To attach great importance to and continuously strengthen party building is a great magic weapon for the Communist Party of China to continue to overcome difficulties, obtain the victory of revolution and construction from small to large, from weak to strong. The Chinese Communists represented by Mao Zedong created and accumulated many valuable experiences in the great project of building the Party mainly including: focus on building the Party ideologically and through the Marxist theoretical education of the majority of Party members, successfully build the Communist Party of China with the vast majority of Party members were peasants into the vanguard organization of the working class in rural areas and war environments; emphasize on reinforcing the building of the Party based on the Party's political line; uphold the principle of democratic centralism of the Party and implement a collective leadership system; strengthen party style building, carry forward the fine style of combining theory and practice, being closely linked with the people, and self-criticism; correctly handle contradictions within the Party and carry out inner-party struggles, insist on starting from the desire for solidarity and achieving unity through criticism and self-criticism to achieve solidarity, as for comrades who made mistakes, adopt a policy of "learning from past mistakes to avoid future ones and curing the sickness to save the patient". After the founding of new China, the first generation of the central collective leadership with Mao Zedong as the core always attached great importance to the Party's construction. The party leadership—through periodical campaigns of rectifying and consolidating—has constantly strengthened the Party's ideological construction, its style construction and organizational construction.

In the new period of reform and opening up and modernization, the second generation of the central collective leadership with Deng Xiaoping as the core held high the banner of "emancipating the mind and seeking truth from facts" and created a great new project for Party building. Deng Xiaoping put forward the task of building our Party into a militant Marxist party, and becoming a strong core that leads the people of the entire country in carrying forward the building of a material and spiritual civilization of socialism, the emphasis that the issue of the leadership and organizational systems is of fundamental, comprehensive, stable and long-term significance and other important guiding ideologies, and in close contact with the Party's basic line in the primary stage of socialism, to carry out the Party's ideological, organizational and style construction, and thus resolved the issue of, indicated what kind of Party should be built in the new historical period and how to build it.

Facing the new century, the third-generation Party central collective leadership with Jiang Zemin as its core continued to push forward the great new project of Party building. He emphasized that we should constantly strengthen and perfect ourselves in the spirit of reform and put forward that we should make our Party a Marxist party armed with Deng Xiaoping Theory, which represents the development requirements of China's advanced productive forces, represents the advancing direction of China's advanced culture, represents the fundamental interests of the overwhelming majority of the Chinese people, who is fully consolidated in ideology, politics and organization and is able to withstand various risks and always keeps ahead of the times, and who leads the people build socialism with Chinese characteristics. To this end, the CPC Central Committee has made a series of decisions on arming the whole Party with Deng Xiaoping Theory, on strengthening the building of an honest and clean government and on strengthening the close ties between the Party and the people.

In the new phase of the new century, the Central Party Committee with Hu Jintao as the General Secretary continues to emphasize pushing forward the Party's construction in the spirit of reform and innovation. In particular, to strengthen the building of the Party's ability to govern and of the advanced nature of the Party, thus the new natures of the great project of Party building has become more prominent.

To stand at the forefront of the times and lead the people to constantly open up a new situation in the career development and to always be the strong leading core of the cause of socialism with Chinese characteristics, the CPC must strengthen its own construction in the spirit of reform and innovation, which is a major strategic task put forward based on the changed conditions of the times, China's economic and social conditions, and the construction status of the Party, and is the fundamental requirement for strengthening Party building in the new situation.

First of all, judging from the perspective of the world, the trend toward multi-polarization and economic globalization is developing in twists and turns with rapid progress in science and technology. The development of high and new technology with information technology as the core has greatly changed people's production conditions, their life styles, international economic and political relations, and the competition for comprehensive national strength based on economic power, with its high scientific and technological content, has become increasingly fierce. Peace and development still remain to be the two major themes in contemporary world. At the same time, there are new developments in regard to hegemonism and power politics. The factors of traditional and non-traditional security threats are intertwined. The dangers of terrorism rise, and peace and development face multiple difficulties and challenges. In the face of opportunities and challenges, the Chinese Communist Party must correctly handle the problems and shoulder down its historic mission. Therefore, the CPC must strengthen itself in the spirit of reform and innovation.

Secondly, judging from the domestic situation, the great practice of over 30 years of reform and opening up and the modernization drive has markedly enhanced our overall national strength. The cause of socialism with Chinese characteristics has made great achievements that have attracted world attention. However, it must be pointed out that our country is still and will be in the initial stage of socialism for a long time and has a large population, a weak foundation and is quite poor in per-capita resources, which are our basic national conditions. The contradiction between the growing material and cultural needs of the people and the backward social production is still the major contradiction in our society. In the new century, China's economic and social development emerges new problems such as urban-rural gap, widening regional disparities, unbalanced economic and social development, resources and environmental bottlenecks, etc. the Party building must carry forward the spirit of reform and innovation, adapt to the new situation and solve new problems.

Thirdly, judging from the Party's situation, the CPC has gone through revolution, construction and reform periods, and is undergoing major changes in regard to its Party members contingency, regarding its position and environment, and its tasks. Broadly speaking, our Party has become a party that leads the people in their struggle to seize the state power, secondly, leads the people to run the state affairs, which is in the status of a ruling party for decades. It has become a party that has led the nation in its construction under the conditions of opening to the outside world and developing socialist market economy. These two major historical changes have collectively reflected all the victories and achievements our Party has made since its establishment and have collectively reflected all the challenges and tests our Party is facing today. In addition, the Party already possesses more than 80 million Party members, the substantial increase in the number of new Party members and the constant succession of new and old cadres in his ranks has added fresh blood to the Party and made the Party's task of self-construction more arduous than ever before.

The bitter historical lessons we have drawn from the fate of some of the world's long-governing great parties and communist parties that have successively lost power are profound. Since the late 1980s and the early 1990s, some major and old parties in the world, which have been in power for decades or even hundreds of years, have successively lost power and some of them even went into decline. There are complicated reasons for this, but fundamentally speaking, the governing performances of these parties can not satisfy the people. These facts tell people that the ruling status of the Party is not inherent or permanent, it is not easy for the proletarian parties to seize power, and it is even harder for them to wield the state power, especially for the long time ruling. Therefore, the CPC must be vigilant in peace time and enhance its awareness of unexpected development. It must persistently examine and discipline itself in the light of development, and strengthen and improve itself in the spirit of reform. It will never be complacent and will never slacken its efforts to sinicize Marxism in China and push forward the cause of socialism with Chinese characteristics.

The Communist Party of China is a Marxist political party. The nature, purpose and historical mission of the Party determine that the Party not only dares and is good at constantly reforming and innovating in the great cause it leads, but also dares and is good at constantly reforming and innovating itself.

To promote Party building with the spirit of reform and innovation, we must take Party building as a systematic project. Take the construction of the Party's governing capability and advanced nature as the main line, adhere to the principle that the Party should control the Party, strictly govern the Party, implement the demands of serving the people, practicability and free from corruption, strengthen ideological construction with a firm conviction as the key points, strengthen organizational construction with a focus on training high-quality Party members and cadres, strengthen style construction with a focus on maintaining the flesh-and-blood relationship between the Party and the masses, strengthen the building of the party systems with a focus on improving democratic centralism, strengthen the construction of anti-corruption and integrity with a focus on perfecting the system of punishment and prevention of corruption, so that the Party will always become a Marxist ruling party that serves the interests of the public and governs for the people, seeks truth and be pragmatic, insists on reforming and innovating, works hard, be honest and clean, be energetic, unified and harmony. Only in this way can the Party maintain its strong creativity, cohesion and combat effectiveness, can it lead the people of all nationalities throughout the country in building an overall well-off society, realize the three historic tasks of promoting the modernization drive, completing the reunification of the motherland, safeguarding world peace and promoting common development, and can it always be the strong core of leadership in the cause of socialism with Chinese characteristics.

Second, strengthening the Party's ability to govern

The construction of its governing ability has been the fundamental aspect of construction of the CPC after it has assumed power. The Party's ability to govern means the ability of the Party to put forward and apply the correct theories, lines, guidelines and policies, lead the formulation and implementation of the Constitution and laws, adopt a scientific leadership system and leadership style, and mobilize and organize the people in administering state and social affairs, economic and cultural undertakings, take effective means in governing the Party, leading state and military affairs, and build a modern socialist country.

Since the Party has assumed power across the whole country, in 1949, its achievements of governance have been obviously demonstrated. The governing capability of the Party can be judged whether it has been able to adapt to the tasks and missions, it has faced. At the same time, we must also see that there are issues which are incompatible with the cause of socialist modernization in the areas of leadership style and governing style, the leading and working mechanism, the qualities and capabilities of leading cadres and leading groups, which have seriously affected the Party's governing image and effectiveness. After the founding of New China, the first generation of the central collective leadership with Mao Zedong as the core emphasized repeatedly that Party members and cadres should learn to manage the country and manage economic construction, and strive to achieve to "be both socialist-minded and professionally competent". Since the 3rd Plenary Session of the 11th Central Committee of the Communist Party of China, Deng Xiaoping closely integrated the actual conditions of reform and opening up and the socialist modernization drive, emphasized that it is necessary to improve the Party's leadership in adhering to the leadership of the Party, put forward the issue of the Party's and the state's leadership structure reform, put forward new requirements for the construction of the Party's governing ability. The third generation central collective leadership with Jiang Zemin as its core closely integrated strengthening the building of the Party's ability to govern with the promotion of socialist modernization and with maintaining the Party's advanced nature, indicating that the Party has a deeper understanding of the construction of its governing capability. The CPC Central Committee with Hu Jintao as general secretary, in face of the profound changes in the world conditions, national conditions and Party conditions, on the basis of a comprehensive summary of historical experiences, starts from the test of governance, the test of reform and opening up, the test of market economy and profound changes in the external environment, continues to vigorously promote the construction of the Party's governing capability. In September 2004, the Decision of the Central Committee of the Communist Party of China on Strengthening the Building of the Party's Ability to Govern adopted by the 4th Plenary Session of the 16th CPC Central Committee comprehensively summed up the major experiences gained by the Party over the past half century and clearly defined the guiding ideology, overall objectives and main tasks for strengthening the building of the Party's ability to govern, which has been a programmatic document for strengthening the Party's ability to govern. In September 2009, the 4th Plenary Session of the 17th CPC Central Committee passed the Decision of the Central Committee of the Communist Party of China on Several Major Issues in Strengthening and Improving Party Building under the New Situation, which defined the general requirements for the Party building and put forward new requirements of enhancing Party building with scientific proficiency, and the strategic task of building, an ever learning Marxist party. The implementation of this decision is of great significance to improve the Party's ability to govern and lead.

In more than half a century of ruling practice, the Communist Party of China has accumulated valuable experience, which are mainly reflected as follows: It is imperative to adhere to the CPC's guiding ideology of keeping pace with the times and guiding its practice with the developing Marxism. We must persistently promote the socialist self improvement and enhance the vigor and vitality of socialism; We must give top priority to governing and rejuvenating the country and regard development as the key to solve all the problems in China; We must uphold the principle of building the Party for the sake of the public and governing for the people, adhere to our flesh-blood ties with the masses; We must adhere to scientific and democratic governance and ruling by law, constantly improve the Party's leadership style and governing style; We must continue to strengthen Party building in the spirit of reform and constantly enhance the Party's creativity, cohesion and combat effectiveness. These experiences as mentioned above are also important guiding principles for strengthening the building of the Party's ability to govern and need to be persisted and continuously enriched and developed in practice.

The building of the Party's ability to govern determines the overall situation of the Party building and the cause of socialism with Chinese characteristics. To strengthen the building of the Party's ability to govern, we must make great effort to improve the Party's leadership system, governing style, organizational form, activity mode and management style, and we must strive to improve the ability to promote scientific development and social harmony. We must strive to build a high-quality leadership team and take the improvement of the leadership and the ability to govern as the core content of building the leading bodies at all levels. According to the requirements of scientific governance, democratic governance and governance according to law, we should improve the thinking and work style of the leading group, improve the leadership skills of leading cadres, improve the leading system, and we must establish the leading groups at all levels into strong leading groups that firmly implement the Party's theories, lines, principles, and policies and are good at leading scientific development. All in all, all above means that we should elevate the level of the entire and mobilize its ranks through enhancing the ability to govern of the leading groups, so that the Party will always become the strong leading core of the cause of socialism with Chinese characteristics.

Third, strengthening the Party's advanced nature

The advanced nature is what the Communist Party of China lives on and where its strength lies. To enhance the building of the Party's advanced nature means that by strengthening the Party's ideology construction, organizational construction, work style construction, system construction and anti-corruption construction, make the Party's theory, line, principles and policies conform to the trend of the times and the requirements of social development and progress of our country, reflect the interests and aspirations of the people of all nationalities across the country so that the Party organizations at all levels can continuously improve their creativity, cohesion and combat effectiveness, always give play to the role of leading nucleus and battle-fighting fortress, drive the majority of Party members to continuously improve their own quality, and always give play to their vanguard and exemplary role, so that the Party will always keep its quality of keeping pace with the times and always keep in the forefront of the times, constantly improve its ability to govern, consolidate its position as a ruling party and accomplish its ruling mission.

Keeping the advanced nature is determined by the nature and purpose of Marxist political party. The Communist Party of China has always attached great importance to maintaining the advanced nature of the Party and always placed the Party's advanced nature construction in a prominent position. The Party has accumulated a series of valuable experiences in the creative practice of maintaining and developing its advanced nature. mainly including: we must accurately grasp the pulse of the times and ensure that the Party always keeps pace with the development of the times; we must take successfully realizing, maintaining and developing the fundamental interests of the overwhelming majority of the people as the starting point and the foothold of the Party's entire work; we must keep the Party's theory, line, principles and policies constantly advancing with the times so as to ensure that the Party's entire work always meets the actual conditions and social development; we must revolve around the Party's central task and strengthen self-construction with the spirit of reform and innovation, so as to ensure that the Party will always lead the development and progress of Chinese society. We must insist that governance over the Party is exercised fully and with rigor, so as to ensure that the Party always enhances its advanced nature. These valuable experiences will long-term guiding affect for further promoting the building of the Party's advanced nature.

To strengthen the building of the Party's advanced nature, we must always do well the basic project of maintaining the advanced nature of the Party members and unremittingly improve the quality of the Party members. The advanced nature of the Party must be reflected in millions of high-quality Party members. The majority of Party members should conscientiously study and observe the Party Constitution and enhance their Party spirit. Party organizations at all levels should establish a regular analysis system of Party members and their spirit, broaden the channels for Party members to serve the masses, build a system for Party members and to contact and serve the masses, improve the long-term mechanism of constantly educating Party members and maintaining their advanced nature so that Party members can truly become the advanced elements who firmly remember their purposes and bear the masses in their minds.

To maintain the advanced nature of the Party, we must promote Party building with the spirit of reform and innovation. We should focus on raising the theoretical level of Marxism in the whole Party, persistently arm the entire Party with the theoretical system of socialism with Chinese characteristics, enhance the ability of the vast majority of Party members, especially Party leading cadres, to use scientific theories to solve practical problems; vigorously push forward the building of inner-party democracy, maximize the innovative vitality of the entire Party, extensively unite the wisdom and strength of the Party, and make the reform and innovation a conscious move by the majority of Party members, especially the leading cadres at all levels. We must vigorously promote the Party's system innovation and make the institutional building permeate the Party's ideological building, organizational and work style building, and constantly improve the institutionalization and standardization of Party building; We should vigorously strengthen the building of leadership groups and leading cadres teams and further improve the pioneering and innovative ability to promote the development of the cause; We should vigorously promote the building of grass-roots Party organizations, further enhance the creativity, cohesion and combat effectiveness of grass-roots Party organizations; We should vigorously promote the building of working style of the Party and the building of a clean government, further enhance the ability to resist corruption and prevent degeneration, and resist risks.

To strengthen the work of building the Party's advanced nature is a long-term historic task that must closely revolve around the Party's historical mission and its central task. In the new phase of the new century, in order to strengthen our work of building the Party's advanced nature, we must closely integrate the practice of implementing the scientific concept of development, the practice of building a socialist harmonious society, the practice of strengthening the Party's ability to govern and the practice of maintaining the Party's flesh-and-blood relationship with the masses of the people, so that all work for the Party's construction can stand the test of practice, history and people.

www.ingramcontent.com/pod-product-compliance
Lightning Source LLC
Chambersburg PA
CBHW031137020426
42333CB00013B/413